W9-COI-460

# INTELLIGENT TUTORING SYSTEMS:

## At the Crossroad of Artificial Intelligence and Education

edited by

**Claude Frasson**

**Gilles Gauthier**

ABLEX PUBLISHING CORPORATION
NORWOOD, NEW JERSEY

Copyright © 1990 by Ablex Publishing Corporation

All rights reserved. No part of this publication may be reproduced, stored in a retrieval system, or transmitted, in any form or by any means, electronic, mechanical, photocopying, microfilming, recording, or otherwise, without permission of the publisher.

Printed in the United States of America

**Library of Congress Cataloging-in-Publication Data**

Intelligent tutoring systems : at the crossroad of artificial
  intelligence and education / [edited by] Claude Frasson, Gilles
  Gauthier.
      p.  cm.
  Papers presented at the Conference on Intelligent Tutoring
Systems, held June 1–3, 1988 in Montréal, Québec.
  Includes bibliographical references.
  ISBN 0-89391-625-0
  1. Intelligent tutoring systems—Congresses.   2. Computer-assisted
instruction—Congresses.   3. Artificial intelligence—Congresses.
4. Educational technology—Congresses.   I. Frasson, Claude.
II. Gauthier, Gilles.   III. International Conference on Intelligent
Tutoring Systems (1988 : Montréal, Québec)
LB1028.5.I553 1989
371.3′34—dc20                                                        89-27542
                                                                         CIP

Ablex Publishing Corporation
355 Chestnut Street
Norwood, New Jersey 07648

# Contents

Contributors    *v*

Preface    *vii*

Introduction    *1*

**1**
Learning Companion Systems    *6*
*Tak-Wai Chan and Arthur B. Baskin*

**2**
Discovery Environments and Intelligent Learning Tools    *34*
*Anne Bergeron and Gilbert Paquette*

**3**
Towards "Interactive Video": A Video-Based Intelligent Tutoring
  Environment    *56*
*Alan P. Parkes and John A. Self*

**4**
Student Modeling and Tutoring Flexibility in the Lisp Intelligent Tutoring
  System    *83*
*Albert T. Corbett, John R. Anderson, and Eric G. Patterson*

**5**
Bypassing the Intractable Problem of Student Modeling    *107*
*John A. Self*

**6**
Discourse Planning in Intelligent Help Systems    *124*
*Radboud Winkels and Joost Breuker*

**7**
SCENT-3: An Architecture for Intelligent Advising in Problem-Solving
  Domains    *140*
*Gordon I. McCalla, Jim E. Greer, and the SCENT Research Team*

**8**

Representing Knowledge about Teaching: DOCENT—An AI Planning System
  for Teaching and Learning   *162*
*Philip H. Winne and Laurane L. Kramer*

**9**

Using Multiple Teaching Strategies in an ITS   *188*
*Fiona Spensley, Mark Elsom-Cook, Paul Byerley, Peter Brooks, Massimo
  Federici, and Claudia Scaroni*

**10**

Finding Errors by Overlooking them   *206*
*Warren Sack*

**11**

20 Years in the Trenches: What have we Learned?   *234*
*Beverly Woolf*

**12**

Three Current Tutoring Systems and Future Needs   *251*
*Patrick Suppes*

**13**

Toward a New Epistemology for Learning   *266*
*John Seely Brown*

Author Index   *283*

Subject Index   *000*

# Contributors

**John R. Anderson,** Advanced Computer Tutoring Project, Department of Psychology, Carnegie-Mellon University, Pittsburgh, PA 15213

**Arthur B. Baskin,** Department of Veterinary Bioscience, University of Illinois at Urbana-Champaign, 1408 West University Avenue, Urbana, IL 61801

**Anne Bergeron,** Département de mathématiques et d'informatique, Université du Québec à Montréal, C.P. 8888, succ. "A", Montréal, Qc. H3C 3P8, Canada

**Joost Breuker,** Department of Social Science Informatics, University of Amsterdam, Herengracht 196, 1016 BS Amsterdam, the Netherlands

**P. Brooks,** Institute of Educational Technology, The Open University, Milton Keynes, MK7 6AA, U.K.

**John Seeley Brown,** Xerox Palo Alto Research Center and Institute for Research on Learning, 3333 Coyote Hill Road, Palo Alto, CA 93405

**P. Byerley,** Institute of Educational Technology, The Open University, Milton Keynes, MK7 6AA, U.K.

**Tak-Wai Chan,** Department of Computer Science, University of Illinois at Urbana-Champaign, 1408 West University Avenue, Urbana, IL 61801

**Albert T. Corbett,** Advanced Computer Tutoring Project, Department of Psychology, Carnegie-Mellon University, Pittsburgh, PA 15213

**Mark Elsom-Cook,** Institute of Educational Technology, The Open University, Milton Keynes, MK7 6AA, U.K.

**M. Federici,** Institute of Educational Technology, The Open University, Milton Keynes, MK7 6AA, U.K.

**Jim E. Greer,** ARIES Laboratory, Department of Computational Science, University of Saskatchewan, Saskatoon, SK. S7N 0W0, Canada

**Laurane L. Kramer,** Instructional Psychology Research Group, Faculty of Education, Simon Fraser University, Burnaby, B.C. V5A 1S6, Canada

**Gordon I. McCalla,** ARIES Laboratory, Department of Computational Science, University of Saskatchewan, Saskatoon, SK. S7N 0W0, Canada

**Gilbert Paquette,** Module science et technologie, Télé-université, 4835 Christophe Colomb, Montréal, Qc. H2J 4C2, Canada

**Alan P. Parkes,** Centre for Research on Computers and Learning, University of Lanccaster, Lancaster LA1 4YR, England

**Eric J. Patterson,** Advanced Computer Tutoring Project, Department of Psychology, Carnegie-Mellon University, Pittsburgh, PA 15213

**Roy Pea,** Laboratory for Advanced Research in Education Techniques, New York University, New York, NY 10003

**Warren Sack,** Department of Information, Université de Paris VIII, 2 rue de la Liberté, 93526 St. Denis Cedex 02, France

**Jacobinj Sandberg,** Department of Social Science Informatics, University of Amsterdam, Herengracht 196, 1016 BS Amsterdam, the Netherlands

**C. Scaroni,** Institute of Educational Technology, The Open University, Milton Keynes, MK7 6AA, U.K.

**John A. Self,** Department of Computing, University of Lanccaster, Bailrigg, Lancaster LA1 4YR, England

**Elliot Soloway,** Department of Electrical Engineering and Computer Sciences, University of Michigan, Ann Arbor, MI 48109

**Fiona Spensley,** Institute of Educational Technology, The Open University, Milton Keynes, MK7 6AA, U.K.

**Patrick Suppes,** Institute for Mathematical Studies in the Social Sciences, Ventura Hall, Stanford University, Stanford, CA 94305-4115

**Radboud Winkels,** Depaartment of Computer Science & Law, University of Amsterdam, Kloveniersburgwal 72, 1012 CZ Amsterdam, the Netherlands

**Philip H. Winne,** Instructional Psychology Research Group, Faculty of Education, Simon Fraser University, Burnaby, B.C. V5A 1S6, Canada

**Beverly Woolf,** Department of Computer and Information Science, University of Massachusetts, Amherst, MA 01003

# Preface

This book follows from the International Conference on Intelligent Tutoring Systems (ITS-88) held June 1–3, 1988 in Montréal, Canada. It contains a selection from the best papers of ITS-88. The authors who have contributed have improved and extended the paper they presented at the conference.

The goal of the conference was to bring together specialists from the fields of artificial intelligence and education, two strong and convergent domains of research which need, more and more, collaborative works. Both disciplines tackle fundamental and ambitious goals and the expertise developed by the two research communities is proving to be complementary and fundamental in contributing to the study of a very complex subject: mental behavior of the human being.

The conference was launched to encourage a close cooperation between the two research communities and to focus on high-level concepts and ideas in order to serve as a strong reference basis for future research. We were also curious to see the state of development of ITS in the world. The response from the international community largely met our expectations: We received 142 communications from 16 countries. To insure a high level at the conference a strong international committee (from eight countries) was set up by Marlene Jones (Alberta Research Council) and Gregor Bochmann (University of Montréal). All contributed papers were assigned to several members of the Program Committee for evaluation. In most of the cases, the papers were reviewed by five referees. In addition, a large number of high-level speakers have been invited to present the State of the Art in different research areas: Jacques Arsac, Patrick Suppes, John Seely Brown, Philip Winne, Elliot Soloway, John Self, Jeffrey Bonar, Beverly Woolf, and Masoud Yazdani. Two panels conducted by Stuart Macmillan and Gordon McCalla including Albert Corbett, Stellan Ohlsson, Elliot Soloway, Patrick Suppes, Beverly Woolf, Marlene Jones, William Clancey, Gerhard Fisher, and David Littman led to stimulating discussions. The success of the conference was greatly due to the contributions of the speakers and the panelists.

Several scientific organizations gave us their support: the Canadian Society for Computational Studies of Intelligence (CSCSI), the Association française pour la cybernétique économique et technique (AFCET), the Association for Computing Machinery (ACM) and its special interest groups SIGART and SIG-CUE, the Inter-American Organization for Higher Education, and the British Computer Society (BCS).

We would like to acknowledge the Natural Sciences and Engineering Research Council of Canada (NSERC), the Fonds pour la formation de chercheurs et l'aide à la recherche (FCAR), and the University of Montréal for their funding and support to the organization of this conference. Thanks to the members of the Program and the Organization Committees: Marlene Jones (Alberta Research

Council), Gregor Bochmann, Jan Gecsei, Gilles Imbeau, Guy Mineau (University of Montréal), Marc Kaltenbach (Bishop University), Robert Godin (University of Québec at Montréal), Roger Hart (Open Systems Group, Victoria), Ehud Bar-On (Israel Institute of Technology), Dick Bierman (University of Amsterdam), Jeffrey Bonar (LRDC, University of Pittsburgh), Lorne Bouchard (University of Québec at Montréal), Jacqueline Bourdeau (CRIM, Montréal), Bernard Causse (University of Pau), Andy diSessa (University of California), Philippe Duchastel (Laval University), Gerhard Fisher (University of Colorado), Jim Greer (University of Saskatchewan), Wayne Harvey (EDC, Newton), Lewis Johnson (University of Southern California), Heinz Mandl (Tubingen University), Stuart Macmillan (SUN Microsystems), Gordon McCalla (University of Saskatchewan), Vitoro Midoro (Istituto Tecnologie Didattiche), Riichiro Mizoguchi (Osaka University), André Ouellet (University of Québec at Chicoutimi), Maryse Queré (CRIN, Nancy), Brian Reiser (Princeton University), Lauren Resnick (LRDC, University of Pittsburgh), John Self (University of Lancaster), Derek Sleeman (University of Aberdeen), Elliot Soloway (Yale University), Hans Spada (University of Freiburg), Georges Stamon (University of Paris-Sorbonne), Harold Stolovitch (University of Montréal), Akira Takeuchi (Kyushu University), Martial Vivet (Université du Mans), Karl Wender (Brunswick University), Beverly Woolf (University of Massachusetts) and Masoud Yazdani (University of Exeter). Thanks also to all the members of the HERON group at the University of Montréal: Samy Bengio, Daniel Gauvin, André St-Gelais, Jean Girard, Soudougou Konaté, Nancy Nadeau, Aziz Ouazzani, Frédéric Plante, François Robillard, and very special thanks to Gilles Imbeau. Finally, we owe a great deal to the support staff at Ablex for their cooperation and constant professionalism.

Claude Frasson
*Département d'informatique et
de recherche opérationnelle
Université de Montréal*

Gilles Gauthier
*Département de mathématiques
et d'informatique
Université du Québec à Montréal*

# Introduction

The evolution from Computer-Aided Instruction (CAI) to Intelligent Computer-Aided Instruction (ICAI) was the first step by which Education and Artificial Intelligence communities began to look at each other's work. The important contributions from artificial intelligence came from the studies on knowledge: knowledge acquisition, knowledge communication, knowledge models, knowledge misunderstanding, expert knowledge, and so on. They address fundamental issues related to the wide and complex domain of education of the human being. We can think of the evolution towards Intelligent Tutoring Systems (ITS) as a step beyond ICAI, leading to new classes of problems and approaches and where learning is at least as important as teaching. ITS involves artificial intelligence concepts including knowledge representation and communication, problem-solving approaches, dynamic student modeling, human cognition, intelligent user interfaces, intelligent help systems, use of strategies, and so on.

As work progresses in these areas, various research has uncovered complex problems requiring fundamental studies. We do need to capture more knowledge about several fundamental components of ITS and several questions arise: What is the influence of the learning environment in an ITS? What are the tools which could improve the learning process? What are the means to obtain a more adequate model of the student? How could we advise and help the student in an intelligent way ? What strategies should an intelligent learning system use? Finally, what have we reached in AI and Education and what is the magnitude of the difficulties in the present ITS research?

This book examines all of the above-mentioned questions. Thirteen chapters address several fundamental aspects of ITS: the learning environment in which the student is placed, the student modeling problem, the planification of the content of instruction, the teaching and learning strategies, and finally we take a look at the near (and not so near) future.

## LEARNING ENVIRONMENT

Tak-Wai Chan and Arthur Baskin (Chapter 1) propose intelligent tutoring systems of a new breed—the Learning Companion Systems (LCS). In the learning environment of such a system, there are three agents involved, namely, the human student, the computer learning-companion, and the computer teacher. The role of the computer learning-companion is to act as a learning companion for the student. To this end the companion performs the learning task at about the same level as the student, and both the student and the companion exchange ideas while being presented the same material by the teacher. The goal of the

1

learning companion is to stimulate the student's learning through the process of collaboration and competition. Two main approaches to the design of the learning companion are considered: simulation and machine learning. The machine-learning approach of LCS could possibly be one of the most interesting application areas of machine learning. The authors present the idea of LCS, illustrate its psychological plausibility for facilitating student learning, investigate its properties, study its design, and discuss some perspectives of the two different learning approaches for the domain of indefinite integration. Finally, the authors outline some perspectives of LCS research.

Anne Bergeron and Gilbert Paquette, in Chapter 2, make a clear distinction between use of artificial intelligence for teaching and artificial intelligence tools for assisted learning. They address the last point, considering tools which can increase the learner's cognitive activity. We see again, as in the previous chapter, a way of motivating the student. The authors describe a system (LOUTI) to design an intelligent discovery learning environment. The AI-based software tools provide a suitable framework for the development of highly interactive environments that combine knowledge representation and processing features. Sample environments are presented: La Ville, High School Chemistry, and Nutrition. Their work constitute an interesting example of an application of artificial intelligence to education.

In Chapter 3, Alan Parkes and John Self consider the potential role of a video-based environment within ITS, in particular to support the modeling stage of apprenticeship learning. So far, the two communities (ITS and interactive video) have concentrated on different stages of the learning process. They describe the requirements of a formalism via which the conceptual and visual content of video material can be discussed, manipulated, generated, and controlled in a user-sensitive way by an ITS. They illustrate these issues by describing the architecture and operation of CLORIS (Conceptual Language Orientated to the Representation of Instructional film Sequences), an experimental video-based ITS.

## STUDENT MODELING

The LISP tutor (Anderon & Reiser, 1985) is one of the best known ITS. It is being used productively both in teaching and research. In Chapter 4, Albert Corbett, John Anderson, and Eric Patterson expose why they would like to modify two aspects of the tutor's behavior (the constraints on the coding order for the code typed in by the student and the tutor's immediate feedback policy) and relate these aspects of the tutorial interaction to the student model. They address issues involved in the implementation of tutorial changes and describe data from one modification—a version of the tutor in which the student and not the tutor controls when feedback is given.

As some researchers have recently questioned both the need for detailed student models and the practical possibility of building them, John Self (Chapter 5) attempts to rehabilitate student models within ITS. He regards it as axiomatic that any *intelligent* tutoring system needs a student model. The author suggests practical guidelines and changes in the philosophical approach (in the form of 4 slogans) which may help in building effective student models. The author stresses that the features of the student model should be linked to tutorial actions, ideally supported by educational evidence.

## ADVISING AND HELP SYSTEMS

The research reported in Chapter 6 is part of the EUROHELP project, which is aimed at the construction of an environment for building intelligent systems for information processing systems. A help system supports the user in handling and mastering an information processing system. Core of this environment is a shell that contains all domain independent procedures and knowledge. A comprehensive help system not only answers questions of users, but also "looks over their shoulders" and interrupts when appropriate. Radboud Winkels and Joost Breuker focus on the generic Coach component of that shell. The Coach has two functions: to assist the user with a current problem and to teach the user about the interactive computer program used. The proposed Coach consists of three layers: (1) A Didactic Goal Generator which generates an overlay of domain concepts that may be taught; (2) a Discourse Planner which constructs didactic discourse strategies; and (3) Tactics which are the terminal elements of strategies. Tactics are the speech acts finally "uttered" by the Coach. The authors present these three layers, discussed in detail, and relate them to general coaching and discourse principles.

The SCENT project, at the university of Saskatchewan, has focused on developing an intelligent advising environment for students learning to program in LISP. In Chapter 7, Gordon McCalla, Jim Greer, and the SCENT Research Team present a status report on SCENT, a summary of recent research contributions and the design of the new SCENT-3 system. SCENT-3 is an architecture for a full scale student advising system. Work on SCENT-3 progresses concurrently on many fronts with new research contributions in dynamic planning and blackboard control, student modeling, strategy judging and diagnosis, and program analysis. The SCENT-3 architecture has been designed to achieve the goal of creating an intelligent advising system for higher order problem-solving activities with minimal domain dependence.

Chapter 8 by Philip Winne and Laurane Kramer concerns the DOCENT project. The long term goal of the project is to build a system that can serve teachers as an expert consultant whose perspective and advice help them take steps which raise the quality of education by improving their teaching. The authors present first the system's architecture with its four sectors. Each of the sectors is related to a major instructional task: developing principles of pedagogy, designing a syllabus for teaching, planning the forms of interaction that comprise instruction, and tutoring students. Then they describe the objectives and architecture of ELI (Expression Language for Instruction), a knowledge representation scheme expressly designed to capture critical aspects of instructional designs, processes, and results.

## STRATEGIES

Fiona Spensley, Mark Elsom-Cook et al. (Chapter 9) describe the DOMINIE system (DOMain INdependent Instructional Environment). DOMINIE is a tutoring system which operates in a number of domains and supports multiple teaching and assessment strategies. The main goal of the system is to teach people to carry out certain tasks using computer-based interfaces. The strategies implemented in DOMINIE are described individually, and then the way in which the current system chooses between strategies is discussed with reference to future directions for research on multiple teaching strategies in intelligent tutoring systems.

Warren Sack (Chapter 10) describes a new method for finding errors in computer programs: the overlooking method. He considers two classes of errors that account for a large portion of novices' programming bugs: (1) detail errors, and (2) coordination errors. Insights gained from the evaluation of the PROUST system (Johnson & Soloway, 1985) are used to point out the weaknesses of the bug identification methods used in PROUST and many other existing debuggers. How the overlooking method could overcome these weaknesses when used for the identification of detail and coordination errors is shown and some concerns regarding the implementation of the overlooking method are discussed.

## WHAT HAVE WE ACCOMPLISHED, WHERE WE ARE GOING?

Beverly Woolf (Chapter 11) attempts to answer these questions. She first distinguishes between work we do as engineers and work we do as researchers using an example from 13th-century architecture. She suggests goals for artificial intelligenge in education, describes some accomplishment since Carbonell's SCHOLAR, presents her own engineering contribution to the problem of providing customized response in an intelligent tutoring system, and finally gives a glimpse of work to be done to get nearer to the goals.

Patrick Suppes, in Chapter 12, first considers three extended examples of tutoring systems: they are interactive theorem provers (for the teaching of elementary logic, of axiomatic set theory and of the foundations of the differential and integral calculus), a system to handle informal calculus derivations, and a program that embodies several mathematical models of different aspects of mastery learning. He then considers what we need and what we may expect of tutoring systems in the next decade or two.

In the last but not the least chapter, John Seely Brown offers us, based on observations of out-of-school learning, his view on the emerging of a new epistemology for learning. He presents examples of the use of situated reasoning strategies both by ordinary people and by experts and compares the learning activities of these to the learning activities of students in schools. Implications of the results are presented for the design of ITS.

It is a challenge to work to achieve the goals set up by Woolf, Suppes, and Brown. It is, however, an important endeavor as it may help to acheive the goal of giving every human being a better access to knowledge. We do hope that, as ITS comes of age, its place will be as foreseen by John Seely Brown.

## REFERENCES

Anderson, J.R., & Reiser, B.J. (1985). The LISP tutor. *Byte, 10*(4), 159–175
Johnson, W.L., & Soloway, E. (1985). PROUST: an automatic debugger for Pascal programs. *Byte, 10*(4), 179–190

# 1
# Learning Companion Systems*

**Tak-Wai Chan**
**Arthur B. Baskin**

## INTRODUCTION

### Why There was One Who Studied with the Prince

In the past in China, there existed a child who studied with the Prince under the instruction of a royal teacher, as mentioned by the Chinese proverb "Studying with the Prince." Why? Perhaps the Queen recognized the importance of *learning companionship*. For whatever reason it evolved, the Prince was clearly expected to learn more effectively with the companion than by learning alone.

Learning Companion Systems (LCS) are a form of intelligent tutoring systems (ITS) in which a computer companion is added to the traditional ITS environment. In developing the LCS model, we have been guided by properties of learning companionship which naturally occur in human learning (Chan & Baskin, 1988).

* The authors would like to thank for support and stimulating discussion with Howard Aizenstein, Alfrida Chan, Peggy Chow, J. Richard Dennis, Jyy-Ing Lee, Ken Smith, Esther R. Steinberg, and Jian-Ping Zhang. We particularly appreciate tremendous help and patience of Lisa Chan throughout the process.

## Learning Facilitation through Peer Interaction in Different Areas

Influence of social interactions on individual cognitive development has also been observed by a number of researchers in different areas. In SOPHIE's game environment (Brown, Burton, & DeKleer, 1982), researchers noticed that "team players are far less self-conscious than a single informant . . . in collecting a protocol of a subject who is working alone, it is extremely difficult to get insights into why he rejects certain moves; subjects usually feel no need to justify why they don't do something. . . . In the two-person team environment, the arguments that naturally arise involve attempts to justify or defeat a proposed move. The record of these justifications provides a rare opportunity to see strategic reasoning unfold and be defended."

In the context of "control" in problem solving, which deals with the resource allocation during problem-solving performance, it seems to Schoenfeld (1985) that Vygotsky's hypothesis about the role of social interaction is plausible: "looking at situations from multiple perspectives, planning, evaluating new ideas, monitoring and assessing solutions in the midst of working problems, and so forth. Where do such behaviors arise, and how does one learn to argue with oneself while solving problems? . . . It seems reasonable that involvement in cooperative problem solving—where one is forced to examine one's ideas when challenged by others, and in turn to keep an eye out for possible mistakes that are made by one's collaborators . . ."

In the studies of cognitive psychology of reading, Goodman (1973) describes receptive language processes in general as hypothesis-based, defining them as "cycles of sampling, predicting, testing and confirming." Spiro (1980) points out that in the dynamic process of reading, "a reader's working hypothesis may be wrong and that at various points during the reading process it may be in a state of limbo, only partially specified, needing more evidence." At some of these intermediate stages, "the reader must back up and rehypothesize about the meaning of a text." But how can such active behavior of the reader be best motivated? It seems to be his need to *convey* his newly learned knowledge, while it is still at a hazy stage, to another agent—his learning companion (Aizenstein, Chan, & Baskin, 1988).

## Psychological Studies of Social Interaction on Cognitive Development

In his work, *Mind in Society,* Vygotsky (1978) hypothesizes that social interactions play a fundamental role in shaping internal cognitive structures. Vygotsky's *zone of proximal development* is the distance (as illustrated in Figure 1.1) between the actual developmental level as determined by independent problem solving and the level of potential development as determined through problem solving under adult guidance or in collaboration with more capable peers. He also points out that the role of imitation is particularly important in this concept

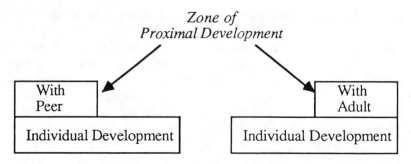

**Figure 1.1. Vygotsky's hypothesis on the zone of proximal development.**

of zone of proximal development. Experiments by Doise and his colleagues (Doise, Mugny, & Perret-Clermont, 1975) have shown that two children working together can successfully perform a task which cannot be performed by children of the same age working alone. Their subsequent experiment (Mugny & Doise, 1978) further indicates that "more progress takes place when children with different cognitive strategies work together than when children with the same strategies do so, and that not only the less advanced but also the more advanced child make progress when they interact with each other." More recent work by Petitto (1985) also illustrates that the approach taken by a pair of students to an estimation task can often be qualitatively different from the approach taken by either student alone. Once the new approach emerges, it then becomes part of their repertoire.

What accounts for the improved cognitive development through interaction with a peer? Doise and his colleagues (Doise, Mugny, & Perret-Clermont, 1975) suggest that such improvement is caused by *social-cognitive conflict*. In the pair situation, the child finds himself confronted with alternative and conflicting solutions which, while not necessarily offering the correct response, may suggest to him "some relevant dimensions for a progressive elaboration of a mechanism new to him" (Mugny, Perret-Clermont, & Doise, 1981). Therefore, it is the active resolution of the cognitive conflict on the learner's part that accounts for the improved learning under the influence of social interaction.

Doise and his colleagues do not further illustrate what constitutes a cognitive conflict. In a broad sense, we can view it as some idea or point of view that arises whenever one agent's response does not completely match with the other agent's knowledge. Unlike a teacher's response, which intends to focus the student back to the supposed correct path, cognitive conflict represents the conflictual dilemma that needs to be reconciled by both agents. Cognitive conflict is not a rare phenomenon, but occurs very often, for it is seldom that two agents' knowledge overlaps completely. When cognitive conflict occurs, the learner is forced to examine his thinking, looking for alternative perspectives hinted at by the conflict, and at the same time keep an eye out for possible relevancies. In a way, both agents need to diagnose and evaluate problems indicated by the cognitive conflict and to justify their own perspectives (Figure 1.2).

### Learning Companion vs. Collaborative Partner

The idea of building a *collaborative partner* to interact with a human student is being explored by Gilmore and Self (1988). This collaborative partner is similar to a learning companion in that

1.  Their learning has to be "psychologically credible," which means that the student must consider the learning performance, by either, whichever's possible for him to emulate.
2.  The role of collaborator or companion can de-emphasize the role of transmitting certified knowledge to students in accordance with the general trend of ITS cited by Gilmore and Self.
3.  The collaborator and the companion are able to make comments about learning skills in order to improve the student's learning skill acquisition.

Learning Companion Systems and the notion of a collaborative partner are different in several important aspects. The collaborative partner, in the form of a machine learning-based partner, emerged from the effort of trying to apply machine learning techniques to dynamically model a student (Self, 1985, 1986). Unlike Gilmore and Self, who do not suggest that collaboration is necessarily more effective than tutorial, our work has been inspired by insights from peer learning. Specifically, we have incorporated cognitive benefits from collaboration as well as competition which occur in peer learning into our LCS design. As part of our effort to explore the cognitive benefits of the learner of LCS, we have identified both simulation and machine learning as two different ways of implementing the companion part of an LCS system.

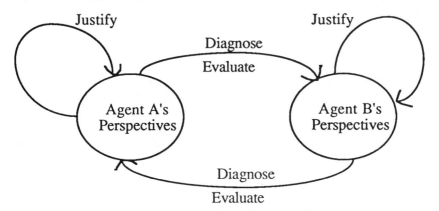

**Figure 1.2.  Cognitive interaction between two learners.**

Our research focuses primarily on exploring an *alternative architecture* in which the usual *two agent model* of ITS, a computer teacher and a human student, is replaced by a *three agent model* consisting of a computer teacher, a human student, and a computer companion. The distinguished notions of computer teacher and computer companion enable the system to interact differently with the student. Integration-Kid (Chan, 1989), a prototype of LCS, adopts a simulation approach to companion learning rather than by first perfecting a machine learning-based companion. In this way, some of the questions raised by Gilmore and Self can be answered. Through the use of a *curriculum hierarchy* to encode concept knowledge about the domain and sets of *rules of behavior* of different agents (Chan, 1989), different learning protocols can be designed in an LCS system, and from which we are able to define what is precisely meant by collaboration and competition. Furthermore, through experience with our prototype of LCS, we are able to test whether the student will accept a computer companion and "learn how to learn" as a result of interaction with the companion.

## DESIGN OF AN LCS FOR INTEGRATION

The design of a Learning Companion System (LCS) involves three agents, namely, the human student, the computer learning companion, and the computer teacher. The role of the computer teacher is to offer examples, guidance, and comments to both the student and the learning companion. The goal of the learning companion is to stimulate the student's learning through the process of collaboration and competition. In order to better illustrate the idea of LCS and discuss the two main approaches to the design of the learning companion, we will describe the application of LCS to the domain of indefinite integration. Since our primary goal is to explore the idea of LCS, we confine ourselves to a subset of indefinite integrations at the level of a first year undergraduate, for example, $\int \cos^5 x \, dx$, $\int e^x \sin x \, dx$, and so on. The prerequisites are some competence with differentiation and algebraic manipulation.

### Indefinite Integration as the Sample Domain

Indefinite integration is a domain which requires heuristic solution and a good deal of resourcefulness and intelligence. Many problems can be solved in a variety of ways—some of which are more efficient than others. Also, this domain is not heavily dependent on other mathematical abilities. In fact, after introducing a technique, students can usually work on a corresponding set of near miss[1] practice problems like those in a textbook without much trouble. Yet

---

[1] Winston's notion of a *near miss* is a sample which does not qualify as an instance of a class for a small number of reasons. Here we refer to a problem set that each selected problem differs slightly from previously selected problems by a small number of features.

**Table 1.1.  Basic Rules of Integrations.**

| | |
|---|---|
| (1) $\int x^a dx = \frac{x^{a+1}}{a+1}$ <br> where $a \neq -1$ | (2) $\int c\, dx = c\, x$ <br> where $c$ is a constant |
| (3) $\int \sin x\, dx = -\cos x$ | (4) $\int \cos x\, dx = \sin x$ |
| (5) $\int \frac{1}{x}\, dx = \ln|x|$ | (6) $\int e^x\, dx = e^x$ |
| (7) $\int c\, f(x)\, dx = c \int f(x)\, dx$ <br> where $c$ is a constant | (8) $\int (f(x) +/- g(x))\, dx =$ <br> $\int f(x)\, dx +/- \int g(x)\, dx$ |

students consistently have more difficulty in taking examinations and in doing miscellaneous exercises than they should despite many hours of working problems, as noted by Schoenfeld (1978). Part of the difficulty lies in their lack of adequate integration of separate concepts and techniques learned and therefore better judgment of the form of integrands.

INTEGRATION-KID is our first LCS system currently in development. The learning companion incorporated in INTEGRATION-KID will be a vehicle for our attempt to examine how a student's learning can be affected through the interaction with a computer companion. For example, when the companion acts as a competitor to the student for those less demanding drill-and-practice exercises (discussed below), we hope that the student can be better motivated than when working alone. For this chosen domain, the difficulty addressed by Schoenfeld should be directly addressed by the learning companion.

**Outline of the Design of Instructional Material**

Similar to the organization of the material in a standard textbook of calculus, the learning activities are divided into five sessions:

(Session a) Introduce the concept of integration.
(Session b) Familiarize with basic rules[2] (Table 1.1).
(Session c) Introduce the substitution method.
(Session d) Introduce integration by parts.
(Session e) Practice miscellaneous exercises..

Learning activities of Session a are rather like a traditional CAI format where teaching material is presented with simple question-and-answer interactions between the teacher and the student. Then, starting from Session b, we introduce the learning companion into the system. In Session b, the student learns to solve problems by applying the basic rules of integration in a rather straightforward

[2] For simplicity, we omit the arbitrary constant of indefinite integration.

way. After a while, the student will realize that there are many problems that cannot be solved just by applying those basic rules right away. Then, in Session c, he will be introduced to a technique, the *substitution method,* which, incorporated with basic rules, allows the student to solve a wider class of problems. Later, in Session d, he will learn *integration by parts,* another powerful technique, to solve another class of integration problems. In the last session, the student by then is already equipped with all the techniques he has learned. However, since the problems are no longer near-miss problems, the student cannot get any hint straight from previous problems.

## THE ROLE OF THE TEACHER AND THE COMPANION

When difficulty or doubt arises, the student may naturally look for the teacher rather than the companion simply because the teacher is the authority on the subject. On the other hand, the student may turn to the companion for assistance in order not to face the teacher with a problem. An important step in the design of an LCS is to know what will actually happen to all the agents, that is, the trilateral relationship involved in the learning activities (Figure 1.3).

### Results from Human Protocol Analysis

We have monitored the activity of a small number of human subjects involved in learning behavior similar to that intended for the Integration-Kid. A protocol analysis of these representative sessions has been used to help design the LCS paradigm. Based on our analysis and Schoenfeld's study (1978), we identified the following general concerns when designing an LCS for integration:

*Educational goal management.* Neither the student nor the companion can be relied upon to know enough about this domain to schedule the major learning objectives in the most effective way. In fact, the tutor may be the only one that could determine the order and the emphasis on a given topic or skill. For example, the human tutor foresees that proficiency of handling basic rules in Session b is critical in the later learning of new techniques or handling more complex problems. In order to achieve the proficiency, the student needs to *overlearn,* that is, practice until he almost *compiles* the knowledge.

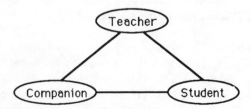

**Figure 1.3.   Trilateral interpersonal relationship of an LCS environment.**

*Stages of learning.* We observe that a student evolves through different stages of learning, for example, in learning a new technique, say, substitution method, first the student takes the teacher's demonstrated example as a template, and in solving his own problem, for each step, he only changes those parts that are needed to be changed—largely maintaining the *syntactic* (form of steps) nature of the problem solution (Figure 1.4a and 1.4b). We call this the *imitation stage.* It seems that the student at that stage tries to acquire all unfamiliar information as much as possible from the demonstrated example. Any mistake he made will be regarded as his misinterpretation of the demonstrated example if it is not the teacher's mistake. After a few problems, the student seems to enter another stage which we call the *developmental stage.* In that stage, the student is getting beyond the burden of syntactic detail. He conceives more about the essential parts of the new technique. For example, his first focus at that stage is "what will be a possible substitution" rather than "remembering that the first step is to find a substitution." Also, later at that stage, the emphasis shifts from accuracy more towards effectiveness. For example, what is a better substitution than another. When the problems are getting more complex, the student needs to integrate the newly learned technique with previously learned knowledge in order to solve those problems. We call this the *integration stage.* In short, the student's learning of this domain seems to evolve from *recognizing* (through the process of imitation) the new knowledge to *gradual increase of control* (applying the new knowledge with older knowledge to solve different problems) over that knowledge.

*Difficulty level of problems.* Managing the difficulty level of problems is an important part of any learning situation. Early failure or prolonged failure can discourage a student unduly. Similarly, problems which do not provide a challenge can reduce motivation. We have also noted opportunities to match the behavior of the companion to the level of difficulty of the problems. For example, problems in Session b are easy; the companion may act as an adversary to arouse stimulation for the student. Problems in Session d are more difficult ones; therefore, the problem solving task is subdivided into decision making and execution, and we adopt the responsibility sharing protocol.

## Defining the Role of the Teacher

The job of the teacher is to generate problems, demonstrate examples, explain the format of learning activities, negotiate with the student (e.g., how many more problems the student will do), and make final justifications of the solution and/or retrospective insightful comments. It is only under rare situations that the teacher would interrupt the problem-solving process—for example, when the problem is expected to be hard and both the companion and the student cannot solve the problem.

$$\int (3x-2)^{234} dx$$

set   $u = 3x - 2$

$$\frac{du}{dx} = \frac{d(3x-2)}{dx} = \frac{d3x}{dx} - \frac{d2}{dx} = 3$$

$$\therefore \quad \frac{du}{dx} = 3$$

$$du = 3 \cdot dx$$

$$dx = \frac{1}{3} du$$

Substitute $u$ into the integration

$$\int (3x-2)^{234} dx = \int u^{234} \cdot \frac{1}{3} du$$

$$= \frac{1}{3} \cdot \frac{1}{235} u^{235}$$

$$= \frac{1}{705} (3x-2)^{235}$$

Figure 1.4a.   Teacher's demonstrated example.

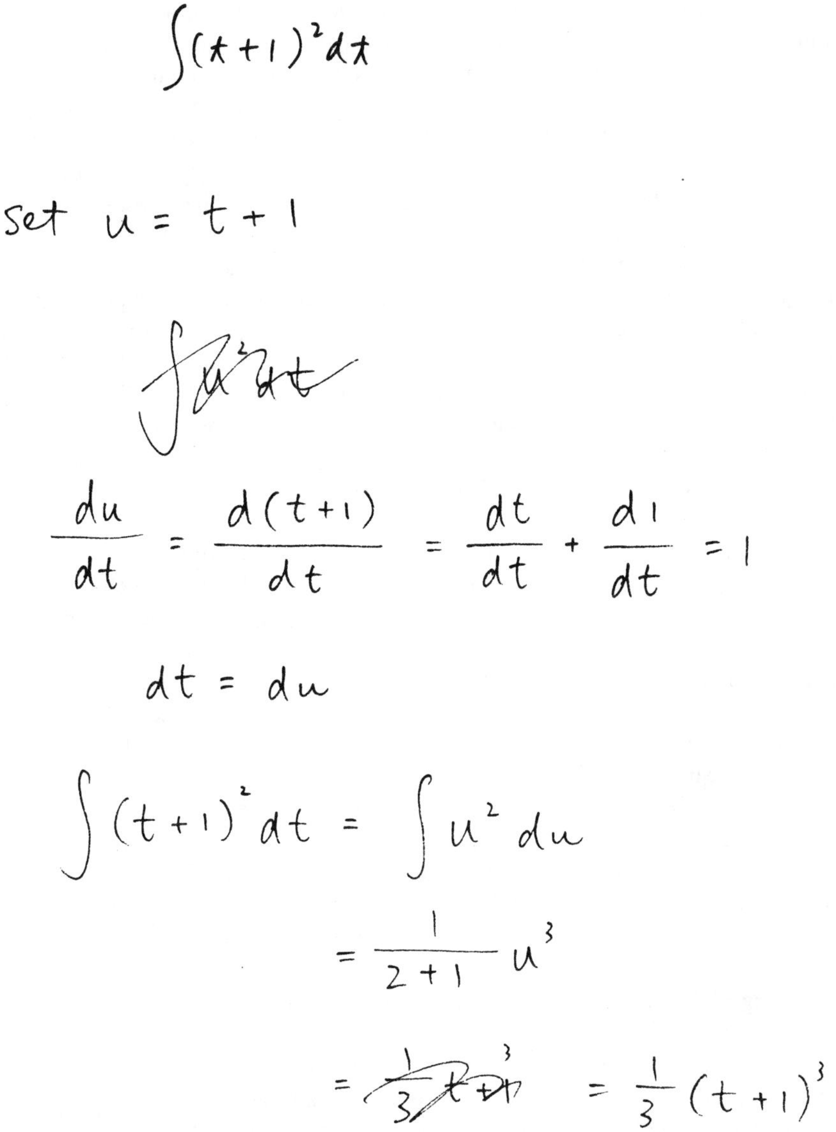

$$\int (t+1)^2 dt$$

set $u = t + 1$

$$\int u^2 \, dt$$

$$\frac{du}{dt} = \frac{d(t+1)}{dt} = \frac{dt}{dt} + \frac{d1}{dt} = 1$$

$$dt = du$$

$$\int (t+1)^2 dt = \int u^2 \, du$$

$$= \frac{1}{2+1} u^3$$

$$= \frac{1}{3} t^3 + 1 \qquad = \frac{1}{3}(t+1)^3$$

**Figure 1.4b.  Student's imitation.**

## Companion as a Competitor

Before a student is able to learn any technique to solve more complex integration problems, proficiency in using the set of basic rules is required. By observing student behavior, we noticed that a student works reliably with problems which are straightforward applications of the basic rules of integration. At the beginning, a student is very careful to choose and apply the proper rule; later on, he can naturally adopt some mental operations, for example, combining two operators into one macro operator, but still he refers to the table of rules frequently.

In Session b, both the student and the companion work on a set of problems offered by the teacher simultaneously but independently. They are requested to work on the problems slowly and accurately. After they have finished, they compare solutions, discover mistakes, and self-correct the mistakes in their own solution. If there remain mistakes not discovered, the teacher points them out. Those correct solutions will receive credits. Then another set of problems is generated by the teacher. Later on, both the student and the companion are required to solve the problems (e.g., $\int (e^x - x^{-3})\, dx$) in one step without consulting the table of basic rules. This additional requirement will encourage the peers to use more macro operations and to memorize the basic rules.

## Working Collaboratively with One Working While the Other Watching

In Sessions c and d, a student learns new techniques in order to solve more complex new integrations. The solution plan in employing these techniques by students can be divided into few phases. For example, in learning substitution method in Session c, the first phase is to choose the right substitution, the second phase is to differentiate the substitution. For more complex problems, this phase also verifies whether the substitution chosen is appropriate. In the last phase the original integration is transformed to a simpler one and then solved. To master these techniques, it is important for the student to have the firsthand experience of solving the whole problem with some external help if needed.

In these two sessions, while one is working on a problem, the other is watching—ready to give suggestions if asked or to critique. If they both run out of ideas, then the teacher may interrupt. The learning activities in this session can be represented by the following network of interaction (Figure 1.5).

## Working Collaboratively via Responsibility Sharing

The problems in Session e are of various levels of difficulty and may require different kinds or combinations of heuristic strategies and techniques. Working on this type of problem, where all goes together, the student has to constantly make a judgment, proceed, then another judgment and so on. At some point in the process, if the solution path looks to be improving, then proceed or seek a heuristic in order to continue; otherwise, back up. About the judgment at that stage, Schoenfeld (personal communication) recommends what he calls the *three phases model:* "Try simple things before you use more complicated techniques, and only when you've exhausted to the possibilities of these do you try some of the *shot in the dark* techniques."

In this session, the protocol of activities for the student and companion (Fig-

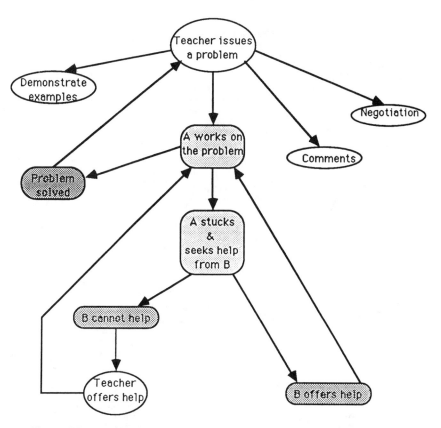

**Figure 1.5. Protocol of activity: one working while the other watching.**

ure 1.6) is negotiation, decision, and working. One is responsible for decision making and the other is for execution, that is, working the problem according to the decision. The negotiation occurs in a rather simple form. The one who will make decisions first suggests a plausible strategy and explains; for example, he suggests using integration by parts and specifies what is $u$ and what is $dv$; then he explains how the problem is similar to the previous one. Then the one who will work on the problem makes a different but plausible suggestion and explains why, if he finds one. Next, the one who is responsible for making decisions decides which suggested strategy to use and the one who is responsible for execution works on the problem according to the decision. This procedure repeats until the next decision point. The roles alternate.

It should be noticed that given a fixed instructional material, it is possible to design other protocols of activities in an LCS. Our choice of these protocols depends on a number of factors described above. Similarly, different domains may have very different design of protocols. Table 1.2 summarizes the protocols of activities.

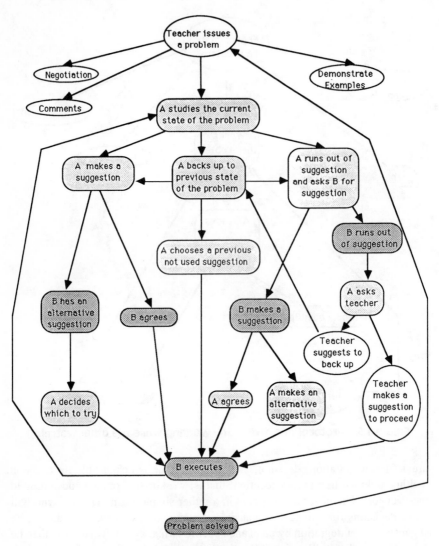

**Figure 1.6.    Protocol of activity: responsibility sharing.**

## EXAMPLES OF LCS INTERACTIONS

The following stylized scenes give an illustration of how the student's learning can benefit from an LCS learning environment with respect to the protocols designed above. More subtleties of the advantages of LCS can be revealed in such scenes.

**Table 1.2.   Summary of Protocols of Activities.**

|  | Same Problems (simple) | Different Problems (near miss) | Different Problems (various) |
|---|---|---|---|
| Working Independently then Comparing (competition) | Session b) | | |
| One Working & One Watching (suggestion) | | Sessions c) & d) | |
| Responsibility Sharing (collaboration) | | | Session e) |

**Scene 1 (Companion Working with Student Watching)**

**Teacher:**      *"Here is a problem, $\int \sqrt{2 - \sin 3t}\, \cos 3t \, dt$, would the Companion try it?"*

**Companion:**  *"$u = 3t$ seems to be a good substitution. Now*

$$\frac{du}{dt} = 3,$$

$$so \; \frac{1}{3}\, du = dt.$$

*Then the original integration*
$\int \sqrt{2 - \sin 3t}\, \cos 3t \, dt$

$$= \int \sqrt{2 - \sin 3t}\, \cos u \, \frac{1}{3}\, du.$$

*Oh ! I don't know how to continue. Do you have any suggestion, Student ?"*

**Student :**      *"How about trying the substitution $u = 2 - \sin 3t$ ?"*

**Companion :**  *"Okay !*

$u = 2 - \sin 3t$

$$so \; \frac{du}{dt} = -3 \cos 3t$$

*. . . .*
*I've got the answer !"*

**Teacher:**      *"Before going further, it is worthwhile to look back over some of the problems we have just solved:*
$\int e^x \cos(e^x + 1) \, dx$ *with substitution* $u = e^x + 1,$

$$\int \frac{x^2 d\,x}{4 - x^3} = \int (4 - x^3)^{-1} x^2 dx$$

with substitution $u = 4 - x^3$,
$\int x^2 e^{(1+x^3)}dx = \int e^{(1+x^3)}x^2 dx$
with substitution $u = (1 + x^3)$, and
$\int\sqrt{2} - \sin3t\cos3t\, dt$ with substitution $u = 2 - \sin3t$."
*There are two interesting observations here:*

*1) All the integrands (e.g. $e^x\cos(e^x + 1)$ in $\int e^x\cos(e^x + 1)\, dx$) are products of two functions where one is simple and the other is more complex, and for every substitution we chose the inside function of the more complex function; for example, $(1 + \chi^3)$ is the inside function of $e^{(1+x3)}$.*

*(2) If the inside function is a polynomial, the polynomial is one degree higher than the simpler function which is also a polynomial. Since differentiation of a polynomial will decrease its degree by one, that may explain why this choice can work; for example, $d(1 + x^3)$ will lead to $3x^2 dx$ and $x^2 dx$ is what we need. Also, it is quite easy to see that when we differentiate $2 - \sin3t$, $\cos3t\, dt$ will drop out.*

Here the student helps the companion by offering an important suggestion. The student is partially involved in the process of solving the problem by watching the companion work and being ready to help. Furthermore, the student can see possibly different strategies for the problem used by the companion. In addition, at this particular scene, the student learns that *picking a correct substitution* is important in solving the problem. Notice that if the companion does not make any suboptimal substitutions (taking $u = 3t$), then a negative example, and thus a piece of useful information, might not be noticed by the student. Moreover, at the end of a set of practice problems, the teacher looks back and offers insightful comments.

**Scene 2 (Student Working with Companion Watching)**

**Teacher:**   *"Let's go on another problem, $\int \dfrac{y + 1}{\sqrt{y}}\, dy$."*

**Student :**   $"\int \dfrac{y + 1}{\sqrt{y}}\, dy$

$= \int (y + 1)\,(y^{-1/2})\, dy$

$= \int (y + 1)\,\dfrac{1}{\sqrt{y}}\, dy$

$u = y + 1$

$\dfrac{du}{dy} = 1$

*Seems no good ! . . . .*
*Companion, how about $u = \sqrt{y}$ ?"*

**Companion:**   *"Sounds good . . . and I cannot see why this is not a plausible choice!"*

**Student:**     *"Thanks! Now,*

$$u = \sqrt{y} = y^{-1/2}$$

$$\frac{du}{dy} = \frac{1}{2}y^{-1/2} = \frac{1}{2}\frac{1}{\sqrt{y}}$$

$$\frac{1}{2}\,dy\,\frac{1}{\sqrt{y}} = du$$

$$dy\,\frac{1}{\sqrt{y}} = 2\,du$$

*Putting back to the integration, we have,*

$$\int (u^2 + 1)2du$$

$$= 2\int (u^2 + 1)du$$

$$= 2[\int (u^2)du + \int du]$$

$$= 2[\,(\frac{u^2}{3}) + u]$$

$$= 2\,(\frac{1}{3}\,y^{3/2} + y^{1/2})$$

$$= \frac{2}{3}\,y^{3/2} + 2y^{1/2}."$$

**Teacher :**     *"Good effort ! However, there exists an alternative way that you both may overlook :*

$$\int \frac{y + 1}{\sqrt{y}}\,dy$$

$$= \int \frac{y}{\sqrt{y}} + \frac{1}{\sqrt{y}}\,dy$$

$$= \int y^{1/2} + y^{-1/2}dy$$

$$= \frac{2}{3}\,y^{3/2} + 2y^{1/2}.$$

*Nevertheless, it is a good practice to look for easy alternatives before committing to a particular way too early. In this case, the rule:*
*$\int (f(x) + g\,(x)\,)dx = \int f\,(x)\,dx + \int g\,(x)\,dx$, that is, integration of sum equals to sum of integrations, tells us that whenever it is possible, split the integrand into sum to obtain simpler integration."*

Here the student was floundering at the beginning in searching for an appro-priate substitution. At one point, he found a substitution $u = \sqrt{y}$, but hesitated. Then he looked for assurance from the companion. The companion did not seem to have a better alternative. Now the student knew that this was not a stupid try as another student would also do that, so he was more secure to carry on. Finally, both the student and the companion missed an easy method. We can see that the companion's feedback is not totally reliable, in contrast to a teacher's. This student appreciates the other easy alternative only when it takes a big effort.

## Scene 3 (Responsibility Sharing)

**Teacher:** *"This, $\int x^2 e^x dx$, is another problem for you both."*

**Companion:** *"Try integration by parts with $u = x^2$ and $dv = e^x\, dx$. This is because we have tried $\int x \sin x\, dx$ with $u = x$ and $dv = \sin x\, dx$, and $\int x^2 \cos x\, dx$ with $u = x^2$ and $dv = \cos x\, dx$. The current problem looks to be the same kind of problems."*

**Student:** *"No objection! So let's take
$u = x^2$, $dv = e^x dx$
so, $du = 2x dx$, $v = e^x$.
Now, $\int x^2 e^x dx$
$= x^2 e^x - \int e^x\, 2x\, dx$
$= x^2 e^x - 2\int x\, e^x\, dx$."*

**Companion:** *"As before, we can continue with $u = x$ and $dv = e^x dx$."*

**Student:** *"I agree, so
$du = dx$ and $v = e^x$, the original integration becomes
$= x^2 e^x - 2\,[xe^x - \int e^x dx]$
$= x^2 e^x - 2\,[xe^x - e^x]$
$= x^2 e^x - 2xe^x + 2e^x$."*

**Teacher:** *"Well done. It is a very good strategy to think of similar problems which have been previously solved in order to tackle the current problem."*

It is easy for one to make decisions hurriedly without careful consideration. However, if one has to defend or to unfold his reasoning process, he is bound to give extra attention to the decision process. Here, the companion explained his reasoning process explicitly to the student. Through looking for other possibilities and justifying the companion's suggestion and his reasoning, the student's view of how to approach the problem is broadened. Furthermore, the correct reasoning was further justified and positively reinforced by the teacher.

## Scene 4 (Responsibility Sharing)

**Teacher:** *"Here is a problem $\int e^x \sin x\, dx$ for you both."*

**Student:** *"I suggest trying integration by parts with $u = e^x$ and $dv = \sin x\, dx$ since the integrand is a product of two different functions; furthermore, there is no obvious choice."*

**Companion:** *"With the same reason, it is also plausible to try integration by parts with $u = \sin x$ and $dv = e^x dx$."*

**Student:** *"I prefer my choice."*

**Companion:** *"Okay! $du = e^x dx$ and $v = -\cos x$, so
$\int e^x \sin x\, dx$
$= -e^x \cos x - \int (-\cos x)\, e^x dx$
$= -e^x \cos x + \int \cos x\, e^x dx$."*

**Student:** *"No progress. Come back and try your previous suggestion."*

**Companion:** *"Okay! $du = \cos x\, dx$ and $v = e^x$, so
$\int e^x \sin x\, dx$
$= e^x \sin x - \int e^x \cos x\, dx$."*

| | |
|---|---|
| *Student:* | *"Again, no progress. Any suggestion, Companion?"* |
| *Companion:* | *"Perhaps, we can continue with $u = e^x$ and $dv = \cos x \, dx$ and see."* |
| *Student:* | *"Okay!"* |
| *Companion:* | *"Now $du = e^x dx$ and $v = \sin x \, dx$, from the last step, we have* |

$$e^x \sin x - [e^x \sin x - \int \sin x \, e^x dx]$$
$$= \int e^x \sin x \, dx."$$

| | |
|---|---|
| *Student:* | *"Strange! This is the original integration. We've been going nowhere! Any suggestion, Companion?"* |
| *Companion:* | *"No!"* |
| *Teacher:* | *"You were on the right track! You may back up to the previous step. Instead of $u = e^x$ and $dv = \cos x \, dx$, try $u = \cos x$ and $dv = e^x \, dx$."* |
| *Companion:* | *"Okay! $du = -\sin x \, dx$ and $v = e^x$. We now have,* |

$$e^x \sin x - \int e^x \cos x \, dx$$
$$= e^x \sin x - [e^x \cos x - \int e^x(-\sin x) \, dx]$$
$$= e^x \sin x - e^x \cos x - \int e^x \sin x \, dx$$

*Moving $-\int e^x \sin x \, dx$ to the left hand side, we get*
$$2 \int e^x \sin x \, dx$$
$$= e^x \sin x - e^x \cos x.$$

*Therefore, $\int e^x \sin x \, dx = (e^x \sin x - e^x \cos x)/2."$*

| | |
|---|---|
| *Teacher:* | *"This is a rather difficult integration. It works because . . ."* |

This problem is particularly difficult because no similar problems have been solved before. In addition, the structure of the integrand gives no hint concerning which is $u$ and which is $dv$. As we can see, both the student and the companion are "shooting in the dark." The teacher had to interrupt and offer help or they might have given up.

## THE KNOWLEDGE AND LEARNING ABILITY OF THE COMPANION

In the LCS environment, both the student and the companion are presented with the same material. As learning goes along, their problem-solving performance improves. That is, with the interaction between them and the demonstrated examples, advices, and comments from the teacher, they acquire new heuristics, refine learned heuristics, associate better related mathematical knowledge, and know better when to apply the heuristics.

If the student is to learn from the companion, the companion's performance must advance along with and be approximately matched to that of the student. In the same way that most students learn a single task with a limited effort, the learning companion's efforts should be limited to a scale similar to that of the student. For example, if a student cannot solve a problem within 10 minutes or after three attempts, he may regard the problem as unsolvable and give up. Likewise, the companion may only be allowed a few attempts at a single problem.

Moreover, the companion has to be at least as advanced as the student. This means that when the problem has become a trivial problem to the student, it must also be a trivial problem to the companion. When the problem is difficult to the student, the companion may either solve the problem or try meaningful effort. For example, in the case of shooting in the dark, the companion uses what he has learned in a disciplined way to approach the problem. Rather like "wild goose chase" which only results in confusion, the effort at least reveals more about the nature of the problem. That is, before any attempt, the companion is able to reason and explain his actions from what he knows and what he has learned.

Even if the companion is limited to a few attempts and is required to have good performance, the companion clearly has an advantage over the student, that is, a good memory. The companion will not forget what he knows and what he has learned. Furthermore, whatever the prior knowledge of the student that a teacher may assume, the companion may also possess such knowledge. For example, it is hard to integrate $\int (\sin x + \cos x)^2 dx$, but after expanding the integrand $(\sin x + \cos x)^2$ into $\sin^2 x + 2 \sin x \cos x + \cos^2 x$, the companion may further use the identity $\sin^2 x + \cos^2 x = 1$ to simplify the integrand while the student might not discover that.

Furthermore, the companion should be able to benefit from a teacher's advice who knows the domain well. The companion can observe the student's work; he can have all the useful background knowledge and related common sense knowledge (e.g., the notion of complexity of an expression) that the student is assumed to have.

## SOME LEARNING TASKS OF THE COMPANION

Since the companion only learns those skills that would be important for the student to learn, the critical problem of building a learning companion is to identify the most important concepts and heuristics to be learned by the human student.

In Session b, if a student is able to write the following integration in one step without hesitation,

$$\int 5\cos x \, dx = 5\sin x$$

$$\int 4e^x dx = 4e^x$$

then he has been acquiring a new macro rule (collapse of operator sequences),

$$\int rf(x) \, dx = r \; eval \; (\int f(x) \, dx)$$

where $r$ is a number, $f(x)$ matches an integrand of the integrations listed in Table 1.1 and *eval* $(\int f(x) \, dx)$ means the evaluated integration of $f(x)$, for example, *eval* ($\int \cos x\ dx$) = sin*x*. According to the basic rules listed in Table 1.1, the sequence of operations would have been

$$\overset{(7)}{\int 5\cos x\ dx} = 5 \overset{(4)}{\int \cos x\ dx} = 5\sin x$$

$$\overset{(7)}{\int 4e^x dx} = 4 \overset{(6)}{\int e^x dx} = 4e^x$$

Therefore, we can see that two elementary steps have collapsed into one. Furthermore, with more practice, a student may write down in one step,

$$\int (5\cos x + 4e^x)dx = 5\sin x + 4e^x$$

Thus an even more powerful macro-rule,

$$\int (rf\ (x) + s\ g\ (x))dx = r\ eval\ (\int f\ (x)\ dx) + s\ eval\ (\int g\ (x)\ dx)$$

the student may have learned. With this rule, three elementary steps have collapsed into one. This also implies that any problem state of the form $rf\ (x)$ and $rf$ $(x) + s\ g\ (x)$ has become a solvable problem state, possibly trivial too, to the student. In the literature of machine learning, such learning techniques (acquiring macro-operators or schemata) have been addressed by several researchers (DeJong & Mooney, 1986; Laird, Rosenbloom, & Newell, 1984).

In Session c and d, sets of near-miss problems corresponding to the intended heuristics are given to the student. For example, as mentioned at the end of Scene 1,

$\int e^x \cos(e^x + 1)\ dx$ with suitable substitution $u = e^x + 1$,

$\int \dfrac{x^2 dx}{4 - x^3}$ $\left(= \int (4 - x^3)^{-1} x^2 dx\right)$ with substitution $u = 4 - x^3$,

$\int x^2 e^{(1+x^3)}\ dx$ with suitable substitution $u = (1 + x^3)$, and

$\int \sqrt{2 - \sin 3t}\ \cos 3t\ dt$ with suitable substitution $u = 2 - \sin 3t$.

A heuristic to learn is:

*if the integrand is a product of two functions, then pick the "inside" function of the more complex function as the substitution.*

After the student notices such a pattern and adapts the heuristic, the teacher may reveal the essential heuristic:

*if the integration is of the form $\int f(g(x)) h(x) dx$ where the $h(x)$ is different from $\frac{dg(x)}{dx}$ by at most a constant factor, then choose the substitution $u = g(x)$.*

This is typically viewed as similarity-based learning with a sequence of positive examples (Michalski, 1983). In Session e, through working the various kinds of practice problems, the student learns metaheuristics (Lenat, 1983), for example, the Schoenfeld's three phases model. Of course, both the student and the companion are taking advice (learning by taking advice or being told; Mostow, 1983; Haas & Gary, 1983) from the teacher—an important source of knowledge acquisition.

## MACHINE LEARNING APPROACH

In this approach, the growing domain knowledge of the companion, which results in improved performance, is acquired from machine learning techniques. We describe some perspectives and constraints in this approach.

### What can a Student Learn from a Machine Learning Based Companion?

The book, *How To Solve It,* by mathematician Polya (1957), which can be imagined largely to be the author's introspective analysis of his own problem-solving process, turns out to be a classic work in teaching problem solving in education. In fact, in providing instructions for how to go about particular tasks we are also providing models for the student for how to go about tasks in general. Papert (1972) has already pointed out that, in teaching children subject material, we are also "teaching children thinking." Being aware of such "meta-teaching," we may provide a more effective educational environment.

Research in machine learning has identified various machine learning techniques. Many of these techniques are inspired by human learning and implemented into computer programs. It is certainly a fruitful effort to explore application perspectives of these researches to education, in particular, in facilitation of students' "learning how to learn." In a machine learning-based LCS environment, the companion explains to the student *how he discovers something and why he speculates something.* By being conscious about the learning behavior in the companion's learning process, the student may acquire "meta-learning" in addition to the domain knowledge. If a student is percipient of such cognitive benefits in his own learning process, he is in fact exploiting and extending the space of possible approaches to a learning task rather than relying on the mysterious "inspiration" or "cleverness." Also, if a student knows explicitly what learning techniques are effective in a given domain, he may transfer those techniques to other domains when appropriate in a self-conscious way rather than by spontaneity. However, we should notice that there may be a paradox in this approach if we control the learning performance of the companion according to the student. Should we ask the student to learn those learning strategies that are not worth learning, for these strategies are ineffective and they lead the student to make mistakes?

## Some Considerations of Machine Learning Techniques for the Machine Learning Companion

Indefinite integration has been the domain of the learning program LEX (Mitchell, Utgoff, & Banejeri, 1983; Mitchell, Keller, & Kedar-Cabelli, 1986; Utgott, 1986). In LEX, the initial knowledge is a set of basic rules of integrations, important techniques (e.g., integration by parts), algebraic term rewriting rules ($\sin^2 x + \cos^2 x \rightarrow 1$), and so on—which all are simply listed as a set of operators. The concept to learn is a set of heuristics that recommend in which problem states the various operators should be applied. Each of these learned or partially learned heuristics is represented as a *version space* (Mitchell, 1977) which is specified by a set of its maximally-general members and a set of its minimally-specific members. While the use of version space is elegant to represent partially learned heuristics, it is not sufficient. For example, it cannot represent advice, such as "modify the integrand," provided by the teacher. Furthermore, a version space in LEX cannot capture exceptional cases. For example, a sequence of training examples $\int x^2 \sin x dx$ , $\int x^2 \cos x dx$ , $\int x e^x \, dx$, and $\int x^2 \ln x$ $dx$, may lead to a learned heuristic of using $u$ to be the monomial and $dv$ to be any transcendental functions. But, for $\int x^2 \ln x \, dx$, it is better take $u$ to be $\ln x$ and $dv$ to be the monomial $x^2$. The other problem of using a version space to represent a heuristic is lacking the intended purpose of the heuristic, which, however, is addressed by explanation-based generalization (Mitchell, Keller, & Kedar-Cabelli, 1986) (discussed below).

To learn a heuristic, a language for describing the generalization, or applicability condition, of the heuristic is important. LEX adopts a grammar for algebraic expressions but does not include composite functions (e.g., $e^{1 + x^3}$). There are two disadvantages of using grammar as description: (a) The description of an integrand is always down to every detail. For example, at some stage of learning, it may be easier to learn the obvious heuristic if the companion has an appropriate abstract language to describe $\sqrt{2} - \sin 3t \cos 3t$ as (product (power sin) cos) rather than (product $((-2 \sin (* 3 t)) 1/2)(\cos (* 3 t)))$; (b) It cannot incorporate prior mathematical knowledge. For example, $\sin x$ and $\cos x$ have very similar properties, not only because they are both trigonometric functions. They have similar properties in differentiation, thus this similarity may extrapolate to indefinite integration too. In fact, it is. Thus, a student may regard $\int x \sin x \, dx$ and $\int x \cos x \, dx$ as similar (so that a solution for one would imply similar solution for another) but will not compare them with $\int x \tan x \, dx$. Another aspect that LEX has not addressed is the metalevel knowledge, for example, being aware of the usefulness of the Schoenfeld's three phases model.

Mitchell, Keller, and Kedar-Cabelli (1986) describe how the Explanation-Based Generalization technique can be employed to generate an operational heuristic (a macro discussed before) of solving integral of the form $\int k \; x^r \; dx$ where $k$ and $r$ are any number and $r \neq 1$ by analyzing the solution of the training example, $\int 7x^2 dx$, and produce an explanation in terms of knowledge about the domain and goal concept. The goal concept is then formulated by generalizing the explanation structure. The main problem of adapting this technique for the companion in this domain is that the companion looks more like a *mathematician* than an *ordinary student*, since most students acquire such macro without realizing they have to prove it. In fact, as Van Harmelen and Bundy (1988) point out, such technique might not even need the example—just use rule 1 and rule 2 from Table 1.1.

As mentioned before, the companion only employs a limited effort of learning a task. Thus any learning techniques which exploit extensive searching or demand a large number of training examples are not appropriate. Furthermore, the learning strategies should reflect human natural preferences in learning. Also the design of knowledge representation should facilitate multiple learning strategies together with shifting of concepts to be learned in different stages of learning.

## SIMULATION APPROACH

In the simulation approach, the increasing skill of the companion is directly coded as part of the companion rather than being produced as a result of machine learning. The simulation companion essentially makes selective use of the complete domain knowledge. The increasing performance of the companion can be derived from a succession of discrete simulation programs, say, a set of rules of behavior, which each simulate a different level of performance. Selection among these programs is made based on the student's performance. Greater responsiveness to the student's increasing skill can be obtained using a knowledge base-driven simulation. In this approach to simulation a single problem-solving engine is given access to an increasingly complete knowledge base. In either approach, any information provided to the student about how the learning takes place must be explicitly included in the simulation.

In order to explore the impact on a human student of a learning companion system, the companion need not actually learn. The image presented to the student must be that of a companion whose skill advances in roughly the same way as that of the student. While machine learning techniques provide a natural explanation ability for the student and an ability to expand the LCS paradigm to a wider domain than hand-crafted simulations of problem-solving performance, the sophistication of the learning companion seems beyond the scope of current learning systems.

## THE SPECTRUM OF LCS

In principle, it is possible to introduce a learning companion to a tutoring system on any domain. In particular, LCS is not restricted to the problem-solving context. A student may be accompanied by a learning companion in learning concepts. For example, in learning the concept of variables in beginning algebra using discovery mode, suppose the student successfully generalizes the pattern $11 + 3 = 3 + 11, 2 + 1 = 1 + 2$, and $100 + 20 = 20 + 100$ to a rule $a + b = b + a$. However, the rule induced by the companion may be a literally different one, $x + y = y + x$. Now the student has to justify this alternative answer.

The wider view of LCS should not be limited to the one described above. In fact, the paradigm of LCS represents a broad spectrum of ITS design due to the possible varieties on the number and the identities of the agents in a LCS. Each of these varieties gives rise to particular cognitive issues in the student's learning.

First, it is possible to have no teacher involved. For example, in learning simple linear equations, the student may provide rules (e.g., distributive rule) and some examples to the learning companion. Then the student may observe how the companion solves the problems and improves performance. In this way, the student *learns how to learn by teaching the learning companion*. In fact, Neves (1978) has developed a system to learn solving linear equations.

At the other extreme, it is possible to have multiple teachers with different persona. For example, there may be a patient teacher and a demanding teacher. The student may choose one of them to respond adapting to his own learning style.

LCS may also be a simulation of peer group learning, which means more than one learning companion with different knowledge level or persona involved in the learning environment. For example, with companions at different levels of performance, the student can compare both suboptimal and optimal performance in learning. Another example is learning with one simulated and one machine learning companion. An interesting case would be that a human student is learning or solving problems collaboratively under competition with another pair of computer-learning agents.

Imagine in the near future as the price of computers falls and the technology of computer networks becomes more accessible, students can learn together through geographically distributed networks of computers (perhaps without a human teacher). We believe that current LCS research is preparing for such an *intelligent futuristic computer classroom*. In particular, LCS research for such a learning environment will probably focus more on the design of dynamically structuring the learning activities which may be monitored by a rather passive computer teacher.

## RELATED LCS RESEARCH UNDERWAY

The spectrum of LCS described above are essentially different LCS environments which vary over the following parameters: domain, number of agents involved, and role of agents (teaching, collaborating, competing, etc.). Apart from the development of INTEGRATION-KID (Chan, 1989), other LCS research underway if the following:

### Perspectives and Implications of LCS Study (Chan, 1989)

*Theory of learning companionship.* We have noticed that LCS environment stimulates more dimensions for student's learning than the traditional *single-teacher oriented* ITS environment (e.g., collaboration and competition). LCS research, we believe, will spawn a lot of studies of cognition and learning. In particular, a *cognitive model of learning companionship* is under development which will form a theoretical basis for LCS research, in particular, for the implementation of the learning companion.

*Counseling.* Apart from learning, the idea of LCS can be applied for counseling. Imagine an AIDS patient who is concerned about the general effects of such a disease and the social impact it brings. He probably prefers to discuss such matters with a knowledgeable peer, a patient with the same disease rather than with a human medical counselor.

*Implication to general knowledge-based systems.* An extrapolation of LCS research will perhaps be the indication that most current expert systems which also care about the user's cognitive benefits apart from offering a solution should have a *separate* component which helps the user justify the recommended solution or motivates the user to obtain a better alternative solution by his own. Critiquing systems (Miller, 1984) can be viewed as an instance from this perspective. Also the role of such a separate component in an expert system seems to be a *natural* environment for an expert system to incorporate a learning agent for knowledge acquisition. Comparison of this perspective with critiquing and apprenticeship systems (Mitchell, Mahadevan, & Steinberg, 1985) is underway.

### Reading Companion System (Aizenstein, Chan, & Baskin, 1989)

Apart from INTEGRATION-KID, another ongoing LCS project is Reading Companion System (RCS) for the domain of medical text. Well-written natural language text is everywhere, in the form of textbooks, magazines, journals, and so on—accumulated over time and written by different authors. In a Reading Companion System, a learning companion is added to a hypertext-like environment. The role of this companion is to engage the student in a peer-style dialogue about what he has read. Aside from the cognitive benefits to the student, this peer-style dialogue also supplements the system's natural language understanding. RCS undergoes three phases of knowledge acquisition in adding new text to the environment. In the first two phases, the system captures a *rough understanding* of a text base using a subprogram called the Knowledge Based Categorization (Aizenstein, 1988) which employs simple natural language processing techniques. In the last phase, the RCS improves its understanding of the text base through the peer-style dialogue with the student. An interesting aspect of RCS is that it takes into account the different strengths and weaknesses of the computer and the human. Most people would agree that a computer is a weak natural language processor but a good data retriever while a human student is a strong natural language understander. Through an interactive, cooperative, and complementary knowledge acquisition system like RCS, both agents—the human student and the learning companion—are benefited by the peer-style dialogue.

## CONCLUSION

In this chapter, we have discussed the preliminary idea of a Learning Companion System. In the learning environment of an LCS, aside from a computer teacher, there is a learning companion which learns along with the student, as a peer. The learning behavior of the companion is either simulated or actual machine learning. Moreover, we have discussed different considerations in the design of an LCS in the domain of indefinite integrations. Finally, we have outlined some perspectives of LCS research. Whether LCS is educational effective remains to be tested. Nevertheless, we believe that LCS, being a new subclass of ITS, will expand and emerge many interesting studies of ITS.

## REFERENCES

Aizenstein, H. (1988). *Knowledge based categorization of pathology text*. Masters Thesis, Department of Computer Science, University of Illinois at Urbana-Champaign.
Aizenstein, H., Chan, T.W., & Baskin, A.B. (1989). Learning companion systems: Using a reading companion for text-based tutoring. (Clinical Cognition Laboratory Tech. Rep. UIUCCL-R-89-1). Department of Veterinary Science, University of Illinois.
Brown, J.S., Burton, R.R., & DeKleer, J. (1982). Pedagogical, natural language and knowledge engineering techniques in SOPHIE I, II, and III. In D. Sleeman & J.S. Brown (Eds.), *Intelligent Tutoring Systems* (pp. 227–282). New York: Academic Press.

Chan, T.W. (1989). *Learning companion systems.* Ph.D. Thesis, Department of Computer Science. University of Illinois at Urbana-Champaign.

Chan, T.W., & Baskin, A.B. (1988, June). Studying with the Prince: The companion as a Learning Companion. *International Conference of Intelligent Tutoring Systems* (pp. 194–200). Montreal, Canada.

DeJong, G., & Mooney, R. (1986). Explanation-based learning: An alternative view. *Machine Learning, 1*(2), 145–176.

Doise, W., Mugny, G., & Perret-Clermont, A. (1975). Social interaction and the development of cognitive operations. *European Journal of Social Psychology, 5*(3), 367–383.

Gilmore, D., & Self, J. (1988). The application of machine learning to intelligent tutoring systems. In J. Self (Ed.), *Artificial intelligence and human learning, intelligent computer-aided instruction* (pp. 179–196). New York: Chapman and Hall.

Goodman, K.S. (1973). Psycholinguistic universals in the reading process. In F. Smith (Ed.), *Psycholinguistic and Reading.* New York: Holt, Rhinehart & Winston.

Haas, N., & Gary, G.H. (1983). Learning by being told: Acquiring knowledge for information management. In R.S. Michalski, J.G. Carbonell, & T.M. Mitchell (Eds.), *Machine Learning* (Vol. 7, pp. 405–428). Los Altos, CA: Morgan Kaufmann.

Laird, J.E., Rosenbloom, P.S., & Newell, A. (1984). Toward chunking as a general learning mechanism. *Proceedings of the National Conference Joint Conference on Artificial Intelligence.* Austin, TX: Morgan Kaufmann.

Lenat, D.B. (1983). The role of heuristics in learning by discovery: Three case studies. In R.S. Michalski, J.G. Carbonell, & T.M. Mitchell (Eds.), *Machine Learning* (Vol. 1, pp. 243–306). Los Altos, CA: Morgan Kaufmann.

Michalski, R.S. (1983). A theory and methodology of Inductive Learning. In R.S. Michalski, J.G. Carbonell, & T.M. Mitchell (Eds.), *Machine Learning* (Vol. 1, pp. 83–134). Los Altos, CA: Morgan Kaufmann.

Miller, P.L. (1984). *A critiquing approach to expert computer advice: ATTENDING.* Marshfield, MA: Pitman Publishing Co.

Mitchell, T.M. (1977). Version spaces: An candidate elimination approach to rule learning. *Fifth International Joint Conference on Artificial Intelligence,* pp. 305–310. Cambridge, MA.

Mitchell, T.M., Keller, R.M., & Kedar-Cabelli, S.T. (1986). Explanation-based generalization: A unifying view. *Machine Learning, 1*(1), 47–80.

Mitchell, T.M., Mahadevan, S., & Steinberg, L.I. (1985). LEAP: A learning apprentice for VLSI design. *Proceedings of the 1985 IJCAI* (pp. 573–580). Los Angeles, CA.

Mitchell, T.M., Utgoff, P.E., & Banerji, R.B. (1983). Learning by experimentation: Acquiring and refining problem-solving heuristics. In R. S. Michalski, J.G. Carbonell, & T.M. Mitchell (Eds.), *Machine Learning* (Vol. 1, pp. 163–190). Los Altos, CA: Morgan Kaufmann.

Mostow, D.J. (1983). Machine transformation of advice into a heuristic search procedure. In R.S. Michalski, J.G. Carbonell, & T.M. Mitchell (Eds.), *Machine Learning* (Vol. 1, pp. 367–404). Los Altos, CA: Morgan Kaufmann.

Mugny, G., & Doise, W. (1978). Socio-cognitive conflict and structure of individual and collective performances. *European Journal of Social Psychology, 8,* 181–192.

Mugny, G., Perret-Clermont, A., & Doise, W. (1981). Interpersonal coordinations and sociological differences in the construction of the intellect. In G.M. Stevenson, & J.H. Davis (Eds.), *Progress in psychology* (Vol. 1, pp. 315–343). New York: Wiley.

Neves, D.M. (1978). A computer program that learns algebraic procedures by examining examples and working problems in a textbook. *Proceedings of the Second National Conference* (pp. 191–195). Toronto, Canada: Canadian Society for Computational Studies of Intelligence.

Papert, S. (1972, Spring). Teaching children thinking. *Mathematics Teaching: The Bulletin of the Association of Mathematics, 58,* 2–7.

Petitto, A. (1985). *Collaboration in problem solving.* Manuscript available from author, University of Rochester.

Polya, G. (1957). *How to solve it* (2nd ed.). New York: Doubleday Anchor.

Schoenfeld, A.H. (1978). Presenting a strategy for indefinite integration. *American Mathematical Monthly, 85*(8), 673–678.

Schoenfeld, A.H. (1985). *Mathematical problem solving.* New York: Academic Press.

Self, J. (1985). A perspective on intelligent computer-assisting learning. *Journal of Computer Assisted Learning, 1,* 159–166.

Self, J. (1986). The application of machine learning to student modelling. *Instructional Science, 14,* 327–388.

Spiro, R.J. (1980). Constructive processes in prose comprehension and recall. In R. Spiro, B. Bruce, & W. Brewer (Eds.), *Theoretical issues in reading comprehension.* Hillsdale, NJ: Lawrence Erlbaum.

Utgoff, P.E. (1986). *Machine learning of inductive bias.* Boston: Kluwer Academic Publishers.

Van Harmelen, F., & Bundy, A. (1988, October). Explanation-based generalization = partial evaluation. *Artificial Intelligence, 36*(3) 401–412.

Vygotsky, L. (1978). *Mind in society.* (M. Cole, V. John-Steiner, S. Scribner & E. Souberman, Trans.) Cambridge, MA: Harvard University Press.

# 2
# Discovery Environments and Intelligent Learning Tools*

Anne Bergeron
Gilbert Paquette

## INTRODUCTION

In the field of artificial intelligence and education, one can make a distinction between *use of AI for teaching* and *AI tools for assisted learning*. On one hand, the system has to model, at least partially, the teacher-student interaction and behavior. On the other hand the system offers tools that can amplify and extend the learner's cognitive activity.

Important work has been done in this second direction that inspire our own work. The microworld approach (Papert, 1980) sees learning as an autonomous constructive process. Using LOGO, a programming language based on AI research, the children construct models about some aspect of the world and develop powerful ideas that can be transferred to other knowledge domains. In Great Britain, researchers like Richard Ennals have used Prolog, another AI language, to explore subjects such as chemistry or history. Using assertion declaration in Prolog, the learner builds a model incrementally and tests new assertions through interrogation of the logic database (Ennals, 1983). Even more related to our work is THINGLAB (Borning, 1981), a system developed at the Xerox Park in the Smalltalk environment. Simulated worlds can be constructed and modified by the learner, and then used for scientific discovery learning. Finally, recent work at the university of Pittsburgh has resulted in discovery worlds such as VOLTAVILLE (Glaser, Raghavan, & Shauble, 1988) where a scientific domain can be explored through the use of inquiry tools.

The LOUPE[1] project team was formed at the end of 1986 by the reunion of

---

\* These projects were developed within the Groupe de recherche sur les Outils Intelligents d'Apprentissage (G.O.I.A.) and received partial funding from the APO-Québec center. Most of the ideas and projects presented here resulted from discussions and team work with different members of the group. We want to specifically note the following contributions: Serge Carrier is responsible for the environment on the forest; Charles Camirand developed the environment on optical lenses; the PRISME language and the PRISME environment were mainly designed by Renaud Nadeau with the help of Martin Longpré. Finally, the nutrition project is the result of the collaboration between Annick Hernandez and Jacques Bordier.

[1]This French acronym stands for "Logiciels-outils utilisés pour l'enseignement," it can be translated as "Software as tools for learning."

two research groups. The first, composed of educators and computer-assisted learning specialists, has undertaken a first phase of the project (Paquette, Bordier, & Labelle, 1986) in which generic software such as spreadsheets and database systems have been used to create learning environments. The second group, composed of computer scientists, has worked to the development of multiparadigm programming environments (functional and object-oriented programming) simple and powerful enough to be used by children as discovery tools (Bergeron & Nadeau, 1986).

So it is not surprising that our work integrates two equally complementary preoccupations: Create computer environments closely tied to children's learning needs and find interesting artificial intelligence applications to education.

## THE LOUPE PROJECT

The project has three main goals:

1. Generate learning units, including both software and other didactic material, where the computer is used as a learning tool.
2. Build an artificial intelligence system for computer-assisted education specialists to create new learning environments.
3. Develop a methodology for the proper use of such tools in the classroom.

The experimental work with children during the first phase of the project confirms the interest of this general approach. It has also shown some severe limitations of traditional generic software used as design systems to build discovery learning environments. This work has enabled us to pinpoint the essential characteristics of our own design system (called LOUTI[2]) and to identify the areas where artificial intelligence ideas and techniques can best be used (Paquette, Bergeron, Bordier, & Nadeau, 1987).

### Computer-Assisted Scientific Discovery

The child is a cognitive system that develops by his own information and knowledge-processing activities. To maximize the child's cognitive development, knowledge-intensive environments are essential to help him explore a situation, construct his own concepts, and discover general laws by his own problem-solving activity.

Science philosophy distinguishes four categories of scientific activities (Pop-

---

[2]This French acronym has a double meaning: "Information Processing Software Tool" and "The Tool."

per, 1961; Langley, Simon, Bradshaw, & Zytkow, 1987): experimental data gathering; search of an "economic" description of the data by means of equations, taxonomies, rules, or qualitative laws; explanation of phenomena by model and theory building; and finally, verification of the laws and theories by prediction generation and testing.

In agreement with many educators, we believe that a certain form of the scientific discovery process can promote the cognitive development of the child (diSessa, 1987). We advocate the necessity and feasibility of a practical initiation to scientific discovery methods very early in school. These ideas have been experimented with both elementary and high school students. From this work with the computer in the classroom, we have built a simplified model of the scientific discovery method that can be used with young children. It can be characterized by five main phases:

1. *Free exploration* to identify the main objects and the variables of the knowledge domain.
2. *Structured exploration* where certain objects and variables are examined more closely and systematically to discover regularities, trends, and exceptional cases.
3. *Hypothesis generation* where an economic description of the data is built in the form of equations, taxonomies, rules, or qualitative laws.
4. *Prediction formulation* to provide for hypothesis testing.
5. *Reviewing,* identifying new knowledge acquired, reinforcing efficient learning strategies, and possibly starting new explorations.

### Description of Learning Environments Based on Generic Software

Ten learning environments, extending on average over 15 one-hour classroom periods, have been developed. Six of them are for elementary school pupils, from age 10 to 12, on the subjects of nutrition, meteorology, Quebec geography, forest, fractions, and numbers and measurements. The other four are for high school students, from age 15 to 17, on the subjects of demography, chemical equilibrium, optical lenses, and stock market. These themes were selected by giving priority to the subjects rated difficult by the teachers. The didactic material was developed interactively with these teachers using successive experimentation with children in the classroom.

Six units have been built using spreadsheets with good graphic capabilities: three with EXCEL on the Macintosh and three others with SUPERCALC on IBM. More recently, three more units have been built using HYPERCARD on the Macintosh. Finally, the nutrition project is a knowledge-based system created on an IBM using the TURBO-PROLOG logic programming language.

Each learning unit is composed of simulations or knowledge bases and knowledge processing tools. An activity guide is provided to the student. A methodological guide proposes strategies to the teacher for the integration of the learning unit in the classroom. The general pedagogic approach is to engage the student in scientific activity through problem solving with the help of the computer tools provided.

As a first example, in the learning unit on *Meteorology* (age 11–12), the student freely explores a spreadsheet containing data on 49 Canadian cities. He familiarizes himself with variables such as latitude, longitude, altitude, wind, temperature, rain, and sunshine statistics. Going on to a more structured exploration, he will sort the cities for certain variables and construct bar graphs to compare pairs of variables. A more precise analysis of the data starts when he formulates a hypothesis such as "the higher the latitude of the city, the colder it is." Looking at predictions derived from this law and not corresponding to known facts, the student will reconsider the hypothesis using other factors. At the end, he will review his activity, assimilating new knowledge, identifying new subjects to explore, and searching for explanations to the laws he has discovered.

As a second example, in the learning unit on *the Forest* (age 10–12), a knowledge base on the Canadian forest has been developed using Hypercard (figure 2.1).

Digitalized pictures and information are written on eight cards describing a tree: general information, bark, leaf, fruit, flower, localization, wood, utility for man. Various tools have been build in Hypertalk to process this knowledge. Children can browse through the stack, sort trees, or select them with a Boolean combination of characteristics. At all times, they have access to online definitions and pictures related to the terminology. At the beginning of the learning unit, each child will adopt a tree. On the street, in a forest expedition or at a botanical garden, he will gather data on his tree, filling an observation sheet and

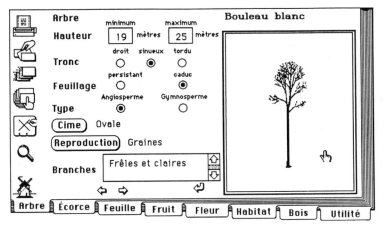

**Figure 2.1.    A stack from the learning unit on the Forest.**

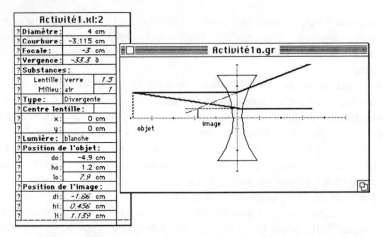

**Figure 2.2.  Windows from the Optical Lenses learning unit.**

transferring it to the computer, bringing his contribution to the collective database. After a free exploration of the database, a classroom discussion will generate hypotheses on tree properties. These hypotheses will be tested using the software tools provided.

As a last example, the learning unit on *Optical Lenses* (age 16–17) involves the student in discovery activities with a simulated optic bench developed using EXCEL (figure 2.2).

With the simulation, he can move, rotate, or distend an object and check the effect on its image through different kind of lenses. He can also modify the path of four light rays and get a feedback on their correctness for a certain lens, discovering concepts like the focus or center of a lens. Finally, he will vary parameters of the lens like diameter, convergence, and focal index, material, environment, or color of light, looking for a relation between the object-to-lens distance and image-to-lens distance. To achieve this, he can use a tool to transfer the simulated observations on a spreadsheet where he can analyze, sort, and graph the data. He can also use different mathematical operations on the variables to build an equation that fits the data.

## Limitations of the Generic Software Approach

For each of the five phases of the scientific method identified earlier, we have evaluated the quality of computer support given to the children.

At the *free exploration* phase, knowledge access and construction is crucial. In some learning units, a simulation generates data; in others a knowledge base is given to the learner; or data is collected by each student and integrated in a collective database.

Each generic software favors some form of access to knowledge that can be unfit to a specific subject domain. Information must be displayed in some rigid way: rows and columns of a predetermined size, cards of a certain format, and so on. This relative rigidity counteracts the very idea of a free exploration where the continuous reorganization of information display is essential. On the other hand the question-answering process with spreadsheets is technically difficult for young children and the form of the questions is quite limited; in Hypercard, it is nonexistent and must be programmed. Finally, spreadsheets and classical database systems can only express factual knowledge. It is not possible to include and interact with logic rules or structured objects. The solution to these problems is in knowledge representation techniques developed in artificial intelligence (Ennals, 1983; O'Shea & Self, 1983).

At the *structured exploration* phase, it is important to support systematic research with a variety of processing and information presentation tools that facilitate the discovery of regularities, trends, or exceptional cases.

Generic software offer very useful functions like information sort, selection, or graphic presentation. But a combined use of these tools will increase the complexity of computer operation, handicapping the learning process. Furthermore, each generic software has a limited set of tools. For many subjects, one would like to use simultaneously different generic software, but that would only increase the time spent on learning computer operation at the expense of the time devoted to learning the subject.

At the *hypothesis generation and prediction testing* phases, the learner needs tools to discover and write down a hypothesis in the form of an equation, a rule, a taxonomy, or a qualitative law. He then has to test how the hypothesis fits a certain set of observations. Then, if he thinks the hypothesis is right, he must engage in prediction generation and testing. These activities imply a back-and-forth movement between the knowledge base or simulation and the hypothesis.

In spreadsheets and classical database systems, no explicit computer support is provided for these operations. All is done through thinking with the help of pencil and paper. When the hypothesis is written down, the learner has to experiment with the same interrogation tools used for structured exploration. The incremental adjustment of an hypothesis with the help of counter-examples is an almost impossible task for a computer novice.

The last *reviewing* phase is essential for knowledge acquisition. The computer support can be provided by existing registering and playback software, but nothing can be done with the interaction data except looking at it. Functions could be built to select the significant events of the computer-learner interaction: question and answers during free exploration, processing and presentation tools used during structured exploration, hypothesis formulation and predictions results. These significant events would constitute a second-order knowledge-base that could be analyzed by the learner and the teacher.

| Phase | Useful functions | Limitations |
|---|---|---|
| 1-<br>Free Exploration | • access and construction of knowledge bases<br>• access to simulations | • rigid display and limited queries<br>• knowledge limited to facts |
| 2-<br>Stuctured Exploration | • sort, selection and mathematical operations<br>• graphic presentation of informations | • complex computer operations<br>• limited processing and presentation tools in each generic software |
| 3 and 4-<br>Hypothesis and Predictions | • queries | • no explicit computer support |
| 5-<br>Reviewing | • register and replay software | • no selection of significant events<br>• no analysis of the interaction data |

**Figure 2.3. Evaluation of computer support.**

To summarize our evaluation (figure 2.3):

1. Generic software presents useful functions such as simulation building, knowledge base construction and query, sort and selection, graphic display.
2. Some important phases of the method are weakly or sometimes not supported at all.
3. Only factual knowledge can be processed.
4. The user interface is aimed for adults and is ill-adapted to discovery learning and cooperative knowledge building.
5. The complexity of computer operation increases the time spent on software initiation and encourages a too-strict guidance of the learner.
6. The interesting functions are usually scattered through many generic software; the use of more than one generic software in the same learning unit can only amplify the complexity of operation.
7. Fundamentally, the tools and interfaces are too far away from the cognitive operations involved in discovery learning, thus creating a computer "noise" that can only reduce the time and attention devoted to the subject domain.

## THE DESIGN OF INTELLIGENT DISCOVERY LEARNING ENVIRONMENTS

With the preceding discussions in mind, we have started the project's second phase aiming at the development of Intelligent Discovery Learning Environments. These environments generalize the possibilities of databases systems, spreadsheets, graphic editors, and programming environments as discovery tools. They give access to the most important forms of knowledge in a chosen domain, allowing dynamic manipulation of knowledge bases. Specifically adapted to children learning, they include knowledge processing tools to support all the phases of a scientific discovery activity.

## Basic Orientations

The work that has been done on learning environments or microworlds (Papert, 1980; diSessa & Abelson, 1986; Lawler, 1987) characterizes learning as an autonomous constructive process of some intellectual structures. Every child has theories, or *mental models,* about the world. The essence of the learning process is the constructive transformation of these models into models that are more faithful, more coherent, more readily accepted, or simply more effective (Solomon, 1986).

Our basic goal is to give maximum support to the child's expression and construction of mental models. The evolution of a mental model can only happen when the learner tries to fit unsuccessfully parts of his actual model to existing conditions (Holland, Holyoak, Nisbett, & Thagard, 1987). So the proximity between the mental model of the student and its external traces using the environment is crucial. For example, an environment providing different meaningful representations of some observations and dynamically adapting changes made by the student will more likely reveal the mental model's mismatches than a unique and static representation.

The scientific discovery activity and the induction and deduction processes we want to support are particular cases of the problem-solving process. We view the child as a problem-solving system that develops his cognitive processes through *observation and discovery learning* (Michalski et al., 1983; Michalski et al., 1986; Langley, Simon, Bradshaw, & Zytkow, 1987). In the spectrum of learning strategies it is this form of learning that maximizes the learner's cognitive activity.

Through this activity, the learner modifies his mental models using *metaknowledge,* and particularly heuristics. It is important that the learning environments we build facilitate the use and improvement of such metaknowledge and heuristics. One way is to embed them in processing tools acting on knowledge. Another way is to favor their use by the choice of appropriate interfaces. A third way is to fully support the reviewing phase of the scientific discovery process we have described earlier. Tools for reviewing will encourage the student to examine his knowledge acquisitions and to pinpoint and reinforce the appropriate metaknowledge responsible for such acquisitions.

It is also essential to construct systems adapted to *group learning.* Even though the construction of adequate mental models is a fundamentally individual activity, the exchange of ideas on a problem and the sharing of information in a group will greatly enhance the validity and the completeness of a mental model.

Integrating this kind of exchange in a computer environment will also solve some problems usually connected with communication, such as defining, naming, detecting analogies, and so on.

## Overview of the Design System

There are many impacts of these issues on the computer architecture of the student environments and of the design system. The variety of information processed requires representation tools flexible enough to allow the treatment of complex concepts composed of structural, factual, procedural, and graphic information. The knowledge base must be dynamic and editable by children: They will be responsible for its evolution both at the level of the content and in the choice of interactions. Finally, the environment must provide tools for observation, for processing and, above all, for defining structures and relations within the area of study.

To reach these goals without the inherent complexity of a huge integrated software, we have discarded the idea of a unique system based on the same tools and interactions for all knowledge domains. LOUTI is a design system for intelligent discovery learning environments where not only the knowledge base, but also the tools, interfaces, and online documentation can be tailored to the knowledge domain, the children's age, and the learning strategies (figure 2.4).

The student environment is an open software where the initiative rests on the learner. The interaction occurs through a dynamic and visual interface built by a designer. In each environment, the student has access to knowledge bases and/or simulations structured by the designer. He can choose various tools to visualize

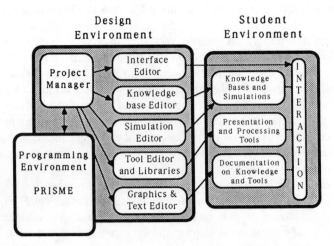

**Figure 2.4.   Functional schemata of the design system.**

and process knowledge and to define, test, and add new knowledge to the system. He also has access to hypertext type documentation on the knowledge domain and tools, such as definitions, procedures, object drawings, or activity description.

Through the project manager, the designer can use the editors to build each component of the student environment. With the interface editor, he can determine the kind of interactions the student will have with the knowledge base, tools, and documentation. With the knowledge base and the simulation editors he can give access to various kind of knowledge in the domain. With the tool editor, he can choose presentation and processing tools in a library, and then combine and modify them in the PRISME programming environment. With the text and graphic editor he can provide online documentation to the student. This design mode gives the designer complete freedom to tailor the student environment to his pedagogic goals.

We will describe further three of the essential elements of this design system: the programming environment, the structure of the knowledge bases, and the tool libraries.

## PRISME: A Multi-Paradigm Programming Environment

In view of the number and the variety of the problems raised by the implementation of LOUTI, the choice—or rather the construction, since none was found to exist—of the development system is crucial. The PRISME development system (Bergeron, Bouchard, & Nadeau, 1988) provides a highly interactive environment suitable for artificial intelligence applications. This system is currently available on the Macintosh microcomputer, thus ensuring that we will effectively reach, in various schools, large audiences for the different projects.

The PRISME language (Nadeau, 1989) is at the heart of the development system. The interpreter for the language features the harmonious integration of three programming paradigms: functional, logic, and object-oriented programming. In the LOUTI environment, the PRISME interpreter is available within the project manager enhancing the functionality of the different editors. One can adapt the library tools to specifics needs; design specialized processing algorithms; and, above all, use the different formalisms available in PRISME to represent declarative or procedural knowledge.

The problems related to knowledge representation are indeed central in the design of exploratory environments. In every discipline, we find a collection of facts, rules, theories, structuring principles, and algorithms as well as descriptions of systems and models. Hence many formalisms can and must be used at the same time. In various fields of AI, notably in education-related research (Borne, 1983; diSessa & Abelson, 1986; Drescher, 1987), similar problems related to knowledge representation and processing gave rise to hybrid programming environments, most of them combining either functional or logic programming to object-oriented features. The next paragraphs show the various benefits associated with the integration of these three paradigms.

*Object-oriented programming.* The object-oriented component of PRISME is inspired by the actor model (Lieberman, 1986). Local values, functions, and clauses may be associated with any object. Specialized objects can be defined interactively and incrementally from more primitive ones through multiple inheritance mechanisms. They can be used in PRISME to structure, with little overhead, a set of functions and clauses. Object programming is an elegant technique to use for partitioning the programming environment, implementing contextual databases (VanCaneghem, 1986), or generic procedures (Abelson & Sussman, 1985).

The initial incentive to include objects in the PRISME programming environment was to provide a natural mechanism for several users to share a same environment—children working on the same project, for instance. As opposed to more traditional functional programming environments, object-oriented programming provides ways to effectively shield local definitions and allows for multiple definitions of the same symbol. One can imagine, for example, different definitions of the primitive "Forward" coexisting in the same graphic environment, each definition designed by a different user.

The object-oriented approach offers interesting solutions to the problems of structured knowledge representation. The class concept (Stefik & Bobrow, 1986), as usually defined in the object-oriented paradigm, allows direct representation of hierarchical and network structured knowledge. Objects can also be used to implement the concept of frames (Minsky, 1975) where information units are described as set of related definitions. Finally, in the design of simulations, objects are used to describe components with states and operators acting on these states—like the LOGO turtle.

In LOUTI, objects are used extensively for the uniform implementation of information processing tools which generalize the operations found in spreadsheets and database systems. Objects are also very useful for coping with more technical problems such as managing animated objects on the screen or implementing direct manipulation interfaces.

*Logic programming.* The PRISME interpreter also supports Horn clauses resolution. The logic component of the language combine naturally with the functional and object-oriented parts. Any object in the system may have a private logic database, and queries directed to that object will be resolved accordingly. Procedures and clauses may be nested arbitrarily, hence any procedure can have access to the current state of the logic database.

The links between knowledge representation and logic programming are well documented. Horn clauses resolution facilitates the construction of deductive databases which combine facts and rules. Furthermore, logic programming is particularly useful for defining simplified "natural language" style interfaces adapted to specific audiences.

## Knowledge Base Architecture

The knowledge base is probably the most important component of a discovery environment. It contains both the initial knowledge provided by the project designer, and the additional information or constructions resulting from user's activity. We opted for a two-level architecture. The elementary level is based on objects and contains the core of factual and procedural information related to the field of study. The structural level allows model construction and exploration by defining concepts and relations over elementary knowledge.

*An object knowledge base.* In a project, the elementary knowledge is represented by a system of *classes* and *instances* (Stefik & Bobrow, 1986). A class defines a set of objects, called instances, that share a certain number of characteristics. Classes can be organized in an inheritance lattice that mirrors the similarities between the sets of instances they describe. Instances of a class can be created at any time, either by the project designer or by the users.

In order to define a class, one must define a certain number of *functions* and *operators.* The functions (often called *attributes*) associated with a class are used to describe factual data either by storing it directly, or by specifying means to compute the information. For example, a class defining a set of *territories* could contain a function *vertices* giving a list of coordinates, and a function *area,* computing territory area according to vertices coordinates. Functions are also used to store default values for potential instances. When an instance is created, it inherits default values, or default procedures, for each function defined in its class.

Each class also contains a certain number of operators. Operators are procedures that can change the values of a function defined in the class. Usual operators include procedures associated with the creation of an instance, edition procedures for the different functions that can modify a stored value or the code that computes it, and extension procedures that allow the definition of new functions associated with a class. Operators can also be used to construct simulations in more specialized environments. For example, if an object has a *position* function, operators can be defined that move the object.

The project designer—eventually assisted by a domain specialist—is responsible of the initial definition of the classes. He might also want to provide the knowledge base with some instances. In the *La Ville* example the initial classes are *territories, people* and transportation graph *nodes.* A sketch definition of *territories* and *people* is provided by the designer, with all the relevant instances of *territories,* but no instance of *people.* The transportation graph *nodes* contain the necessary information for the application of graph traversal algorithms, and several instances are initially available.

On the other hand, if the suitable operators are provided, children can edit a class by adding new functions or by redefining existing functions; they can interactively create instances and specify the values associated with the relevant functions. This kind of interaction, the importance of which may vary from one environment to another, can involve programming activities with redefined or user-defined primitives.

*The structural level.* Structures are (sub)sets or relations defined on sets of instances from the knowledge base. Structure definition is probably the most interesting interaction in a specific environment, and is mainly done by the users. This kind of interaction is tightly linked to model construction and exploration. It provides ways to organize and describe sets of instances, and to observe the evolution of those structures according to new or changing information.

The base structure is the *set.* The class definitions initially provide some universal sets of instances sharing the same characteristics. Subsets of these universal sets can be defined by specifying a predicate. This predicate usually involves the values of the functions defined in the class and provides an effective membership decision procedure. For a fixed state of the knowledge base, defining a set is equivalent to a query over a set of instances. On the other hand, each set is automatically updated following any modification of the knowledge base. Sets can grow or become empty, and relations between sets will generally change over time. In this dynamic perspective a set definition is more a *concept* than a query.

*Relations* can be defined between instances of the same set or of different sets. As with sets, relations are defined using predicates involving function values and will mirror the changing states of the knowledge base. Relations can also be predefined—like the adjacency relation between transportation graphs in *La Ville*—or user defined like "living in the same street."

In each environment, tools are provided to follow the evolution of the structures currently defined. Figure 2.5 shows two versions of the same sets corresponding to two states of a knowledge base. Directed edges correspond to inclusion relations between sets—some edges are missing for readability.

Structure definition, and their automatic updating, allow the user to experi-

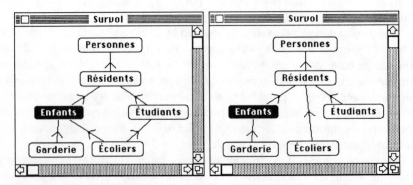

**Figure 2.5.   Reorganizations of sets following knowledge base modifications.**

ment and test different organizations or different models. These constructions react dynamically to changes or extensions of the knowledge base and the system gives immediate feedback on these modifications. Our assumption is that this approach will help establish links between the mental models of the learners and formalizations constructed using the system.

## The Tool Libraries

One of the main features of LOUTI is to supply the project designer with a large variety of information processing tools that act on defined structures. He can choose any subset of tools from the libraries and add them to a particular environment. Since all tools are implemented using PRISME objects, the designer can easily adapt any tool to specific needs using inheritance mechanisms.

Tools are usually triggered by users using menus provided by the designer and are then linked to a selected set or relation. These links will be kept by the system unless otherwise specified. Each defined structure can be linked simultaneously to several tools; each tool linked to a structure will immediately react to any change in the structure or, more generally, to any change in the knowledge base.

*Presentation tools.* Presentation tools are currently the largest set of available tools. The system provides the usual spreadsheet like tables, editable cards with hypertext facilities, and a vast selection of graphical tools, including pictograms and animated presentations. To meet specific educational needs, we also developed presentation tools that handle sets, trees, and networks.

When structures linked to presentation tools are modified, the immediate reaction of the tools allows the user to watch on the screen the evolution of some local or global characteristics of the structures. For example, Cartesian graphs will redraw according to edited information, new pictures or shading will appear on a map, and so on. The combined use of several tools linked to the same structure—tables, charts, animations—allow the confrontation of different point of views: One can study, for example, the effect of modifying a local information on a global graph involving all instances of a set.

*Processing tools.* Most of the classical processing or defining tools usually available in spreadsheets or database software are defined through the operators and the structures of the knowledge base: Adding or modifying information is accomplished through instance creation and edition, defining attributes with computed formulas can be achieved by function definition, and selection or query correspond to set definition.

To these basic operations, the libraries add tools for mathematical and statistical data processing, sorting, and curve fitting. We also developed specialized tools acting on relations allowing property analysis, partial order sorts, computing equivalence classes, and partitioning and graph traversal algorithms. Finally, some tools can modify the knowledge base, either by calling operators defined in a class, or by the generation of instances having specific characteristics. This feature has been used to implement simulations related to random phenomena.

## SAMPLE ENVIRONMENTS

We will now describe three of the student environments that are being developed in parallel with the design system. The subject domains are the city, high school chemistry, and nutrition.

### La Ville

La Ville offers elementary school children a means of exploring and describing their immediate physical and human environment (typically the immediate vicinity of the school). They can, for example, define subgroups of the population and their interrelations, study the relations between these groups and various territories, define and classify varieties of land uses, or analyze constraints connected with movement within a transportation network.

The environment supports graphic, factual, strategic, and conceptual information pertaining to a neighborhood (Figure 2.6); it provides tools for defining and processing this information; and, finally, it offers a multiuser interface designed for the exchange and sharing of information local to each user.

Maps of the target neighborhood are available in the system. These maps are digitalized from urban land-use maps. We have selected from the original maps the lot divisions, the streets names, as well as indications of the function of

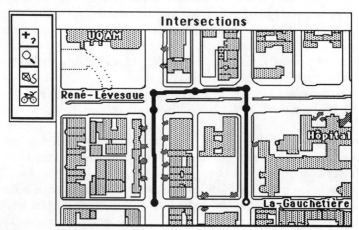

**Figure 2.6.    A map from *La Ville* with a car's shortest path between two intersections.**

certain public buildings. Graphs of the major transportation network, as well as the adjacency relation of territories with these networks, are similarly integrated in the system to allow automatic processing of movement within the neighborhood.

This information is normally completed by the different users. They can define, locate, and identify services, commercial and industrial centers, green spaces, and types of residence. They can similarly complete the information on the transportation network: one-way streets, pedestrian streets, traffic lights, crosswalks, bus routes, and train or subway stations. Finally, they can register in the system as residents or visitors and define suitable characteristics (and their values) for different kind of people.

The environment is completed by tools for presenting and processing available information. The most impressive of these is the graphic screen that offers fast-moving scrolling through the maps, zooming effects, interactive selection of territories, and animated tracing of paths subjects to constraints (shortest-paths or user-defined constraints like "safest-paths").

## High School Chemistry

Another example of scientific discovery environments is being developed on the subject of high school chemistry. Matter is diversified and complex, but it can be classified on the basis of a small set of properties on which the others are based. The series of findings from middle-age alchemy to atomic-based chemistry are among the best achievements of the scientific method. The student will engage in a simplified but similar problem-solving activity, starting from external properties such as color or taste, up to periodic properties based on an atomic model.

A knowledge base on chemistry is organized as a hierarchy of sets. At the beginning there are three primitive sets in the environment: *elements, compounds* and *reactions*. The learner can define subsets, modify set attributes, create new elements to any defined set, and select an active set for further study. He can also select or build an assertion stating a hypothesis relating attributes.

Different tools can be used to visualize the active set in the form of tables, cards, curves, networks, set diagrams, pie charts, atomic models, periodic chart. With these display tools, the learner will explore the knowledge base, identify its variables, and start guessing some relations between them.

During hypothesis formation, he can use induction tools like ordering, classifying, making modification to sets of observations, identifying trends between variables, comparing and adjusting assertions to observations. He can also use deductive tools for consistency checks with known facts and assertions or for predictions generation and testing.

With the display tools the learner can see different representations of the basic sets and their subsets, elements, and attributes. Choosing good representations is an important heuristic (Polya, 1964) that the student will have to master. When

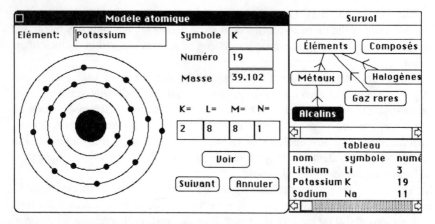

Figure 2.7.   A partial classification of the chemical elements.

he has chosen the right presentations tools, the learner will engage in a more meaningful exploration. He can also use ordering and classifying tools to reveal important similarities and differences that will lead to new set definition. Figure 2.7 shows the result of such an activity where a classification of the chemical elements is partly achieved.

The general heuristic here is called *conceptual clustering* in machine-learning literature (Michalski, Carbonell, & Mitchell, 1983). The learner can now go on with conceptual clustering and try to characterize more precisely the classes he has defined. For example, looking at a table representation of reactions of the form *alkali + halogen,* he can peek at the properties of the resulting compounds and find that they are all salts.

Another strategy uses heuristic tools inspired by the models built in the BACON programs (Langley, Simon, Bradshaw, & Zytkow, 1987) and the analysis of scientific discovery that led to their construction. In shifting from heuristics in a machine-learning program to heuristic tools in a student-driven discovery environment, we take into account the fact that the learning system is now a student responsible for the control strategy managing tool selection. We have to provide the right tools and interfaces that will make strategies transparent and meaningful.

For examples, the student can first select two variables, graph the observations, and guess the general trend. Then he can use a tool to verify the trend between the two variables. If the result is that the variables are inversely (directly) proportional, he can add a column to the observation table showing the product (quotient) of the variables and check if it is constant. If the trend seems linear, quadratic, or periodic, he can try curve fitting and adjust parameters to find a suitable equation.

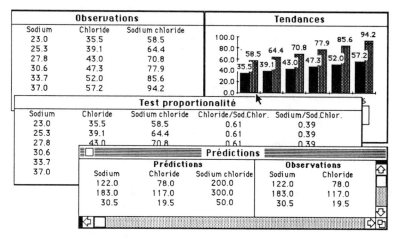

**Figure 2.8.    Use of induction tools.**

The use of such tools in figure 2.8 reveals the law of definite proportions for this set of reactions leading to the formulation of two assertions:

Chlorine   = 0,61 * Sodium-Chloride
Sodium     = 0,39 * Sodium-Chloride

Afterward, the learner must test these assertions against known facts and assertions, or new predictions.

**Nutrition**

A last example of a knowledge-based environment is being developed on the subject of nutrition. this is a subject where children often have largely false models about what is good nutrition. Through interaction with the environment, it is hoped that they will learn not only facts about food but also gain better theories about good nutrition.

The knowledge base contains information on over 500 foods: classification, nutritive value, historical and geographical comments, pictures and special characteristics like taste or color. The knowledge base also has definitions about meals (initially breakfast, lunch, snack, and dinner) and rules that define the concept of balanced nutrition, currently based on the Canadian Nutrition Guide.

The system first builds a model of the dietary needs of each user by asking questions about his age, sex, height, weight, and food preferences. With these facts, it computes his daily requirements with respect to energy, proteins, fat,

Voici, Sébastien, un menu pour une journée qui correspond à peu près à tes besoins:

| | |
|---|---|
| Petit déjeuner: | 1/2 pamplemousse;<br>1 jus d'orange nature;<br>1 tranche de pain grillée; beurre d'arachide. |
| Collation: | 1 jus de pomme;<br>1 muffin au son. |
| Boîte à lunch: | 1 tranche de pain de seigle;<br>2 tranches de saucisson de bologne;<br>1 tomate;<br>1 verre de jus frais de pamplemousse. |
| Collation: | 1 morceau de fromage cheddar; eau. |
| Souper: | 1 yogourt nature;<br>brochet, sauce au beurre;<br>riz blanc, carottes;<br>1 morceau de gâteau des anges;<br>1 verre de lait. |

Ce menu comprend:

| Énergie: | 8578 kj |
|---|---|
| Protides: | 80 g |
| Lipides: | 52 g |
| Glucides: | 321 g |
| Calcium: | 776 mg |
| Fer: | 16 mg |
| Complexe B: | 2,5 mg |
| Vitamine C: | 130 mg |

Alors que tes besoins sont:

| Énergie: | 8402 kj |
|---|---|
| Protides: | 24 g |
| Lipides: | ≤ 251 g |
| Glucides: | ≥ 151 g |
| Calcium: | 800 mg |
| Complexe B: | 18 mg |
| Vitamine C: | ≥ 40 mg |

Figure 2.9.   A menu proposition by the Nutrition program.

carbohydrates, vitamins, and minerals. Online documentation and previous non-computer activities will have familiarized the children with these concepts.

Each student can then compare his food habits with his needs by asking an analysis of what he has eaten on a particular day or week. The system will display a table and a graph comparing the nutritive value of food ingested with the particular needs of the student, show which particular food are responsible for a bad adjustment, or propose some alternative that can restore a better balance. The student can also ask the system to build menus satisfying constraints such as containing or excluding certain food or averaging a determined amount of calories (Figure 2.9).

The knowledge base is extensible, the students can add facts and assertions about food to the knowledge base, define new food categories or concepts such as vegetarian or party meals. These new definitions can be used in any query, including the construction of menus subject to user-defined constraints.

## CONCLUSION

The design of discovery environments for young children is still a pioneer task. After several experimentations with environments based on generic software, we were able to gain a larger perspective on both the educational and computer science problems involved in the conception of intelligent discovery environments. This resulted in the construction of software tools based on artificial intelligence techniques. These tools provide a suitable framework for the development of highly interactive environments that combine knowledge representation and processing features.

Problems related to knowledge representation are central and we have chosen to first tackle them from a pragmatic point of view. Using the different representation tools provided by the PRISME environment, we created a knowledge base model suitable for dynamic interaction. This model allows for the interactive definition of sets, the definition and modification of elements and functions, and the definition of relations involving these sets. We still have to test the effective power of this model to capture relevant knowledge in various domains and to support the different phases of elementary scientific discovery.

Initially constructed around tools usually available in generic software and deductive databases, the system now offers a large variety of information processing tools specifically designed with educational applications in mind. We also want to extend the tool libraries in several directions. One such direction is the development of interaction analysis tools available to both the students and the instructors. Another is providing the system with more sophisticated tools for the elaboration and verification of conjectures.

We discussed three examples of discovery environments designed within this project. In the light of these experiments, we hope to adjust a protocol that will facilitate interaction among the various specialists required for the construction of discovery environments: educators, content specialists, computer specialists. Following pedagogical objectives, one can determine the types of structures (sets and relations) definable in the environment, as well as the tools for acting on them. These choices allow the project designer, advised by the content specialist, to establish initial class definitions. This process is done with the help of a high-level project manager which allows interactive editing of the knowledge base and of the interface. Finally, specialized tools are adapted from general tools and may require more computer expertise.

## REFERENCES

Abelson, H., & Sussman, G.J. (1985). *Structure and interpretation of computer programs.* Cambridge, MA: The MIT Press.
Bergeron, A., Bouchard, L., & Nadeau, R. (1988). A multi-paradigm development system for exploratory environments. *CSCSI Conference Proceedings,* Edmonton, Canada.
Bergeron, A., & Nadeau, R. (1986). Building microworlds in an object-oriented LOGO. *LOGO 86 Conference Proceedings,* Boston, MA.
Borne, I. (1983). Les objets dans Logo. *Journée d'étude sur les L.O.O., BIGRE No37.* Le Cap d'Agde, France.
Borning, A. (1981). The programming language aspects of THINGLAB, a constraint-

oriented simulation laboratory. *ACM Transactions on Programming Languages & Systems, 3,* 353–387.

diSessa, A. (1987). Artificial worlds and real experience. In R. Lawler & M. Yazdani (Eds.), *Artificial intelligence and education* (Vol. 1, pp. 55–78). Norwood, NJ: Ablex.

diSessa, A., & Abelson, H. (1986). Boxer: A constructible computational medium. *Communications of the ACM, 29,* 9.

Drescher, G.L. (1987). Object-oriented LOGO. In R. Lawler & M. Yazdani (Eds.), *Artificial Intelligence and Education* (Vol. 1, pp. 55–78). Norwood, NJ: Ablex.

Ennals, R. (1983). *Beginning micro-Prolog.* New York: Harper & Row.

Glaser, R., Raghavan, K., & Shauble, L. (1988). Voltaville, a discovery environment to explore the laws of DC circuits. *ITS-88 Conference Proceedings.* Montréal, Canada.

Holland, J.H., Holyoak, K.J., Nisbett, R.E., & Thagard, P.R. (1987). *Induction, processes of inference, learning, and discovery.* Cambridge, MA: MIT Press.

Langley, P., Simon, H.A., Bradshaw, G.L., & Zytkow, J.M. (1987). *Scientific discovery, computational explorations of the creative processes.* Cambridge, MA: MIT Press.

Lawler, R.W. (1987). Learning environments: Now, then and someday. In R. Lawler & M. Yazdani (Eds.), *Artificial intelligence and education* (Vol. 1, p. 1). Norwood, NJ: Ablex.

Lieberman, H. (1986). Using prototypal objects to implement shared behavior in object oriented systems. In *OOPSLA '86 Proceedings.*

Michalski, R.S., Carbonell, J., & Mitchell, T. (Eds.). (1983). *Machine learning I.* Palo Alto, CA: Tioga.

Michalski, R.S., Carbonell, J., & Mitchell, T. (Eds.). (1986). *Machine learning II.* Los Altos, CA: Morgan Kaufmann.

Minsky, M. (1975). A framework for representing knowledge. *The psychology of computer vision.* New York: McGraw-Hill.

Nadeau, R. (1989). Intégration de trois paradigmes de programmation. Computer Science Master's Degree thesis (draft), Université du Québec à Montréal, Montreal, Canada.

O'Shea, T., & Self, J. (1983). *Learning and teaching with computers, artificial intelligence in education.* Brighton, England: Harvester Press.

Papert, S. (1980). *Mindstorm: children, computers and powerful ideas.* New York: Basic Books.

Paquette, G., Bergeron, A., Bordier, J., & Nadeau, R. (1987). Un environnement de conception pour l'apprentissage par le traitement des connaissances (Research report). APO-Québec, Montréal, Canada.

Paquette, G., Bordier, J., & Labelle, M. (1986). Logiciels-outils utilisés pour l'enseignement (Projet LOUPE) (Research report). APO-Québec, Montreal, Canada.

Polya, G. (1964). *Mathematical discovery: On understanding, learning and teaching problem solving.* New York: Wiley.

Popper, K.R. (1961). *The logic of scientific discovery.* New York: Harper & Row.

Rees, J., & Clinger, W. (1986). Revised Report on the Algorithmic Language SCHEME. *SIGPLAN Notices, 21*(2), 2–41.

Solomon, C. (1986). *Computers environments for children.* Cambridge, MA: The MIT Press.
Stefik, M., & Bobrow, D. (1986). Object-oriented programming: Themes and variations. *AI Magazine, 4,* 4.
VanCaneghem, M. (1986). *L'Anatomie de Prolog.* Paris: Inter Editions.

# 3
# Towards "Interactive Video": A Video-Based Intelligent Tutoring Environment*

Alan P. Parkes
John A. Self

## INTRODUCTION

The aim of this chapter is to consider the potential role of video within intelligent tutoring systems (ITS) and to describe a prototype implementation illustrating our ideas.

Both the ITS and interactive video (IV) communities claim to offer the prospect of radical improvements in learning but so far the dialogue between he two communities has been minimal. The reason for this is that the two communities have concentrated on different stages of the learning process, as can be seen by considering the apprenticeship model of learning (Collins, Brown, & Newman, 1987), which both the ITS and IV communities implicitly follow.

The apprenticeship model distinguishes four stages of teaching/learning:

1.  Modeling—in which the apprentice repeatedly observes the master executing (or modeling) the target process.
2.  Coaching—in which the master guides and helps the apprentice during attempts to execute the process.
3.  Fading—where the master reduces his participation as the apprentice becomes able to perform the target skill.
4.  Reflecting—where the apprentice applies self-monitoring skills to improve his performance at the target skill.

The ITS community has concentrated mainly on coaching, rather less on fading, and hardly at all on modeling and reflecting; the IV community has concentrated mainly on modeling, rather less on reflecting, and hardly at all on coaching and fading. ITS designers have been mainly concerned with developing pedagogical techniques for intervening constructively (coaching) during the performance of some skill. Fading occurs naturally as the need for intervention diminishes, but more often the student is moved on to a more complex skill with the level of

* The CLORIS system was built by Alan Parkes as part of his PhD research which was supported by the Science and Engineering Research Council (SERC) and Logica (Cambridge) Ltd. The authors' present research in this area is supported by SERC.

coaching remaining constant. Only recently, in systems such as AlgebraLand and ARK, has reflection been emphasized but usually the student receives no tutorial help during this stage. On the other hand, IV is used mainly to provide illustrations of some process for the student to observe. Videotape may also be used to provide recordings of student performance for self-reflection. The tutorial (coaching and fading) strategies associated with IV, however, are usually primitive, being based on conventional author language branching techniques. If the coaching/fading and modeling/reflecting stages could be decoupled, then the ITS and IV communities would be safe to ignore one another. Unfortunately, in general they cannot, as we will see.

Collins et al. develop their apprenticeship model for *cognitive* skills, such as reading, writing, and mathematics, where video sequences of expert performance may not be very insightful. They are concerned to emphasize the benefits of externalizing previously tacit cognitive skills so that the traditional apprenticeship methods can be applied. They distinguish between cognitive skills and physical skills, the latter being considered the traditional domain of apprenticeship methods. (The three examples they give of where apprenticeship methods are still used are tennis coaching, learning foreign languages at Berlitz, and receiving training in medical diagnosis). Such domains, they say, are characterized by having a target process which (a) is external and thus readily available to both teacher and student for observation and comment, and (b) bears a relatively transparent relationship to concrete products.

If the target process has these characteristics then it would be adequate, in the modeling stage, for the student to observe the process in action, for real or on film. But most target skills (including the examples mentioned above) do not have these characteristics: Most skills have both cognitive and physical aspects, and even those aspects which are directly observable are liable to the misinterpreted or not noticed by students. In any case, executing skills often results in nonvisible states.

There are additional problems with real-life apprenticeship which video-based apprenticeship may help overcome:

1.  In real-life, many skills (e.g., emergency operations) cannot be interrupted to permit the learner to ask questions.
2.  Learners may be reluctant to ask 'on-line' questions.
3.  If questions are not raised when relevant, then misunderstandings may propagate as execution continues, problems may be forgotten by the time execution is finished, and post-execution tutoring cannot relate to within-execution questions.

However, research on learning from film and television has shown that such media do not adequately support the modeling stage of apprenticeship (Lauer, 1955; Fraisse & Montmollin, 1952, who showed that about one-third of the visual content is immediately forgotten and the remainder lacks precision). Indeed, it is an assumption of interactive (really, reactive) video designers that viewers will benefit from reviewing video material.

A more questionable assumption of the IV community is that viewers have the metacognitive skills to know when and what they need to review. This needs empirical study but we feel sure that viewers will need tutorial assistance for adequate modeling from video material to occur. As Collins et al. remark, "a learning environment in which experts simply solve problems and carry out tasks, and learners simply watch, is inadequate to provide effective models for learning."

This, then, is the principal role we see for video within ITS—to support the modeling stage of an apprenticeship mode of teaching, that is, to help learners build conceptual models of a target skill prior to attempting to execute it, such conceptual models serving as advance organizers providing a structure for interpreting the coaching sessions. But building such conceptual models will not, in general, occur through the passive observation of video material; it must be promoted by tutorial interactions about the "meaning" of the material.

In the following sections we describe CLORIS (Conceptual Language Orientated to the Representation of Instructional film Sequences), an experimental video-based ITS, intended to illustrate these issues.

## THE METHODOLOGICAL BASIS OF CLORIS

(A brief outline of work detailed previously: Parkes, 1986a,b,c and 1987).

### A Video-based ITS Scenario

A learner faces a video screen, holding a pointing device. On the screen a short description of the aims of a sequence of (moving) film is given. The sequence begins. From now to the end of the sequence, the learner can interrupt the film, at any point, and enter into discussion with the system about that film, such discussion being about:

1. The event which is *in progress* at the interrupted point (e.g., "What is actually happening now?"); in terms of its place in the temporal chain of events on view (e.g., "Why was $x$ done *before $y$?*); its wider context (e.g., "Tell me more about . . .") and why and how it was done.
2. The objects which are on the screen at the interrupted point: by *selecting* (i.e., by clicking the pointing device on the screen image of the object) e.g., "What is $x$ for?" "Tell me more about $x$"; "Show me some examples of $x$ being used . . ."; "Show me a better view of $x$."

The system responds using: (a) generated *natural language* explanations; (b) generated *graphics overlays* and *annotations*; and (c) further *stills* and *sequences,* all being the subject, if required, of further interactions as described above.

In addition to this, the learner can use the system directly as a retrieval tool by asking questions, in some form, for example, "Show *x.*" Note that this retrieval function could be utilized by *another* ITS system, to which *this* one is an *intelligent image and film retrieval tool.*

## The Requirements of the System

In order to achieve these levels of interaction, a system needs access to the following:

1.  A body of *domain knowledge* describing the *concepts, objects, and events* for a particular domain in question, and providing access to the *background information* (Parkes, 1987) necessary to facilitate discussing moving films.
2.  A body of *descriptions relating the terms used in (1) to images in storage,* and *specifications of the interrelationships among those images*—to facilitate learner/system manipulation of *networks of related images.*
3.  A collection of *rules for the generation of multi-media "explanations".* This can involve constructing sequences (i.e., from existing *shots* and *scenes* (Monaco, 1977)), editing existing sequences, or coordinating the use of language, graphics, and film.

The architectural realizations of the three requirements have been separated because:

(a)  The *domain knowledge* exists independently of any medium which may be used to portray examples of that knowledge, and a particular concept or event may be visually representable in a multitude of ways.
(b)  *Images in storage* should be described separately because:
    (i)  Sequence material may not actually feature in that available, or there may be a mixture of stills and sequences.
    (ii)  Sequence material is, ultimately, a collection of still frames, and despite the fact that frames may be part of a sequence, they can also be used for other purposes (Parkes, 1986b).
    (iii)  The system should support the facility for *browsing* by the learner through sets of related stills.
    (iv)  The stills descriptions relate the domain knowledge to images, ultimately to *frame addresses,* and objects depicted in images to *on-*

*screen positional information* (e.g., *polygons*) representing, in some coordinate system, the location of the objects on screen when that frame is on display.

(c)    The *film rules* are *context and domain-independent.*


## The Meeting of the Requirements

***Events, instants and frames.*** We should not assume that because the videodisc is ultimately a collection of individually addressable images, one's conceptual description of it should start at those images. It can be seen from the above scenario that the *still* image has at least two interdependent uses:

1.    *As a picture in its own right—a photographic* depiction of objects from some domain, for example, a micrometer—which can be the subject of discussion as to the visual and/or conceptual aspects of those objects, giving access via some structure to other depictions, examples and so on thereof.

2.    *As an interrupted "moment" from a moving film,* that is, an event "in progress" (McDermott, 1982), in which case its fuller meaning requires not only (1) above, but the situation in the film at that time, for example, "In this picture the Engineer *is cleaning* the micrometer." Note that the interpretation of pictures in this way is not restricted to those taken from a moving film, for example, "Here is a photograph of a man *running*"—the man is shown "frozen" in a certain position: One *infers* that he was actually running when photographed.

So, in addition to the description of the *objectively-visible* aspects of stills (Parkes, 1988) suggested by (a) above, conceptual description of moving film requires higher level structures than the individual frames themselves. The argument is, in fact, analogous to that given by Turner (Turner, 1984, Chapter on Temporal Logic) who argues that description of *events* in terms of *instants* (c.f. the *frame*) should proceed from our conceptualization of those events, and not from the instants, which only possess meaning by virtue of the events they constitute.

***Event structures and "settings."*** What, then, are these structures we should describe? By way of illustration, an example can be considered, using a brief sequence of film (from a London University Audio-Visual Centre demonstration disc) also considered in earlier work (Parkes, 1986a, 1988).

The narrative content of the sequence can be briefly described as follows:

An engineer sits at a work bench. In front of him is a small case, from which he takes, then cleans, a micrometer. He moves a small piece of metal to the front of the bench and measures it with the micrometer. He writes the reading in a small notebook also located on the bench.

Now see Figure 3.1. This mapping shows the way in which the events in the "micrometer film" are portrayed by *settings*.

Intuitively, a setting is a group ($> = 1$) of frames sharing the same visual description (in practical terms, this includes frames which have differences deemed to be irrelevant). *In terms of the event structure of the film*, the setting is the minimal element of description, that is, the level below which description is, *at the level of events*, unnecessary. This means that all the frames within a setting which is a member of a series of settings realizing an event will share the same event meaning (determined by the particular film in which the setting is being used).

Referring to Figure 3.1, take setting $D$ as an example. In this setting, the rods of the micrometer are shown moving apart. In the film this setting is on display for 6.6 seconds (i.e., occupies some 150+ frames—at 25 f.p.s). The only changes in the frames in $D$ concerns the distance between the rods—in each and every frame the learner could point to the same screen locations to indicate the same objects. Moreover, the same objective *logical* description applies to each and every frame in the setting—each shows the slightly parted rods of a particular micrometer. Now consider the actions. The *unscrew collar* one, for example, is shown by:

1. Setting $B$.
2. A *cut* to setting showing *close-up* of hands of engineer.
3. A *cut* to setting $D$ showing the rods.

In setting $D$ the rods are moving, *but the engineer is not shown explicitly carrying out the action*, only its effects are shown. If the film were to be interrupted by the learner at this point, the system could quite reasonably say: "The Engineer is loosening the collar," but it would be unwise to say this if such a picture was arbitrarily retrieved as a still from the disc. The emphasis concerning the *meaning* of the picture has changed in and out of the moving film context—an excellent illustration of both the interaction between, and the need for the separation of, the descriptions of the stills and events. Furthermore, it is this *separation* which facilitates the exploitation of the full potential "meanings" of the still frame. This reflects the assumption (Parkes, 1988) that the still frame has a *continuum of meanings:* from the *objectively visible* (a depiction of a configuration of specific objects), through *event-selectable* (when one of many events could be chosen as the one which the picture shows a "moment" of), to *event-determined* (the frame is the result of interrupting a moving film, or further information is given, so that the chosen event is predetermined).

***The settings structure.*** Consider now the relationship between the settings themselves. $C$ is, in effect, a *zoom in* of $B$, while $D$ is a *zoom in* of $C$, and thus, transitively, a *zoom in* of $B$. There are other relationships suggested by *zoom outs, pans,* and *tilts* (see Monaco, 1977, for a glossary of film terms).

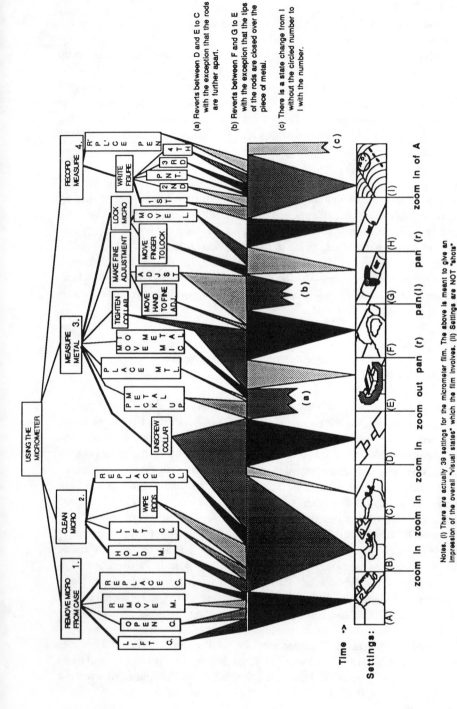

**Figure 3.1. The Mapping between the event hierarchy and the (simplified) settings.**

(a) Reverts between D and E to C with the exception that the rods are further apart.

(b) Reverts between F and G to E with the exception that the tips of the rods are closed over the piece of metal.

(c) There is a state change from I without the circled number to I with the number.

Notes. (i) There are actually 39 settings for the micrometer film. The above is meant to give an impression of the overall "visual states" which the film involves. (ii) Settings are NOT "shots" (i.e. the portion of film from "cut" to "cut"). In general, the shot is unsuitable as the minimal element at the level of events, due to the many-to-many mapping between shots and events (for example, settings A, B and C actually constitute one shot).

62

## X $\underline{Zi}$ Y (Zoom in)

X is a zoomed-in version of Y i.e. some detail from the setting Y has been represented in full screen size in X.

Example: C $\underline{Zi}$ B.

## X $\underline{Zo}$ Y (Zoom out)

The inverse of $\underline{Zi}$ i.e. Y is a zoomed-in version of X.

Example: $C_1$ $\underline{Zo}$ D.

## X $\underline{M}$ Y (Modified)

X and Y are the same settings save for some change. The actual change is difficult to quantify, but we wish this definition to apply to changes which preserve some non-empty sub-setting common to both.

Example: I $\underline{M}$ $I_1$.

## X $\underline{MZi}$ Y (Modified zoom-in)

X is a zoomed-in version of Y with modifications (as for $\underline{M}$) which affect the image in X. There must be a setting (though not necessarily existing as such) Y' such that Y' $\underline{Zi}$ Y => X $\underline{M}$ Y'.

Example: B $\underline{MZi}$ A.

## X $\underline{MZo}$ Y (Modified zoom-out)

The inverse of $\underline{MZi}$.

## X $\underline{Pl}$ Y (Pan-left)

X is a left pan of Y i.e. a setting which, in the (visible) world which Y is a part of, is located to the left of Y.

Example: $E_1$ $\underline{Pl}$ F.

## X $\underline{Pr}$ Y (Pan-right)

The inverse of $\underline{Pl}$.

Example: F $\underline{Pr}$ E.

Note: Settings in the examples are as in Figure 3.1. $C_1$, $E_1$, and $I_1$ are the resulting settings described in notes (a), (b), and (c) in Figure 3.1. (See Parkes, 1988, for all the setting relations.)

**Figure 3.2. Some of the setting relations described.**

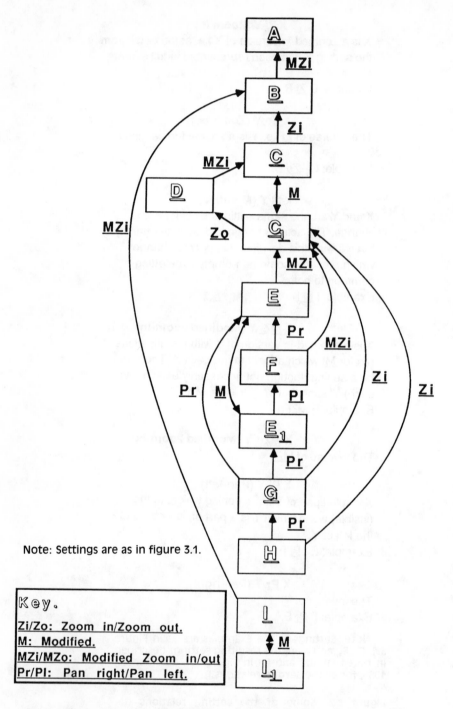

Note: Settings are as in figure 3.1.

Key.

Zi/Zo: Zoom in/Zoom out.
M: Modified.
MZi/MZo: Modified Zoom in/out
Pr/Pl: Pan right/Pan left.

Figure 3.3.    Simplified settings structure for the micrometer film.

Figure 3.2 gives a brief description of some of the setting relations (Parkes [1988] describes all of the relations, which include "overlapping" and "modified" pans and tilts).

Such relations can exist independently of the moving film scenario. Imagine a database of stills representing paintings. It would be quite feasible to show *details* from a painting by means of *zoom in* pictures: among those zoom ins would be those which were *pans* (or *tilts*) of each other, and so on. The structure which, for a collection of settings, maintains the details of the *setting relations* between any two of those settings is called the *settings structure*. For a diagrammatic simplified representation of the settings structure for the micrometer film see Figure 3.3.

The settings structure provides a way of accessing alternative views of the same object(s) in the still frame situation, and also provides a basis for the making of temporal inferences when the settings are part of the temporal chain in the moving film—a simple example: The book appears in setting *A*, but does not appear again until written on (setting *I*). Following backup the settings chain facilitates finding (and *showing*) the appearance and location of the book. The settings structure was influenced by the *temporal relations transitivity table* (Allen, 1981), in that an algorithm, based on Allen's, can be used to take advantage of the relational properties of the setting relations (e.g., *zooms*—in or out—are *transitive*) in order to propagate a fully specified settings structure from a skeletal specification provided by the describer. This is briefly discussed later.

***Temporal event hierarchies.*** Reconsider Figure 3.1 and, in particular the micrometer film event hierarchy. The informal interpretation of such a hierarchy can be seen in the *clean micro* example:

*Cleaning the micrometer involves:*

1. Holding the micrometer.
2. Lifting the cloth.
3. Wiping the rods.
4. Replacing the cloth.

Note that each of the sequence of actions is an *event* in itself, and might have other actions as its subordinates—as in *measure metal*.

Thus, an interruption in any of these subevents can be described: "The Engineer is cleaning the micrometer, and at this time is . . ." and so on. The interpretation of an event as being true of all its subevents is called *downward-hierarchicality* (Shoham, 1986) and is an important inference requirement of the type of system envisaged here.

## THE CLORIS SYSTEM ARCHITECTURE

CLORIS has been developed to demonstrate the applicability of the methodological basis as outlined above. (It is written in Poplog Pop-11 on a Sun,

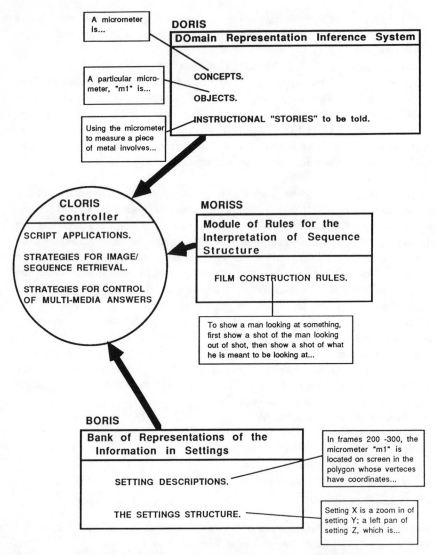

**Figure 3.4. Overview of the CLORIS system architecture.**

using a Philips VP-410 Laservision disc player, a Philips CM8533 monitor, and a Felix Link interface.) CLORIS consists of a *controller* module (also called CLORIS) and three representation modules. Two of the modules use the *conceptual graph* formalism (Sowa, 1984) as their basic *building block*. This notation was chosen because it is programming language- and domain-independent, is well suited to describing objects, concepts, and events in a uniform notation, and has clear psychological, philosophical, and semantic foundations.

The three representation modules will now be described (see Figure 3.4).

## DORIS: DOmain Representation Inference System

The purpose of this module is to provide the conceptual descriptions of the concepts, objects, events, and instructional *stories* to be told in a domain. The constructs utilized are as follows (note that the constructs are entered as shown, except that the *conceptual graphs* are entered in the *linear form,* as shown in Figures 3.7 and 3.9).

*A Type Hierarchy*
- the definitional hierarchy of type labels used in the system. This is actually a *lattice,* since some types have common supertypes (e.g., a PET-CAT is both a PET and a CAT)
- a domain independent *skeletal* form of this resides permanently in the CLORIS system, to which a describer adds the terms for his domain.

*Types, Relation and Schemata Definitions*
- are as given in Sowa, 1984 (for an example, see Figure 3.5).

*Event Frame Rules*
- describe the causality aspects of an event in terms of (conceptual graph) *preconditions, simultaneously caused* and *persisting* states (see Figure 3.6)

*Script Abstractions*
- based on the work of Schank (Schank & Abelson, 1977).
- abstractions describing a *stereotypical sequence of events,* for example, the sequence of tasks in the micrometer film above. The overall form is basically *Schankian,* but they take more advantage of the temporal hierarchies as discussed earlier (see Figure 3.7).
- they make no reference to films or any other media, since they exist independently of any means used to convey their information content.

## BORIS: Bank of Representations of the Information in Settings

This module exists to relate the terms defined in DORIS to sets of still images in storage. The settings are described by *setting descriptions* (see Figure 3.8).

In some cases, that is, a database of unique still images, each frame would require a separate setting description. As has been pointed out, however, one often finds that a setting description can apply to several—usually contiguous— frames.

The setting description has up to three dimensions:

1. *The visual, or logical.* Propositional accounts (in conceptual graph form) of what the setting (objectively) *shows.* Figure 3.8 shows an example where only simple object identifiers have been used, but in general, we would expect to find descriptions of *objectively visible states* involving the objects

*schema for MICROMETER(x) is*

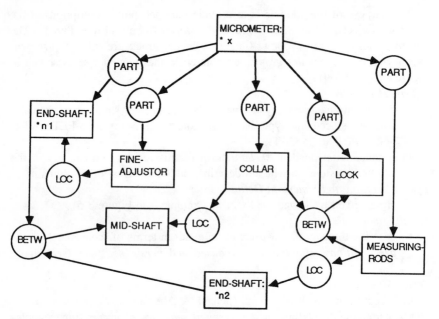

"A micrometer has a fine adjustor, a collar, a lock, and measuring rods. The collar is located between the two end shafts of the micrometer, on the mid shaft. The fine adjustor is located on one end, the rods on the other. The lock is between the collar and the measuring rods."

Note that Schemata are PLAUSIBLE, not logically correct descriptions. For the necessary conditions of a type one uses TYPE DEFINITIONS. Schemata can be specialised (by restricting some, or all, of the nodes to refer to SPECIFIC INDIVIDUALS). In these cases a schema becomes a PROTOTYPE. For example, the particular engineer in the film and the particular micrometer he uses are described by prototypes.

**Figure 3.5.   A schema for the concept "MICROMETER."**

in the setting. For example, the statement "the thumb is touching the collar" would be acceptable, providing that this statement could be seen to be true *in each and every frame of the setting, when that frame is viewed out of context.* All object identifiers in a setting description should be *individualized.* This reflects the assumption that the *describer* has sufficient information to state which *particular objects* are in the setting. However, this is not to say that the subsequent *viewer* (or *learner*) can make the determination in this way. The viewer may require further information from the *system* to do this.

2.  *The Physical.* This dimension represents information about the physical

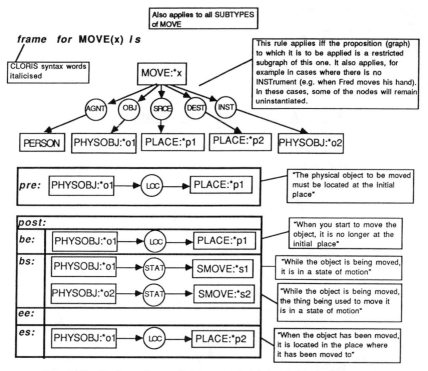

Figure 3.6.   A simple event frame rule.

location of the objects in the setting *in terms of their locations on the screen* (see Figure 3.8).

3.  *The Spatial, or Geographical.* Here is represented the information necessary to construct the *settings structure,* that is, (some of) the setting relations holding between the setting being described and others. The information is used by a *constraints propagation algorithm* to traverse the settings structure network, suitably restricting, where possible, the number of setting relations applying between pairs of settings. Thus, the describer need only specify a subset of the whole settings structure.

Note that any, or all, of the above dimensions may be omitted from any particular setting description.

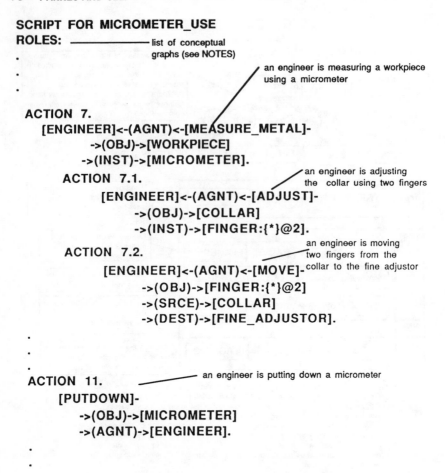

SCRIPT FOR MICROMETER_USE
ROLES: ———————— list of conceptual
      .                      graphs (see NOTES)

      .                                              an engineer is measuring a workpiece
                                                     using a micrometer
      .

  ACTION 7.
    [ENGINEER]<-(AGNT)<-[MEASURE_METAL]-
        ->(OBJ)->[WORKPIECE]
      ->(INST)->[MICROMETER].
          ACTION 7.1.                          an engineer is adjusting
                                                the  collar using two fingers
              [ENGINEER]<-(AGNT)<-[ADJUST]-
                  ->(OBJ)->[COLLAR]
                ->(INST)->[FINGER:{*}@2].
                                              an engineer is moving
          ACTION 7.2.                          two fingers from the
              [ENGINEER]<-(AGNT)<-[MOVE]- collar to the fine adjustor
                  ->(OBJ)->[FINGER:{*}@2]
                  ->(SRCE)->[COLLAR]
                  ->(DEST)->[FINE_ADJUSTOR].

      .
      .

      .
  ACTION 11.          ————————  an engineer is putting down a micrometer
      [PUTDOWN]-
          ->(OBJ)->[MICROMETER]
          ->(AGNT)->[ENGINEER].

      .
      .

      .

> Notes: As there is only one engineer, micrometer etc., the type labels can be left
> without variables i.e. the label "ENGINEER" refers to the same engineer throughout
> the script. If there were two, then say, "ENGINEER:*x" and "ENGINEER:*y" would
> have to be used to indicate which one was involved in particular actions. Similarly,
> since we are concerned with only one micrometer, there is no need for a "roles"
> specification including such information as "COLLAR:*c" is part of "MICROMETER:*m,
> while "COLLAR:*c1" is part of "MICROMETER:*m1" etc.

**Figure 3.7.   (Part of) the script ABSTRACTION for the micrometer film.**

**MORISS: Module Of Rules for Interpreting the Structure of Sequences**

In general terms, this module is given a conceptual representation of a "chunk"
of knowledge, and produces a coordinated multimedia "explanation" of that
knowledge. This will involve not only the *generation* of new sequences to satisfy

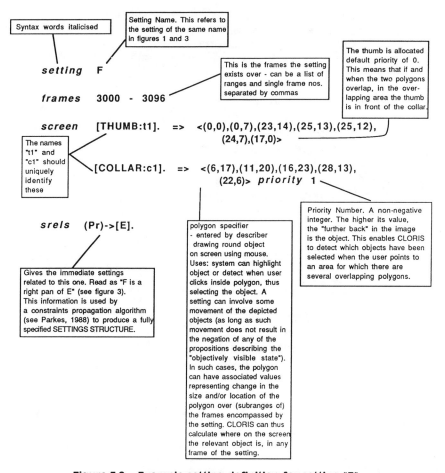

**Figure 3.8.   Example setting definition for setting "F".**

some narrative specification, but also the use of still images, graphics, and generated natural language to communicate dynamic concepts (for example, a frame from setting *D*—discussed above—could be shown, with graphical annotation, to describe what happens when the collar is *tightened*). At present, the MORISS module is only rudimentary, and its development is a subject of the first author's current research.

## OPERATION OF THE CLORIS SYSTEM

CLORIS exists to demonstrate the realisability of the above scenario. CLORIS displays sequences, monitors user activities and interruptions, answers questions

**SCRIPT APPLICATION FOR MICROMETER_USE**
**[ENGINEER]** => **[ENGINEER:e1]**
**[MICROMETER]** => **[MICROMETER:m1]**
**[CASE]** => **[CASE:c1]** ⟵ role assignments for this application.
The individualised type labels (e.g. "MICROMETER:m1")are used by CLORIS
to retrieve prototypes so that type labels in the application can be suitably restricted
(e.g. the micrometer "m1" has a collar called "c1") - these restricted versions will be the ones featuring in the SETTING DESCRIPTIONS.

- The frames over which the action takes place. Also used to retrieve the SETTINGS for the action.

**ACTION  7.  2999-3477**

**ACTION  7.1.  2999-3202**

**[TIGHTEN_FOR_OBJ]->(INST)->[FINGER:{ff1,th1}].**

Note that "TIGHTEN_FOR_OBJ" is a subtype of "ADJUST".

**ACTION  7.2.  3203-3211**

**[MOVE]->(OBJ)->[FINGER:{ff1,th1}].**

This graph can be joined to the corresponding graph in the ABSTRACTION (figure 7), and along with restrictions provided by the expanded role assigments (see above), the resulting graph constitutes a specific description of this action in the context of the particular film sequence.

This action (and all its subordinates) has been (linearly) deleted from the realisation. Note that the abstraction simply says that the micrometer is put down. The extra information here says it was put in the case (using the left hand).

**ACTION 11. cut**
  **[PUTDOWN]-**
    **->(DEST)->[CASE]**
    **->(INST)->[HAND:e1rh].**

Note also that actions can have some subordinates marked "cut" even if they themselves are (partly) present in the film.

Notes. (i) A given ABSTRACTION can have any number of associated APPLICATIONS.
(ii) The describer need not re-specify the whole of the information present in the ABSTRACTION. For example ACTION 7 is not specified at all being, save for the necessary RESTRICTIONS, identical to ACTION 7 in the abstraction (figure 7).
(iii) The type of any label in CLORIS is given by its type hierarchy position. Thus, labels which are subtypes of type EVENT in the above script are used to retrieve EVENT FRAME RULES for which they are subtypes.

**Figure 3.9.  (Part of) the script APPLICATION for the micrometer film.**

(including *retrieval*—see Parkes, 1988) and discusses any part of the film or any still image which the user desires. The output from the system is:

*Generated Natural Language*
- this uses a *conceptual graph to English* generator. Example outputs can be seen on pp. 77–79.

*Textual and Graphical Annotation*
- highlighting and labeling them (from the *setting polygon specifiers*—see Figure 3.8).

*Further Stills and/or Sequences*
- including replays of the same sequence (or parts thereof), and short explanatory sequences or example stills, and so on.
- *stills:* by interpreting the settings structure to find suitable *close-ups, long-shots* of a particular object or "scene."
- *sequences:* by consulting DORIS for event descriptions, these being mapped onto existing sequences, or used as a basis for the generation of new ones (via MORISS).

CLORIS also uses a *learner-model* (Clancey, 1986) to guide its discussion with a particular learner. The present model is, however, rudimentary, and consists of a record, for a given user, of the level of explanation reached for each concept in the domain.

Finally, since the CLORIS system is required to *discuss the events in a moving film, relate those events to the domain material, to other sequences and to stills portraying them, and be capable of discussing the event in progress at any stage in a moving film,* the constructs called *script applications/instantiations* are introduced. Any script *abstraction* in DORIS can have any number of *applications* associated with it (since a piece of narrative can, in general, be represented by various pieces of film). The application is derived from the abstraction, but presents a more detailed breakdown of the events involved, in respect of the particular *actors* and *props,* ultimately relating those events to start/end disc locations where *film phrases* showing those events can be found. Since film realization of events can involve the nonrepresentation of certain events from the sequence—so called *linear deletion* (Carroll, 1980)—on the understanding that the viewer will infer their presence, the application allows such events to be specified (with their full details being derived from the abstraction). Figure 3.9 shows a part of an application.

At compilation time, CLORIS forms mappings between:

1. The storage independent DORIS scripts and the storage dependent CLORIS applications. This involves the *filling in* of role and prop *slots,* and so on.
2. The application and the settings used in the film sequence to which that application refers: By associating the actions of the application with the settings encompassed by the *frame-ranges* of those actions.

It is on the above mappings that the system's dialogue about a piece of film is based, for it is:

1. Via the terms used in the application that the DORIS module can be used to derive explanations for those terms.
2. Via the settings in BORIS that the graphics can be generated, objects selected and highlighted, user selection of objects detected, object names used

to obtain DORIS descriptions and so on, other views of objects and related objects obtained etc.

At the present time, the user input takes the form of selection (by mouse device) from hierarchically organized pop-up menus (which appear, as does all input and output, as overlays on the video screen) of predefined question types. An overview of the CLORIS menu system can be seen in Figures 3.10 and 3.11.

## CLORIS and Question Answering

Since allowing the user complete freedom of input was deemed to be beyond the scope of our research, a methodology upon which to base a question-answering system not involving natural language input was required. Obviously, an approach was needed which did not allow the restricted forms of *input* to unduly restrict the *questions which the user was permitted to ask.* In view of the visual nature of the material, and the facilities for graphical interfaces available with computer-controllable videodiscs, it seemed that the optimal approach would involve *selection,* by the user, of questions from preprepared question types, the precise meaning of a *specific* question then being dependent on the *particular context* in which the question is asked. Some work on question answering facilities based on this type of approach is described by Hartley and Smith (1988), but proves, with the domain being UNIX mail, to have insufficiently detailed question types for use in more "real-world" types of domains.

Hartley and Smith derive the basis for their question classification scheme from research into question answering by Lehnert (1977), Lehnert's approach being to say that typical *how* and *why* categorizations are far too broad, and there are subdivisions within each category. One might, for example ask, "How do you get to London" and be asking for a detailed list of directions—a so-called *procedural how* question, or one might ask the same question and expect to be told, say, "by bus." Lehnert's original typology has been usefully refined by Hughes (1986), in Hughes' area of interest, that is, that of providing *expert systems* with more realistic explanation capabilities. Essentially, it is on Hughes' work that the CLORIS style of question answering is based. The useful distinctions made between *how* and *why* questions as each relating differently to *states* and *events* (e.g., we may ask "how" a state came about, and mean *"what event caused it?"* while we may ask "why" an event is done and mean *"what state does that event cause"*) in Hughes' work were a major influence on the CLORIS question-answering model.

To briefly set the scene, CLORIS operates by allowing the user to interrupt the moving film and ask questions by selecting options from pop-up menus. As can be seen from Figure 3.10, the selection at the *"Interruption Menu"* determines whether the questions are about objects, states, or events. The more interesting questions are those regarding the last two of these, and so such questions will be discussed here.

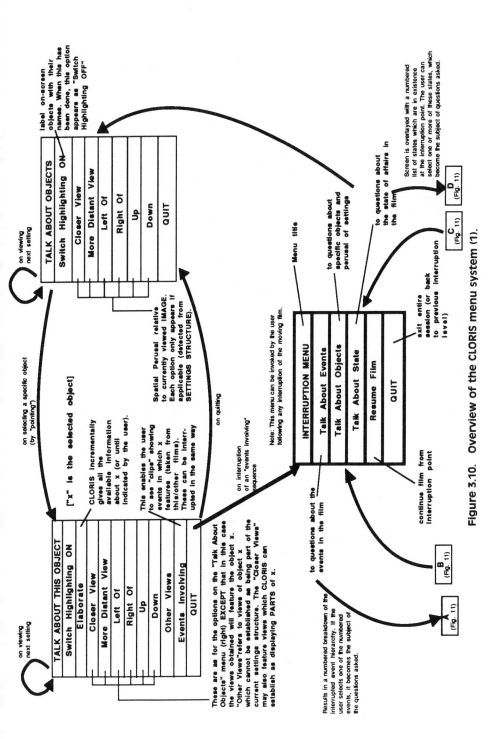

**label on-screen** objects with their names. When this has been done, this option appears as "Switch Highlighting OFF"

**on viewing next setting**

**TALK ABOUT OBJECTS**

| Switch Highlighting ON |
| Closer View |
| More Distant View |
| Left Of |
| Right Of |
| Up |
| Down |
| QUIT |

**Spatial Perusal** relative to currently viewed IMAGE. Each option only appears if applicable (detected from SETTINGS STRUCTURE).

**on selecting a specific object** (by "pointing")

**["x" is the selected object]**

CLORIS incrementally gives all the available information about x (or until indicated by the user).

This enables the user to see "clips" showing events in which x features (taken from this/other film). These can be interrupted in the same way.

**on viewing next setting**

**TALK ABOUT THIS OBJECT**

| Switch Highlighting ON |
| Elaborate |
| Closer View |
| More Distant View |
| Left Of |
| Right Of |
| Up |
| Down |
| Other Views |
| Events Involving |
| QUIT |

These are as for the options on the "Talk About Objects" menu (right) EXCEPT that in this case the views obtained will feature the object x. "Other Views" refers to views of object x which cannot be established as being part of the current settings structure. The "Closer Views" may also feature views which CLORIS can establish as displaying PARTS of x.

**on quitting**

**on interruption** of an "events involving" sequence

**INTERRUPTION MENU**

| Talk About Events |
| Talk About Objects |
| Talk About State |
| Resume Film |
| QUIT |

**Menu title**

Note: This menu can be invoked by the user following any interruption of the moving film.

**to questions about specific objects and perusal of settings**

**to questions about the state of affairs in the film**

Screen is overlayed with a numbered list of states which are in existence at the interruption point. The user can select one or more of these states, which become the subject of questions asked.

**D** (Fig. 11)

**C** (Fig. 11)

**exit entire session (or back to previous interruption level)**

**continue film from Interruption point**

**B** (Fig. 11)

**to questions about the events in the film**

Results in a numbered breakdown of the interrupted event hierarchy. If the user selects one of the numbered events, it becomes the subject of the questions asked.

(Fig. 11)

**Figure 3.10. Overview of the CLORIS menu system (1).**

75

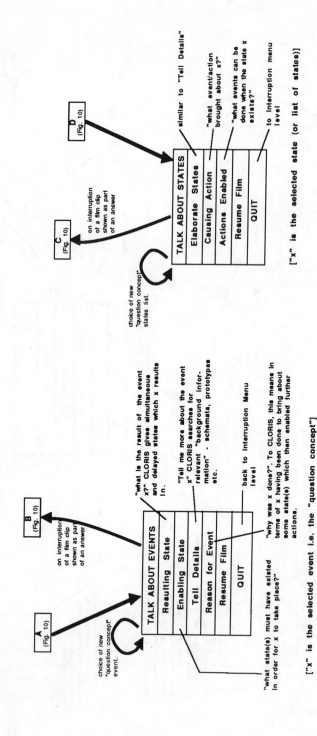

**Figure 3.11.  Overview of the CLORIS menu system (2).**

**TALK ABOUT STATES**
- Elaborate States
- Causing Action
- Actions Enabled
- Resume Film
- QUIT

similar to "Tell Details"

"what event/action brought about x?"

"what events can be done when the state x exists?"

to interruption menu level

["x" is the selected state (or list of states)]

on interruption of a film clip shown as part of an answer

choice of new "question concept" states list.

**TALK ABOUT EVENTS**
- Resulting State
- Enabling State
- Tell Details
- Reason for Event
- Resume Film
- QUIT

"what is the result of the event x?" CLORIS gives simultaneous and delayed states which x results in.

"Tell me more about the event x" CLORIS searches for relevant "background information" - schemata, prototypes etc.

back to Interruption Menu level

"Why was x done?". To CLORIS, this means in terms of x having been done to bring about some state(s) which then enabled further actions.

on interruption of a film clip shown as part of an answer

choice of new "question concept" event.

"what state(s) must have existed in order for x to take place?"

["x" is the selected event i.e. the "question concept"]

A (Fig. 10)

B (Fig. 10)

C (Fig. 10)

D (Fig. 10)

76

On selection of "Talk About Events," the user is given a detailed hierarchical numbered breakdown of the event structure of the interrupted event. An actual example of such a breakdown is reproduced, in part, here (the film was interrupted in setting $C$):

> *(1) Fred is prepare_to_measuring the workpiece using the micrometer.*
> *(2) Right forefinger and right thumb has been moved from the fine_ adjustor to the collar by Fred.*
> *(3) The collar is being loosen_for_objed by Fred using right forefinger and right thumb.*
> *YOU CAN SEE;*
> *Upper rod and lower rod have between them distance. Sincreasement of distance.*
> *Right forefinger and thumb is being used to loosen_for_obj the collar.*
> *Movement of right thumb and right forefinger on the collar.*
> *Movement of the collar.*
> *(4) The workpiece is going to be gotten by Fred.*

The following points should be raised about the example:

1.   It is appreciated that the "natural language" is far from "natural"! This was not an express concern of our research, but the aim was to provide an understandable level of output. In particular, note that some words (e.g., "prepare_to_measure") come directly from the internal descriptions, which is what CLORIS does if there is no entry for the internal label in the lexicon.

2.   The tense of each sentence represents its temporal location with respect to the lowest level interrupted event—in this case (3).

3.   For the lowest level interrupted event, CLORIS attempts to say what, about that event, the viewer can actually *see* (the "YOU CAN SEE" part of the output). Though not very well expressed, it should at least be clear what CLORIS means by the above output (note that CLORIS doesn't include any object which cannot be directly *seen*—interruption of the film in the same event but in a subsequent setting ($D$), will result in an identical hierarchy, but only the first two sentences of the "YOU CAN SEE" part above). We would more naturally say "Fred is loosening the collar, and *you can see* his thumb and forefinger doing the loosening," that is, CLORIS "knows" that the fingers are the *instrument* of the action. Similarly, we would say "*you can see the distance* between the rods increasing." These are *explanation* issues, rather than deficiencies in CLORIS' inference processes. Note also that the scripts, in themselves, do not represent such detailed causality; the inferences made come from the intersection between what is known to be on the screen (from the *setting description*), the event underway (the instantiated *script application*), and the background temporal and causal information about the event(from the appropriate *schemata* and *event frame rules*). In conjunction with these, CLORIS uses knowledge about what are objectively visible states to infer what was happening (in visual terms) at the interruption point.

The user can select any item of the numbered hierarchy (by locating somewhere in the text of the sentence and "clicking" a "mouse" button), which then becomes the event on which subsequent questions (until a change or "quit") are based. This is how the CLORIS question-asking situation always operates for events (and *states*—see below): the selected items become, in Hughes' (1986) terminology, the *question concept,* for example, an abstract *conceptual dependency* (in the case of CLORIS, a *conceptual graph*) structure which can be used to *probe* the knowledge structures available to the system for the answer. Subsequent references to the *question concept,* therefore, can be taken to mean "the conceptual graph from which the selected sentence was derived." Figures 3.10 and 3.11 give an overview of the processing requirements for the question types, but, by way of example, the output for the answers to two questions will be presented, the first is a question about *events,* the second concerns *states.*

Referring again to the numbered hierarchy above, suppose the viewer selects item number (3), and invokes the "Talk About Events Menu," selecting the "Reason for Action" option (see Figure 3.11). This course of action represents the question "why is Fred 'loosen_for_objing' the collar." To CLORIS, the reason for performing an action is to bring about a state which will facilitate some other action in the future. Thus, this question involves a forward traversal of the script application, searching (via the *event frame rules*) for an event with a *precondition* which matches the *persisting post-conditions* of the selected event (the "question concept"). One of the "reasons" returned by CLORIS for this is (again, in CLORISese!) that the action is being done to bring about the following state:

*The workpiece has width of 16.01. Distance is the distance between upper rod and lower rod and is greater than width of 16.01*
*(i.e., to make the distance between the rods wide enough to accommodate the workpiece).*

CLORIS then adds that this state needs to be brought about to facilitate the following action:

*Fred is going to move_for_obj upper rod and lower rod to the workpiece using left hand and right hand*
*(i.e., the rods are going to be moved so that they are about the workpiece—this is the definition of "move_for_obj").*

Now let us consider an actual example of a question from the "Talk About States" menu. On selection of the appropriate option from the "Interruption Menu," the viewer is then presented with a numbered list of generated sentences representing the state of affairs at the interruption point. A part of such a list can be seen here (for an interruption point in setting *A* when Fred has taken the micrometer out of the case, and replaced the case on the desk):

*(1) Sopenment of the case.*
*[i.e. the case is open—Fred does not close it before replacing it].*
*(2) The case is at the desk*
*[for a time it was not—he was holding it].*
*(3) Fred is holding the micrometer using the left hand*
*[Because he has taken it out of the case].*

Again the viewer is able to select a numbered item (in fact, with states *several* items can be selected), which then becomes the *question concept.* Suppose the user selects number (1)—"the case is open." This now becomes the state which the user wants to ask questions about. Thus, in our example here, the question concept is the graph for "the case is open." As in the case above for events, the user can now invoke the corresponding question menu—"Talk About States" (see Figure 3.11). The user now selects the "Actions Enabled" option. This option means "what action/event is facilitated by the *question concept state,* or in this specific example "*what actions can be carried out because the case is open?*" Thus, this question causes CLORIS to search the script *forwards in time from the point in the film at which the question concept came into existence, until an event is found which has preconditions which match the question concept.*
The answer actually given by CLORIS is:

*The state "sopenment of the case" existed because Fred has uncased the micro-meter from the case using the left hand.*
*(Note the use of the past tense to indicate that the action facilitated by the state has already taken place.)*

In all cases where a *visual state* or *event* is part of the answer to a question, CLORIS also gives the user the option to actually *see* it taking place. It will be noted that this option only appears when an event or state can be shown (it would *not* appear if, in the case of an event, the event which was the answer to our question had been *linearly deleted* from the sequence, and did not appear—with exactly the same *individual instantiations—*in *another film sequence*).
Some final points should be borne in mind:

1.  The use of the menu-based question typology does not reflect a complete commitment to such an approach; the idea is to show the scope of CLORIS' question answering abilities.
2.  The examples given are of a simple nature, and only for exemplary pur-poses. One can, however, imagine the application of such a question-answering facility in a wide range of domains, where it would be important to know how and why states came about, and why actions were being done (the operation of complex machinery in engineering domains, for example).
3.  At the present time, CLORIS outputs all information available to it (in particular, in the answering of questions such as those above, CLORIS

searches for *all* possible answers). The reader will appreciate that with a suitable *user-modeling* component, or a specific *instructional strategy*, some of the information would not appear (in particular, some states and the lowest levels of the event hierarchies would be omitted).

Of course, one cannot do full justice to a highly visual and interactive system by showing a few examples. Photographic and textual descriptions of CLORIS in operation can be found in Parkes (1988).

## DISCUSSION

All the standard concerns of ITS research and development have to be reinterpreted within a video-based ITS, as we can see by considering the three main components of conventional ITS, the domain knowledge, the learner model, and the tutoring procedure.

The ITS axiom that we cannot tutor what we do not know about implies that a video sequence cannot be the subject of a tutorial discussion unless the ITS has access to symbolic descriptions of the video content (descriptions which are totally lacking in ordinary IV). As we have seen with CLORIS, these descriptions should include representations of the particular video (in settings), representations of the video narrative (in scripts), and representations of the background knowledge necessary to understand the narrative (in schemata).

Again, as ITS research emphasizes, these knowledge representations should be related to the cognitive processes by which viewers understand video. There is a long tradition of film analysis on which we may draw. (Some of this analysis is surprisingly "cognitive" for its time. For example, Kuleshov and Pudovkin [see Carroll (1980)] write in terms of "expectations, inferences and associations" to explain how viewers come to "see" different things when an identical film sequence is shown in different contexts.) Film understanding relies on cultural and conventional factors and these influence even the most banal video sequence. The micrometer video, for example, uses pans and zooms to shortcircuit the "what should be noticed?" question and uses cuts to distort the real-time sequence. It is only to be expected that students will occasionally misinterpret such subtleties, especially as students have different background knowledge and different abilities for understanding film (Salamon, 1979).

The tutoring procedure has two additional problems with which to contend. First, while the student is actually viewing the video material, the ITS has no evidence to justify tutorial interventions and must rely on student-initiated interruptions for clarifications and on computer-initiated post-video questions. Secondly, the ITS has to determine how to make use of video material during tutorial discussions—how to select or edit appropriate coherent sequences, as indicated by the learner model.

## CONCLUSIONS

We have argued that merging ITS and IV technology may lead to considerable enhancements to an apprenticeship approach to teaching and learning. Video material may be used within the modeling stage of apprenticeship learning but this is not likely to be fully effective unless the controlling computer system has access to representations of the knowledge and skills illustrated by the video material. With such representations, video-based intelligent tutoring systems may use video material much more flexibly. For example, Collins et al. stress that a global view of a skill should be presented before local views—the same video sequence may be used, if intelligently manipulated, to convey both the global view of a process and a fine-grained analysis of the individual components of the process.

A prototype video-based ITS, CLORIS, has been implemented to assess the validity of the methodological assumptions underlying the video-based scenario of learner-orientated discussion about pictures and moving film. Further research is needed on: (a) the suitability of various interaction styles; (b) desirable dialogue management strategies for intelligent multimedia systems (e.g., to coordinate different media in explanations); and (c) the special requirements of learner modeling in video-based systems. These are the subject of present experimental studies with CLORIS.

## REFERENCES

Allen, J. (1981, August). An interval-based representation of temporal knowledge. *Proceedings 7th International Joint Conference on Artificial Intelligence* (pp. 221–226). University of British Columbia, Vancouver, Canada.

Carroll, J.M. (1980). *Toward a structural psychology of cinema.* The Hague: Mouton.

Clancey, W.J. (1986). Qualitative student models. *1st Annual Review of Computer Science, 1,* 381–450.

Collins, A., Brown, J.S., & Newman, S.E. (1987). Cognitive apprenticeship: Teaching the craft of reading, writing and mathematics. In L.B. Resnick (Ed.), *Cognition and instruction: Issues and agendas.* Hillsdale, NJ: Lawrence Erlbaum.

Fraisse, P., & Montmollin, G. de. (1952). Sur la mémoire des films. *Revue Internationale de Filmologie, 9,* 37–68.

Hartley, J.R., & Smith, M.J. (1988). Question answering and explanation giving in on-line systems. In J. Self (Ed.), *Artificial intelligence and human learning: Intelligent computer-aided instruction* (pp. 338–360). London: Chapman and Hall.

Hughes, S. (1986, December). Question classification in rule-based systems. *Proceedings of the 6th Annual Technical Conference of the British Computer Society Specialist Group on Expert Systems.* Brighton, England.

Lauer, S. (1955). Some factors influencing the effectiveness of an educational film. *British Journal of Psychology, 46*(4), 280–292.

Lehnert, W.G. (1977). *The process of question answering.* Hillsdale, NJ: Lawrence Erlbaum.

McDermott, D.V. (1982). A temporal logic for reasoning about processes and plans. *Cognitive Science, 6,* 101–155.

Monaco, J. (1977). *How to read a film.* New York: Oxford University Press.

Parkes, A.P. (1987). Towards a script-based representation language for educational films. *Programmed Learning and Educational Technology, 24,* 234–246.

Parkes, A.P. (1986a). *The analysis and description of a sequence of educational film* (Tech. Report 28). University of Lancaster, Department of Computing, Centre for Research on Computers and Learning, England.

Parkes, A.P. (1986b). *Temporal and conceptual factors influencing the design of a representation language for educational motion films* (Working paper). University of Lancaster, Department of Computing, Centre for Research on Computers and Learning, England.

Parkes, A.P. (1986c). *An overview of the architecture of a computer system with which a trainee can discuss the conceptual and visual content of educational film* (Tech. Report 29). University of Lancaster, Department of Computing, Centre for Research on Computers and Learning, England.

Parkes, A.P. (1988). *An artificial intelligence approach to the conceptual description of videodisc images.* Doctoral Thesis, University of Lancaster, England.

Salamon, G. (1979). *Interaction of media, cognition and learning.* San Francisco: Jossey-Bass.

Schank, R.C., & Abelson, R.P. (1977). *Scripts, plans, goals and understanding.* Hillsdale, NJ: Lawrence Erlbaum.

Shoham, Y. (1986, July). Reified temporal logics: Semantical and ontological considerations. *Proceedings of the 7th European Conference on Artificial Intelligence* (pp. 390–397). Brighton, England.

Sowa, J.F. (1984). *Conceptual structures: Information processing in mind and machine.* Reading, MA: Addison-Wesley.

Turner, R. (1984). *Logics for artificial intelligence.* Chichester, England: Ellis Horwood.

# 4
# Student Modeling and Tutoring Flexibility in the Lisp Intelligent Tutoring System

**Albert T. Corbett**
**John R. Anderson**
**Eric G. Patterson**

## INTRODUCTION

The Lisp Intelligent Tutoring System is a program that provides assistance to students as they work on Lisp coding exercises (Anderson & Reiser, 1985). The program presents problem descriptions and as the students type answers, the tutor monitors the solutions and stands ready to provide assistance at each step. The tutor has been in use in an introductory Lisp course at Carnegie-Mellon University each term since the fall of 1984. While the lesson material has been revised and extended over the years, and now consists of approximately 240 exercises covering the first 12 chapters of an introductory Lisp text (Anderson, Corbett, & Reiser, 1987), the basic architecture of the tutor and the nature of the tutorial interaction have remained essentially unchanged. Thus, the Lisp tutor represents a relatively large and stable intelligent tutoring system.

The tutor was developed to serve as a "real-life" application of the ACT* model of skill acquisition (Anderson, 1983). The tutor's design and behavior are based in large part on the principles of this model, as is described in more detail below. One goal of the tutor, of course, was to teach LISP more effectively, but a second goal was to collect detailed data with the tutor on the course of skill acquisition in a natural setting. The tutor has proved successful in both endeavors. Two evaluation studies, for example, have indicated that working with the tutor is more effective than doing the same exercises "on your own" in a Lisp environment (Anderson, Boyle, & Reiser, 1985; Anderson & Reiser, 1985). In one study, students using the tutor completed the exercises in a little over half the time required by the students working on their own and scored equally well on a posttest. In the other study, students completed the exercises 30% faster and scored 43% higher on a posttest. The tutor's effectiveness, as indicated by these global measures of time-on-task and posttest success, provides some general confirmation of the underlying theory. However, the data provided by the tutor on the course of acquisition bear more directly on the theory. As students interact with the tutor, it generates log files containing a time-stamped record of the students' overt responses and the abstract coding rule that governs each response. As is described below, these coding rules are the basic units of skill acquisition in ACT* and the theory makes some predictions about the time-course of acquisition. For example, there should be a large speed-up in application of a rule from the first to second use, followed by a subsequent more gradual speed-up. This prediction is confirmed by the results (Anderson, 1987a, in press; Conrad & Anderson, 1988).

While the tutor has reached a stable configuration and is being used productively both in teaching and research, there are several reasons why we would like to create substantially different tutorial interactions. First, the theory underlying the tutor has undergone revision since the tutor was first developed (Anderson & Thompson, in press). Second, while the tutor is more effective than "learning on your own," it is not as effective as a human tutor (Anderson & Reiser, 1985; Bloom, 1984). Third, some students complain about aspects of the tutor and believe they would be happier with modifications in the tutorial interaction. We have begun to tackle the task of implementing tutorial changes and in this paper would like to address issues involved in such a task. Specifically, we will focus on the impact of one component of the tutor, the student model, on the tutor's behavior and implications for modifying that behavior. We will begin with a brief description of the tutor's current behavior, followed by the principles that gave rise to the tutor. Then we will discuss the architecture of the tutor, the role of the student model in governing the tutor's behavior, and the implications for modifying the tutor. Finally, we will describe some data from one such modification: a version of the tutor in which the student and not the tutor controls when feedback is given.

## MODEL TRACING AND THE TUTORIAL INTERACTION

The tutor employs a *model tracing* paradigm to provide assistance to students. In this approach the tutor attempts to model the steps that a student might take in solving a problem and uses the information to evaluate the student's responses. Thus, while the student is working, the tutor in lock-step simulates the steps that a knowledgeable student could take in writing the code. In addition, it models errors that students make at each step on the basis of known misconceptions. By comparing the students' response to the set of possible legal actions and the set of known erroneous actions, the tutor is able to recognize whether the student is on a correct solution path, appears to be suffering from a known misconception, or has typed something unrecognizable, and is able to provide feedback accordingly.

Figure 4.1 provides some "snapshots" of what it is like to work with the tutor. Figure 4.1a depicts the terminal screen shortly after the student has begun working on an exercise in which a function called *ends* is to be defined. One possible solution to this exercise looks like this:

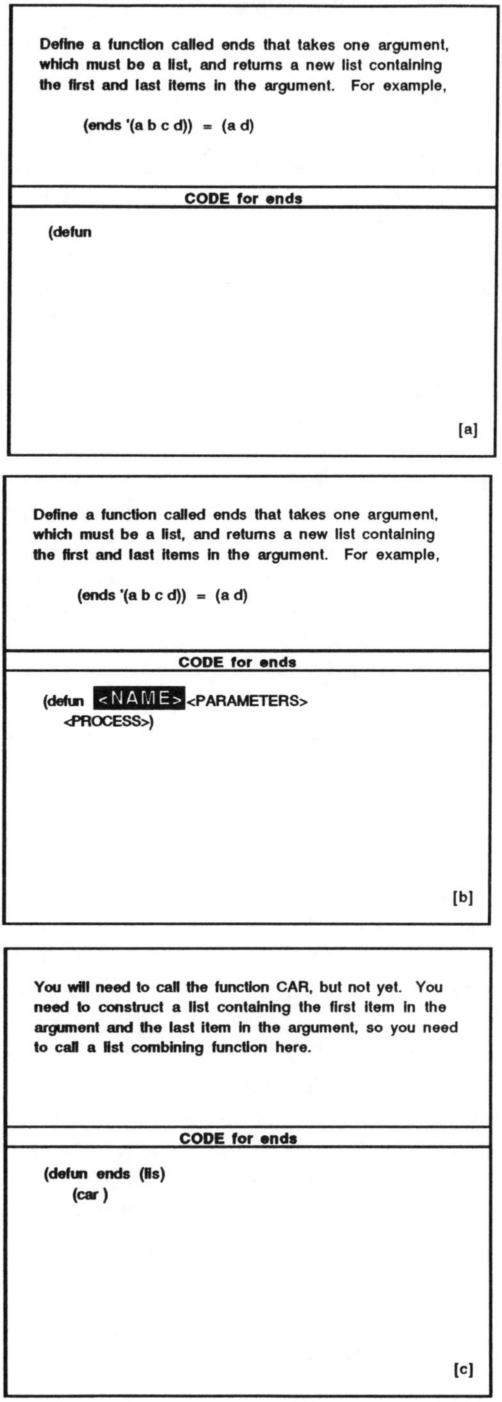

Define a function called ends that takes one argument,
which must be a list, and returns a new list containing
the first and last items in the argument.  For example,

(ends '(a b c d)) = (a d)

---

**CODE for ends**

(defun

[a]

---

Define a function called ends that takes one argument,
which must be a list, and returns a new list containing
the first and last items in the argument.  For example,

(ends '(a b c d)) = (a d)

---

**CODE for ends**

(defun <NAME> <PARAMETERS>
    <PROCESS>)

[b]

---

You will need to call the function CAR, but not yet.  You
need to construct a list containing the first item in the
argument and the last item in the argument, so you need
to call a list combining function here.

---

**CODE for ends**

(defun ends (lis)
    (car )

[c]

**Figure 4.1.** Three "snapshots" of the terminal screen as a student codes the
function *ends* with the tutor.

*(defun ends (lis)*
  *(cons (car lis) (last lis)))*

At the beginning of each exercise, the problem description appears in the tutor window at the top of the screen, while the code window at the bottom of the screen is blank. In this figure the student has already begun by typing a left parenthesis and the symbol *defun*. Once the student has typed a delimiter, in this case a space, the tutor recognizes the response is correct and creates a template on the screen for a call to the operator *defun*. As shown in Figure 4.1b, the tutor fills in a right parenthesis that balances the left parenthesis and puts three angle-bracket symbols on the screen. These angle-bracket symbols represent subgoals that the student must satisfy, more specifically, they represent arguments of *defun* which must be expanded (replaced with code). The student is constrained to write the code in a left-to-right and top-down fashion, so the tutor immediately highlights the next symbol which must be expanded and the student continues typing.

The tutor continues to monitor the student's responses, essentially on a symbol-by-symbol basis. As long as each symbol lies on a known solution path, the tutor continues highlighting nodes and creating function templates where appropriate, and the student continues along without interruption. However, if the student types a symbol that does not fall on a known solution path, the tutor interrupts with feedback. For example, Figure 4.1c depicts the screen after the student has typed the function name, *ends,* and the parameter list and has begun working on the body of the function. This figure shows the reaction of the tutor when the student makes a mistake, in typing *car*. This error suggests that the student has not decomposed the task correctly and the tutor attempts to describe what the current goal should be.

As long as the student makes errors that the tutor can recognize, it will let the student continue trying to expand a goal symbol. However, if the student repeatedly makes errors that the tutor cannot recognize or if the student repeatedly makes the same type of error, the tutor will tell the student what code would work in that step, explain why, and fill in the code for the student. The student also has the option at any point of asking the tutor for two types of information. First, the student can ask the tutor to provide a hint about the current goal. In this case the tutor provides a description of what needs to be done, but not how to do it. Second, the student can ask the tutor what to do next, in which case the tutor will tell the student what the next step is, explain why, and fill in the code for the student.

After completing each exercise, the student enters a Lisp environment, in which he or she tries the code that was generated and is also free to explore. Then when ready, the student proceeds to the next exercise.

## ACT* AND THE TUTOR'S DESIGN

The tutor's behavior as described in the prior section reflects both general assumptions of the ACT* theory and observations of students learning to program in LISP (Anderson, 1987b; Anderson, Farrell, & Sauers, 1984; Pirolli & Anderson, 1985). ACT* is a general theory of cognition, but only a few of its assumptions are relevant to tutoring.[1] These assumptions were in turn distilled into a set of tutoring principles by Anderson, Boyle, Farrell, and Reiser (1987).

One central assumption is that problem-solving behavior is hierarchically structured. A problem represents a goal that can be solved by decomposition into subgoals. For example, the template in Figure 4.1b indicates that the goal of defining a function can be satisfied by typing *defun* and setting three subgoals: (a) coding the function name, (b) coding the function parameters, and (c) coding the process or body of the function. Some goals can be directly satisfied by the execution of a rule (e.g.,the first two subgoals in our example). Figure 4.2 (p. 94) depicts the hierarchical goal tree that underlies the task of defining the function *ends*.

The nodes in this figure represent goals and the branches are labeled with code symbols that are generated in satisfying the goals. As can be seen, when *defun* is coded, three subgoals are set (the arc at this juncture in the figure indicates that each of these subgoals must be satisfied). This goal structure represents three different solutions to the exercise, since the CODE-PROCESS goal can be satisfied by any of three code symbols, *cons, list* or *append*. Each of these three symbols gives rise to a unique subgoal structure that must be satisfied. One tutoring principle is derived from the hierarchical goal-structure assumption: A tutor should make the goal structure explicit.

An important cluster of assumptions, giving rise to several tutoring principles, concerns the representation and acquisition of knowledge. ACT* distinguishes between declarative and procedural knowledge. It assumes that knowledge underlying a skill is encoded in declarative form initially, on the basis of communication or observation. Declarative knowledge can be encoded readily, but does not lead directly to behavior. Instead, behavior requires procedural knowledge. Procedural knowledge is represented as a set of independent IF-THEN rules called *productions*. An English translation of some production rules that students learn early in LISP programming would be:

(1)   IF the goal is to define a function called *name*
         that accepts *n* arguments and performs the task *process*
      THEN code a call to *defun*
      and set subgoals to code.
         (a)   the function name *name*
         (b)   a list of *n* parameters
         (c)   the process *process*

(2)   IF the goal is to form a list
         by inserting *newitem* at the beginning of
         an existing list *oldlist*

---

[1] These assumptions are not unique to ACT*, but are shared by a variety of cognitive theories.

THEN code a call to CONS
and set subgoals to code
  (a)   *newitem*
  (b)   *oldlist.*

In the course of skill acquisition, the declarative knowledge that is encoded is applied by means of general problem-solving productions. This application of declarative knowledge is relatively slow, but results in the formlation of domain specific productions (e.g., the examples above) that can be applied more rapidly. With additional experience, productions become stronger and give rise to larger-order productions. These assumptions concerning skill acquisition give rise to several tutoring principles: Instruction should be presented in the context of problem solving, the student's knowledge should be represented as a set of productions and the grain size of the representation should be adjusted with learning.

Finally, ACT* assumes that skill acquisition and performance depends on a limited-capacity working memory. This assumption gives rise to the general principle that working memory load should be minimized. Along with some specific production-learning assumptions discussed below, it also gives rise to the principle that error feedback should be presented immediately.

Although the tutor as described here has proven generally effective, there are two aspects of its behavior that we would like to manipulate experimentally, the constraints on coding order and the immediate feedback policy.

## Coding Order

Students are constrained by the tutor to expand goals left-to-right and depth-first. These constraints do not represent a general principle of problem-solving in ACT*, but represent a generalization based on observations of students learning Lisp (Anderson, Farrell, & Sauers, 1984). The tutor itself deviates from the generalization under some circumstances. For example, when a student creates a helping function in an exercise, the tutor imposes a breadth-first expansion; that is, the student completes the top-level function before defining the helping function. In some exercises students refer to local variables before declaring them, which violates left-to-right goal expansion. The tutor also recognizes that students may deviate from strictly top-down goal expansion. For example, imagine an exercise in which students have to define a function called *remove-last* that removes the last element of a list, for example, (*remove-last '(a b c d)*) returns (*a b c*). This function can be defined as follows:

```
(defun remove-last (lis)
        (reverse (cdr (reverse lis)))) 
```

The body of this function is nonobvious to novices, even when students understand what the functions *cdr* and *reverse* do. The function reverses the list, deletes the resulting first element, and then flips the list back again. The tutor contains coding productions that generate this code top-down, but if a student flounders at this point, the tutor branches to mean-ends analysis planning productions that derive the solution in a different order. The first means-ends production that applies recognizes that *cdr* is the only known function that deletes a list element. The second production recognizes that the list should be reversed before *cdr* is called, since *cdr* only deletes an element from the front of a list. A final means-ends production then recognizes that the resulting list should be reversed again. Conceivably, if students implicitly work through this plan, they would deviate from top-down code generation.

Our chief motivation for relaxing coding-order constraints is that some students complain about the restrictions on coding order. Relaxing the restrictions and observing when students deviate from the standard order may provide additional evidence on the development of coding productions.

**Immediate Feedback**

There are several reasons for manipulating the timing and control of feedback. Anderson, Boyle, Farrell, and Reiser (1987) proposed that feedback be provided immediately in skill acquisition for practical as well as theoretical reasons. Two practical reasons for immediate feedback are that it saves time and frustration on the part of the student by reducing floundering and that it simplifies the model tracing task. On the other hand, there are several practical reasons for varying from the principle. Some students complain about immediate feedback, in part because they don't like being interrupted and in part because they would prefer to find and fix mistakes themselves. In addition, human tutors do not necessarily intervene immediately when mistakes are made (Fox 1988; Lepper & Chabay, in press) and the effectiveness of immediate feedback varies (Kulik & Kulik, 1988).

An additional reason for varying feedback, however, is that the learning assumptions of ACT* have changed. Previously in ACT* production formation was based on a working memory trace of the problem-solving episode. That is, production formation was based on all that transpired between the initial setting of a goal and the action that satisfied it. Optimal production formation required both the presence of relevant information in working memory and the ability to filter out irrelevant information. Since immediate feedback reduces floundering, it reduces the load on working memory (by reducing the size of goal-satisfaction episodes) and fosters the formation of appropriate productions. Since the Lisp tutor was developed, however, assumptions have been elaborated and revised concerning the initial proceduralization of domain-specific productions (Anderson & Thompson, in press). In the revised formulation, production formation is based on working memory data structures representing the initial goal and ulti-mate solution and not on a trace of the entire goal-satisfaction episode. As a result, production formation is no longer directly related to the size of the episode (amount of floundering), and immediate feedback is no longer viewed as crucial in production formation.

## MODEL TRACING AND THE TUTOR'S ARCHITECTURE

The tutor's architecture can be analyzed into three basic components: domain knowledge (the student model), tutoring rules, and the interface (cf. Sleeman & Brown, 1982; Wenger, 1987). One might guess that the characteristics we wish to manipulate, coding order and immediate feedback chiefly involve the interface and pedagogical component. However, because of details of the tutor's architec-ture, these aspects of the tutorial interaction are closely tied to properties of the student model.

### The Interface

Currently the tutor's interface is fairly simple. It is responsible for accepting the student's code and displaying the code on the screen. It is not responsible for maintaining an internal representation of the student's code. The interface ac-cepts expressions from the student roughly a symbol at a time and does some syntactic checking. For example, it ensures that students do not embed illegal syntactic characters within atoms and ensures that students type a left parenthesis at the beginning of function calls. (Note that the interface must have information on correct solutions to perform the latter task.) If the input satisfies these syntac-tic constraints the interface passes it through for checking. Communication in the other direct, from the tutor to the interface is accomplished by means of a symbol table, which is described below. At the end of each cycle, the interface converts the symbol table to Lisp code for display on the screen, sets the cursor on the appropriate goal symbol, and awaits a new input.

### The Student Model

As specified by the tutoring principles, the student model is implemented in the form of a production system. The complete set of correct rules for writing code is referred to as the *ideal student model* and represents the instructional objectives of the text and tutor. The student model also includes a *bug catalog*—a set of incorrect rules that reflect known misconceptions. In modeling student behavior, the production system is given a specification of the function to be written (analogous to the English description provided the student) and the top-level goal of coding the function is added to a goal stack. In each cycle a goal is pulled from the stack and the set of production rules is compared to the goal and the problem description. This comparison process results in a set of productions, called the *conflict set,* that match the problem state and therefore could be applied. This set always contains one or more correct rules and generally contains one or more buggy rules. The student's input is then compared to this set. If the input matches the coding action of a correct production, that production "fires." It adds an expression to the symbol table which represents the student's solution and may add goals to the goal stack.[2] No tutorial action is taken, and control is returned to the interface. If the student's input does not match a correct production, then the tutorial component responds.

## The Tutorial Component

The tutorial component consists of a set of simple rules that apply when the student makes a mistake. If the student's input matches the coding action of a buggy production, then a feedback message associated with the production is presented. If the input does not match any production, the tutor cannot diagnose the error and indicates this to the student. If the student makes two errors at a goal that cannot be diagnosed or triggers the same buggy production three times, the tutor assumes the student is floundering and provides a correct code symbol along with an explanation. In each case, after the student hits the *return* key, control again passes to the interface.

In addition to providing error feedback, the tutorial component performs a second function we call *knowledge tracing.* As the student solves exercises, the tutorial component maintains an "overlay" model of the student's knowledge of Lisp coding. For each correct production in the student model, the tutor maintains a probability estimate that the student has the production correctly encoded. The student's first response at each goal, correct or incorrect, is used to modify the estimate for a correct production in the conflict set. These probability estimates do not influence the tutor's response to error, but are used to select exercises and to decide when a student is ready to move on to a new topic. (See Corbett and Anderson, in press, for additional implementation details and an evaluation of knowledge tracing.)

---

[2] This is an oversimplification since not all productions generate code. Some only modify the goal structure or the problem description and, as described earlier, some productions model planning processes. However, these productions are not directly relevant to the topic of modifying the tutorial interaction.

## Implementation of Model Tracing

One difficulty with model tracing within the framework described above is that production systems have high computational costs (due to pattern matching demands) and require an unrealistically high level of computational resources to keep up with students in real time. A second difficulty with model-tracing concerns the disambiguation of students' responses, since under some circumstances, a student's response may match more than one production instantiation. For example, consider the function call

(+ (car lis1) (car lis2))

Since the ordering of arguments to the function + is unimportant, the tutor will allow the student to code the two arguments in either order. Thus, when the goal is set to code the first argument, there are two viable production instantiations, each of which codes *car*. When the student types *car*, it is not possible to determine which argument the student is coding. This ambiguity could be resolved in the next cycle when a variable is typed. However, to postpone resolution for a cycle, it would be necessary for the production system to follow both possible branches. That entails matching the student's next response to the subgoal of each production, which increases the amount of matching required.

## PROBLEM COMPILATION

Both of these difficulties can be resolved when it is recognized that model tracing does not require online execution of the production system while the tutor is running. The tutor's ability to recognize correct solutions and standard bugs depends on the student model, since the tutor is only presented a problem description and not a solution. However, it is possible to run the production system model ahead of time as long as a trace of the run is stored that retains whatever information is relevant to tutoring. In this way the cost of pattern matching in identifying relevant rules can be borne ahead of time. Once those rules have been identified and stored in a data structure, it is easy to match the student's response to the rules and have the tutor respond accordingly. This process, referred to as *problem compilation,*[3] not only enhances the efficiency of modeling, but as an added benefit, enables functional modifications in the student model at relatively low cost.

---

[3] A similar process is described in Sleeman, 1983.

## Implementing Problem Compilation

There is one substantial difference between running the production system on-line and running it ahead of time. Most of the exercises in the tutor can be solved in more than one way and some have literally hundreds of acceptable solutions. Thus a goal tree representation of the student model's potential behavior contains or-nodes (e.g., the CODE-PROCESS node in Figure 4.2). When the student model is being run online and an or-node is encountered, it is only necessary to follow the branch selected by the student. When the model is run ahead of time, however, it is necessary to follow each branch at an or-node so that subsequently the tutor can follow the student down any branch that is selected. Thus, problem compilation requires the exhaustive representation of alternative expansions of the goal tree and the resulting data structures can become quite large.

The need to expand the goal tree exhaustively poses an additional complication in representing mutual constraints among productions. Whenever there is more than one production that satisfies a goal, the production selected will almost certainly constrain the way at least one other goal in the problem is satisfied. This can be seen in the body of the function *ends*. Three different functions, *cons, list,* or *append,* can be employed to construct the required list of two elements. Not surprisingly, the subsequent code for the two elements is different in each case:

```
(cons (car lis) (last lis))
(list (car lis) (car (last lis)))
(append (list (car lis)) (last lis))
```

In this example the components of the code that co-vary are hierarchically organized. That is, whichever function is chosen at the top-level goal here, *cons, list,* or *append,* determines the correct code at the subgoals (the correct arguments). It is easy to represent such hierarchically organized constraints in a goal tree. (Each branch at a choice point only represents legitimate actions at the subordinate goals.) However, it is sometimes the case that mutually dependent code is not hierarchically organized. In iteration, for example, variable initializations and loop actions are not hierarchically ordered (at least in the tutor's student model) but the initial values assigned to variables interact with the order in which loop actions are performed and the nature of the variable updates. When a goal tree containing such constraints is exhaustively expanded by the student model it is essential that some convention be adopted for marking the constraints.

One solution to this problem, adopted by Anderson and Ross Thompson, in compiling problems for the tutor, is to represent the student model traces not as a goal tree, but as a depth-first expansion of the goal tree. An example of such a representation is presented in Figure 4.3.

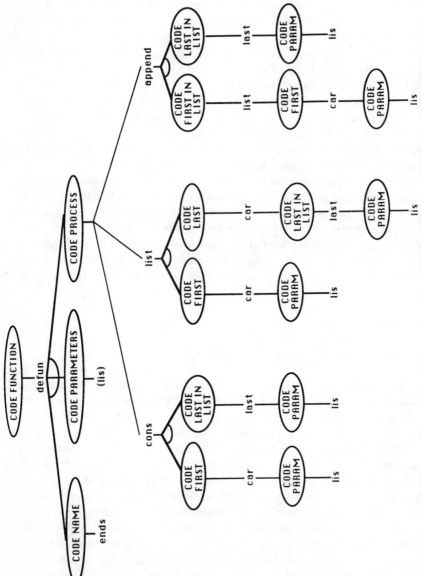

**Figure 4.2.** The goal structure of the function *ends*. Goals are represented as oval nodes. Branches are labelled with code symbols that are generated by productions in satisfying the goals. (Circular arcs indicate points at which multiple subgoals are created, each of which must be satisfied.)

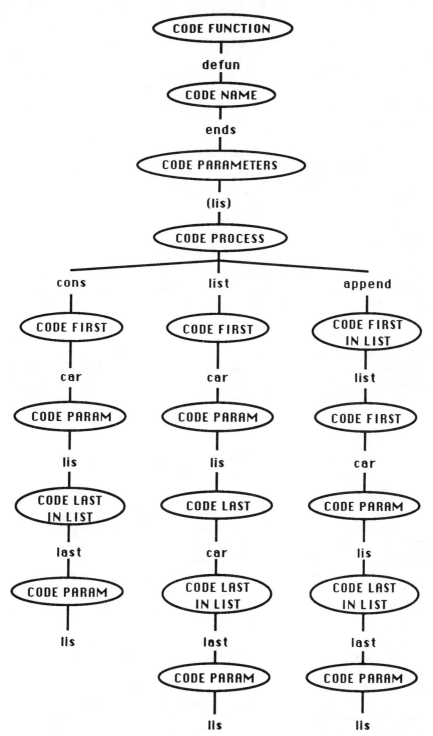

**Figure 4.3.** A depth-first transformation of the goal structure for the function *ends*.

The effect of this transformation is that temporal relations are represented hierarchically. If goal B follows goal A temporally, then goal B is structurally a descendent of goal A. The advantage of this is that coordinate goals in the basic goal tree become hierarchically arranged and any mutual constraints among goals can be easily represented. The disadvantage of this solution is that identical substructures may be represented redundantly on various branches in the tree. Even when branches are allowed to converge whenever possible, an exhaustive depth-first expansion of an and-or goal tree may be larger than the corresponding and-or goal tree itself.[4]

## Problem Compilation and Tutoring Flexibility

There are at least two advantageous side effects of problem compilation. First, it becomes relatively inexpensive to search multiple steps down alternative branches in the goal tree when necessary to process ambiguous responses. Second, it becomes relatively inexpensive to modify the behavior of the tutor by effectively modifying the student model. The production system is no longer running online as the tutor is at work. Instead, a relatively simple interpreter exists which accepts the trace structure as input and simulates the running model. As a result, it is possible to simulate a new model without changing the production system by writing an interpreter that accepts the same data structure, but behaves differently.

## MODIFYING THE TUTORIAL INTERACTION

As is suggested in the preceding section, much of the tutor's complexity resides in the student model. The interface and tutorial components are fairly simple, as is the communication between components. Given this architecture, the tutorial characteristics we wish to manipulate, coding order and immediate feedback, depend heavily on characteristics of the student model. In particular, input order is not an optional attribute of the interface, but is governed by properties of the student model, because the student model rather than the interface determines what the student can do next. Since the student model can only expand goals top-down, depth-first, and left-to-right, the student is constrained to type code in that order.

A further characteristic of the student model has a strong impact on the nature

---

[4] Alternative solutions to the space demands of representing trace structures are being pursued in other tutoring projects. Skwarecki (1988) describes a tutoring project that employs a more compact goal tree. Anderson and Ray Pelletier are developing a more efficient production system interpreter that should be fast enough to run online in tutoring, eliminating the need for compiled solutions.

of the tutorial interaction. The student's knowledge of Lisp is represented at about the finest grain size that has functional meaning in lisp. Roughly speaking, it models performance at the level of the individual symbol (modeling at a finer level of analysis would essentially be of typing rather than Lisp coding). This has a direct impact on the tutor's behavior, because in model tracing the immediate feedback principle actually specifies that feedback should be given after each production firing. Thus, the tutor's symbol-by-symbol feedback is not strictly a consequence of immediate feedback, but a consequence of applying immediate feedback to a student model of minimum grain size.

In summary, important aspects of the tutorial interaction depend directly on features that are built into the student model. In principle, then, modifications in the tutor's behavior require a recoding of the student model. This is an important realization because the student model, which currently consists of approximately 1200 rules for generating correct and incorrect code, represents about 75% of the code involved in the tutor. Fortunately, we can implement model tracing in a way that makes modification of the student model a less imposing task than this statistic suggests.

To relax the tutor's input and feedback constraints, we need to dissociate the tutor's interface component from the student-modeling component and to revise the tutorial component. We are following a multistage plan in accomplishing this task. The first step is to isolate the interface functions from the modeling functions. To do this, we have introduced a true structured editor into the tutor. It provides editing commands that allow the student to enter code in any order and to delete code they have entered. The editor assumes the responsibility of maintaining a symbol table representing the student's code and ensures that the code is syntactically legal, but has no capability for checking the code is functionally correct. The structured editor provides code templates with angle-bracket symbols that are similar to, though not uniformly identical to the tutor's templates.[5] As in the case of the tutor, the student can only enter code by expanding angle-bracket symbols on the screen, but the student is able to select the next angle-bracket symbol to be expanded, to generate arbitrary angle-bracket symbols (as long as they are structurally legal), and to embed existing code or angle-bracket symbols in a template for a higher-level function call, and so has control over the order in which the code is generated.

---

[5] For example, many functions such as + and *list* can take a variable number of arguments and the editor has no information on what the student intends. Thus, while the tutor generates templates with the correct number of argument nodes for the solution, the editor simply generates one argument node when the function is first called and generates a new argument node each time an earlier one is expanded until the student finally deletes the last empty argument node.

## Student-controlled Feedback

Having introduced the editor, the next step is to integrate it with the student-modeling and tutorial components to enable feedback. In our initial research with the revised architecture, we have implemented a student-controlled tutor, in which students not only control the order in which they input code, but also when feedback is given. In this tutor students can type code, make whatever changes they want, and ask for feedback from the tutor at any point. The transition from tutor-controlled feedback to student-controlled feedback is a fairly small one. Instead of feeding each unit of code to the student-model and tutorial component as it is typed, the code is buffered in the editor's symbol table and matched to the student-model only when the student requests help. Problem compilation is important in converting to student-controlled feedback largely for the purpose of resolving ambiguity. As described earlier, there are some situations in which a student's response may match more than one correct step that the tutor is prepared to take. Further ambiguity can arise in the student-controlled tutor since students can deviate from left-to-right input order and as a result, may have unexpanded template symbols in the middle of their code when they ask the tutor for help. Problem compilation makes it convenient to resolve both types of ambiguity by looking ahead through the rest of the student's code.

In the student-controlled tutor, the student can request three types of help. As in the standard tutor, the student can ask for a hint at any unexpanded goal and the student can ask for an explanation at any goal. A third option is provided the student in this version of the tutor, however. At any time the student can ask the tutor to check over all the code that has been written so far. At that point the tutor checks over the code in the same top-down, left-to-right sequence that it ordinarily would. The tutor ignores any unexpanded template symbols it encounters by skipping over the corresponding nodes in the goal tree. If no errors are found, it tells the student that everything is fine so far. If no errors are found and the code is complete, the tutor advances the student to the Lisp window just as in the standard configuration. If an error is detected, however, the tutor gives the same feedback as it would in the standard condition and removes the erroneous code from the screen. The tutor does not check any farther and any code that is down or to the right is popped out of the solution and into a separate buffer (since leaving it in place might suggest to the student that it is correct and in the proper position). We have begun collecting data with this version of the tutor, and preliminary results are described below.

## Further Developments: Restoring Tutor Control

As data is collected with the student-controlled tutor, we have also begun work on the next phase in our project: restoring the ability to evaluate code on a symbol-by-symbol basis, while allowing students to deviate from the standard input order. Restoring symbol-by-symbol evaluation will allow us substantial flexibility in implementing tutor-controlled feedback rules. In addition, it will enable greater flexibility in knowledge tracing. In the standard tutor, knowledge tracing is based on the student's first coding attempt at each goal. Under the code-buffering implementation of the student-controlled tutor, however, the model-tracing and knowledge-tracing mechanisms only have access to the state of the code when the student requests help, with no record of the order in which the code is entered and no record of deletions and revisions the student made. Symbol-by-symbol evaluation will restore maximum information to the knowledge-tracing mechanism.

Since the fully-expanded goal tree is available for each exercise as a result of problem-compilation, we can implement symbol-by-symbol evaluation by means of a purely structural mapping of editor symbols onto goals. As described earlier, the editor generates code templates much like those created by the productions in the student-model. For example, when the student types a call to *defun* the editor generates the template *(defun ⟨name⟩ ⟨parameters⟩ ⟨process⟩)*, which is identical to the template generated by the production that codes *defun*. While the angle-bracket symbols created by the editor do not, strictly speaking, represent goals in a correct solution, they do correspond closely to those goals. Thus, the solution to integrating the editor with model-tracing is to map each node in the editor symbol table, as it is generated, to goals in the compiled solution tree. This mapping allows us to continue evaluating code on a symbol-by-symbol basis, even if the student diverges from depth-first left-to-right expansion and even if the student makes mistakes.

If there is a single solution to an exercise, each editor node will map to at most one goal in the solution tree. If an exercise has more than one solution, then editor nodes below a choice point will map to multiple goals on various branches. Issues arise concerning such mappings to multiple branches, but these issues can be readily resolved. First, a given input may satisfy goals on multiple paths. For example, if the student begins the body of *ends* by typing *(cons (car . . .)*, the symbol *car* matches a goal on two branches. In this case, we can identify the appropriate branch, because only one branch involves *cons*. However, the same disambiguation is not possible if the student begins the body as follows: *(⟨function⟩ (car ⟨list⟩) ⟨other-expressions⟩)*. Since the entire goal tree has been expanded through compilation, though, there is no particular reason to perform the disambiguation. The appropriate branch will emerge as the student continues typing.

A second issue in multiple mappings also arises. Suppose the student types the following code: *(cons (car lis) (car (last lis)))*. The first three symbols match one branch in the tree and the latter three symbols match a branch from a different solution. In light of the theoretical assumption of top-down goal expansion, when such conflicts arise, we will disambiguate them in favor of the higher-level code. Given this resolution, each time code is added to the editor table at or below a branch point, it is necessary to check downstream nodes to see if previously consistent code is now on a mismatching branch. On the other hand, each time code is deleted from the symbol table, it is necessary to check downstream to see if previously inconsistent code is now on a consistent branch.

Thus, while computational complexity is introduced, we can return to something approximating the input cycle of the original tutor. On each cycle, new code is matched to a production conflict set at some goal (or more than one set if the code maps to more than one goal), any new editor nodes are mapped to goals in the tree, and finally downstream code is checked when the modified node falls below a branch point.

A final issue concerning this structural node mapping concerns bottom-up coding. Although the editor expands code templates in a top-down fashion, much like the tutor, it is possible, by means of an editor command, to generate code bottom up. (This command takes an existing lisp expression or angle-bracket symbol and embeds it as the first argument of a new function call template.) To the extent that students deviate from top-down expansion, a purely structural mapping will lead to code mismatches. For example, if a student coded the body of *ends* bottom up, he or she would being by coding *lis*. This symbol would be structurally mapped to the CODE-PROCESS goal, at which it does not match any production. Eventually, as the student completes a bottom-up expansion, the code would be recognized, but at intermediate states the tutor would fail to recognize it as a possible solution. If we find this happening frequently it would warrant moving to a more complex goal-mapping scheme which makes reference to the content of the goals. As the student types symbols under this system, the tutor would search the goal tree for goals that match the input and are topologically consistent with the structure of the editor table. Thus, if the student stated by typing *lis* the tutor would tentatively map the input to the six CODE-PARAM goals in the goal tree. If the student then embedded this symbol in a call to *car*, that is, (*car lis*), only four topologically consistent mappings would remain (i.e., mappings that would not require the subsequent deletion of code). Such a system would enable more immediately accurate evaluation of bottom-up coding, but at higher computational expense.

The immediate code evaluation process described in this section enables us to implement a variety of tutor-controlled feedback rules. One option, of course, is to restore the standard tutor's policy: Inform the student of errors immediately and require that each step be accomplished correctly. However, symbol-by-symbol evaluation does not necessitate immediate feedback. One structural alternative that might prove less disruptive is to provide feedback on the basis of larger order units, for example, complete function calls.

Another option is to make feedback timing contingent on the type of error made. For example, given the demonstrable effect of working memory limitations on coding errors (Anderson & Jeffries, 1985), it would be ideal to present feedback messages immediately only when the benefit of the message outweighs the cost of disrupting working memory. One rule that would approach this goal and would be fairly easy to implement given the knowledge tracing mechanism, would be to delay feedback on "slips," (errors in which a student fails to fire a well-learned production) that do not seriously disrupt the goal structure of the exercise. An alternate scheme to minimize working memory disruptions would be to provide immediate notification when an error is made, but not to insist on immediate correction. Such a tutor would signal that an error has been made by displaying the error in a distinctive font, but leave it up to the student when a correction is made. Under this system it is up to the student to evaluate the relationship of the error to his or her current goal structure and to choose the optimal time to suspend goal expansion and correct the error.

## Multiple Errors

A final issue deserves comment before we consider the preliminary data from the student-controlled tutor. If we deviate from immediate feedback and error correction, then students will be generating code with more than one error. When the student requests help, a decision will be required concerning the error on which to comment.

The student-controlled buffering approach described above answers this question implicitly. Given the standard student-modeling mechanism, when the student asks the tutor to check over the code, the tutor checks it top-down, depth-first, left-to-right, and provides feedback on the first error encountered. Indeed, if the student asks for goal-specific feedback (a goal hint or explanation of correct code), the tutor checks over the code from the beginning. If an error is encountered before reaching the target goal, the tutor will instead provide feedback on the earlier error. In part this is because it could be difficult to continue tracing down to the target goal once an error is made. However, another important reason concerns the content of the feedback itself. Given the operation of the standard tutor, the feedback messages, including the goal reminders, bug diagnoses, and descriptions of correct code assume that the upstream code is correct and that there is no code downstream. These messages may mislead students if these assumptions are violated. Currently, we are keeping the standard feedback messages in the new implementations for two reasons: experimental control and efficiency. We want to keep the content of feedback constant as we vary its control and timing to avoid confounding the factors. However, another important consideration is that there are more than a thousand feedback messages to be modified. We would like to determine that an alternative to immediate feedback and error correction is effective before tuning this body of messages accordingly.

## TESTING STUDENT-CONTROLLED FEEDBACK

As described earlier, our initial research in varying the nature of the tutorial interaction employs problem compilation to implement a tutor that gives the student more control over the coding process in two ways. First, we have relaxed the constraint on input-order so that the students can generate code in any order they wish. Second, in the new tutor, students have control over when feedback is presented. We have collected data with this tutor for the first two lessons of the tutor's curriculum. The first lesson introduces basic arithmetic and list functions, the structure of function calls, and variables. The second lesson covers function definitions.

Thirty-four subjects took part in this study of student-controlled tutoring. Half the students used the standard immediate-feedback tutor, while half used the new student-controlled-feedback tutor. Students in both conditions, completed the first two lessons in the tutor curriculum and then took a cumulative quiz. One student dropped out in the immediate-feedback condition and one student in the student-controlled condition failed to complete the two lessons in the allotted time, leaving 16 subjects in each group.

**Evaluation Measures**

Two measures of tutor effectiveness are of interest: Performance on the final quiz and time to complete the lessons. There was no difference between the two groups on the quiz; the mean score for both groups was 83% correct. However, there was a reliable difference in time to complete the exercises: Subjects in the immediate-feedback condition required an average of 2.9 minutes to complete each exercise, while subjects in the student-controlled condition required 4.3 minutes, $t(30) = 3.9$, $p < 0.001$. Part of this time difference may reflect the fact that the subjects in the student-controlled condition were working with the true structured editor which is necessarily more complicated than the constrained interface in the standard version of the tutor. However, as described in the next section, students are doing additional processing in the student-controlled condition (in catching their own errors) and part of the time difference may reflect that extra processing.

**Processing Measures**

The log files in the student-controlled condition can be used to address three issues concerning interface design in programming tutors: (a) when do students request feedback; (b) to what extent do students deviate from top-down, depth-first, left-to-right coding; and (c) to what extent do students catch their own errors when immediate feedback is suspended?

In answer to the first question, subjects in the student-controlled condition showed an overwhelming inclination to complete their code before requesting feedback. Students asked the tutor to "check over the code" a total of 661 times across the exercises in both lessons and in 646 of these cases their code was complete, though not necessarily correct. Students also requested a goal-hint 33 times and a goal-explanation 39 times and these requests necessarily require the tutor to give feedback on partial code. Even when these goal-specific requests are included, however, the proportion of tutoring requests that involved partial code is still relatively small (12%). This suggest that students could be happy with a tutor that does not provide feedback on partial solutions but only on complete code, as for example in the case of Proust (Johnson & Soloway, 1985).

Examination of those instances in which students request tutoring on partial code also provides indirect evidence on the issue of coding order. In no case did any of these partial solutions show evidence of right-to-left, breadth-first, or bottom-up coding. To obtain direct evidence on this issue, however, it is not sufficient to simply examine the state of the code when a student asks the tutor for assistance. Rather, it is necessary to trace through the students' complete interaction with the editor, which we did for the second lesson. Subjects never deviated from depth-first coding in these exercises, although the structure of the exercises provided relatively few opportunities to distinguish depth-first vs. breadth-first coding—a total of three per subject. Across the 16 subjects using the student-controlled tutor and the seven exercises in lesson two, however, there were about 400 goals which required subgoals and hence could be satisfied in a bottom-up rather than top-down fashion. In addition, there were about 450 opportunities for the students to complete goals in a right-to-left rather than left-to-right fashion. Detailed inspection of the editor interactions revealed only five cases in which a goal was completed in a bottom-up fashion and just one case in which goals were completed in right-to-left order.

It should be noted that these results concerning tutoring requests and coding order may hinge on the relative simplicity of the exercises under study here. As functions become more complex, students may show more inclination to have the tutor confirm parts of the code before proceeding with the rest. Similarly, as functions become more complex, there may be some payoff for jumping around and filling in the parts the student is sure of before tackling the more difficult parts of the solution. Moreover, this pattern of results may be specific to the functional quality of Lisp and may not generalize to more procedural languages (or to more procedural operations, such as iteration, encountered in later Lisp lessons). However, at least for the early lessons, the top-down, depth-first, left-to-right interface of the standard tutor seems entirely adequate.

In answer to the final question, analyses of the log files suggest that subjects are catching and correcting their own errors in the student-controlled condition. Across both lessons, the tutor caught reliably more bugs per exercise in the immediate feedback condition, 1.15, than in the student-controlled condition, 0.83, ($t(30) = 2.48$, $p < .05$). This suggests that subjects in the student-controlled condition are catching their own errors, though again, this is only indirect evidence since it is conceivable that students are being more cautious and making fewer errors in the student-controlled condition. Detailed inspection of the editor interactions in lesson two confirmed the conclusion, however. In that lesson students detected and revised a total of 86 errors, while the tutor detected 165 errors. Of these 86 errors students revised, 49 (57%) were corrected, while the remaining 37 (43%) are changed to a different error.[6] Thus, there may be some benefit in deviating from symbol-by-symbol assistance in tutoring. It should be noted though, that in addition to correcting errors (and "miscorrecting" errors) students also changed correct code symbols 21 times (changing them to alternative correct symbols 9 times and "discorrecting" them 12 times). Thus, of all the spontaneous changes students made, 20% were changes to correct code.

A final issue we examined concerns the relative position of the coding revisions the subjects made. Gray and Anderson (1988) investigated the code revisions students made when writing fairly difficult iterative search functions in Lisp. They found that subjects are most likely to change code at the goal they are currently working on or have just completed and are next most likely to go back and change code at a goal superordinate to the current goal. They are relatively unlikely to change code at other goals. For example, suppose a student is typing code in the standard order and has reached this point in coding a solution to *ends:*

```
(defun ends (lis)
    (list (car lis) (car (last ⟨list3⟩)))))
```

Gray and Anderson found that the student would be most likely to change the symbol *last,* next most likely to change the second instance of *car,* or the occurrences of *list* and *defun,* all of which satisfy superordinate goals of the current goal, and least likely to change any of the other symbols in the code. The detailed analyses of lesson 2 revealed the same pattern for the simpler functions in the current experiment. Sixty-one of the students changes (57%) were at the current goal, 31 (29%) were at superordinate goals and 15 (14%) were at other goals. In addition, the probability that a revision actually corrects an error varied with the position of the correction relative to the current goal. Fifty-one percent of the changes at the current goal corrected an error, while only 42% of the changes at superordinate goals and 33% of changes at other goals corrected errors.

These results suggest that a more optimal tutor might track students' responses all the way down to leaf nodes in the goal tree but only provide feedback as the students pop back up through the tree. Such a tutor would (a) allow students editing freedom while working on incomplete subgoals; (b) check each subgoal after it is complete, providing feedback and ultimately answers where necessary; and (c) move the student forward after each subgoal is complete. A

---

[6] The data in this section exclude errors that would not register as such in the immediate feedback tutor, for example, errors that were corrected by deleting characters before typing a delimited and certain syntactic errors that are caught by the interface rather than the student model.

tutor with this control structure may not save much time relative to the student-controlled tutor; since students make most changes on the way down through the tree, they would still be making almost as many productive and unproductive changes as if the tutor never intervened. However, such a tutor would have the advantage, relative to the standard tutor, of allowing students to catch whatever errors they are likely to catch, while providing feedback as soon as possible on errors that the student is not likely to correct.

# REFERENCES

Anderson, J.R. (1983). *The architecture of cognition.* Cambridge, MA: Harvard University Press.

Anderson, J.R. (1987a). Production systems, learning and tutoring. In D. Klahr, P. Langley, & R. Neches (Eds.), *Production system models of learning and development.* Cambridge, MA: MIT Press.

Anderson, J.R. (1987b). Skill acquisition: Compilation of weak-method problem solutions. *Psychological Review, 94,* 192–210.

Anderson, J.R. (in press). Analysis of student performance with the LISP tutor. In N. Fredericksen, R. Glaser, A. Lesgold, & M. Shafto (Eds.), *Diagnostic monitoring of skill and knowledge acquisition.* Hillsdale, NJ: Erlbaum.

Anderson, J.R., Boyle, C.F., Farrell, R., & Reiser, B.J. (1987). Cognitive principles in the design of computer tutors. In P. Morris (Ed.), *Modelling cognition.* New York: Wiley.

Anderson, J.R., Boyle, C.F., & Reiser, B.J. (1985). Intelligent tutoring systems. *Science, 228,* 456–462.

Anderson, J.R., Corbett, A.T., & Reiser, B.J. (1987). *Essential Lisp.* Reading, MA: Addison-Wesley.

Anderson, J.R., Farrell, R., & Sauers, R. (1984). Learning to program in LISP. *Cognitive Science, 8,* 87–129.

Anderson, J.R., & Jeffries, R. (1985). Novice LISP errors: Undetected losses of information from working memory. *Human-Computer Interaction, 22,* 403–423.

Anderson, J.R., & Reiser, B.J. (1985, April). The Lisp tutor. *Byte, 10*(4) 159–175.

Anderson, J.R., & Thompson, R. (in press). Use of analogy in a production system architecture. In S. Vosniadou & A. Ortony (Eds.), *Similarity and analogical reasoning.* New York: Cambridge University Press.

Bloom, B.S. (1984). The 2 sigma problem: The search for methods of group instruction as effective as one-to-one tutoring. *Educational researcher, 13,* 3–16.

Conrad, F.C., & Anderson, J.R. (1988). The process of learning Lisp. *The Proceedings of the Tenth Annual Conference of the Cognitive Science Society.* Montréal, Canada.

Corbett, A.T., & Anderson, J.R. (in press). The Lisp intelligent tutoring system: Research in skill acquisition. In J. Larkin, R. Chabay, & C. Sheftic (Eds.), *Computer assisted instruction and intelligent tutoring systems: Establishing communications and collaboration.* Hillsdale, NJ: Erlbaum.

Fox, B.A. (1988). *Cognitive and interactional aspects of correction in tutoring*. (Tech. Rep. #88-2). University of Colorado, Institute of Cognitive Science, Boulder, CO.

Gray, W., & Anderson, J.R. (1988). Change episodes in coding: When and how do programmers change their code? In G. Olson, S. Sheppard, & E. Soloway (Eds.), *Empirical studies of programmers: Second workshop* (pp. 185–197). Norwood, NJ: Ablex.

Johnson, M.L., & Soloway, E. (1985, April). PROUST: An automatic debugger for Pascal programs. *Byte, 10*(4) 179–190.

Kulik, J.A., & Kulik, C.C. (1988). Timing of feedback and verbal learning. *Review of Educational Research, 58,* 79–97.

Lepper, M.R., & Chabay, R.W. (in press). Socializing the intelligent tutor: Bringing empathy to computer tutors. In H. Mandl & A. Lesgold (Eds.), *Learning issues for intelligent tutoring systems.* New York: Springer.

Pirolli, P.L., & Anderson, J.R. (1985). The role of learning from examples in the acquisition of recursive programming skill. *Canadian Journal of Psychology, 39,* 240–272.

Skwarecki, E.J. (1988). Improving the engineering of model-tracing diagnosis. *The Proceedings of the International Conference on Intelligent Tutoring Systems* (pp. 215–221). Montréal, Canada.

Sleeman, D.H. (1983). Inferring student models for intelligent tutor-aided instruction. In R. Michalski, J. Carbonell, & T. Mitchell (Eds.), *Machine learning.* Palo Alto, CA: Tioga.

Sleeman, D.H., & Brown, J.S. (1982). *Intelligent tutoring systems.* New York: Academic Press.

Wenger, E. (1987). *Artificial intelligence and tutoring systems.* Los Altos, CA: Morgan Kaufmann.

# 5
# Bypassing the Intractable Problem of Student Modeling*

## John A. Self

### INTRODUCTION

In a review of the 1987 Artificial Intelligence and Education Conference, Sandberg (1987) summarized a general opinion that

> detailed user models do not necessarily enhance the capability of an intelligent tutoring system . . . good teaching can do without a detailed user model, because in good teaching serious misconceptions are avoided, and errors will be repaired on the spot . . . it is debatable whether the cost of constructing very detailed, complex user models that are runnable and have to be maintained all the time is worthwhile in terms of the gain in teaching efficiency.

The aim of this chapter is to rehearse the arguments for student models in intelligent tutoring systems and to present a less bleak prognosis of the possibility of actually constructing them.

Opinions such as the above derive from two sources:

1. Preconceptions about the potential roles of student models.
2. Theoretical and practical difficulties in building and using student models.

For the former, we offer some alternative, possibly more productive, views of the potential roles of student models; for the latter, we describe some more realistic, practically achievable, and useful goals for student modeling. In the next section, the student modeling problem is reviewed and in the following section some possible ways forward are suggested.

*The U.K. Science and Engineering Research Council has supported the work of Michael Twidale, Steve Payne, Helen Squibb, David Gilmore, and myself. Logica (Cambridge) Ltd. and British Telecom have been involved in some of the projects. Other members of the University of Lancaster's Centre for Research on Computers and Learning (in particular, Peter Goodyear, Jim Ridgway, and Rachel Rymaszewski) will recognize the influence of their thoughts on this chapter.

# THE STUDENT MODELING PROBLEM

A pure version of the student modeling problem might be the following:

*Tutor:*    What is the integral with respect to x of

$$x^4 / (1 + x^2)$$

*Student:*   $x + x^3 / 3 + \tan x$
*Tutor*    (thinks: How did she get that?): . . . .

A standard ITS approach might be to identify the set of allowable transformations and to study student protocols to build a catalogue of associated mistransformations. If there are $m$ possible transformations ($m \approx 30$ in this case), $n$ mistransformations for each of these (say, $n \approx 5$) and up to $p$ steps to a solution (say, $p \approx 10$), then there may be up to $(m*(n + 1))^p$ paths to analyze (about $10^{24}$), which is clearly intractable.

We can, of course, eliminate the combinatorial explosion if we ensure that $p = 1$, as in the Lisp tutor (Anderson & Reiser, 1985), constraining the student to the smallest analyzable step, with the consequent imposition of a rigid tutorial style. However, we still have the considerable difficulty of determining an appropriate "grain" of detail in defining the (mis)transformations. It is relatively easy to interrupt a student if she appears to be putting the clauses of a COND in the wrong order, but much harder to realize that she is doing so because she has confused the "if-then-else" semantics with a "production-system-like" semantics, where all the true conditions would be simultaneously acted upon.

Advocates of student models would wish to go beyond the analysis of student performance in terms of surface mistakes. They would like to isolate the underlying misconceptions which are the "cause" of the mistakes, because remedying such misconceptions might eradicate a whole set of mistakes. But defining, representing, and recognizing such misconceptions is even more difficult than identifying a procedural mistake.

And then, some would say, the $p = 1$ restriction and the usual ITS analysis of student-input on a sentence-by-sentence basis represents a very weak view of student problem-solving. Students do not always solve problems as finite automata, responding only to the state they are in—they develop goals, plans, and strategies. And indeed they should, and our ITS student models should ideally include descriptions of these, to permit discussions with students at this level. Unfortunately, such goals are often malformed, idiosyncratic, and difficult to identify automatically. For example, Unix experts know all sorts of hacks for achieving goals not normally associated with the Unix commands actually used.

This would imply that our student model needs access to quite specific information about the student's prior knowledge. This prior knowledge may be such that an ITS would not have any a priori reason for associating it with the topic of the tutorial. For example, Shrager's studies of how people learned by experimentation how to operate a programmable toy showed that they drew analogies with other programmable devices, clocks, and so on (Shrager, 1987). It is difficult to imagine ITSs having access to commonsense knowledge of clocks and thousands of similar objects just in case a student should happen to draw an analogy with them.

We know also that students' learning is influenced not only by their general prior knowledge but also by the more immediate learning context. For example, students attempting physics problems draw surface analogies with immediately preceding problems (Kolodner, 1983). This, of course, implies that student models should ideally maintain an episodic memory in order better to provoke productive analogies and to understand the source of mistaken analogies.

And not only will students have different prior knowledge and learning experiences, but they will have personal learning preferences, styles and strategies. Again, ideally these should be modeled, so that an ITS may present material in a way appropriate to the individual's learning abilities and perhaps to address weaknesses in those abilities.

Perhaps the student has particular interests, or an unusual social background, or some personality characteristic, which, if it were represented within the student model, might be used to individualize the instruction.

In this way, the "student modeling problem" expands—from computational questions, to representational issues, through plan recognition, mental models, episodic memory to individual differences—to encompass, it would seem, almost all of cognitive science. One reaction to this is to conclude that ITS research, and especially student modeling, is important precisely because many fundamental cognitive science questions have to be addressed.

Another reaction is to conclude that the student modeling problem is overwhelming difficult, that with the current state of knowledge there is no possibility of satisfactorily addressing most of these cognitive science questions, and therefore that ITS development had best proceed without student models at all. I hope to show that this last conclusion is not justified.

## BYPASSING THE STUDENT MODELING PROBLEM

It is not essential that ITSs possess precise student models, containing detailed representations of all the components mentioned above, in order to be able to tutor students satisfactorily. If we back off from the grand vision and adopt more realistic aims, then solutions for some aspects of the student modeling problem are practically attainable and useful. This approach will be described under four "slogans":

## Slogan 1: Avoid guessing—get the student to tell you what you need to know

The problem illustrated above with the symbolic integration question—that is, of inducing a student's (mis)conceptions from a problem-solution pair—may be, for ITS, a nonproblem. Using a pencil and paper, students do indeed occasionally, through bravado or a misplaced sense of style, write solutions down "by inspection," although this is very much against the recommendations given in modern classrooms. And with the older teletype-like interfaces to ITSs, students may well have been sorely tempted to omit intermediate steps to avoid laborious, error-prone typing. But imagine how a student would solve symbolic integration problems with a modern WIMP interface.

She might be presented with a menu of transformations to apply. With any transformation (e.g., integration by parts), she might be able to map the general form of the transformation onto the specific example by selecting parts of the example using the mouse, for example, to let $u = 1 / (1 + x^2)$ of the above example. Maybe there would be a "do_it" key to ensure there were no clerical slips. Perhaps the steps of the solution would be displayed in an appropriate tree structure, making it possible to see how the various steps relate to one another and to return to previous steps, if desired.

The process of problem solving is so much easier than with older interfaces (and with pencil and paper) that we may expect students to be much less inclined to omit intermediate steps. But, more importantly, with careful design the interaction may provide the ITS with precisely the information that it needs to model the problem-solving process, for example, to understand how the student proposes to apply integration by parts—information that is often difficult to infer even from a complete step-by-step solution. Ideally, the information is provided by the student, naturally and voluntarily, while problem solving (and not in response to some interventionist ITS).

So rather than attempting to develop better ways of inferring missing steps, a better goal for student modeling research might be to design interactions through which the information needed for building student models is provided nonintrusively as an intrinsic part of problem solving.

It might immediately be objected that this would only provide us with information about individual steps and not information about the "goals and strategies," which we have indicated it is more important and useful to model. An experiment reported by Singley (1987) shows that this is not necessarily so.

He designed a system to help students learn to solve algebra word problems about rates of change. He provided a menu of available operators and a solution window. With the first version of the system it was found that students performed badly at solving problems, mainly because they became muddled as to where they were. As a result, a "goal window" was included in which a student was required to "post" the goal(s) she was working on before selecting operators.

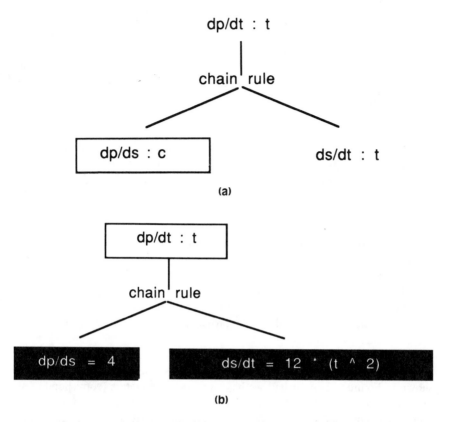

Figure 5.1. Two images of the goal-posting window (from Singley, 1987).

For example, in Figure 5.1(a) the "dp/dt : t" at the root of the tree denotes that she is trying to find dp/dt in terms of t. The "chain rule" is the proposed operator which, before it can be applied, needs two subgoals to be satisfied, namely "dp/ds : c" and "ds/dt : t." An open box around a node indicates the goal currently being worked on, and a closed box (Figure 5.1(b)) indicates that a goal has been satisfied.

The hypothesis is that, for example, when she sees the two closed boxes then she will have less difficulty in recalling that she was trying to apply the chain rule, which will improve problem-solving and learning performance. But it may be that the overhead of "goal-posting" actually interferes with problem solving. Experimental studies showed that, under the conditions Singley specified,

1.  Goal-posting improved problem-solving performance, in that operator selections were made faster, there were fewer "illegal" selections, and the solutions found were shorter.

2. Performance was improved even after the goal window was remove—that is, students had not just benefited from a temporary technological crutch but had learned some problem-solving skills.

3. The improvement transferred to other kinds of (admittedly similar) problem, indicating that the skills learned were not problem-specific tricks but were more generally useful.

One possible conclusion from this experiment is that we should include a goal window in our problem-solving environments and that this will facilitate student learning, thereby reducing the need for any "intelligent tutoring" and hence student modeling. However, the interpretation I would make is that it may be possible to design such environments so that students provide precisely the information ITSs need for student modeling and have difficulty in inducing from performance (namely, information about goals).

There are two main research questions (which my colleague Michael Twidale and I are investigating):

1. How can the information provided by interactions with a goal window be used by an ITS to carry on discussions about the student's goals?

2. What kind of language should be provided for the student to communicate her goals?

We have implemented a prototype logic tutor, a screen image of which is shown in Figure 5.2. As usual, we have a menu of operators (corresponding to rules of inference) and a solution window. In addition, we provide a set of plan schema (one or more with each operator, indicating what goal the operator may help achieve, and some, for example, "contradiction," which are independent of particular operators). Pointing to a plan schema shows an abstract form of the plan, which can be instantiated to the problem at hand if the student wishes (in the figure the student may be about to instantiate the X of the plan schema to Q and the Y to R). Selecting a plan causes the instantiated form of the plan to appear in the "goal window." The student may then select components of this plan to work on, which may of course call up further subplans. The student's progress through the plans is automatically marked in the goal window (the tick indicating achieved plans, the arrow pointing to the current goal).

The student's selection and use of plans is monitored by the system. The system may intervene if a plan is deemed inappropriate, writing a message in the "message window." As usual, it is difficult to say precisely what use an ITS should make of its knowledge of student goals, when it should intervene, and how it should express its interventions.

The use of plan schemas is not a general solution to the problem of providing a language through which the student may express her goals. We had previously experimented with the use of a menu of (about 30) stock phrases (e.g., "in order

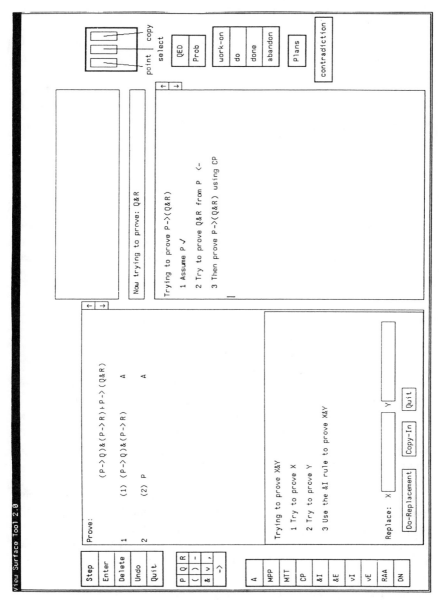

**Figure 5.2. Monitoring plans in a logic tutor.**

113

to," "it follows that," etc.) from which the student could select and build up a natural language plan of any desired complexity. We believed that the selection of phrases would considerably ease the parsing problem. It turned out that students could so express plans in this domain, and that they could be parsed relatively easily, but that there were unfortunately too many ambiguous phrases (e.g., "from x and y," meaning "from lines x and y of the proof so far," or "using proof rules x and y," and so on). However, we are optimistic that the technique of phrase selection to express logical arguments may be adequate in other domains. For example, we are looking at the possibility of using the technique to express causal arguments in economics, where clauses are usually of the form "x leads to y," with numerous paraphrases.

**Slogan 2: Don't diagnose what you can't treat**

The grand ambition to build high-fidelity student models can easily obscure the fact that, in practical terms, student models by themselves achieve nothing. Student models are merely data for the tutoring component of ITSs. It follows that there is no practical benefit to be gained from incorporating in our student models features which the tutoring component makes no use of, and there is no point the ITS laboring to identify such features.

However, this assumes that our tutoring component is given and that we have only to inspect its code to discover the features that our student model needs to identify. This is not so: Our understanding of tutoring expertise is not deep and it is indeed a prime function of student modeling to drive this understanding. The division of an ITS into the standard "subject, student, tutor" modules is an explicatory device, not a guideline for ITS implementation. Mobus and Thole (1988) seem to regret the fact that "their identification in current systems is difficult or even impossible to obtain because their knowledge bases are often not as clearly separated as theory postulates." In my view, the student model and tutoring procedure should be developed in tandem, not separately. Any proposed feature of a student model should be explicitly linked with existing educational evidence which justifies it.

One implication of this suggestion is that the development of the tutoring component is no longer to be left as an intuitive afterthought. Its contents are to be brought out into the open, so that we may assess their implications for student modeling and their educational rationale. This, indeed, is happening. For example, Clancey (1987), Mizoguchi, Ikeda, and Kakusho (1988), and Woolf (1988) all give details of tutoring procedures. In general, the implications are that, in practical terms, we can be much less demanding of our student models and that the educational rationale is somewhat ad hoc.

Imposing the ⟨feature : processing : evidence⟩ test, suggested above, I suspect would render many of the discussions on student models irrelevant. For example, the original genetic graph proposal (Goldstein, 1982) suggested overlaying a description of the student's "learning preferences" on the links, where these preferences seem to be described in terms of "his need for repetition, his degree of forgetfulness, and his receptivity to advice." What use the tutoring component was to make of this information, and on what basis, was left to intuition.

The same difficulty arises with most proposals to incorporate some description of "learner styles" in student models. These proposals invariably quote Pask's holist/serialist distinction (Pask, 1976) but are quite unable to point to any other learner styles which can be reliably identified by ITSs and which can be associated with demonstrably effective differential treatments by ITSs.

As regards the idea that other individual differences, describing intellectual abilities, cognitive styles, academic motivation, and personality characteristics should be represented within student models, then the literature on aptitude-treatment interactions, reviewed by Corno and Snow (1986), is not encouraging. They conclude that further research is needed to identify likely aptitude variables and that, in any case, "practical systems can use no more than a few control variables for adaptive purposes" (e.g., two, perhaps intelligence and motivation, for human teachers).

## Slogan 3: Empathize with the student's beliefs, don't label them as bugs

The general perception, reflected in the Sandberg quote above, that student models in ITS are for *remediation* presents a serious philosophical problem. It is the arrogant, "tutor knows best" style of ITSs which alienates classroom teachers more than any technical shortcomings. The standard ITS approach of first defining a body of certified knowledge and then devising ways to correct students' understanding so that it conforms to it does not accord with the philosophies of epistemologists, with or without an educational orientation. For example, Piaget urged us to appreciate that a child's understanding was never merely wrong but that it made sense to him in his own terms, if we as teachers could but understand those terms. And philosophers of science, such as Popper, have argued that the history of the development of scientific knowledge demonstrates that we ought to regard all knowledge as provisional and potentially falsifiable.

The idea that student models are for remediation is implicit in both standard approaches to student modeling, the "mal-rule approach" and the "expert system overlay approach." Here I will concentrate on the former.

In the mal-rule approach, two sets of productions are defined: a "correct" set, which if applied to the problem at hand gives a correct solution, and a "mal" set, which consists of deformed versions of the correct productions. If a member of the mal set is used instead of its associated correct rule, then an incorrect solution will (usually) be obtained. Of course, the aim of the ITS is to eradicate any mal-rules which may exist in the student's head (anything "mal" clearly needs treatment).

Apart from philosophical misgivings, there are practical and theoretical problems with this approach:

1.    To label something as incorrect and in need of remediation, an ITS needs to know what is to be deemed "correct." Consequently, the mal-rule approach is, in principle, only possible where such a knowledge representation can be specified, that is, in closed-world, formal domains (such as subtraction and Lisp programming), and even there there may be many equivalent effective representations.

2.    A mal-rule is to be understood as one which is systematically applied instead of the correct rule. But how "systematic" does a mal-rule have to be to qualify as a mal-rule? In an attempt to discover whether it is in fact the case that "there is great systematicity in the appearance of [algebra] errors" (Resnick, Cauzinille-Marmeche, & Mathieu, 1987), Payne and Squibb (1987) analyzed student errors in solving linear algebraic equations. While they considered that they could identify 99 different mal-rules, over 90% of them were used on less than 50% of the occasions when they could have been used (and by the original Brown & vanLehn (1980) guidelines would not have qualified as mal-rules at all).

3.    The empirical data will indicate that some mal-rules are more common than others. It requires a theory of "mal-rule generation" to explain why this is so. As Payne and Squibb (1987) point out, it is difficult to see how syntactic mechanisms (such as repair theory [Brown & vanLehn, 1980]) can explain why the transformation:

A: $Mx + N - > [M + N]x$
(e.g. $3x + 4 = 5x + 2 - > 7x = 5x + 2$)

is more common than:

B: $Mx + N - > [M + N]$
(e.g. $3x + 4 = 5x + 2 - > 7 = 5x + 2$)

[This is so even when there are multiple x's in the equation: the bias is to be expected when there is only one x.] The intuition that A is "more sensible" amounts to a belief that student models need to include descriptions of (partially formed) conceptual knowledge in addition to purely procedural knowledge.

4.    How consistent are mal-rules across different populations? Payne and Squibb (1987) found very little overlap between the most common mal-rules at three different schools (in fact, the five most common mal-rules at the three schools gave 13 different mal-rules). This suggests that theories of mal-rule generation need to take more account of educational experience and context than they currently do.

5.    The developers of lists of mal-rules have many decisions to make. In an

algebra study, for example, do we abstract over integers (but 0 and 1 are surely special cases), do we abstract over operators, do we consider permutations (e.g., Mx + N, N + Mx) the same, and so on? The tally of mal-rules depends on such decisions. Too many mal-rules leads to a vacuous theory and computational inefficiency: Too few mal-rules obscures data which may be of theoretical importance.

6.   In general, there is a difficult knowledge representation question which has been preempted by the mal-rule terminology. Production rules may be suitable for modeling procedural skills in closed, formal domains, but it is difficult to see how, even in principle, the mal-rule approach could be applied to address misconceptions deriving from inappropriate analogies, such as those identified by Shrager (1987), mentioned above.

7.   Finally, and referring back to slogan 2, even if we could reliably identify mal-rules, what should an ITS do about them? According to Pintrich, Cross, Kozma, and McKeachie (1986), "once a bug has been accurately diagnosed, an instructional prescription follows naturally", but recently, Sleeman (1987) has discovered that "even though [his system] has a model for a student's problem solving it has not so far proved possible to remediate very effectively."

If student models are not primarily for remediation, then what other role may they have? In a recent review (Self, 1988), I identified 20 different uses that had been found for student models in existing ITSs. The largest class of uses was indeed to do with remediation—but the next largest was what I called "elaborative," that is, to do with leading the student to elaborate or refine his current knowledge, not necessarily because a "bug" had been identified and not necessarily towards some prespecified target knowledge. This is the role that I would encourage for student models.

Sandberg's assertion that "good teaching can do without a detailed user model, because in good teaching serious misconceptions are avoided" is doubly misleading. First, good teaching involves much more than the avoidance of misconceptions. Secondly, teaching activities other than remediation, for example, provoking a student to question her own beliefs, would benefit from having a detailed user model.

To escape from the remediationist view of student models, it may perhaps help if we consider that student models are intended to describe not what students "know" but what they "believe." The former encourages ITS designers to impose value judgments about the correctness or otherwise of this "knowledge." Beliefs, on the other hand, are always provisional and liable to be changed if their justifications are seen to be inadequate or their implications seen to be unreasonable. The student modeling problem then becomes one of identifying what a student believes, and if possible why, the beliefs being represented in their own terms, not with respect to some target knowledge. The role of student models would then be to help ITSs to provoke students to consider the justifications and implications of their beliefs.

**Slogan 4: Don't feign omniscience—adopt a "fallible collaborator" role**

The proposed change of ITS style, from knowledgeable remediator to empathetic belief elaborator, is not made solely on philosophical grounds. There are also practical reasons for such a change.

For most of the subjects which we would like our ITSs to address, describing a "correct' knowledge base, together with an adequate description of potential student misconceptions, is a practical impossibility. To attempt to conceal this under a facade of omniscience is a risky business.

Most studies of human tutoring that I have seen have concentrated on elucidating how a tutor makes pedagogic use of his own subject matter knowledge. It would be interesting to know how human tutors help students in situations where they lack subject matter knowledge. (My own experience is that this situation prevails over the first!)

Clearly it *is* possible for tutors to respond appropriately to questions for which they do not know the answers: "Why are cooling towers the shape they are?" "Are all modern aeroplanes powered by turbines?" "How can mercury be a metal?" and so on. We can respond in a variety of ways, such as giving suggestions about where to find relevant information, joining in an attempt to answer the question by reasoning from shared "common sense" knowledge, probing the student's preconceptions behind the question, and so on. In many ways, these would be better responses than direct answers even if we were able to give them, because, of course, they go beyond mere factual knowledge to address problem-solving and learning skills which are, one hopes, of general utility. Is it possible for an ITS to play a similar role?

We have been toying with the idea of building an ITS which deliberately does not have the knowledge which the student is endeavoring to acquire. For example, to take a somewhat artificial situation, imagine that the student and the ITS have access to a database giving details of the properties of all the chemical elements, and that the student is trying to discover why certain elements are called "metals," some "nonmetals" and others "semimetals." The ITS would not itself know the rules (if any) which map sets of properties onto these classifications. The student may ask for specific information ("What is the boiling point of mercury?"), probe hypotheses ("Are all metals solid?"), offer thoughts ("Maybe all nonmetals are soft"), make strategic comments ("Let's look at magnetic properties"), ask for specific help ("List the boiling points we've seen so far"), seek general help ("What next?") and so on.

The role of the ITS is to act as a collaborator in this endeavor, by giving (or indeed taking) strategic advice, derived not from its prior knowledge of the concepts concerned, but from its understanding of how to set about developing such hypotheses in general and its knowledge of the particular information which the student has asked for. The perceived style of the ITS is all-important: If the system were to say "Those last two metals were both shiny—perhaps they all are," this would have to be understood by the student not as an unsubtle hint (the tutor knowing perfectly well that all metals are shiny), but as a genuine, hopefully useful, but possibly mistaken, comment.

How could it be made to work? The ITS needs to be able to work out what a student may reasonably be expected to infer (or not to infer) from the data she sees. In other words, in this case, the ITS needs a machine learning program capable of inferring concepts from examples in a psychologically plausible way. The ITS would use such a program in two ways: First, for building a student model describing the student's beliefs about the concepts (again, as above, these are not to be judged by the ITS as correct or not, but, if necessary, as "interesting" or justified by the evidence or not), and secondly, to work out which information would enable it (the ITS) and, it is to be hoped, the student to refine those beliefs, in particular, to find information capable of falsifying them.

We adapted the focusing algorithm for concept learning to try to build these student models (Gilmore & Self, 1988), but we encountered three particular problems:

1.   We had underestimated the volume of prior knowledge which such an ITS would need. Only with AI machine learning programs does the closed world assumption hold. Students bring to bear all sorts of "common knowledge" (such as that "temperatures are precisely given, but colors are imprecisely described in English," "boiling points are related to melting points but probably not to conductivity") which an ITS would need access to, even if it is not to know specifically what is to be learned by the student. Perhaps the approach of explanation-based learning would have been a better choice than the similarity-based learning of focusing. Explanation-based learning emphasizes the role of domain knowledge in promoting learning from a single example, rather than by generalizing over several examples.

2.   The perceived setting was too sterile: We could not imagine many students being sufficiently motivated to explore the database in the way assumed. Learning concepts is not an abstract game: Concepts are learned for a purpose (to help solve problems or to make sense of a story, say). Without knowing why the student is trying to discover what a metal is it is not possible for an ITS to determine whether her beliefs about the concept are adequate for the present purpose. Conceptual learning needs to be embedded within a problem setting.

3.   We had little idea of how to support collaborative dialogues, in which both participants are to be seen as of "equal status," or whether students would, in fact, welcome such a style of interaction with a computer. The benefits claimed for human-human collaboration (e.g., Slavin, 1983) may result more from social and motivational effects than process effects, and may therefore disappear even if the student-computer collaboration is carefully designed.

However, the exercise was productive in two ways. First, it showed that educationalists were more responsive to the idea of a computer collaborator than to that of a computer tutor. Of course, "collaborative learning" is very much in vogue in modern classrooms and we may simply have triggered a positive reaction. On the other hand, they may have grounds for believing that students learn more productively by discussing problems with peers than by being tutored by "experts" such as themselves.

Secondly, it caused us to rethink the role of a student model. In a conventional ITS, the student model is an internal data structure purporting to describe the student which is used furtively by the ITS to determine tutorial actions. (Incidentally, it is questionable whether such a student model is legal—in the U.K., at least, all data about individuals has to be registered with the Data Protection Registrar and accessible to the individuals concerned!) In a collaborative ITS, there is no need to hide the student model from the student—in a sense, it represents a shared understanding of the problem and with the more "open" philosophy, it may well help, or challenge, the student to be aware of what the system thinks she believes.

Indeed, it would be a salutary principle to insist that all student models be made open to the student. This might benefit ITS design by reducing the temptation to include crude, ad hoc classifications, and, more importantly, may lead to educational benefits as it might well provoke the student to reflect on her own understanding. To promote student reflection and to foster collaborative learning it would not be necessary to develop the high-fidelity student models needed for remediation.

A collaborative interaction may also help the student develop a more favorable self-image and a better view of how knowledge is acquired. Instead of being perpetually corrected, with the imputation of incompetence or stupidity, she may see how her own understanding reasonably develops. A "knowledgeable" ITS commenting that "that is a perfectly reasonable misconception but . . ." would be seen as patronizing: A collaborative ITS would carry the same message without needing to verbalize it.

In a related exercise, we are considering whether it may be possible for an ITS to understand, and comment upon, a student's strategy, without attempting to understand the subject matter. With the AlgebraLand system (Foss, 1987), a student solves algebra problems and has the search space displayed graphically to reflect upon. AlgebraLand does not attempt to tutor the student. But by analyzing the shape of the search space and simple syntactic properties of the nodes of the graph (and *not* by trying to understand the problem-solving process in depth), it is possible to determine potentially useful features of the space, such as when students tend to abandon a solution path, where they tend to back up to, which nodes seem to be a source of difficulty, whether the search is in any way systematic, and so on. Consequently, it may be possible for an ITS to give strategic advice to a student, from the evidence of structural properties of the search space.

We are looking at the ways students use hypertext systems, for example, containing a classical Greek dictionary, to answer questions such as "Describe the main adversaries faced by Jason in the Argonautica." It is clearly not possible to apply machine learning techniques to learn, as students would, from reading the dictionary text. We are hoping to be able to make sufficient sense of their search spaces, without understanding any of the subject matter, to enable an ITS to give strategic advice to students.

However, there is an apparent logical flaw in the argument that ITSs do not need subject knowledge, but rather knowledge of strategic learning skills, so that ITSs may promote the learning of those strategic skills, which we may consider more important than mere factual knowledge. For, by a similar argument, perhaps ITSs do not need learning skills either, but rather knowledge of how to develop learning skills (and so on). But for all practical purposes, and I suspect for all theoretical ones too (for the skills at "higher" levels may not be significantly different from those at lower ones), there are only a very small number (e.g., 2) of such levels.

## CONCLUSIONS

This review of the role of student models in ITSs is intended to show that, while research in student models is potentially capable of embracing almost all the problems in cognitive science and that there is therefore no realistic possibility of building student models which meet all the objectives of ITS designers, there are nevertheless several ways in which, by changing our design principles and our philosophical approach, we may build ITSs in which student models play a significant role.

Several suggestions have been made, perhaps the most important of which are:

1. To design student-computer interactions in which the information needed (especially about the student's goals) by the ITS to build a student model are provided naturally by the student while using the ITS, and does not have to be inferred by the ITS from inadequate data.
2. To explicitly link the proposed contents of student models with specific tutorial actions, ideally supported by educational evidence, in order to clarify what is really needed (and not needed) in the student model.
3. To avoid viewing student models solely as devices to support remediation, which is often perceived as implying a behaviorist philosophy of learning and which often cannot be satisfactorily achieved anyway because of various difficulties with the "mal-rule" approach to student modeling.
4. To use student models "constructively" by regarding the contents as representing student beliefs, with no value judgments imposed by the ITS, the ITS's role being to help the student elaborate those beliefs.
5. To make the contents of the student model open to the student, in order to

provoke the student to reflect upon its contents and to remove all pretense that the ITS has a perfect understanding of the student (and that ITS designers should build systems which proceed as though they do).

6.   To develop ITSs which adopt a more collaborative role, rather than a directive one, for then the style corresponds to a better philosophy of how knowledge is acquired and we do not have to seek such a high degree of fidelity in the student model.

*It is not often that any man can have so much knowledge of another, as is necessary to make instruction useful.* (Samuel Johnson (1752), *The Rambler,* p. 87)

## REFERENCES

Anderson, J.R., & Reiser, B. (1985). The Lisp tutor. *Byte, 10,* 159–175.

Brown, J.S., & van Lehn, K. (1980). Repair theory: A generative theory of bugs in procedural skills. *Cognitive Science, 4,* 379–426.

Clancey, W.J. (1987). *Knowledge-based tutoring: The GUIDON program.* Cambridge, MA: MIT Press.

Corno, L., & Snow, R.E. (1986). Adapting teaching to individual differences among learners. In M. Wittrock (Ed.), *Handbook of research on teaching* (pp. 605–629). New York: MacMillan.

Foss, C.L. (1987). Productive thrashing in a computerized tutoring system. *Proceedings of the Third International Conference on Artificial Intelligence and Education.* Pittsburgh, PA.

Gilmore, D.J., & Self, J.A. (1988). The application of machine learning to intelligent tutoring systems. In J.A. Self (Ed.), *Artificial intelligence and human learning* (pp. 179–196). London: Chapman and Hall.

Goldstein, I.P. (1982). The genetic graph: A representation for the evolution of procedural knowledge. In D.H. Sleeman & J.S. Brown (Eds.), *Intelligent tutoring systems* (pp. 51–77). London: Academic Press.

Kolodner, J.L. (1983). Towards an understanding of the role of experience in the evolution from novice to expert. *International Journal of Man-Machine Studies, 19,* 497–518.

Mizoguchi, R., Ikeda, M., & Kakusho, O. (1988). An innovative framework for intelligent tutoring systems. In P. Ercoli & R. Lewis (Eds.), *Artificial intelligence tools in education* (pp. 105–120). Amsterdam: North-Holland.

Mobus, C., & Thole, H. (1988). *Tutors, instructions and helps* (Absynt Report 3/88). University of Oldenburg, West Germany.

Pask, G. (1976). Styles and strategies of learning. *British Journal of Educational Psychology, 46,* 128–148.

Payne, S.J., & Squibb, H.R. (1987). *Understanding algebra errors: The psychological status of mal-rules* (CeRCLe Tech. Report 43). University of Lancaster, England.

Pintrich, P.R., Cross, D.R., Kozma, R.B., & McKeachie, W.J. (1986). Instructional psychology. *Annual Review of Psychology, 37,* 611–651.

Resnick, L.B., Cauzinille-Marmeche, E., & Mathieu, J. (1987). Understanding algebra. In J. Sloboda & D. Rogers (Eds.), *Cognitive processes in mathematics* (pp. 169–203). Oxford: Clarendon.

Sandberg, J.A.C. (1987). The Third International Conference on Artificial Intelligence and Education. *AICOM, 0,* 51–53.

Self, J.A. (1988). Student models: What use are they? In P. Ercoli & R. Lewis (Eds.), *Artificial intelligence tools in education* (pp. 73–86). Amsterdam: North-Holland.

Shrager, J. (1987). Theory change via view application in instructionless learning. *Machine Learning, 2,* 247–276.

Singley, M.K. (1987). The effect of goal posting on operator selection. *Proceedings of the Third International Conference on Artificial Intelligence and Education.* Pittsburgh, PA.

Slavin, R.E. (1983). *Cooperative learning.* New York: Longman.

Sleeman, D.H. (1987). Some challenges for intelligent tutoring systems. *Proceedings of the International Joint Conference on Artificial Intelligence, 87.* Milan, Italy.

Woolf, B.P. (1988). Representing complex knowledge in an intelligent machine tutor. In J.A. Self (Ed.), *Artificial intelligence and human learning* (pp. 3–27). London: Chapman and Hall.

# 6
# Discourse Planning in Intelligent Help Systems*

**Radboud Winkels**
**Joost Breuker**

## INTRODUCTION

The research discussed here is part of the EUROHELP project. This project is aimed at the construction of an environment for building *Intelligent Help Systems* (IHSs) for "Information Processing Systems" (IPSs, i.e., interactive computer programs). Core of this environment is a shell that contains all domain-independent procedures and knowledge. The major task of a developer of a help system for some specific IPS will be to fill the shell with a representation of the domain concepts (commands, syntax, methods of object reference, etc.). It is often believed that modern, well-designed IPSs have such a self-evident structure and such "understandable" (metaphoric) interfaces that help seems superfluous. A good user interface is supposed to have help implicitly wired in. For instance, the famous Apple Macintosh interface looks so self-evident, that novice users soon feel quite comfortable. However, experienced users complain about its modularity and inaccessibility of its elementary processes. In other words, the Mac is hiding the fact that the electronic world is differently shaped than the real world. The real-world metaphors break down very soon and even impede the acquisition of skill and insight into an IPS. With even more advanced and versatile software (e.g., NoteCards, HyperCard), users already need Intelligent Help to guide them in what they could use it for, let alone *how* to use it (see also Breuker, 1988).

Within the EUROHELP project a prototype Help System for Unix Mail exists and several new prototypes of Help System Modules have been built and tested for other domains. Specifications of the entire shell have been written, and in April 1989 a second version will be implemented. In this chapter we will focus on the construction of a generic Coach that is part of this shell, but we will begin with a short description of what a full IHS consists of (cf. Breuker, Winkels, & Sandberg, 1987; Breuker, Baaren, Winkels, & Duursma, 1987).

---

* The research is partially funded by the ESPRIT Program of the European community under contract P280. The project encompasses an effort of about 100 man-years over a 5-year period, of which 4 years have been spent now. Partners in the project are: CRI, DDC (Denmark), ICL, University of Leeds (U.K.), Courseware Europe, University of Amsterdam (The Netherlands). We would like to thank Jacobijn Sandberg for her contributions to the research described.

## THE ARCHITECTURE OF AN INTELLIGENT HELP SYSTEM

The most important goal of Intelligent Help Systems is to support the task performance of the IPS users. This is different from normal Intelligent Tutoring Systems: Their primary goal is to teach the user (not without reason called *student*) knowledge in a specific domain. Of course, teaching the user the domain of IPSs in general and the particular IPS she is working with enables (better) performance. Likewise, using the IPS correctly, facilitates learning about the inner workings of the system. Still, teaching in IHSs is basically *opportunistic,* occasion-driven.

IHSs support users both in a passive and in an active way: The user may ask a question concerning the IPS, or the Help System may infer a need for information from the users performance. This means that a help system should have the role of a human coach, who looks over the shoulder of the user to interpret her performance, interrupts when things go wrong, or when there is an opportunity to extend the repertoire of the user, and who is able to answer questions in the context of current use of the IPS. The latter is crucial, because many users—in particular novice users—often are not aware of problems, and if they are, they do not know how to describe them (Fischer, Lemke, & Schwab, 1985). This is one important reason why question-answering help systems, which do not interpret user performance, have a very limited functionality (e.g., UC [Wilensky, Arens, & Chin, 1984]; AQUA [Quillici, Dyers, & Flowers, 1986]). Online monitoring the performance of the user entails many conceptual and computational problems, but these are not qualitatively different from those in intelligent coaching in general (e.g., Sleeman & Brown, 1982; Anderson, Boyle, & Yost, 1985; Self, 1988).

Because user needs may either be identified by the system or by the user, EUROHELP consists of a *Question Interpreter* and a *Performance Interpreter.* To circumvent the problem of interpreting questions in natural language (Lehnert, 1978; Wilensky et al., 1984), question frames are used. For each type of question (Lehnert, 1978; Hartley & Smith, 1988) a text frame is presented for which the user supplies the objects.

The question interpretation problem may be reduced by relying on the linguistic competence of the user, the performance interpretation problem presents itself in its full glory. In normal coaching (training) the system presents a problem to the student. However, in IPS performance the user poses the problems (tasks) to herself. Finding out whether something goes wrong is highly dependent on identifying the intentions of the user. Therefore, the Performance Interpreter contains a *Plan Recognizer* and a *Planner,* which cooperate in such a way that the former works bottom-up and provides constraints to the latter in generating currently feasible plans. Plans may not only be wrong or impossible, they may be highly inefficient.

Both Question and Performance Interpreter can consult a detailed *User Model* to help them identify possible problems or needs for information. The User Model basically is an overlay of the Domain Representation, augmented with information on the use of certain commands, and so on.

Once a possible need for information has been identified, the *Diagnoser* will have to explain it in terms of either a lack of knowledge or a misconception on the part of the user. Although generative diagnosis by systematic perturbations of correct domain knowledge is certainly beyond the current state of the art for domains of any complexity (cf. Clancey, 1986), the diagnosing can be reasonably constrained by the current goal of the user and the User Model.[1]

If the Diagnoser does find such an explanation, a formal description of the current user need is sent to the *Coach*, who will plan an intervention to meet this need (next section). The *Utterance Generator* will transform the result of this planning process to natural language or some other means of representation.

Figure 6.1 summarizes the described architecture.

The next section will deal with the Coach in more detail.


## THE COACH

As mentioned earlier, the Coach of a Help System has two functions: to assist the user with a current problem (support task performance) and to teach the user about the IPS. The scope of these functions is different. Learning goals are long term goals, while the HELP function is a very local one. Therefore we distinguish *global needs,* that is, the knowledge to be acquired about a particular IPS, and *local needs,* which state the current problem of the user. Whenever a local need can be related to a global need, that is, the user is supposed to be able to learn from the information presented, the Coach should teach; otherwise it simply presents the required information (Help), without expecting this information to be remembered.

Presenting information consists of a sequence of "communication acts" or *tactics.* This sequence is the result of a planning process that takes into account what to say, when, and how, given the identified problem of the user (i.e., the local need). This is what a *teaching strategy* is about. Current Intelligent Tutoring Systems contain more or less fixed, prewired teaching strategies (e.g., Sleeman & Brown, 1982; Wenger, 1987; Self, 1988). In an existing EUROHELP system—a Help System for Unix-Mail—coaching strategies are also prewired in the form of fixed frames in which topics (what to say) can be inserted. However, the large variety of potential local needs requires a more generative approach. As literature (e.g., Ohlsson, 1986) and empirical data show: There are no *fixed* coaching strategies. They are flexibly generated as a function of the current

---

[1] If the Plan Recognizer is not able to establish the current goal, multiple hypotheses about misconceptions can often be ruled out by asking the user about what she intends to accomplish.

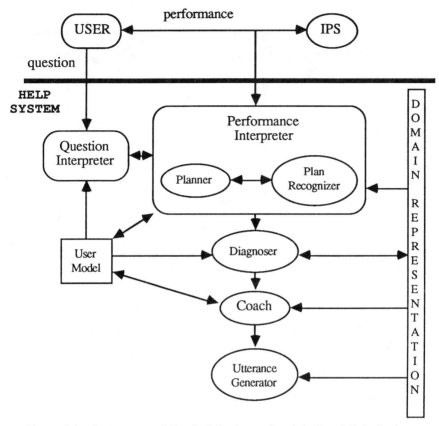

**Figure 6.1.   A summary of the Architecture of an Intelligent Help System.**

problem and state of knowledge of the user. Therefore, there is a very recent
tendency to construct flexible, multileveled *didactic planners* for intelligent
coaching systems (e.g., Elsom-Cook, 1987; Macmillan, 1987; Woolf & Murray,
1987).

The structure of the Coach consists of the following three layers (see Figure
6.2), which are similar to those proposed by Woolf and McDonald (1984), but
with more functional differentiation.

1.  *Didactic Goals* Form an overlay of the Domain Representation of the IPS,
    and provide a didactic view of the domain.
2.  *Discourse Strategies* are planned to meet specific users problems in specific
    situations.
3.  *Tactics* are the terminal elements of the strategies. They are communication
    acts that can be "executed" right away, with a specific goal (i.e., to change
    something in the mind of the user).

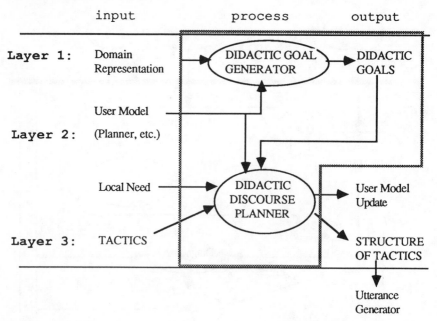

**Figure 6.2. Input, output, and processing of the Coach. Components of the Coach are in CAPITALS.**

These three layers will be discussed in more detail, but first we will describe shortly the methodology we use for our research.

**Research Methodology**

Research has taken two parallel routes: an empirical route and a model construction route. The empirical route consists of several mock-up experiments, in which human tutors simulate Help Systems. They guide users of an IPS through computer terminals: one on which they can monitor the users performance, another with which they can communicate with the user. This empirical route tries to identify in a bottom-up way how human coaches plan their strategies and what tactics are employed. The model construction approach is top-down: It is aimed at the development of prescriptive notions about effective coaching, that is, it specifies "(psycho)logical" concepts, derived from notions about optimizing knowledge acquisition (cf. Didactic Goal generation). Model construction consists of designing and implementing a domain independent Coach which, fed with a local need and access to knowledge structures (domain representation, user model, performance and coaching histories, current state of the IPS), constructs a strategy, which bottoms out in a sequence of tactics.

The two approaches complement one another. The empirical data keep the model "honest" and "ecologically valid." The model construction not only provides an interpretation framework for the empirical data, but also "criticizes" these data, in the sense that human coaches are not necessarily behaving in an optimal way for two reasons. The first reason is time constraints. The on-line coaching does not allow the coaches to carefully plan their actions. There is often backtracking. This leads us to the second reason: The coaches are not expert in coaching-by-teletype. Their "normal" way of expressing themselves is constrained. Moreover, there are large individual differences between coaches, and we want to have some semi-external criterion to select styles and strategies that appear to work. This can partially be abstracted from the empirical data, because the users provide thinking-aloud protocols, which show in which way the actions of the coach are understood. The "ideal model" is another framework to evaluate the usefulness of these empirical data.

Various empirical studies have been conducted (e.g., Bison & van der Pal, 1985, on Unix Mail; Winkels, Sandberg, & Breuker, 1986; and Rengel, Sandberg, & Winkels, 1988, on Unix Vi) leading particularly to a refinement and modeling of Tactics. A number of typical coaching strategies have been identified, most of which focus on correcting and expanding operational knowledge (*skill*).

The model construction has lead to an initial design and implementation of the Discourse Planner in Prolog (Winkels, 1987). A new version has been built using InterLisp on a Xerox machine.

## Didactic Goals

The first layer of the Coach consists of Didactic Goals. Their major function is the specification of knowledge which can be acquired by a user/student by applying some learning principle. The learning principles will be specified in the form of types of relations between concepts. In this sense, Didactic Goals have a similar representation format as *genetic graphs* (Goldstein, 1979). For a particular user the Didactic Goals consist of relations between knowledge the user already has and new topics in the domain.

We distinguish four types of didactic relations:

- *Generalization—Specification:* Some concepts are more general than others. They share attributes, but the more specific one has extra attributes. All the shared ones can be transferred from the general concept to the more specific one if the Coach explicitly mentions this specification relation. This facilitates acquisition. In general the direction of teaching will be from general to specific, also from a performance point of view. More general commands are more readily applicable than specific ones.

- *Abstraction-Concretion:* When certain system procedures are reasonably well practiced by the user (*skill*), it is time to explain some underlying, hidden objects and models, that is, introduce some support knowledge (*insight*): *abstraction.* Also, it may be desirable to illustrate an explanation of how part of a system works (support knowledge) by telling the user how he can use it (operational knowledge), thereby specifying a *concretion* relation.
- *Inversion:* Instead of transferring shared attributes, inversion allows one to transfer the inverse of attributes, for example, "X is the opposite of Y."
- *Analogy:* Explaining domain concepts by using metaphors.

A *Didactic Goal Generator* interprets the Domain Representation to identify these didactic relations. For instance, some specification relations can be deduced from and through the *isa* and *part-of* hierarchies of objects. Concepts higher up in the isa hierarchy are more general than concepts lower down. System procedures that affect objects higher up in the part-of hierarchy are more specific than those affecting objects lower down.[2]

The generalization-specification relations, as the inversion relations,[3] can be generated as soon as the Domain Representation for a specific IPS is ready. They are fixed, user-independent didactic goals, and resemble genetic graphs. The abstraction-concretion relation, however, is user-dependent and will have to be generated "on the spot." The need for abstraction will have to be inferred from the operational knowledge the user is supposed to have acquired (as reflected in the User Model). This will mainly be the case for the (hidden) objects and models the user has used or been referring to without (explicitly) knowing so. For instance, in the Unix Vi domain, the user has been issuing the commands "delete" and "put" several times, without knowing anything about "buffers" (the common hidden objects of these commands). Then the concept of a "buffer" will become a Didactic Goal—which, in turn, might trigger telling about how to address these buffers, so giving some new operational knowledge (concretion).

## Discourse Strategies

Once a user problem has been identified, a *local need* is sent to the Coach. Four types of local needs are distinguished, corresponding to the four functions of coaching:

- *error:* when a user issues a nonexecutable command or performs in a way diagnosed as not intended (REMEDIATE)

---

[2] For more detail, see Breuker, Winkels, and Sandberg (1986).

[3] The analogy relation is a special one, with special problems. Real-world analogies are likely to introduce misconceptions. Therefore we are thinking of special IPS metaphors. Discussion of these metaphors is outside the scope of this paper.

- *occasion for reminding:* when there is an opportunity to remind the user of something she is not expected to know very well (REMIND)
- *occasion for expansion:* when there is an opportunity to introduce new knowledge (EXPAND)
- *lack of feedback:* when the feedback of the IPS is assumed to be insufficient for a user (PROVIDE FEEDBACK).

Besides the type, local needs contain the immediate cause of the problem (user performance and/or a question) plus the diagnosis: a lack of knowledge or a misconception concerning some domain topic; one or more attributes of a concept; some aspect of the current system state, and so on. These topics cannot be hard-wired in the domain representation (like the Bite-Size architecture; Bonar, Cunningham, & Schultz, 1986), because i.a. for a shell this representation has to be generic. The topics of the diagnoses can be considered *minimal* topics. The Coach may decide to tell the user some more, for example, to prevent future overgeneralization or possible conflicts with unmentioned higher-order user goals (cf. Luria, 1987). Therefore a *topicalization* process expands these minimal topics to situation and user specific topics (see Winkels & Sandberg, 1987). Still, topics tend to be rather small in Help Systems.[4]

Given a local need, the Discourse Planner first tries to find a strategy to meet the current user need in a library of stereotypical ones (cf. *skeletal plans,* Friedland & Iwasaki, 1985). If it does find one, the strategy is instantiated to the current situation, and the "planning" process is finished. If it does not find one, or if the stereotypical ones have already been tried (as can be seen from a coaching history of the current session), general, fallback strategies will be used. These require real planning through the application of heuristic *refinement rules.* The conditions of these rules refer to the User Model, the Didactic Goals, the Coaching History, the current state of the system, and, of course, to the local need. They form the implementation of some of the Coaching Principles that will be discussed in the next section.

A general strategy consists of five parts:

- *Announcement:* As the name indicates to announce that the Help System is going to say something, and possibly to *signal* the content of the message. If the immediate cause is neither a question nor an error, the user may be asked for permission to interrupt.
- *Context:* Specifies the context of the new information. The Coach may refer to the user's performance (*performance history*), to something it has said

---

[4] Cf. "relevant knowledge pool" in database query systems (McKeown, 1985). In these systems there is no performance context to guide topicalization. Only when the user of a Help System asks a question completely out of context, the Coach can be compared to a database query system (one with a User Model).

before (*coaching history*), or to knowledge the user is considered to possess (the *User Model*). Besides linking old to new knowledge, the context-part of a strategy can be used to justify and explain the interruption for example, by referring to an error the user made.

- *New Information:* The most important part of any strategy, the goal of the interaction. Here the topic of the local need is explained, either in operational terms or by providing support knowledge.
- *Consolidation:* Meant to consolidate the new knowledge by allowing practice and giving examples.
- *Evaluation:* In the final phase the Coach tries to see whether the user understood everything that happened in the previous four phases. Usually a simple question will suffice; only after a lot of new information and an intensive consolidation phase can one think of a true test.[5]

The result of the planning process is a hierarchical structure that ends in tactics (see Figure 6.3 for an example). Tactics are directly executable communication actions that have a specific goal (see Table 6.1). They consist of a communication part (e.g., "To give you an example") which embeds the topic of discourse (e.g., "2dd deletes two lines from the current line"). This topic can be a domain topic (see above), or a reference to the communication or learning process itself (e.g., "Did you understand what I just said?").

We distinguish six tactics aimed at transferring domain knowledge (the upper part of Table 6.1) and also six for guiding the communication (lower part of Table 6.1).

The tactics intend to change something in the mind of the user, but whether this change is expected to be lasting or not, is decided at the strategic level. If the new information can be linked to existing knowledge, as reflected by the User Model (i.e., if the new topic is part of the Didactic Goals), the Coach will decide to do some real coaching. The strategy chosen or planned will be a coaching strategy and the User Model will be updated afterwards. If however, the new information is beyond the reach of the user, pure Help will be given (a stripped version of the coaching strategy will be picked) and the User Model will not be updated. The actual content of the updating, if any, will be determined by the tactics.

The output of the Discourse Planner is then fed through an Utterance Generator, which takes care of lexical, syntactic, and text-semantic issues like pronominalization and ellipsis.

---

[5] In principle the user can adjust the Help System in such a way that it functions like a pure Intelligent Tutoring System (through the so called "style parameters"), in which case the Didactic Goals specify the curriculum. This would make the consolidation and evaluation phases much more important.

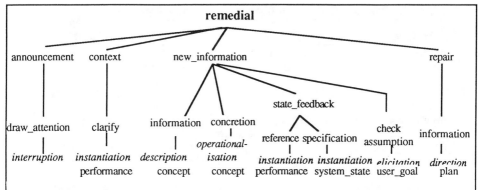

**Figure 6.3.** Simplified example of the tacticstructure of a stereotypical strategy: A remedial for the case of a user who issues a command she is not supposed to know (according to the User Model). Tactics are printed in italics.

## Coaching Principles

The basic principles for Coaching in Help Systems are the following (NB: They are all formulated for the normal situation, i.e. the user of the IPS is primarily task-oriented. If the user states she wants to be taught, the Help System should behave much more like a pure tutoring system.):

- *Be opportunistic:* Because the user provides the task and problems, the Coach has to look for opportunities to teach the user something new. An ideal opportunity is when the user makes an error, but suboptimal performance provides another one. When a user shows she masters part of the IPS, that too may lead to the introduction of new functionality or hidden models (see p. 130). Finally, questions may, of course, lead to real coaching. A side effect of this principle is that the new knowledge will be directly applicable most of the time. This promotes retention (see also Brown, Burton, & de Kleer, 1982). In the case of questions this may require constructing an example, thus providing context.

   The Didactic Goals are the anchor points for opportunistic coaching. They form the *global needs* of the user (see beginning of this chapter). In a real tutoring situation, the Didactic Goals would completely specify the curriculum in a *top-down* way. The Coach would pick the next Didactic Goal, call the Discourse Planner to plan a strategy to take the new knowledge across, execute the plan, and so on. In that case, the three layers would, in fact, be specifications of one another (cf. Woolf & MacDonald, 1984). But in a "normal" circumstance for Help Systems, the user sets the goals and prob-

Table 6.1.   Type of Tactics, Their Goals, and Canonical Forms.

| Type of Tactic | Goal | Canonical Form |
|---|---|---|
| description | information | "I will describe [what]" |
| direction | information | "I instruct you [how] to achieve [what]" |
| | application | "I instruct you [when] you can achieve [what]" |
| operationalization | concretion effect | "Practically, it means: [that]" |
| limitation | distinction | "You may think [this], but it only [that]" |
| | caution | "You think you can [when] achieve [this], but it can only [when]" |
| extension | generalization | "You may think [this], but it also [that]" |
| | | "You think you can only [when] achieve [this], but it can also [when]" |
| instantiation | example | "I show you an example" "I will show you" |
| | clarification | "I tell you [what] you just did" |
| | specification | "I tell you [what] you will see" |
| | reference | "I tell you [where] you are" |
| | | "I tell you [what] the current state is" |
| elicitation | check assumption | "Can you tell me [what]" |
| retorical | state assumption | "I assume [that]" |
| question | check understanding | "Do you understand [what] I just said" |
| | check acquisition | "Are you still with me" |
| | | "Do you understand [what] I have told you" |
| | | "Do you remember [what] I told you" |
| evaluation | motivation | "My opinion about your performance is [that]" |
| signalling | metacommunication | "I am going to tell you about [this] in [this] way" |
| interruption | drawing attention | "May I have your attention" |

Note: the [ ] denote propositions that refer to the actual situation.

lems, and the Didactic Goals can only guide the opportunistic coaching (*bottom-up*). This preoccupation with performance can also manifest itself when the Coach has to choose between several possible expansions of the users knowledge. If it, for instance, can choose between providing some support knowledge through an "abstraction," or introducing more operational knowledge through a "specification," the task-support orientation will be more likely to press for the operational knowledge.

- *Be conservative:* Because the user is primarily task-oriented, the Coach should not bother the user too much with interactions with the Help System. This means that, unless there is good reason or a good opportunity (see above) to interrupt the user, the Help System should not do so. If it does interrupt, it should justify this by referring to the users performance and explaining the relation to the new information (unless the user asked a question, of course).
- *Be concise:* If the Coach does interrupt, it should be as concise as possible for the same reason. Besides being to the point, that is, not introducing unnecessary topics, specifying didactic relations between concepts will also promote conciseness.
- *Explain relation to existing knowledge:* to facilitate acquisition of new information. This applies to all tutoring systems. The Didactic Goals are the result of this principle.
- *Be informative:* Do not explain topics the user is already assumed to know about. This too is common to all tutoring systems (e.g. Burton & Brown, 1982). It also promotes conciseness.
- *Alternate support-operational knowledge:* Not only should the Coach provide both support and operational knowledge (Clancey, 1983), he should also alternate them. Operational knowledge provides the user with information on *how* to achieve certain goals; support knowledge not only functions as support for understanding and remembering operational knowledge, but reflects a conceptual model as well. It enables the user to "reason from first principles," thereby deducing her own operational knowledge. This indicates that the ratio support/operational should grow over time. With a naive user, the Coach should provide more operational knowledge, with a more experienced user, it should gradually provide more support knowledge. The Didactic Goals, that is, the abstraction-concretion relations between domain concepts, take care of this variation and ratio shift. The Discourse Planner too decides whether to formulate information in operational terms or in terms of support knowledge.
- *Be precise:* or "it is better to prevent than to remediate." This entails i.a. specifying conditions, mentioning unexpected effects of commands, and so on. The topicalization principles are based on this general coaching principle.

These coaching principles are realized by discourse strategies that the Discourse Planner uses to communicate with the user. Besides these, their are two special principles that have only to do with discourse, not with coaching per se:

- *Be polite:* Announce any interruption (except answers to questions). Human tutors do not always do this, but a machine should.
- *Signal content:* If the Coach is about to cover more than one or two topics, he

will signal this first. This has to do with the sequential nature of natural language. An other way might be to number several steps of an explanation, and so on. The Utterance Generator handles part of this problem.

## CONCLUDING REMARKS

The results described in the previous sections may appear obvious and, for all practical purposes, adequate. However, the design and construction of the Discourse Planner didn't follow a smooth path. When our investigations on coaching strategies started in 1986, there was ample recognition of the fact that such strategies were hard or impossible to identify. Educational research had little to offer (cf. Ohlsson, 1986); the state of the art in constructing intelligent teaching systems consisted of fixed solutions;[6] empirical data of human tutorial dialogues—as we have collected these ourselves—showed an almost endless variety, which lent itself to an almost similar variety of interpretations. It appeared that coaching is not some fixed expertise, where for each problem there is a ready-made solution, as in analytic problem solving (Clancey, 1985), but coaching requires much more flexibility and rather consists of the synthesis (planning) of solutions. The Discourse Planner presented here does just that, and has given us more insight into the nature of coaching strategies.[7]

From the last section on Coaching principles it follows that coaching strategies do not differ principally from normal discourse strategies. Only the aim of coaching strategies is different: to realize a long lasting effect in the mind of the subject. Viewing coaching strategies as a subset of normal discourse strategies enables us to elaborate on theoretical frameworks developed in the field of research on human discourse. Fortunately, this kind of research has a long and respectable tradition (e.g., rhetorics). In the last decade theoretical frameworks have emerged that focus on the selection and sequencing of topics of discourse, that is, the "what," and "when" to say things, which precedes syntax and discourse semantics. The principles of topic selection and sequencing are not uniform. Some appear to be related to the semantics of the domain of discourse (e.g. McKeown, 1985); others are based upon the information management required for human serial processing (e.g. Reichman, 1981; Clark & Havilland, 1977). Within the EUROHELP project we started to investigate the relations between general principles of discourse and didactic discourse on the one hand, and the relations among the different didactic principles themselves.

---

[6] With the notable exception of the design of "Socratic dialogues" (Stevens & Collins, 1977).

[7] Meanwhile the EUROHELP Coach has also been applied in an ITS for teaching systematic diagnosis in fysiotherapy (the FysioDisc system: cf. Winkels, Achtoven, & Gennip, 1988). Without substantial alterations it worked well in this completely different domain.

# REFERENCES

Anderson, J.R., Boyle, C.F., & Yost, G. (1985). The geometry tutor. *Proceedings of the 9th International Conference on Artificial Intelligence* (pp. 1–7). Los Altos, CA: Morgan Kaufmann.

Bison, P., & van der Pal, F. (1985). *Using UNIX-Mail: An experiment in on-line tutoring.* (Internal report). University of Amsterdam, Holland.

Bonar, J., Cunningham, R., & Schultz, J. (1986). An object-oriented architecture for intelligent tutoring systems. *Proceedings of the first annual conference on Object Oriented Programming, Systems, Languages and Applications.* New York: Association for Computing Machinery.

Breuker, J.A. (1988). Coaching in Help systems. In J. Self (Ed), *Artificial intelligence and human learning. Intelligent computer-aided instruction.* London: Chapman & Hall.

Breuker, J.A., Baaren, J.v.d., Winkels, R.G.F., & Duursma, C. (1987, December 8–10). *Principles and practice in knowledge representation in EUROHELP.* Paper for workshop on "Knowledge Representation for Help Systems for Unix," University of California, Berkeley.

Breuker, J.A., Winkels, R.G.F., & Sandberg, J.A.C. (1986). *Didactic goal generator.* Deliverable 2.2.3 of the ESPRIT Project P280, "EUROHELP." University of Amsterdam, Holland.

Breuker, J.A., Winkels, R.G.F., & Sandberg, J.A.C. (1987). A shell for intelligent Help systems. *Proceedings of the 10th International Joint Conference on Artificial Intelligence, 1,* pp. 167–173.

Brown, J.S., Burton, R.R., & de Kleer, J. (1982). Pedagogical, natural language and knowledge engineering techniques in SOPHIE I, II and III. In D. Sleeman, & J.S. Brown (Eds.), *Intelligent tutoring systems.* New York: Academic Press.

Burton, R.R., & Brown, J.S. (1982). An investigation of computer coaching for informal learning activities. In D. Sleeman & J.S. Brown (Eds), *Intelligent tutoring systems.* New York: Academic Press.

Clancey, W.J. (1983). The epistemology of a rule based system—a framework for explanation. *Artificial Intelligence, 20,* 215–251.

Clancey, W.J. (1985). Heuristic classification. *Artificial Intelligence, 27,* 215–251.

Clancey, W.J. (1986). Qualitative student models. *Annual Reviews Computer Science, 1,* 381–450.

Clark, H.H., & Havilland, S.E. (1979). Comprehension and the given-new contract. In R.O. Freedle (Ed.), *Discourse Processes: Advances in research and theory.* Norwood, NJ: Ablex.

Elsom-Cook, M. (1987, May). *Discourse for tutoring.* Paper presented at The Third International Conference on Artificial Intelligence and Education. Pittsburgh, PA.

Fischer, G., Lemke, G., & Schwab, T. (1985). Knowledge-based help systems. *CHI'85 Proceedings,* pp. 161–167.

Friedland, P.E., & Iwasaki, Y. (1985). The concept and implementation of skeletal plans. *Journal of Automated Reasoning, 1,* 161–208.

Goldstein, I.P. (1979). The genetic graph: A representation for the evolution of procedural knowledge. *International Journal of Man-Machine Studies, 11,* 51–77.

Hartley, J. R., & Smith, M.J. (1988). Experiences in explanation giving in the EUROHELP Project. In J. Self (Ed.), *Artificial intelligence and human learning. Intelligent computer-aided instruction.* London: Chapman & Hall.

Lehnert, W. (1978). *The coaching of question answering: A computer simulation of cognition.* Hillsdale, NJ: Erlbaum.

Luria, M. (1987). Goal conflict concerns. *Proceedings of the Tenth International Joint Conference on Artificial Intelligence, 2,* 1025–1031.

Macmillan, S. (1987, May). *Dynamic instructional planning: Global planning.* Paper presented at The Third International Conference on Artificial Intelligence and Education, Pittsburgh, PA.

McKeown, K.R. (1985). Discourse strategies for generating natural-language text. *Artificial Intelligence, 27,* 1–41.

Ohlsson, S. (1986). Some principles of intelligent tutoring. *Instructional Science, 14,* 293–326.

Quillici, A.E., Dyer, M.G., & Flowers, M. (1986). AQUA, an intelligent UNIX advisor. *Proceedings of the 7th European Conference on Artificial Intelligence, II,* 33–38.

Reichman, R. (1981). *Plain speaking: A theory and grammar of spontaneous discourse.* Doctoral dissertation. Bolt Beranek and Newman Inc.

Rengel, B., Sandberg, J.A.C., & Winkels, R.G.F. (1988). *A long-term experiment for Unix-Vi.* Deliverable 2.5.3 of the ESPRIT Project 280, 'EUROHELP'. University of Amsterdam, Holland.

Self, J. (Ed). (1988). *Artificial intelligence and human learning. Intelligent computer-aided instruction.* London: Chapman & Hall.

Sleeman, D., & Brown, J.S. (Ed). (1982). *Intelligent tutoring systems.* New York: Academic Press.

Stevens, A., & Collins, A. (1977). The goal structure of a Socratic tutor. *Proceedings of the Association for Computing Machinery Annual Conference.*

Wenger, E. (1987). *Artificial intelligence and tutoring systems.* Los Altos, CA: Morgan Kaufman.

Wilensky, R., Arens, Y., & Chin, D. (1984). Talking to UNIX in English: An overview of UC. *Communications of the ACM, 27.*

Winkels, R.G.F. (1987). *PSP—A Prototype Strategy Planner for IHSs.* Deliverable 2.2.4 of the ESPRIT Project 280, 'EUROHELP'. Memo 81 of the VF-Project "Knowledge Acquisition in Formal Domains." University of Amsterdam, Holland.

Winkels, R.G.F., Achthoven, W.A., & Gennip, A. van (1989). Methodology and modularity in ITS design. In *Proceedings of the fourth International Conference on AI and Education.* University of Amsterdam.

Winkels, R.G.F., Sandberg, J.A.C., & Breuker, J.A. (1986). *Coaching strategies and tactics of IHSs.* Deliverable 2.2.2 of the ESPRIT Project 280, 'EUROHELP'. Memo 78 of the VF-Project "Knowledge Acquisition in Formal Domains." University of Amsterdam, Holland.

Winkels, R.G.F., & Sandberg, J.A.C. (1987). *The EUROHELP Coach: A Progress Report.* Deliverable 2.5.1 of the ESPRIT Project 280, 'EUROHELP'. Memo 94 of the VF-Project "Knowledge Acquisition in Formal Domains." University of Amsterdam, Holland.

Woolf, B., & McDonald, D.D. (1984). Context dependent transitions in tutoring discourse. *Proceedings of AAAI 1984,* Los Altos, CA: Morgan Kaufmann.

Woolf, B., & Murray, T. (1987). A framework for representing tutorial discourse. *Proceedings of the Tenth International Joint Conference on Artificial Intelligence, 1,* 189–192.

# SCENT-3: An Architecture for Intelligent Advising in Problem-Solving Domains*

Gordon I. McCalla
Jim E. Greer
SCENT Research Team*

## INTRODUCTION

The issues underlying the construction of intelligent educational systems are currently the subject of intense research. Several collections of papers have already been produced (e.g., Sleeman & Brown, 1982; Yazdani, 1984; Kearsley, 1987) and at least one textbook (Wenger, 1987) has been written in an effort to try to integrate the many diverse threads of this multidisciplinary effort. One lesson that emerges from this research is the importance of focusing investigations by limiting study to manageable but nontrivial domains.

For the past six years, research into intelligent tutoring systems at the University of Saskatchewan has been focused on the SCENT (Student Computing ENvironmenT) project. The long-term objective of SCENT is to produce a flexible, responsive computing environment to support the needs of instruction in computer science. The shorter-term goal has been to construct an intelligent advisor to aid novice Lisp programmers. A prototype SCENT advisor has been designed and implemented (McCalla, Bunt, & Harms, 1986). It is one of many such program advising systems recently developed, including PROUST (Johnson & Soloway, 1984), the Lisp Tutor (Anderson & Reiser, 1985), TALUS (Murray, 1986), Lisp-Critic (Fischer, 1987), and PITS (Looi, 1987). Although there are many interesting points of similarity and contrast between the SCENT advisor and these other systems, this chapter is not concerned with delving into these comparisons except where such discussion arises naturally. The main pur-

---

* Participating members of the SCENT Research team include Bryce Barrie, Barb Brecht, Rick Bunt, Judy Escott, Xueming Huang, Marlene Jones, Mary Mark, Teng Ng, and Paul Pospisil.

* Thanks go to Chris Stang for the creation of a package for doing data analysis of Lisp code, to Ken McDonald for providing the means for automatically collecting the data in the first place, and to Berni Schiefer and Dan Zlatin for their input into the SCENT project during its early days. Janelle Harms was instrumental in developing the SCENT-1 prototype, the basis for all that has followed. The funding provided by the Natural Sciences and Engineering Research Council of Canada, through ongoing operating grants and an equipment grant, is gratefully acknowledged.

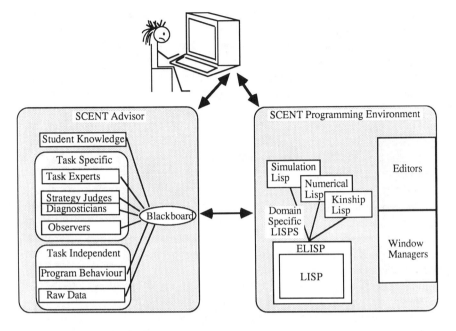

**Figure 7.1.   SCENT-1-Architecture.**

pose is to show how the architecture underlying SCENT has been generalized into a new architecture called SCENT-3, and how it might be used more widely than simply for program advising.

In order to provide some context for a discussion of SCENT-3 it is first necessary to discuss the initial SCENT prototype (SCENT-1) in somewhat more detail. The prototype is domain-specific and task-dependent, dealing only with Lisp programs to solve certain kinship problems such as finding the eldest ancestor of an individual in a kinship tree, finding his or her siblings, producing a sorted list of all of his or her descendants, and so on. The SCENT-1 prototype has been further restricted in that most of the issues dealing with the user interface have not been considered. The prototype is asked only to determine the strategies (usually various recursive strategies, in contrast, for example, to the largely iterative programming plans of PROUST) that may underlie a student's program and to diagnose misconceptions in these strategies.

Despite these restrictions on the initial SCENT-1 prototype, what remains is still substantial and interesting. Of most interest is the architecture underlying the prototype, (Figure 7.1). It is based upon the notion of cooperating entities communicating through a shared blackboard (Erman, Hayes-Roth, Lesser, & Reddy, 1980). These entities are grouped into different conceptual levels, ranging from low-level entities that perform traces and structural analyses of student code, through observers that look for patterns in these lower-level analyses, to higher-level strategy judges that look for evidence of the use of particular strategies, diagnosticians that look for strategy bugs, and task experts that foreground certain lower-level entities relevant to a particular task and judge the results produced by such entities. There is a student knowledge level, which has been trivialized in the SCENT-1 prototype, but which has been a major focus of more recent investigations.

The experience in building SCENT-1 has shown that this architecture can make for relatively easy prototyping of a program advising system tailored for a particular set of tasks. It also can make it easy to expand and modify the initial prototype to achieve more sophisticated performance. Unfortunately, SCENT-1 has proven to be quite rigid in its approach to debugging and quite brittle when confronted with unexpected deviations in the student's use of Lisp, when trying to recognize unknown strategies, or when faced with new tasks. It also is very limited in its abilities to interact with the student—only a trivial student model and student history are maintained, and no tutoring strategies have been incorporated. Finally, it has no real ability to understand the cognitive processes by which students may have devised their programs, and hence no way of knowing about the deeper cognitive processes that often affect surface behaviour.

These limitations have led to a series of "SCENT-2" investigations aimed both at understanding more clearly what is required to overcome SCENT-1's limitations and proposing actual techniques for overcoming them. Teng Ng (1987) has looked at the blackboard component and devised a plan-based control scheme that allows a range of debugging strategies to be modeled. Xueming Huang (1987) has constructed a new component for SCENT that takes a knowledge-based approach to discovering the equivalence of code segments, thus enhancing SCENT's ability to handle a variety of usages of Lisp. Bryce Barrie (1989) has developed an approach to strategy judging that allows strategies to be recognized at a variety of levels of detail, thus giving SCENT the capability of dealing with a strategy at coarser grain sizes even if the details of the strategy are unknown to the system. Using a similar notion of granularity, Paul Pospisil (1988) has enhanced and generalized the knowledge base of strategic misconceptions, making the diagnosis process much more robust. Judy Escott (1988) has carried out a study with a large number of student programs that convincingly demonstrates how students use analogy in devising solutions to new tasks. She has also proposed a model for recognizing such analogies, which is important if SCENT is to understand the cognitive processes of students as they learn. Barb Brecht (1988) has been investigating how to recognize the importance of various instructional goals, and then how to choose among them, in dispensing advice to the student. Preliminary results from her work indicate that a planning approach to instructional design is an effective technique.

All of these investigations have been carried out more or less independently, and have only been loosely coordinated with one another. They have also left a number of loose ends. It has become imperative that a new, comprehensive architecture for SCENT be developed which accounts for the results of this work, and which can help to coalesce some of the loose ends. This is the role of the SCENT-3 architecture. The remainder of this chapter contains a brief overview of the new architecture and shows how the various SCENT-2 research projects can be accounted for in the new architecture. Finally, the chapter concludes with some speculations on the generality of the SCENT-3 approach, and discusses the many open research issues currently underway and yet ahead in the SCENT project.

## THE SCENT-3 ARCHITECTURE

As in SCENT-1, the fundamental organizing principle underlying the SCENT-3 architecture is that distributed, communicating processes called "entities" can cooperate to perform various aspects of the program advising task. These include monitoring student input; analyzing student knowledge, strategies, and misconceptions; and designing instruction for the student. The entities are grouped into six relatively independent components with control mediated by a blackboard control and data structure. Various knowledge bases are associated with individual components; some are shared among components, while others are shared globally through the blackboard.

The six components comprising the SCENT-3 architecture include (a) the interface, (b) the instructional planner, (c) the student model manager, (d) the cognitive analyst, (e) the domain knowledge analysts, and (f) the student response analyst. Some components, such as the student response analyst that carries out most of the activities of SCENT-1, have been elaborated in great detail, while others are in the early stages of research. Figure 7.2 illustrates the general architecture of the SCENT-3 system.

### The Blackboard

A blackboard-based architecture was selected for the SCENT-3 system for a number of reasons. The blackboard data structure promotes relatively easy and rapid prototyping of the system components. Direct interfaces between components disappear since each component places its output on the blackboard and derives its input from the blackboard. Such an architecture permits separating out control from the definition of the components, thus allowing each entity to have a declarative task description. This occurs because the blackboard mediates requests for resources, initiating entities in which preconditions are met and that adhere to the overall plan for execution. The use of blackboard control in an instructional context is not unique to SCENT (see, for example, Macmillan & Sleeman, 1987).

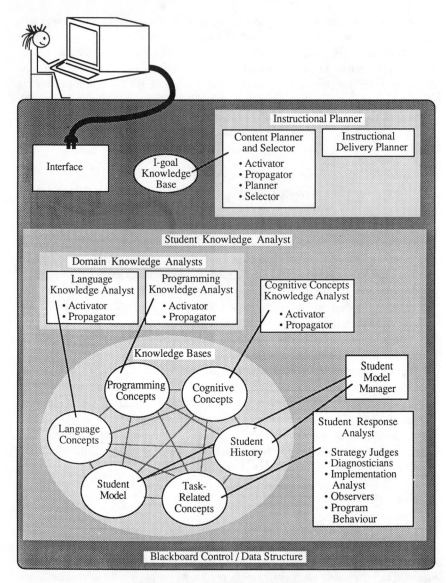

**Figure 7.2. Scent-3-Architecture.**

The SCENT blackboard has been designed and implemented by Ng (1987; Ng & McCalla, 1988). The blackboard control component is designed to capitalize on the definite stages carried out by human tutors as they analyze a student's code. This standard sequence of stages (aimed at identifying student misconceptions and understanding student programs) may be represented in a plan that can

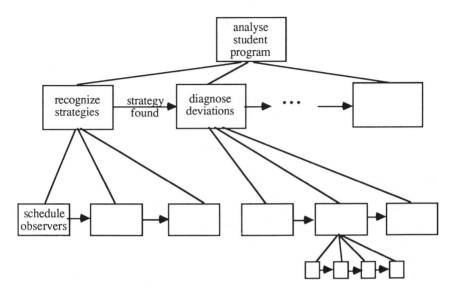

**Figure 7.3.   Structure of a Blackboard Debugging Plan.**

be executed to actually do the program analysis. Various plans can be created to represent various styles of debugging. The execution of its plans is dynamic, enabling the system to manage catastrophic and serendipitous events. Dynamic replanning allows both recovery from unanticipated negative events and opportunistic actions based on new discoveries.

Based on the plan architecture used in the ELMER route planning system (McCalla, Reid, & Schneider, 1982), the blackboard plan structure has a hierarchical organization, with higher-level plans corresponding to large debugging steps such as "recognize strategy" or "diagnose deviations," and lower-level plans corresponding to more specific steps such as "schedule entities at the observer level" (see Figure 7.3). The execution of such a plan proceeds from plan step to plan step as information posted on the blackboard (by entities executed in any given plan step) indicates that a transition should be made. Opportunistic transitions from a higher level plan can be made when information suggests that the activities of this plan and all of its descendants is no longer relevant (e.g., that the strategy has now been recognized so there is no need to continue to schedule lower-level entities to help to recognize the strategy). Error recovery also will be needed if catastrophes occur that prevent the system from completing a plan step (e.g., no strategy can be recognized).

This architecture has proven to be very useful in providing just the right amount of control to the SCENT debugging process. Using this approach, the blackboard controls the class of entities being executed (e.g., strategy judges), but not which particular entity in this class is appropriate (e.g., the "tail-end-recursion strategy judge"). This latter choice is still made by the entities themselves in true distributed fashion.

This blackboard architecture seems to be readily adaptable to the needs of SCENT-3, requiring only the creation of new plans that schedule entities to debug the student's program, entities to reason about the implications of these bugs at the cognitive and domain levels, and entities to produce appropriate instruction. Some more general issues regarding blackboard control need to be carefully considered before embarking on wholesale application of the blackboard philosophy to SCENT-3. Since certain components, such as the interface and instructional planner, are driven by the need for real-time interaction with the student, it might prove beneficial to remove these components from blackboard control and permit their execution to proceed in parallel with the remaining components. Another concern stems from the possible interaction of domain knowledge with control. The extent to which control of the tutoring enterprise is affected by the domain is not clear at this time. Despite these tradeoffs, the benefits to prototype development with a plan-controlled blackboard architecture are significant. Independent prototyping of entities may proceed without great concern for their data or control interactions.

**The Interface**

Interface issues are of primary concern in a full-fledged intelligent tutoring system. A mechanism for accurate communication with the student is essential. In the Lisp programming domain, however, student input to the system often takes the form of segments of Lisp code. For this reason, the addition of a natural language understanding system for SCENT has remained a low-priority need. On the other hand, natural language output in the form of advice to the student requests for information, or new task descriptions is necessary.

Efforts to date have not emphasized the interface to SCENT, although a number of interface tools for course developers have been constructed. These tools facilitate knowledge base construction and revision through a graphical menu-based interface to the student response analyst.

**Student Knowledge Analyst**

Four subcomponents of the SCENT-3 architecture comprise the student knowledge analyst. These include the student response analyst, the domain knowledge analysts, the cognitive analyst, and the student model manager.

*The student response analyst.* The goal of the student response analyst is to examine the Lisp program a student has created in response to a programming task, and to produce a description of the strategies the student has used and the bugs he or she has made (including errors in the use of Lisp and logical errors) in that program. It is a component of SCENT that has been considered in great detail. Much of the original SCENT-1 architecture now resides inside this component, and several of the SCENT-2 investigations have been concerned largely with elaborating subcomponents of the student response analyst. This component of SCENT-3, being the closest in some sense to the student input, is the most dependent on both the domain of instruction and the specific task being worked on by the student. The component uses a number of different subcomponents to carry out its mandate, including a program behavior component, a set of observers, an implementation analyst, a group of diagnosticians, and a set of strategy judges.

*Program behavior and observers.* The lowest level subcomponent of the student response analyst is a program behavior module that carries out various traces and produces various cross-reference charts relating to the student's Lisp program. These are then analyzed by a set of entities called observers which look for interesting patterns in the traces and cross-reference charts. Observations such as "recursive call detected," "null test predicate in cond," or "list constructor applied to recursive result" can prove useful to other subcomponents of the student response analyst, and allow these other subcomponents to reason at a level more abstract than the primitive code level. Although the role of the program behavior entities is similar to that in SCENT-1, some enhancement of observers (described below) is underway.

*The implementation level analyst.* The implementation level analyst (Huang, 1987; Huang & McCalla, 1988) considers another level of program analysis. The purpose of this entity is to determine functional equivalence and deviations between two segments of Lisp code, a capability that further insulates the strategy judges and diagnosticians from idiosyncratic uses of Lisp, in that they need only deal with canonical Lisp forms. Typically the pair of code segments under scrutiny consists of an ideal code segment (as would be found in a preferred solution) and a student code segment (which may or may not be functionally equivalent to the ideal code). These segments are peeled back layer by layer, first trying to match the two segments at the top-level of bracketing, and then plunging into the nested subfunction calls.

The matching is done using a knowledge base consisting of a discrimination network (such as the one shown in Figure 7.4), which represents the implementation analyst's knowledge of Lisp forms. Nodes at the higher levels of this graph represent categories of Lisp operations (e.g., "list construction functions") and the lower levels represent specific forms that implement these categories (e.g., "cons," "append"). The ideal code segment is filtered through this network until it is matched at some specific lower level node called the "pit node" that represents the most precise interpretation (I) of the ideal code. The student code segment is then matched against the pit node to see if it is the same; if not, variation (V) and deviation (D) links are traversed from the pit node looking for known perturbations of the ideal code that might match the student code. What-

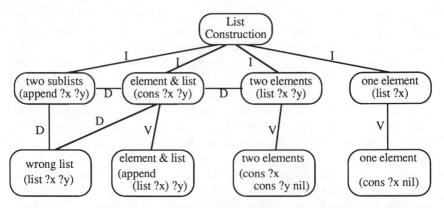

**Figure 7.4.   A Portion of the Implementation Analyst's Discrimination Network.**

ever is found (an exact match, no match, a deviation or a variation) is then reported. For example, given an ideal code segment such as "(cons a nil)" and a student code segment "(append (list a) ())", the pit node would be identified as "(cons ?x ?y)" which is V-linked to "(append (list ?x) ?y)". The code segments would be judged equivalent with the variation "cons" = "append(list)".

This approach to detecting functional equivalence of ideal and student code is efficient and robust, provided that the discrimination network contains a pit node corresponding to an implementation of the ideal code. When the ideal code cannot be found in the discrimination network, attempts are made to partition the ideal code (e.g., a Lisp "cond" statement would be partitioned into test-action pairs). Pairings with similarly partitioned student code segments can produce partial or complete matches. If partitioning fails as well, the knowledge-based approach to functional equivalence is abandoned and a theorem prover is invoked.

The primary research contribution of this approach results from the combination of knowledge-based and theorem-proving approaches to identify functional equivalences and deviations. Although the task was similar to that undertaken in TALUS (Murray, 1986), the implementation level analyst differs from TALUS by utilizing a knowledge-based approach for locating equivalences and deviations. Further, this component is supported by the knowledge-based pairings of ideal and student code carried out by strategy judges and diagnosticians (described next) which means that only relatively small Lisp segments will need to be compared. Most other program transformation and theorem proving approaches such as TALUS and LAURA (Adam & Laurent, 1980) must consider the equivalence of entire programs.

*Strategy judges and diagnosticians.* Strategy judge entities and diagnostician entities within the student response analyst are charged with the responsibility of recognizing domain-specific strategies and misconceptions in the student's solution to a programming task. Strategy judges attempt to determine whether student responses exhibit strategies consistent with predetermined "ideal" strategies. In the context of SCENT, a strategy is a description of a technique that a student might use in solving a problem or part thereof. A strategy is recognized if and only if the system can account for a specific aspect of student behavior in terms of such a description. Strategies differ from Proust's notion of plans (Johnson & Soloway, 1984) in that strategies represent the student's actual behavior without making definite conclusions about the student's intentions.

Strategies for accomplishing a task may differ in terms of the way data structures are accessed or changed. For example, code implementing a selection sort versus a bubble sort would represent different sorting strategies. Similarly, an iterative and a recursive solution to a problem would represent different control strategies. A general rule of thumb to identify two code segments as strategically variant might be that no simple transformation can make them match. Although it can be correctly argued that tail-end recursion and iteration are merely syntactic transformations, these are indeed differing strategies from a pedagogical perspective. Clearly strategies are an artifact of the body of knowledge to which they apply, and as such require domain specific knowledge for identification.

SCENT-2 research by Barrie (1989) has concentrated on an approach to strategy judging that allows flexible and robust strategy recognition to be carried out. The core of this recognition system is a hierarchical semantic network of objects that represent strategies. Strategy objects are connected by relations of two types: the "abstraction" relation, which connects specific, specialized strategy objects to more general strategy objects; and the "aggregation" relation, which links component-parts or substrategies to an aggregate strategy.

Strategy objects in this hierarchy are based on knowledge of experts' Lisp programming, and on studies of the actual behavior of novice Lisp programmers (Escott, 1988; Soloway & Woolf, 1980). This includes research into student usage of both appropriate and inappropriate programming techniques. By drawing upon these sources, we have been able to represent hierarchies for both preferred strategies and perturbed strategies in Lisp programming.

The principal hierarchy (a fragment of which is shown in Figure 7.5) describes the global strategy for Lisp programming at various levels of abstraction detail. Each object in the principal hierarchy spawns an aggregation hierarchy of substrategies, producing at each principal strategy object another hierarchy orthogonal to the principal hierarchy. A sample aggregation hierarchy fragment that elaborates the principal hierarchy object "Cdr Recursion" is shown in Figure 7.6. The composite bidimensional abstraction and aggregation network of strategy hierarchies is used as a representation structure for Lisp programming-strategy knowledge.

The root of the principal hierarchy is the strategy object "Lisp-Program" (Figure 7.5). All other objects in the network are attached to this object, either by

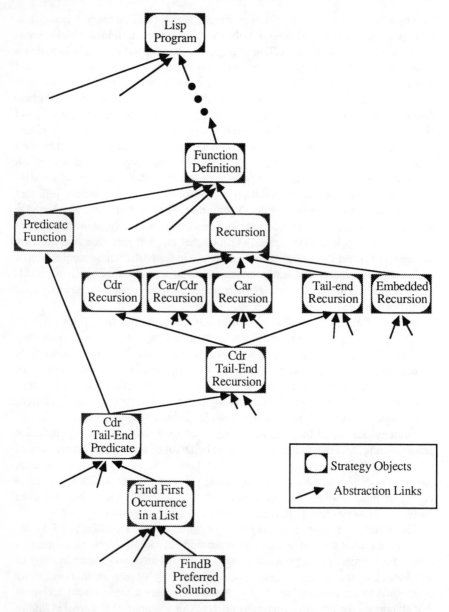

**Figure 7.5. A Fragment of the Principal Hierarchy for Strategy Judging.**

abstraction relations within the principal hierarchy, or indirectly through a combination of abstraction and aggregation relations. Below "Lisp-Program," specialized strategies describe particular types of Lisp programs. Since the most common way to solve a programming problem is to construct one or more

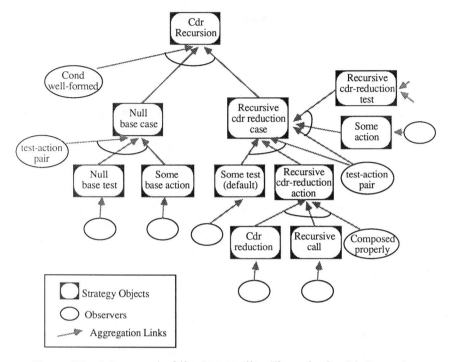

**Figure 7.6.   A Fragment of the Aggregation Hierarchy for Cdr-Recursion.**

function definitions (using defun), the object "Function-Definition" is of particular interest. This object corresponds to any student program that defines a Lisp function. Function definitions can be categorized in a variety of ways, depending upon the way in which the function body is implemented.

An important distinction among Lisp functions is whether or not they are recursive. Understanding the subtlety of recursive programming often causes confusion for Lisp novices. Recursive functions in Lisp can be car-recursive, cdr-recursive, or car-cdr-recursive. Car, cdr, and car-cdr recursions are further specialized according to other criteria such as tail-end versus embedded recursions; whether or not the values returned from the recursion are combined using composition; and the type of values returned by the function (distinguishing predicate functions, selector functions and builder functions). The principal hierarchy bottoms out at preferred strategies for specific tasks.

The aggregation dimension of the network permits the representation of component parts that constitute principal-level strategy. For example, as shown in Figure 7.6, a strategy such as "cdr recursion" contains a cluster of component-part substrategy objects (not in the principal hierarchy) such as a "Null base case" strategy to detect the end of a list, and a "Recursive cdr reduction case" strategy properly integrated using a "cond" statement (detected by an observer). Each of the substrategy objects has its own clusters of subparts (finer-grained component parts). For example, the cdr reduction case contains two clusters, one where the recursive cdr reduction is in the test of some test-action pair, and another where the recursive cdr reduction is in the action of some test-action pair. Strategies continue to be decomposed down to primitive strategies which are recognized ultimately by direct observations on student code through observer entities (with the assistance of the implementation level analyst).

In addition to the standard interpretation of abstraction and aggregation relations, these two types of links can also be interpreted as a "granularity" relation, useful for robust, fail-soft recognition. Strategies are detected in student code by matching aspects of their code to the lowest possible (most specialized) level in the network. If a program can be identified, for example, as "Find First Occurrence in a List" then identification has been successful to a very fine grain size. If the program can only be identified as "Cdr recursion" then the granularity of the classification is coarser. This, of course, implies that objects (frames) higher up in the hierarchy must have qualitatively different recognition abilities than do objects lower down in the hierarchy; that is, they must be able to recognize a strategy at their level of abstraction even if none of their finer-grained descendant objects is able to recognize the strategy.

This bidimensional representational scheme seems to be able to characterize the important human capability of selective attention to detail by capturing the notion of granularity in knowledge. Substantial work has been recently devoted to a more formal exploration of this granularity-based approach to knowledge representation (Greer & McCalla, 1988). Following on this work and the research of Barrie (1989), granularity hierarchies have assumed an even more central role in strategy representation and recognition in SCENT-3 prototypes currently under development (Greer & McCalla, 1989; Greer, McCalla, & Mark, 1989).

The use of granularity in classifying strategy objects identifies the degree of correspondence between a preferred strategy and an actual student program. Because of the ability to recognize coarser-grained strategies, a student's program can be at least partially understood in every case. This understanding stems from guaranteed recognition of strategies at some sufficiently coarse grain size in the principal hierarchy along with possible partial recognition of some aggregate subparts at finer grain sizes. Heuristics determine the most probable strategies being employed in the student's program on the basis of these two types of recognition.

The most important contribution made by this granularity-based approach is through added robustness in strategy judging. The system never fails to find some strategy in the student's code, even if that strategy exists only at a coarse level of granularity. The level of granularity at which recognition occurs also provides a measure of the confidence with which a strategy is identified.

Diagnosticians are called in to assist the strategy judges when strategies cannot be identified at the finest grain size. Pospisil (1988) has investigated the diagnosis aspect of the student response analyst in the context of kinship Lisp. Frequently students' programs contain deviations, variations, or spurious or incomplete code. The diagnosticians are able to fill slots corresponding to typical code "perturbations" in the strategy objects. If a strategy cannot be recognized at the finest grain size as a correct program, it may be recognizable at the finest grain size if some typical code perturbation is permitted. This gives strong evidence that the student is using a particular strategy, but has a specific (precisely identified) problem with adaptation of the strategy. Diagnosticians are organized into their own granularity hierarchy (cross-linked to the strategy judge hierarchy), an organization of programming bugs that is analogous in purpose to the bug graphs for subtraction employed in BUGGY (Brown & Burton, 1978). This provides the diagnostic component with the ability to recognize general bugs, even if recognition of specific bugs fails. The separation of diagnosticians from strategy judges and their organization into distinct (albeit related) hierarchies is consistent with the assumption in SCENT-3 that there may be an organization of bugs that is not simply a reflection of the organization of strategies. This has yet to be conclusively proven, however.

Empirical evaluation of the performance of hierarchically-organized strategy judges and diagnosticians has been conducted using 93 student Lisp programs for three different programming tasks (Barrie, 1989; Pospisil, 1988). General coarse-grained strategies were correctly recognized in all of the programs. Strategy diagnoses at a fine grain size agreed with those of an expert human tutor in 76% of the programs. In the remaining programs the system's diagnosis was slightly more conservative than that of the human tutor, usually deciding upon strategies which were more general (more coarse-grained) than those judged by the human tutor. The system arrived at a completely erroneous judgment of the student's strategy in only 4% of the programs. These results are very encouraging, especially in light of the fact that no student model or student history information was used in these diagnoses.

*The domain knowledge analysts.* The student response analyst provides considerable evidence to the system regarding the specific strategies and errors that students manifest in their interactions with the system. This knowledge is embedded in a knowledge base of programming concepts and language concepts relatively specific to the task the student has been working on. The purpose of the domain knowledge analysts is to extract this task specific knowledge and to generalize it into task-independent domain knowledge bases. Research into this aspect of SCENT-3 is much more preliminary than the investigations into the student response analyst. Nevertheless, the general requirements for the domain knowledge analysts are becoming clear, as are their main activities. In particular, in the Lisp programming domain there appear to be two domain knowledge bases, one for language concepts and the other for programming concepts.

The language concepts knowledge base is a hierarchy containing at its lowest levels the details of Lisp syntax, at middle levels the basic semantic notions such as prefix form and bracketing and quoting semantics, and at upper levels more subtle knowledge such as parameter binding mechanisms and scope rules for function calls. Although the language knowledge hierarchy is itself task-independent, linkages with concepts in knowledge bases used by the task-specific student response analyst must be known. This implies that at least some knowledge of prototypical tasks must be contained in the language knowledge hierarchy. It also suggests that there must be an initial phase where language knowledge concepts that have directly arisen in the student's solution to a programming task are activated using these linkages.

Once these initial concepts are activated, the language knowledge analyst must evaluate the implications on the rest of its knowledge, that is, it must propagate inferences from these initially activated concepts throughout the hierarchy. For example, if the student does not seem to understand the use of quoted arguments, it is probable that he or she does understand that Lisp arguments are normally evaluated. Propagation within this hierarchy is clearly not automatic, and considerable domain knowledge must be used. The problem of propagation within domain knowledge hierarchies is being actively researched by Brecht (1988).

The general programming knowledge base includes knowledge of programming concepts independent of language. Concepts in this knowledge base include recursion and its specializations, general parameter passing schemes, general scope rules, and so on. It is unclear how students develop this language-independent general programming knowledge, or indeed whether this knowledge appears only after learning many programming languages. Regardless, the programming concepts knowledge base can be used for reasoning about deep conceptions and misconceptions students may have with respect to general programming. Students apparently promote certain knowledge from the language concepts knowledge base to the programming concepts knowledge base using some genetic operators. Linkages reflecting this interconnection (possibly similar to those used in the genetic graph of Goldstein, 1982) must be kept. Much more research is needed in this area.

As above, an initial activation phase along the linkages connecting language knowledge to programming knowledge must be carried out, followed by a propagation phase to determine the implications on the rest of the programming concepts knowledge base. This process, too, is being investigated in the limited domain of recursion by Brecht.

*The cognitive analyst.* This component of the SCENT-3 architecture focuses on general cognitive strategies (problem-solving heuristics) used by students. These cognitive strategies are presumed to be relatively independent of the problem-solving domain. Examples of such cognitive strategies include problem decomposition, means-ends analysis, reasoning by analogy, deductive reasoning, inductive reasoning, and so on. Use or misuse of these cognitive strategies is frequently evident in student responses. Links from the student response knowledge bases as well as from the domain knowledge bases seem to connect to the cognitive strategies network. The exact nature of this overlap, how to represent the interconnections among these knowledge bases, and the implications of this overlap are not yet well understood. However, analogy, one particular type of cognitive strategy, has been studied in some detail.

Evidence of analogy guiding the development of successive student solutions to a series of Lisp programming tasks has been accumulated by Escott (Escott, 1988; Escott & McCalla, 1988). Data was collected from 48 students who were attempting to solve four different Lisp problems, requiring strategies that ranged incrementally from simple tail-end recursion through to complex double recursions. The final solution to one problem was compared to the first solution to the next harder problem, looking for evidence of analogy and for evidence that poor use of analogy may have caused errors. The evidence for use of analogy was strong, as was the evidence that errors were caused by inappropriate use of analogy. In fact, 75% of the students used an incorrect analogy at least once, and of the 248 nonsyntactic errors that appeared, 100 could be attributed to incorrect analogy.

This research confirms that the cognitive strategy of analogy is important in Lisp programming situations, and suggests that recognizing a badly used analogy is an important aid to tutoring. Escott has categorized four different types of bad analogy, and has designed a model for automating the recognition of analogies from sequences of student code (kept in the student history). Once a bad analogy has been recognized, it can be used to activate concepts in the cognitive concepts knowledge base. As in the domain knowledge analysts, propagation of conceptions and misconceptions must then be carried out within the cognitive concepts knowledge base. Attaching computational precision to the cognitive concepts knowledge analyst promises to be one of the greatest research challenges as SCENT-3 is more fully fleshed out.

*The student model manager.* The student model manager in SCENT-3 maintains for each student an individualized student model (essentially an overlay on the various knowledge bases of the student knowledge analyst) and a student history (a record of the interactions carried on between the student and the advisor). Although this component has not been the subject of in-depth research so far, several points should be emphasized. First, strictly speaking, all the activations and propagations carried out through the various student knowledge analyst knowledge bases will actually be kept in the student model, since they represent the concepts and misconceptions of a particular student. Second, the student model and student history are used by most other components in the system, and are especially important to the instructional planner. Third, the student model manager has a very active role in maintaining the student model and student history, including the need to reorganize information from time to time, something that should be done intelligently so that relevant information is not lost. A final point is that much of the student knowledge analyst could be considered to be conceptually part of the student modeling process, since in a very real sense the efforts of all the other subcomponents are aimed at coming up with a precise analysis of the student's particular state of knowledge, that is, at the creation of the student model. The preference in SCENT-3 has been to separate out most of the knowledge analysis components from the student model manager, and limit this component to more of a bookkeeping role.

*The instructional planner.* The instructional planner must decide what to present to the student and how to present it. The SCENT-3 architecture recognizes this duality, and separates the instructional planning process into two phases: first, planning the content of instruction, a task carried out by the content planner and selector subcomponent of the instructional planner; and, then, planning the delivery of the content, a task that is the responsibility of the instructional delivery planner, another subcomponent of the instructional planner. Research into this component is currently underway, being carried out by Barb Brecht (1988). In fact, the primary focus of Brecht's research is on the content planner and selector, and interest in activation and propagation within the domain knowledge bases and the cognitive knowledge base arises mainly as a by-product of the need for this information in the planning and selection of content. The bulk of this section will be devoted to discussing the content planner and selector.

Central to the role of the content planner and selector is the notion of "instructional goal." An instructional goal (I-goal) is a goal that the SCENT-3 system wants to achieve, for example, to have the student learn some concept or to remove a misconception that the student may have. There can be many different kinds of I-goals and they can relate to each other in a variety of ways. For instance, they may be mutually reinforcing. Thus, domain specific I-goals such as "have the student learn recursion" or "have the student understand the list data structure" may mutually reinforce cognitive I-goals such as "have the student learn better problem decomposition skills" or "have the student refine his/her analogical reasoning skills." I-goals may also be incompatible with one another, for example, "correct student's misconception about tail-end recursion" may not jibe with "have the student learn complex recursion." Another interaction among I-goals is that they can be decomposed into sub-I-goals. For example, achieving the instructional goal "have the student learn recursion in Lisp" has as component subgoals "have the student learn about the use of base cases," "have the student understand recursive cases," and "have the student understand composition and coordination of returned values." I-goals also can have prerequisite I-goals. For example "have the student learn recursion in Lisp" has as prerequisite the I-goal "have the student learn about calling functions in Lisp." The complex interconnections among I-goals are kept in the I-goal knowledge base, which is a more sophisticated version of the AND/OR, multilevel prerequisite graphs used in a Lisp tutoring system that preceded the SCENT project (see McCalla, Peachey, & Ward, 1982).

The task of the content planner and selector is to use the information in the I-goal knowledge base in conjunction with the information provided by the student knowledge analyst to formulate a plan of I-goals individually tailored for a given student, and then to select a particular I-goal (or I-goals) from this plan as the active content to be delivered. Primary I-goals for this plan are selected on the basis of shortcomings in the student's knowledge recognized in the student model. The plan is then elaborated and structured largely according to constraints imposed by the I-goal knowledge base. Thus, the plan may also be hierarchical, based on subgoal information from the I-goal knowledge base. Any given I-goal in the plan may also have associated with it parallel I-goals, attached on the basis of information from the I-goal knowledge base about what goals are mutually reinforcing. An open research problem is what to do about incompatible I-goals, which will force the selection process to make very difficult choices.

Once a plan has been created, it must be executed. This requires the selection of an appropriate I-goal (or I-goals) from the plan. This selection is based on what parts of the plan have already been delivered, and what level of instruction is desired (I-goals at the top of the plan or more specific lower level I-goals). The information needed to make this decision can be found in the student history and student model, although exactly how to apply this knowledge is still the subject of research. Once the appropriate I-goals have been selected they are passed to the delivery planner to be turned into relevant instruction to which the student must respond.

After the student has responded, and the student knowledge analyst has carried out its activities resulting in an updated student model, the instructional planner takes over again. Its first task is to analyze how changes in the student model (i.e., the new nodes that have been activated in the various student knowledge bases) affect its plan. This requires a two-phase activation and propagation scheme similar in nature to those used within the student knowledge analyst. The activation process marks specific I-goals in the I-goal knowledge base that are affected by new knowledge about the student (using links connecting the I-goals to concepts in the domain knowledge bases and cognitive concepts knowledge base). Marked I-goals are then appropriately propagated along prerequisite, subgoal, and reinforcement links in order to determine the full impact of student knowledge on I-goal knowledge. The semantics of the subgoal and prerequisite links determine the nature of these propagations (e.g., if the student is having problems with a concept related to an I-goal, all I-goals for which this is a prerequisite might now be problematical). Once the implications on I-goal knowledge have been understood, it is then relatively easy to see what parts of the plan are affected. Some student problems will only have minor effects, thus allowing the plan to be continued. Others will have major effects, which may require patching the plan or even entirely replanning the instruction. Various approaches to patching and replanning are being evaluated by Brecht, including the dynamic blackboard-based instructional planning techniques of

Macmillan and Sleeman (1987), the error recovery techniques developed for route planning discussed in Ward and McCalla (1982), and the dynamic planning approach to instruction developed by Peachey and McCalla (1986).

The important point about the content planner and selector is that maintenance of an individualized student model and use of dynamic planning techniques allows the content of instruction to be tailored, within the limitations of the system, precisely and flexibly to the needs of the student.

Before leaving the instructional planner, a few remarks should be made about the delivery planner. The delivery planner must translate an instructional goal (or goals) into appropriate instruction. This requires it to choose an overall form of instruction (e.g., assign problems, embark on question-answer sessions, provide direct help, give the student a hint), and then to plan out a specific sequence of actions that will achieve the instructional goal(s) (e.g., give the student the eldest ancestor problem to work on, or tell him/her about the logic error in his/her recently completed program). The exact nature of the delivery planning process has not been studied so far in SCENT. Nevertheless, it is clear from the work of Woolf (1987), Winne (1987), and others that it is important to incorporate into this process notions of pedagogy, instructional strategies, and tactics, cue selection, and cognitive mediation. This will require the delivery planner to use knowledge from the student model, the student history, and other components of SCENT-3.

## SUMMARY OF CONTRIBUTIONS

The SCENT-3 advisor constitutes a large-scale effort to design and implement a general and operational intelligent tutoring system in a nontrivial domain. Its main contributions are:

- the integration of many kinds of knowledge into one model
- a modularized approach allowing incremental development and change
- the incorporation of flexible control and information sharing capabilities into the model
- the development of approaches to dealing with cognitive knowledge and instructional planning, aspects largely downplayed in other research into intelligent tutoring.

More specific contributions include

- the use of student knowledge, domain knowledge, cognitive knowledge, and knowledge about instruction in the advising process
- the creation of knowledge bases and components that accurately partition these various kinds of knowledge
- blackboard mediated communication among the components of the system
- dynamic planning to achieve flexible system control and responsive instruction

- the widespread use of propagation and activation schemes that use existing knowledge structures to guide inference
- robust recognition of student strategies and errors through the use of granularity.

In addition, the SCENT-3 architecture has potential for gracefully achieving domain- and task-independence. Although it appears that the student response analyst must be changed from domain to domain, as must the knowledge bases used by system, the procedures carried out by most of the components should survive largely unchanged. The cognitive analyst and instructional planner should be readily transportable to a new domain. Of course, only further research will be able to fully prove out these intuitions.

A vigorous research program into the many issues surrounding SCENT-3 is ongoing. This research is integrating ideas from artificial intelligence, cognitive science, and education. In the near term, research efforts will be mainly directed at development the domain knowledge analysts and the instructional planner to the point that a fully integrated SCENT-3 prototype can be implemented. In the longer term, the cognitive concepts analyst, and the interface component will be investigated so that a completely usable SCENT prototype can be developed. Concurrently, efforts are underway to use the architecture to develop a training system in another domain.

The problems confronting the development of intelligent educational systems should not be underestimated. Very difficult, extremely large issues must be tackled, issues that will not be fully resolved in the near term. There are many different perspectives on how to deal with these issues. Thus, there are psychologically motivated investigations into cognitive modeling, engineering-oriented attempts to build commercial instructional systems, education-based research into teaching and learning with immediate applicability to classroom, use, and artificial intelligence investigations elaborating computational structures underlying the process of instruction. The SCENT project's motivations are to take an artificial intelligence research approach, with relatively less emphasis on issues of immediate practicality, classroom applicability, or cognitive verisimilitude. Thus, the main contributions of SCENT lie in the artificial intelligence research ideas that the project has explored, with any contributions to engineering, education, or cognitive science an additional benefit.

## REFERENCES

Adam, A., & Laurent, J. (1980). LAURA: A system to debug student programs. *Artificial Intelligence, 15,* 75–122.

Anderson, J.R., & Reiser, B.J. (1985). The LISP tutor. *Byte, 10*(4), 159–175.

Barrie, J.B. (1989). *Using granularity hierarchies for strategy recognition.* Master's thesis, University of Saskatchewan, Saskatoon, Canada.

Brecht, B. (1988). *Deciding what needs to be said: Instructional planning for intelligent tutoring systems* (ARIES Research Report #88-6). University of Saskatchewan, Department of Computational Science, Saskatoon, Canada.

Brown, J.S., & Burton, R.R. (1978). Diagnostic models for procedural bugs in basic mathematical skills. *Cognitive Science, 2,* 155–192.

Erman, L. D., Hayes-Roth, F., Lesser, V. R., & Reddy, D. R. (1980). The HEARSAY-II speech understanding system: Integrating knowledge to resolve uncertainty. *Computing Surveys, 12*(2), 213–253.

Escott, J.A. (1988). *Problem solving by analogy in novice programming.* Master's thesis, University of Saskatchewan, Department of Computational Science, Saskatoon, Canada.

Escott, J.A., & McCalla, G.I. (1988). Problem-solving by analogy: A source of errors in novice programming. *The Proceedings of the International Conference of Intelligent Tutoring Systems,* pp. 312–319. Montreal, Canada.

Fischer, G. (1987). A Critic for LISP. *Proceedings of the 10th IJCAI Conference,* pp. 177–184. Milan, Italy.

Goldstein, I. P. (1982). The genetic graph: A representation for the evolution of procedural knowledge. In D. Sleeman & J.S. Brown (Eds.), *Intelligent tutoring systems* (pp 51–78). London: Academic Press.

Greer, J.E., & McCalla, G.I. (1988). Formalizing granularity for use in recognition. *Applied Mathematics Letters, 1*(4), 347–350.

Greer, J.E., & McCalla, G.I. (1989, August). A computational framework for granularity and its application to educational diagnosis. *Proceedings of the International Joint Conference on Artificial Intelligence (IJCAI),* pp. 477–482. Detroit, MI.

Greer, J.E., McCalla, G.I., & Mark, M.A. (1989, May). Incorporating Granularity-Based Recognition into SCENT. *Proceedings of the Fourth International Conference on Artificial Intelligence and Education (AI-Ed),* pp. 107–115. Amsterdam.

Huang, X. (1987). *Finding language errors and program equivalence in an automated programming advisor* (M.Sc. Thesis, Research Report 87-13). Saskatoon: University of Saskatchewan, Department of Computational Science.

Huang, X., & McCalla, G.I. (1988). A hybrid approach to finding language errors and program equivalence in an automated advisor. *The 7th Biennial Conference on the Canadian Society for Computational Studies of Intelligence,* pp. 161–168. Edmonton, Canada.

Johnson, W.L., & Soloway, E. (1984). Intention-based diagnosis of programming errors. *Proceedings of the 5th Annual Conference of the American Association for Artificial Intelligence (AAAI),* pp. 162–168. Austin, TX.

Kearsley, G.P. (1987). *Artificial intelligence and instruction: Applications and methods.* Reading, MA: Addison Wesley.

Looi, C.K. (1987). *Heuristic code matching of Prolog programs in a Prolog intelligent teaching system* (Research Report). University of Edinburgh, Scotland.

Macmillan, S.A., & Sleeman, D.H. (1987). An architecture for a self-improving instructional planner for intelligent tutoring systems. *Computational Intelligence, 3*(1), 17–27.

McCalla, G.I., Bunt, R.B., & Harms, J.J. (1986). The design of the SCENT automated advisor. *Computational Intelligence, 2*(2), 76–92.

McCalla, G.I., Peachey, D., & Ward, B. (1982). An architecture for the design of large scale intelligent teaching systems. *Proceedings of the 4th Biennial Conference of the Canadian Society for Computational Studies of Intelligence*, pp. 85–91. Saskatoon, Canada.

McCalla, G.I., Reid, L., & Schneider, P.F. (1982). Plan creation, plan execution and knowledge acquisition in a dynamic microworld. *International Journal of Man-Machine Studies, 16*, 89–112.

Murray, W.R. (1986). Automatic programming debugging for intelligent tutoring systems. *Computational Intelligence, 3*(1), 1–16.

Ng, T.H. (1987). *Dynamic planning of blackboard focus shifts in an automated debugging system* (M.Sc. Thesis, Research Report 87-3). Saskatoon: University of Saskatchewan, Department of Computational Science.

Ng, T.H., & McCalla, G.I. (1988). A plan-based approach to blackboard control in an intelligent tutoring system. *International Computer Science Conference on AI Theory and Practice '88*, Hong Kong.

Peachey, D., & McCalla, G.I. (1986). Using planning techniques in intelligent tutoring systems. *International Journal of Man-Machine Studies, 24*(1), 77–98.

Pospisil, P.R. (1988). *Diagnosing strategy errors in SCENT*. Master's thesis. University of Saskatchewan, Saskatoon, Canada.

Sleeman, D., & Brown, J.S. (Eds.). (1982). *Intelligent tutoring systems*. London: Academic Press.

Soloway, E., & Woolf, B. (1980). *From problems to programs via plans: The content and structure of knowledge for introductory LISP programming* (COINS Tech. Report 80-19). Amherst, MA: University of Massachusetts.

Ward, B., & McCalla, G.I. (1982). Error detection and recovery in a dynamic planning environment. *Proceedings of the 2nd Annual Conference of the American Association for Artificial Intelligence (AAAI)*, pp. 172–175. Pittsburgh, PA.

Wenger, E. (1987). *Artificial intelligence and tutoring systems*. Los Altos, CA: Morgan Kaufmann.

Winne, P.H. (1987). *A framework for development theories about instructional effectiveness*. College of Education Invitational Conference on Cognition and Literacy in a Changing Society, University of Saskatchewan, Saskatoon, Canada.

Woolf, B. (1987). Representing complex knowledge in an intelligent machine tutor. *Computational Intelligence, 3*(1), 45–55.

Yazdani, M. (Ed.). (1984). *New horizons in educational computing*. New York: Wiley.

# 8
# Representing Knowledge about Teaching:
# DOCENT—An AI Planning System
# for Teaching and Learning*

Philip H. Winne
Laurane L. Kramer

## INTRODUCTION TO THE PROJECT

Education is an investment in one of our most important natural resources—people. Every day, children spend nearly two-fifths of their waking time in educational programs and, if their experiences are to build useful foundations for children's futures, we must assure that teaching is as effective as it can be. Both the public and the profession perceive that research can help. For example, the American Educational Studies Association's *Pride and Promise: Schools of Excellence for all the People* (1984), one of a spate of recent reports reflecting on the state of American education, noted:

> [Teacher] preparation programs must rest on a research base of knowledge about classrooms and instruction, and knowledge about education, otherwise new teachers will have no professional knowledge to practice. (p. 37)

Despite this and other calls for teacher education to insure that teachers-in-preparation are informed by knowledge from research, the father of research on teaching, N. L. Gage, concluded in his 1985 book, *Hard Gains in the Soft Sciences—The Case of Pedagogy,* that:

> generations of teacher education students have been given inadequate grounding in how to teach. They have not been taught how to organize a course, how to plan a lesson, how to manage a class, how to give an explanation, how to arouse interest and motivation, how to ask the right kinds of questions, how to react to students' responses, how to give helpful corrections and feedback, how to avoid unfair biases in interacting with students — in short, how to teach. (pp. 27–28)

* This work was supported by grants from the Social Sciences and Humanities Research Council of Canada (#411-09-0085), Simon Fraser University, and Sun Microsystems of Canada, Ltd.

Perhaps teacher education programs only should set the stage for beginning teachers to acquire research-based expertise? If so, we might expect newly certified teachers would acquire and improve their knowledge of research-based principles for teaching while on the job. Unfortunately, opportunities for such growth appear meager. The U.S. Department of Education's 1986 pamphlet, *WHAT WORKS: Research about Teaching and Learning*, reports:

> *Research Finding:* Teachers welcome professional suggestions about improving their work, but they rarely receive them.
> *Comment:* When supervisors comment constructively on teachers' specific skills, they help teachers become more effective and improve teachers' morale. Yet, typically, a supervisor visits a teacher's classroom only once a year and makes only general comments about the teacher's performance. (p. 52)

Thus, supervision for newly certified teachers is meager and is apparently insufficiently grounded in specific findings from research. If we could increase opportunities for supervision, what kind of supervision seems best? Clark (1988) suggests a model of consultation, characterizing a good consultant for teachers as one who

> has experience and a perspective different from that of the client, and engages this expertise in the service of the client's own ends. A consultant seldom solves major problems, but often contributes important pieces to the client's own solutions . . . who leave[s] something interesting and provocative to think about as the clients continue to wrestle with the complexities of the local problematic situation. (p. 6)

In part, Project DOCENT begins a program of research and development that will break trail in this challenging territory (see also Winne, 1989).

*What is a docent?* Webster's Ninth New Collegiate Dictionary gives this definition:

> *DOCENT*   1. a college or university teacher or lecturer
> 2. a person who conducts groups through a museum or art gallery.

Adopting this metaphor for the system suggests features it should have if it is to consult with teachers about how to teach more effectively.

A university lecturer commands deep and broad knowledge about a paradigm. Such knowledge includes disciplinary knowledge per se plus methodological procedures that can be used to investigate, verify, and modify disciplinary knowledge. In DOCENT, disciplinary knowledge corresponds to research-based and first-hand experiential information about teaching. Methodological expertise would assist teachers in adapting research-based principles to local problems that arise in the their classrooms.

As a guide, a docent introduces visitors to interesting displays. We assume that novice teachers are interested in expertise which will help them become more effective teachers and that such expertise is available in research and from experienced teachers. A docent also makes information about displays memorable and gives to visitors knowledge they can carry away from their visit to the gallery. DOCENT will assist novice teachers in this respect by helping them to script plans for teaching. These can be output as notes, overheads, worksheets, and other materials which teachers commonly use in lessons. Finally, a docent addresses visitors' questions and satisfies their curiosity. DOCENT has a direct facility for serving as an expert system, fulfilling this requirement. In general, DOCENT should be responsive to a novice teacher's interests and needs by suggesting interesting and verified pieces that fit into the large, complex, and idiosyncratic puzzle of how to teach effectively.

## DOCENT'S ARCHITECTURE

The current design for DOCENT partitions the system into four sectors, each of which corresponds to one major task relating to instruction: developing principles of pedagogy, designing a syllabus for teaching, planning the forms of interaction that comprise instruction, and tutoring students. Each sector includes four components. *Knowledge bases* bank information which figures directly in the instructional task assigned to a sector. An *archivist* receives information from a teacher or a student user or from another sector, catalogs and stores it in a format unique to that sector's knowledge base(s), and fetches information in response to specific requests by people or by another program in DOCENT. *Reasoning engines* approach goals which are set by a person or which a reasoning engine may develop itself. Because these programs perform the tasks allocated to a sector, sectors are named after their reasoning engines. *Interfaces* provide specially adapted formats that ease communications and guide exchanges of information between teachers and students, on the one hand, and DOCENT on the other.

### Sector PEDAGOGUE

This sector's reasoning engine, PEDAGOGUE, answers queries about teaching effectiveness and creates principles of instruction that are predicted to be effective under specified conditions. These tasks can be set either by a teacher or by the sector called PLANNER. The knowledge base which supports these functions is the LIBRARY and its archivist program is the LIBRARIAN. The LIBRARY and a scheme for representing knowledge about teaching are the main topics of this chapter; they are described more thoroughly in subsequent sections.

The interface INQUIRER will link a teacher to this sector. Using INQUIRER, teachers can ask straightforward questions of the LIBRARIAN, such as, "What information is there about motivating students to do homework?" Teachers also can address problems for which PEDAGOGUE develops principles, for instance, "How can I motivate my top students to do the enrichment exercises?"

## Sector SYLLABUS

This sector's job is to coordinate the subject matter to be taught with instructional objectives that describe tasks in which students recall and demonstrate competence with knowledge. The archivist program in this sector is SOCRATES. It works in and among four knowledge bases.

The CURRICULUM knowledge base will contain information about the scope and sequence of curriculum topics plus a description of curriculum material that is required by the jurisdiction in which a teacher works. The DISCIPLINARY WEB knowledge base will store facts about the disciplinary structure of knowledge of a topic. Thirdly, the OBJECTIVES WEB knowledge base records information about tasks that involve a subject matter and what students do with it, that is, instructional objectives.

The reasoning engine SYLLABUS will select, integrate, and fuse information from these three knowledge bases and, occasionally, will query the LIBRARIAN for other needed information. With these sources, SYLLABUS will create this sector's fourth knowledge base, CONTENT LAYOUT, a complex representation of a syllabus of knowledge and skills in terms of prerequisites and corequisites, core and enriching parts of content, examples, elaborations, and crosslinks among topics within lessons and across units of lessons that allow navigating throughout the subject matter.

The interface program that will links a teacher to SYLLABUS and to SOCRATES is called MAPPER. Teachers will use MAPPER to create or flesh out information in any of the knowledge bases, or weight material's importance according to their own preferences. MAPPER also will provide means for teachers to adjust the information in CONTENT LAYOUT developmentally over the course of lessons and tutorials.

## Sector PLANNER

This sector's main job is consulting interactively with a teacher. Together, PLANNER and the teacher will design instruction comprising lessons so that students reach set goals and the lesson conforms to criteria of effectiveness (e.g., time, content covered). Because it seeks to create effective designs, PLANNER also helps the teacher evaluate agendas for lessons and routines that comprise agendas and other features of instruction. Teachers will design plans and work with PLANNER to analyze teaching using the interface program SCRIBE.

PLANNER draws on three knowledge bases in its own sector. As well, PLANNER requests specific information from the PEDAGOGUE sector, to insure that plans are solidly grounded in empirical knowledge about effective instruction; and SYLLABUS's sector, to guarantee that lessons and tutorials incorporate appropriate subject matter content and organize it well.

Two of PLANNER's knowledge bases accumulate evaluative data about the instructional setting. They share a common archivist, TELLER. In the aggregate, these two knowledge bases provide a basis for continuous formative evaluation of instructional processes and outcomes. This allows PLANNER to identify past deviations and forecast future deviations of actual instruction from planned instruction. One of these knowledge bases is STUDENT DATA and it has two partitions. The first partition cumulatively tabulates data about individual student's achievements, motivations, styles of learning, and behavior. The second partition reflects similar information about groups of students, such as the degree of cooperation evidenced in a small group or the performance of a group which the teacher uses as a basis for gauging the class's overall mastery of content (a steering group; Dallöff, 1971). Data for the first partition are provided to DOCENT by the teacher, using the interface program EVALAUTOR, and by TUTOR. Data for the second partition are recorded by the teacher.

The second of PLANNER's knowledge bases containing evaluative information is an inventory of INSTRUCTIONAL DATA. It also has two partitions. The first contains data about the correspondence between aspects of a lesson as planned and instruction as actually implemented and adapted. The second partition of INSTRUCTIONAL DATA records data that measures the outcomes of actual instruction relative to goals set for a lesson or parts of a lesson. All these data are gathered during or after instruction, and entered in INSTRUCTIONAL DATA by the teacher, using EVALUATOR, or by TUTOR.

The third knowledge base in PLANNER's sector is PLANS. Before a teacher begins to work with DOCENT, PLANS will be stocked with a collection of "seed" instructional tactics (Winne, 1985, 1987), routines and agendas (Leinhardt & Greeno, 1986), and models of teaching (e.g., Joyce & Weil, 1986). Seeds will supply some initial structure for teachers when they work with DOCENT to develop experimental formats for teaching or trial agendas which TUTOR may follow in developing a tutorial session. As the teacher works with DOCENT over time, seeded structures will be adapted and extended as the teacher annotates and stores for future reference those instructional events that have demonstrated empirical value for reaching particular objectives. Two other important items will be included in these records: tolerances for deviations of actual instruction from planned events, and connections between instructional events and students' mediation of them. In short, PLANS becomes a growing repository of what works in a teacher's particular situation, a record that teachers can return to as they develop and adapt their own repertoires for teaching.

PLANS' archivist program is called COLLECTOR. SCRIBE provides the interface.

## Sector TUTOR

This sector will provide students with tutorials that address small, focused parts of content that was covered or introduced in a teacher's lesson(s). Its reasoning engine, TUTOR, consists of rules and heuristics that are unique to managing tutorials and to collecting data about a student's participation in instruction in tutorials.

The knowledge that TUTOR needs to tutor effectively depends on all the functions carried out in the other three sectors of DOCENT. Because of the extensive computation involved in searching and processing very large knowledge bases, it presently is not practical for these sectors to be "up, running, and fully involved" during a tutorial. However, the architecture of DOCENT readily lends itself to selecting relatively tiny, well-defined subsets of information from the other sectors' knowledge bases that apply to a single 20–30 minute tutorial. Consequently, the knowledge bases and reasoning engines can be pared and imported into the TUTOR sector just prior to tutorials (e.g., the morning before), thereby lowering demands for computational resources to levels that can be handled feasibly, paralleling the notion of virtual processing. With data in the form the student's responses to tutoring, TUTOR will be able to develop, evaluate, and adapt a tutorial script interactively.

The LAB interface that provides a student with a window into TUTOR will contain several modules. PostOffice will give students and their teacher access to electronic mail. Logbook, Notebook, and Quizzer will be modifications of the teacher's SCRIBE and MAPPER programs. In their LAB versions, these programs will be "soft" tutoring tools, soft in that direct instructional intervention by TUTOR is minimal unless a student asks for help. Logbook will post assignments from the teacher or TUTOR and chart a student's mastery developmentally. Here, based on research into metacognitive skills in self-regulated learning (Corno, 1986), TUTOR will subtly guide students to develop macro-level self regulation. Students will use Notebook to rework new information and to organize it as a cumulative hypertext of notes. TUTOR will "softly" help students develop micro-level metacognitive skills of self-regulation, study skills (Weinstein, Goetz, & Alexander, 1988), and strategies for spatially representing information (Holley & Dansereau, 1984). Quizzer will give students a facility to develop and take self-tests while, in the background, TUTOR helps students review content. Teacher2 is the interface for direct tutorial instruction provided by TUTOR. It will use hypertext and graphic facilities to communicate with students about content and to reflect their cognitive interactions with instructional events (Winne, 1989).

With this introduction to the overall system, we turn now to a more detailed description of the the LIBRARY. Following this, we describe the Expression Language for Instruction (ELI), the knowledge representation scheme we have developed to serve our approach to knowledge engineering and which underlies representations throughout DOCENT. Finally, we sketch software systems that are used to carry out knowledge engineering to stock the LIBRARY.

## THE LIBRARY

The LIBRARY is a metaphorical building of three floors which houses information about instruction. The first floor shelves knowledge about instruction drawn from published studies about instructional research. The second floor will be stocked with expertise about teaching gleaned from experienced teachers. The third floor will contain conjectures, grounded on entries on the first and second floors, that are computed by PEDAGOGUE.

A global schema for an entry in the LIBRARY consists of three clusters of information: (a) conditions describing the context within which instruction takes place, (b) the events that constitute instruction, and (c) outcomes that resu lt from the instruction described in the entry. Each of these three facets of instructional activities will be recorded in a degree of detail that a library user will be able, in a nearly strict sense of the term, to clone the design (Perkins, 1986) of an instructional event. By design, we mean something special which will be the topic of the penultimate section.

Information in the LIBRARY is represented in the Basal Language for Encoding Educational Processes (see Kramer & Winne, 1988). The process of translating information from educational research and teacher's expertise into ELI requires a human translator and an artificially intelligent software system, the Knowledge Acquisition Tool for Instruction (KATI), currently under development. ELI and KATI will be described in some detail after specifying more about the nature of knowledge shelved in the LIBRARY.

### First Floor—Research Knowledge Base

Each entry on the first floor of the LIBRARY is a precise translation from a single published study in the domain of educational research. A study has four components: (1) citation, a simple database entry; (2) research design, a detailed description of people, static variables, and measures which make up an experiment; (3) processes, a precise and elaborate record which operationally defines the instructional intervention in terms of the dynamic events in the study; and (4) results, the consequences of enacting instruction. The citation component is self explanatory. Each of the remaining components is considered more fully.

***Research design.*** This component reflects the overall structure of the experiment, identifying independent and dependent variables as well as other static elements of instruction and its setting. These data provide a first approximation of a study's relevance to particular instructional situations and allow a teacher to replicate features of the study in a classroom. For example, a study's fit to the students whom a teacher is teaching rests on an exhaustive description of the study's participants in terms of age, prior knowledge, demographic characteristics, and so forth. Similarly, a teacher may want to take advantage of sophisticated instruments used in a study to assess learners' growth in achievement or motivation. This requires a complete operational description of those measures, including how they are scored and how scores are scaled for interpretation.

***Processes.*** The dynamic processes by which instruction is carried out in a study are crucial aspects of instructional expertise. Once a teacher knows instruction's "parts," these parts must be choreographed to create an ordered flow of interactions which constitute teaching. Thus, the exact sequence, timing, duration, and other features of actions which specify when, how, and in what manner teaching unfolds are recorded from a study. For instance, research demonstrates that there is considerable delicacy in the processes by which students in small groups should interact to maximize their learning and motivation, and to optimize the smoothness of the classroom's operation. Specifying these interactions from a study using ELI would record rules that, for example, govern when a student should seek help from a groupmate, how students share tasks, and when and how a teacher intervenes to provide guidance.

***Results.*** Results indicate whether and to what degree instructional interventions are effective. The LIBRARY will record two different senses of results. First, we believe that teachers want to know in absolute terms the level and variance of students' achievements, attitudes, or behaviors which are associated with an instructional intervention. Second, teachers want to know how these absolute levels of performance compare to those which can be achieved by adopting other practices. To achieve these two ends, ELI records information about the scale on which an outcome is measured, the mean level of an outcome for both the treatment and comparison groups, and statistics describing the variance of outcome scores within each group. Internally, the various scales which researchers use to measure effects in separate experiments will be transformed to a standard metric having a mean of 70 and a standard deviation of 10. This will allow reports to teachers such as: "The treatment in which students read the advance organizer boosted an average student's score on a multiple-choice test from 70 to approximately 78. Without the treatment, the usual range of scores which includes two-thirds of the class is 60–80 (20 pts.). The advance organizer treatment expanded this range to 62–91 (26 pts.). While most students' correctly answered about 8 more items, there were a few students whose scores remained in the lower part of the range."

## Second Floor—Teacher's Knowledge

Entries on the first floor of the LIBRARY probably will be partially inappropriate for at least three reasons. First, to the extent that information is available in research articles, first-floor representations will describe the setting, treatments and outcomes of instruction as very fine-grained patterns of discrete variables. Although this is precisely what is needed for PEDAGOGUE to reason, these descriptions are of a different order than teachers' (Hook & Rosenshine, 1979). Second, it is rare for a single study to address more than one theoretical domain, combining in one investigation concerns about, say, problem solving and motivation. Teachers' concerns typically blend across domains. Third, to make inroads into theoretical matters, researchers exercise extensive experimental controls to minimize perturbations in the instructional activities they investigate in an experiment. Teachers, however, often face such perturbations and sometimes are the causes of them. On these counts and probably others, research studies alone will not suffice as a basis for characterizing the kinds of instruction that teachers deliver in classrooms.

To extend and elaborate the sorts of knowledge which research can provide, we plan also to stock the LIBRARY with knowledge about teaching which will be acquired from master teachers. In addition to providing knowledge to address the problems just noted, master teachers likely will be able to extend the LIBRARY with knowledge not found in research. Kinds of extensions needed include knowledge about planning for instruction that extends over time and across curriculum areas, and which is sensitive to multiple, externally imposed constraints; about effective routines and sequences of teaching events; about orchestrating multiple overlapping events in lessons; and about catering simultaneously to a wide variety of student interests, abilities and problems.

Problems in stocking this second floor of the LIBRARY are substantial. The first and most daunting is that of securing these sorts of knowledge from expert teachers. Usual knowledge engineering methods are not feasible if our goal is representativeness and scope since these methods would require thousands of hours to observe lessons, interview teachers, and analyze the resulting protocols in order to distill what teachers know about instruction and how to do it. We propose procedures that stock this floor in a bootstrap fashion.

First, formal research is now emerging which reports what expert teachers know and how they practice this knowledge (e.g., Berliner, Clarridge, Cushing, Sabers, & Stein, 1988; Peterson & Comeaux, 1987). As these studies appear, they can be incorporated directly into the LIBRARY as are findings from other research. Second, at least some classic knowledge engineering with a small number of master teachers is crucial. The focus of this work will be to characterize forms of knowledge that teachers have, and which DOCENT requires, rather than to gather this knowledge per se. In this work, we can build on other's research into the nature of expert teachers' knowledge (for a review, see Clark & Peterson, 1986).

Based on the results of these first two attacks on the problem of capturing master teachers' knowledge, we plan to extend the KATI system which the research staff uses to translate information from research articles. This modified and extended version of KATI, T-KATI, will be an artificially intelligent knowledge engineering tool that teachers can use solo to represent their knowledge about teaching for the LIBRARY. If we can entice teachers to use T-KATI, we can substantially reduce resources needed to stock the LIBRARY's second floor. As well, T-KATI will provide kernels for the interfaces which teachers will use to interact with DOCENT.

Finally, resources for teacher education such as videotapes and transcripts already exist. Once preliminary knowledge engineering has created a framework for T-KATI, these resources can be tapped in a manner paralleling published studies.

## Third Floor—Computed Conjectures

Unlike the first two floors, the third floor of the LIBRARY is created by PEDAGOGUE. It will contain quasiknowledge about instruction that has been bred from parent entries shelved on the first and second floors. At present, we envision three types of computed conjectures. DO-principles will characterize what teachers might consider putting into plans for instruction. DON'T-principles will suggest instructional events and tactics that should be avoided because PEDAGOGUE forecasts they either produce unwanted interactions during teaching or lead to undesirable consequences for students' achievements. LOOK-FOR-schemata describe patterns of instructional events that teachers will be encouraged to seek out as a lesson develops. Rather than propose actions, LOOK-FOR-schemata will play roles as triggers for teachers to consider alternative teaching actions.

The granularity and scope of these principles will vary as a function of the number of studies upon which they draw and the details included in the original studies. DO- and DON'T-principles will have essentially the same components as a translation of a study: a context which describes as precisely as possible when the principle is applicable; details about how to implement the principle; and descriptive statistics about outcomes that are projected. LOOK-FOR-schemata will present constraints in the same way as DO- and DON'T-principles.

DO- and DON'T-principles and LOOK-FOR-schemata will be useful to novice teachers in direct proportion to the degree of detail that they supply. Consider an example: "Make sure that feedback given to students is informative." While this has the form of a principle, it lacks information of the sorts that novice teachers are likely to need. To be useful, a principle must contain enough detail to be operational. For example:

*Constraints:*   task = applying a procedure with several steps
proficiency = recently presented and not mastered
context = students are writing answers to exercises

*Action:*   1.   indicate in writing whether the answer is right or wrong for each exercise
2.   if the exercise is wrong:
    a) name the error
    b) write out a rule to check for the error
    c) illustrate how the checking rule is applied
    d) name the trigger that fires the checking rule

*Extension:*   write a statement of praise that refers to steps in the rule for solving the problem correctly

Computed conjectures will interleave with one another and with entries on the other floors of the LIBRARY. The principle just illustrated would have links to at least two other topics: (1) a LOOK-FOR-schema for recognizing the transition from the initial acquisition phase to the phase in which skills are composed and automaticity is achieved; (2) a DO-principle describing how to provide informative feedback in that phase of instruction.

## THE EXPRESSION LANGUAGE FOR INSTRUCTION

Information stocked in the LIBRARY is based on a knowledge representation scheme expressly designed to capture critical aspects of instructional designs, processes, and results. Several demands which the scheme must satisfy already have been implied, namely, the needs to: represent fine-grained detail, characterize the kinds of instructional events reported in educational research and carried out in real classroom activities, and provide a common medium of exchange among DOCENT's sectors. Here, we describe more fully the full set of objectives we sought to meet in developing the scheme, and the architecture of the scheme itself.

### Objectives in Representing Knowledge about Teaching

The first objective ELI must meet is to represent information precisely and thoroughly, that is, with a *very* fine grain. Three advantages follow from this. First, the paradigm which guides educational research requires that attributes of participants in research, variables, and events be defined meticulously in terms of measurements and operational manipulations. Thus, omitting these details from representations of information about instruction would intrinsically lower the validity of a representation.

Another advantage of very fine granularity in representing knowledge about teaching is that it helps PEDAGOGUE avoid inappropriate synthesis across studies. For example, suppose one study shows that presenting an advance organizer before students read a passage increases comprehension, but a second, generally similar study shows no effect. Do these studies cancel one another? Not necessarily. For instance, the difficulty of the text may vary across studies, and the studies' dependent variables may be different measures of comprehension. A better synthesis of these two studies may be this: When students read lengthy passages that present unfamiliar concepts in difficult technical terms, an advance organizer which relates the new concepts to familiar concepts increases comprehension of general principles; short passages of this sort do not require an advance organizer to assure students' comprehension. This more precise statement resolves a potential conflict by stepping down levels in a hierarchy of details. A less obvious, but equally useful result of this approach is that a teacher can be advised against writing an advance organizer when material is either relatively familiar to students or short. Such reasoning could not occur without details about the studies.

Finally, research on novice teachers' lesson plans shows them to be shallow and unelaborated (e.g., Leinhardt & Greeno, 1986; Peterson & Comeaux, 1987). These findings about novice and expert teachers copy the results of other research on the differences between novices' and experts' representations of knowledge. To deepen and elaborate novice teachers' plans, the LIBRARY must contain details about how instruction is enacted.

The second objective sought in representing the information presented by a published study is to minimize inferences that a translator might be invited to make. We aim to equate a translation of a study stocked in the LIBRARY with all the explicitly stated, factual aspects reported in a study. Investigations into methodologies for researching teaching effectiveness (Dunkin & Biddle, 1974; Evertson & Green, 1986) demonstrate persuasively that when observers in classrooms make inferences about instructional events, distortions creep into data which lessen the validity of those observations. The same holds true for representations developed from "observations" of published studies. Beyond lessening the validity of information recorded from a single study, distortions in the information represented from multiple studies would have a further disastrous effect—this would create a breeding ground for serious mistakes when PEDAGOGUE aggregates and reasons across entries in the LIBRARY. Thus, ELI provides a medium for recording precise, operationally defined information about the events of instruction. Entities needed to record speculations, conjectures and inferences are planned to be included in the scheme as entities called hypotheticals, but hypotheticals will not be accessible by translators who enter information about research studies.

A third requirement of ELI is that it must have the capacity to adapt to the several interfaces teachers will use to interact with parts of DOCENT. Since teachers and experimenters operate with different vocabularies and organize knowledge differently, this is not a small problem. We return to this problem in subsequent sections describing KATI and T-KATI.

A fourth criterion set for ELI is to represent imprecision validly. Researchers' reports of studies as well as teachers' descriptions of practice use natural language which allows fuzzy expressions such as "several" and "approximately." Furthermore, most studies are designed to extend a line of prior research and, thus, some components of instruction may be referenced in a publication but not described. Such unspecified components need to be fleshed out, when possible, by referring to another study or to the teacher's knowledge base.

A fifth objective for ELI is the need to represent generic concepts. This poses a slightly different issue from imprecision in that there is a set to which specific items belong, but no particular member can be identified. For example, a question on a pretest which asks sixth grade students to rate their attitudes about mathematics asks about mathematics generically. No constraints are placed on content except for those that might be inferred by knowing the grade level of respondents. Nor does the question specify a particular type of task (completing worksheets, reading textbooks, doing homework, cooperative small groups), what mathematics should be compared to in assessing attitude, what the specific attitude is, or any of a host of other particulars that educational research demonstrates are important in predicting whether students will approach tasks that involve mathematics or choose to do mathematics if given an option to do something else.

## Dominant Aspects of Knowledge about Instruction

Classroom lessons include wide variations in types of human interactions, deliberate individualization of goals for students, and differences in curricula. Experimental research also is extremely heterogeneous, in part because experimenters constantly explore for original knowledge. We presume that there must be some features of commonality across all these experiences. Otherwise, human teachers and researchers could neither learn about the domain of teaching nor communicate their experiences meaningfully to one another. Nonetheless, the diversity of concepts which characterize educational phenomena poses a significant challenge to representing knowledge.

In order to capture this diversity, ELI is founded on a set of primitive objects structured as frames. Supplementing the basal frames are a range of quantifiers which provide means to describe the qualities and properties of the things and events represented by frames. To develop patterns among frames, ELI includes a second set of objects that relate frames, called structured objects, and a set of operators for building more complex objects from basal frames and structured objects.

Educational phenomena also are characterized by a second aspect that challenges the ability to represent knowledge about them—plasticity. As new research is done and new models of teaching are created, there will be new forms for events in instruction which could not have been foreseen when ELI was created.

ELI has been devised to accommodate plasticity by its method of building up descriptions for highly evolved, complex entities from primitive elements. By revaluing the attributes in a primitive component of one complex event, for instance, by changing the communicative role in a small group from information-giver to information-seeker, variations in the character of a complex social grouping can be made readily. In general, virtually all changes are confined to upper levels in the organizational hierarchy of objects in the system. Consequently, as new approaches to teaching and new research interests arise, they can be represented in the system by creating new composites at the high levels without having to introduce fundamental changes to basal elements or to the system itself. Moreover, since the low level elements for representing knowledge are modular and can be placed in explicitly stated relationships to one another, additions at mid-levels in the system of representation will have predictable influences on other representations in the overall system. In short, by adopting a technique in which complex objects are built from a wide-based set of primitives, we have accommodated the plasticity of knowledge in education while simultaneously providing a controlled mechanism for growth in the breadth of representations.

The primitive elements which comprise ELI were developed from a lengthy analysis of both classroom behavior and research studies. ELI's objects and operators provide a robust and expressive vocabulary which DOCENT's modules can share. The basal levels of the scheme, however, are far better suited to computer than to educator or researcher. Users' needs, therefore, were met by creating a upper-level terms and templates that are grounded on the primitive level. In the set of interfaces planned for DOCENT, the user only rarely needs to descend into the basal level to represent knowledge about instruction.

The next section discusses ELI's basal level first by briefly overviewing elements of the knowledge representation scheme and then illustrating selected features of it in a short example.

## The Architecture of ELI

The Expression Language is constructed in successive layers that represent information units of increasing complexity and specificity, that is, instances of abstract representative units. The most primitive layer of ELI consists of frames and data entry forms. More complex information is represented by combining these to form structured objects. In addition, special operators allow frames and structured objects to be combined dynamically from simpler ones, and are used to identify explicit relationships between abstract entities and instances of these entities in the real world.

*Data entry forms* are simple structures, uniform throughout the scheme, by which qualitative and quantitative information about an object can be recorded. Numerical quantifiers that indicate, for example, the number of homework exercises assigned, are entered using the NUMBER data entry form. This form provides slots that can be filled with either an integer or real, but also adapts to imprecise data by allowing numbers to be entered as a range, or to be modified by greater than ($>$), less than ($<$), approximately ($\sim$). The MODIFIERS data entry form provides a list of dimensions such as precision, clarity, loudness, difficulty and creativity. A dimension can be attached to a frame or object, and a number from 1 to 5 is entered to describe the degree to which the object is modified. The meaning of a degree for each dimension is defined carefully to guide the encoder and to provide an basis for English translation in output. In general, the degrees use a scale of 1=poor, 3=average, 5=excellent. Other data entry forms include DESCRIPTIVE STATISTICS, TIMING, and PHYSICAL DIMENSION.

*Frames* represent a basal component of an educational phenomenon or process which cannot be decomposed further into meaningful, independent components. Examples of frames included are: PERSONAL QUALITIES, CLIMATE, DEMOGRAPHICS, GROUPING, INFORMATION, PHYSICAL MOVEMENT, and TOPIC. Slots on a frame identify dimensions along which instantiations of the frame may vary. Values for slots are specified either by selecting one or more choices from a menu, each of which represents an educationally significant alternative, or by using a data entry form.

*Structured* objects configure basal frames and other structured objects according to patterns typical of educational processes. Objects represent the first level of increasing complexity. For instance, a chapter in a social studies textbook, among other features, has a specific organization, is about a particular subset of the curriculum, and has particular physical characteristics. It would be described using an INFORMATION structured object on which specific slots appear for information type, curriculum and physical presentation. A structured object always includes slots requiring at least two frames or other structured objects, and may include menus and data entry forms which are locally relevant. The main role played by structured objects is to define relationships among frames and other objects nested within it.

Actions are of necessity composed of multiple frames or objects. Thus, all processes are represented on one of two key structured objects. The first is ACT which identifies a single discrete action. It has simple case grammar slots such as actor, verb, object, and recipient; plus it has slots for entering adverbs and information about the duration and relative timing of its parts. The verbs allowed in ELI describe primitive actions performed by people, groups, and media such as films or computer games. Verbs are hierarchically structured. DO is one parent and has four offspring: ACQUIRES, GIVES, THINKS, and MOVES. Offspring of GIVES, for example, are WRITES, DRAWS, STATES, and DEMONSTRATES. The second parent, HAVE, has two offspring: KNOWS and FEELS. Verbs appear only in the ACT structured object.

The second complex structured object used to capture process is ACTIVITY. It builds on the acts composing it to create a unifying entity that articulates aspects in an entire educational process. ACTIVITY links together frames and other structured objects, including subactivities, to describe participants in the activity, the ongoing dynamics within which these people interact, the affective climate of the activity, standards to be met by teachers and by students, tasks in which each participant engages, and the organization of those tasks.

An intrinsic feature of structured objects is that they purposefully have been defined to represent in single units basic patterns for aspects of education which may appear superficially different. For example, the structured object REQUEST FOR INFORMATION was designed to describe all situations in which a person supplies information in response to some stimulus, regardless of whether that stimulus is an oral question in class or in a small group, an exercise on a student's worksheet, an item in a self-test at the end of a chapter, a teacher's quiz, an attitude inventory, or a commercially published standardized intelligence test. Using the same underlying objects for such superficially diverse phenomena allows the inference engines in DOCENT to address underlying similarities among apparently different situations. Thus, for example, because the underlying dimensions are the same, a research study which determined that a particular form of question was more effective in measuring retention on recall tests can be matched to a teacher's in-class oral review and incorporated in plans generated by PLANNER.

Data entry forms, frames, and structured objects compose the basic level of ELI. Also at the basic level are two mechanisms for combining these basic objects to fit a given situation.

*Joints* take frames and structured objects as arguments in forming a more complex object of the same type (e.g., a more complex INFORMATION frame built of other INFORMATION frames). The new entity which is created by joining arguments can receive values for its slots in two ways: by the execution of predefined rules attached to the slot of a constituent entity, or as a direct specification by a translator who is instantiating knowledge. Several different joints are available, each describing a different internal organization for the new object. The weakest joint is UNION which collects objects into a set but imposes no organization on the resultant object. For example, a DEMOGRAPHICS frame might be used to describe an individual or a homogeneous group such as five grade 7 boys 11–12 years old from a lower socioeconomic background who are reading at or below fifth-grade level. Once several demographics frames have been created, they can be UNIONed to describe a complex heterogeneous group as a frame. Other joints include COMPLEMENT, SEQUENCE, and PATTERNED SERIES. *Relationships* do not create a new entity. Rather, they specify qualitative connections between previously defined entities. TEMPORAL relationships specify the timing of two activities relative to one another. PATTERN relationships describe abstract organizations of objects and concepts such as a set of ideas and their relative importance in a chapter. INFORMATION relationships identify dimensions about information that are important in teaching and learning such as the difference between paraphrased versus verbatim recall. MODIFIER relationships compare two objects along dimensions defined in the MODIFIERs data entry form such as appropriateness (e.g., behavior A is more appropriate than behavior B), complexity, correctness, difficulty, likelihood, and similarity.

The layers of ELI described thus far define its full expressive power—nothing can be expressed within ELI that cannot be expressed using these mechanisms. The extensive details and intricate formats which ELI requires in order to represent information about instruction are necessary for the scheme to meet the needs outlined earlier. However, ELI's structure also imposes unacceptable burdens. For example, after a careful reading of a complicated research article, it can take an expert in ELI more than 20 hours to represent information from the study. Given that the LIBRARY should be stocked with thousands of entries, the process of representation must become much more efficient. Another problem reflects ELI's representational power: the scheme offers sufficient flexibility such that more than one valid representation can be developed for the same information in an article. To avoid overwhelming an already complicated process for reasoning, representations must be standardized. Thus, to make the process of representing knowledge about teaching more efficient, more generally comprehensible to educators, and more uniform, two additional layers of ELI have been developed, each of which defines common patterns found in education.

*Terms* will make up a 500–1000 word lexicon of largely precoded ELI representations for common elements in the natural language of researchers and teachers. For example, "multiple-choice test" is a term defined on the REQUEST FOR INFORMATION structured object previously mentioned. A term collects the various frames or objects that will be required to define it according to the proper relationships. Further, each term fixes certain slot values which may not be altered. For example, a multiple-choice test is always a test in which items present answers to be selected from options. As well, terms can lock out certain slots so that values cannot fill them. For instance, the type of item can not involve students in ordering options, so this slot is locked out. Terms also identify slots that must be completed to describe a particular instance of a test, such as the topic of the test, and set default values such as assigning one point for a correct response so that a translator need only confirm this slot value for a given instance of the term. Fixes, locks, options, and defaults may be set for slots on several objects comprising the term. In addition, rules attached to optional slots may further constrain or otherwise alter values of the slots within or between terms. For example, if the topic of a multiple-choice test is not achievement but attitudes, then the scoring default is automatically altered.

*Templates* are complex internal configurations of terms plus the component objects and relational operators which comprise terms. Templates create expectations about additional information that usually is needed to create a thorough description of a pattern in research or teaching. Like structured objects, templates are frequently nested. Unlike the other components within ELI, templates are defined top down, from the more general to the more specific. The purpose of templates is to boost the accuracy of representations; first, by placing critical details that need to be captured in a representation within a context and, second, by constraining elements of ELI. Thus, templates contribute to making terms more comprehensible.

Consider, for example, the templates relevant to the term multiple-choice test. "Test" is itself is a term defined as one kind of request for information, and is represented by a template with two slots:

Kind:    checklist, edit, short-answer, multiple-choice, free recall . . .
About:   topic, affects, attribution . . .

The list of items opposite "About" is extended during a translating session to include any instructional materials already defined. Rules attached to the template define the relevance of other templates. For example, selecting multiple-choice and either topic or any instructional materials activates the following template:

Number of items:
Information in the premises:
# of options:                [default 4]
Information in the options:
Selected by:                 recalling, applying rules, inferring
Expected Answer:

Each slot in the template has a predefined pattern for completion which may be very simple, as for the integer number to be entered in the first slot, or may require the translator to complete other templates such as the information templates that would be required to describe the premise and options within an item of the multiple-choice test.

### An Example of a Representation in ELI

To illustrate the interplay of ELI's components, we sketch an activity commonly found in classrooms and research. Students individually read a passage from a social studies text. Next, they form into small groups of mixed ability levels to discuss the text. Finally, they individually complete recall tests about the passage and a questionnaire about their attitudes toward fellow group members. The example will illustrate the use of various features in ELI and, in particular, the interrelationships of templates, terms, and the more primitive levels. In the interests of space only a few steps will be shown in their entirety. As noted previously, representations would begin with top-level templates and proceed down toward more primitive levels.

Representing any activity commonly begins by identifying the participants. In this case there are two boys, one of high ability and one of low ability; two girls, also of high and low ability; and a teacher. Since the group is not homogeneous, information about each member is first represented separately on the DEMO-GRAPHICS frame to record characteristics such as age, grade, ability, and, for the teacher, professional experience. The DEMOGRAPHICS frame for each member is then linked via the PARTICIPANT structured object with the test results which were used to determine their ability level. Each individual has now been characterized. A joint, UNION, is then used to create the small group by joining the four students to form a new entity.

The next stage is normally to characterize the instructional materials used by the participants in instruction. This is accomplished by entering a phrase built from ELI terms according to a pattern established by a template:

*Brazil* is 1000 word expository text about social studies.

*Brazil* is a label, invented and entered by the translator, to identify this unique instance of the term "expository text" and it will be used later in the representation of this instructional episode whenever this particular text is referred to. Each term in the phrase (expository text, word, social studies) identifies a subset of ELI with its own fixes, locks and options. The translator describing the text is then led to enter further knowledge and to confirm defaults. An underlying ELI INFORMATION structured object is created with the following settings:

*Brazil* = INFORMATION STRUCTURED OBJECT
Information: 1000 words, semantic, expository, explicit, factual, description
Topic: social studies, South America, government, imports, exports, culture
Presentation: 2 pages, standard formatting

Phase one of the activities, where students read the text, is described by using one of the act templates. The user enters a simple sentence:

Students read *Brazil* to self.

Additional templates needed to complete all of the information deemed appropriate would be flagged. For example, the directions template can be invoked which allows ELI sentences that paraphrase the directions given to students. For example:

> Students read *Brazil* carefully.
> Students not allowed read *Brazil* more than once.
> Students search for main ideas of *Brazil* and supporting details in *Brazil*.

"Main ideas of" and "supporting details in" are ELI terms which define relationships between instances of information in a text.

The next phase of the activity, the small group discussion, is more complex. In addition to describing the task that the group is set, in a manner similar to the directions above, it also is necessary to describe as much detail as possible about interactions that occur within the group setting. Special terms and templates are designed to reflect this type of knowledge. A common group rule, for instance, is:

> Student criticize ideas.
> Student not criticize group members.

"Criticize" is a term provided as verb in the ACT template but which is represented internally in ELI as "dissatisfaction with" whatever fills the object case of the ACT. This rule for the group members' interaction is meant to apply to all members of the group, and this is recorded. It is also possible to describe particular tasks or responsibilities assigned to individual members of the group. Since these are rules and expectations for behavior, it is important that they are clearly separated from the actual behaviors which students perform in the group. The use of templates ensures that the standards for behavior are clearly labeled as such and also that the standards are associated with the actual processes of the activity to which they apply. In addition, slots on the template ensure that the manner is described in which standards were conveyed to the students. It then becomes possible to compare which standards or directions have the most beneficial results.

The final activity in the sequence was the testing. Since a multiple-choice achievement test was already illustrated, here we will illustrate the attitude inventory. Students were asked to rate how well they liked each group member after the small group experience. This is an example of the term "rating scale" which activates a template that is completed for one item as follows:

> Number of items:      1
> Given:                Student likes high ability boy.
> Minimum on scale:     1

Maximum on scale:     7
Dimension:            agreement
Relation to:          self


## Acquiring Knowledge about Instructional Events: KATI

The terms and templates which form ELI's upper levels define the major elements of a control structure for the Knowledge Acquisition Tool for Instruction (KATI), a smart software system which staff can use to translate into ELI the descriptions of instruction that studies present in the natural language of researchers. To assist with translations, KATI calls on the knowledge about expected relationships and prototypical patterns of educational processes that is embodied in the definitions of terms and templates to guide a translator to enter information from the article in a top down manner. This process is further assisted by additional knowledge about the structures and patterns of educational research that is encoded into the software. PEDAGOGUE's interface, INQUIRER, also will derive from this control structure.


## KNOWLEDGE ENGINEERING ON THE FLY: T-KATI

The problem of developing a scheme for representing teachers' knowledge which supplements knowledge in research studies and which teachers can use comfortably adds a major task to our agenda. We propose a two-step procedure which extends ELI and KATI so that the second floor of the LIBRARY can become well-stocked with useful and valid knowledge.

The first step applies the popular version of Turing's test. A small sample of teachers will plan and teach small units about a set of curricular topics. We will collect their plans and videotape their lessons. After teaching, we will work with these teachers to obtain analyses of their plans and of the videotapes. The protocols emerging from these sessions will be treated as "research studies" and encoded using KATI and ELI. These representations and the teachers' original protocols then will be given to blind judges for analysis. If ELI and KATI can represent instructional events authentically, the judges should be unable to detect differences. Passing this test establishes that ELI and KATI provide a medium for representing knowledge and lines of reasoning that teachers use to plan and to analyze actual instruction. Over a cycle of such studies, ELI and KATI will be modified and extended to take a first step toward insuring that DOCENT can validly represent what teachers do.

The second step in the process investigates whether ELI's and KATI's representations of research studies can be transformed into descriptions which teachers find clear and informative. In this series of studies, a group of teachers will be given research articles and asked to develop two products. The first product will be a factual account of what happened in the study. The second product will describe an implementation of this information in a plan for instruction. These same articles also will be encoded in ELI and KATI and then "unparsed" to produce English-like paragraphs. The paragraphs will be given to a second group of teachers as raw material to be implemented in a plan for instruction. Finally, both group's plans will be given to blind judges for analysis. If plans produced by teachers using original research articles exhibit features paralleling those produced by teachers using ELI-based representations, this establishes that ELI provides a medium for representing knowledge found in research which teachers can transform into concrete plans for teaching.

Based on products of this program of research into teacher's perceptions and characterizations of instruction, we propose to design and implement a teachers' version of KATI, T-KATI. T-KATI will be an artificially intelligent knowledge engineering system that teachers can use "on their own" to represent their knowledge about teaching for DOCENT. If we can entice teachers to use T-KATI, this will substantially reduce resources that otherwise would be needed to stock the LIBRARY's second floor. T-KATI also will form the kernel of the interface through which teachers will interact with the PLANNER sector of DOCENT. Importantly, since T-KATI also is grounded in ELI, this insures that PEDAGOGUE will be able to access knowledge on the second floor of the LIBRARY.

## THE DESIGN OF INSTRUCTION

Earlier, we reserved a special meaning for the term *design*. Having described items shelved in the LIBRARY, we now address in more abstract terms what knowledge in the LIBRARY is about. We base this description on a scheme proposed by Perkins (1986) which maps knowledge onto the concept of a design. Perkins suggests that "active knowledge that one thinks critically and creatively about and with, not just passive knowledge." (p. xiii) can be configured as a design in four dimensions: structure, objectives or purposes, model cases or illustrations, and arguments that explain or evaluate. We hypothesize that construing knowledge about teaching as a design will provide novice teachers with information of the kinds needed to make their consultations with DOCENT useful. Our medium for discussing these issues is the case of a teacher giving feedback to a student after the student has worked out a mathematics problems on a worksheet.

*Structure* reflects the parts and materials which make up instructional events, the pattern of those parts, and their properties and qualities. ELI excels in recording structural features of knowledge about educational processes.

For the case of feedback, ELI specifies in detail the categories of information it contains, such as whether merely the correct answer is given or this plus information about whether the student's error should be attributed to carelessness, a hard exercise, lack of knowledge, or luck. ELI also specifies the conditions under which feedback is provided, such as the timing of feedback relative to a student's work and the types of errors which trigger feedback. As well, it characterizes properties of how feedback is delivered, such as whether it is written on the student's worksheet versus spoken supportively; or whether it is a suggestion versus a command to rework the exercise.

*Objectives* for instruction take two forms. In the predictive case, an objective is an expectation about an effect or a following state which is expected to emerge when one knows or exercises information. In the retrospective case, having information or having exercised information, one examines a state of affairs and recognizes that it meets a criterion which, had that criterion been in mind beforehand, would have been an objective in the predictive sense.

The teacher's feedback can fulfill one or several objectives. It can identify for the student which steps of the work were correct and which were incorrect. It can redirect the student's explanation for failure from negative feelings about low ability to a case of not having applied a plan for solving the problem. These illustrate predictive objectives. Retrospectively, a teacher may observe that, while providing feedback, there was time during which to create a follow-up exercise which invites the student to rehearse information in the feedback just provided.

Entries in the LIBRARY's 1st floor specify objectives retrospectively in the form of results. PEDAGOGUE will predict teaching practices based on this factual evidence. Objectives of the predictive sort appear on the second floor as recordings of teacher's experience, and on the third floor in the form of LOOK-FOR schemata.

*Model cases* are concrete illustrations that manifest key and critical features of a design for instruction or demonstrate how the design works. Model cases lend to a design a measure of reality. Translators can deposit model cases in the LIBRARY as literal expressions transcribed from articles. For instance, from a study by Elawar and Corno (1985, p. 164), a model case of one type of feedback is: "Juan, you know how to get percent but the computation is wrong in this instance . . . Can you see where? (the teacher has underlined the location of errors)."

Since researchers exercise extensive control over the events of instruction, model cases from research articles may strip out features of instructional events that teachers consider critical. In other words, model cases from published studies may be weak model cases. We propose two remedies in an attempt to reconstitute the fullness of model cases. First, designs for instructional events that are shelved on the LIBRARY's second floor, developed jointly by teachers and T-KATI, can be cross-indexed through ELI with model cases taken from research articles. This will elaborate weak model cases. The second remedy likely will be much more satisfying. As teachers use DOCENT, over time they will develop their own catalog of locally relevant model cases. These, also, will be cross-indexed through ELI.

*Arguments* that explain and evaluate knowledge rest on theoretical principles that are justified by a logic governing a paradigm and validated by empirical evidence. They also address advantages and disadvantages for a design.

Referring back to the example from Elawar and Corno's (1985) study, suppose the research demonstrates that feedback of the kind illustrated contributes to boosting Juan's computational skill. An explanatory argument might be speculated as: Feedback having this structure helps Juan to induce a pattern recognition procedure that describes when he needs to monitor his computation for errors. An evaluative argument might concern the fact that having to underline every error on a classroom of students' worksheets is far more time consuming for the teacher than having students carry out this task by exchanging papers.

On the explanatory fork, ELI and its higher-level manifestations in KATI and T-KATI excise explanatory terms as much as possible. Nonetheless, because terms which operationally define structures and functions are infused with theory, explanatory arguments can be reconstructed. For instance, if Elawar and Corno's study included a dependent measure of whether students monitored computational accuracy as they worked out worksheet problems, and if students' scores on computation correlated with scores for monitoring, then an explanatory argument such as the one speculated about in the preceding paragraph can be pieced together.

An alternative to building explanations out of the representations is to develop another representation scheme which expresses theoretical accounts explicitly. For the time being, this tack is unexplored.

On the evaluative fork, ELI represents evaluative arguments directly in the form of results associated with instructional events. ELI also sets the stage for teachers to evaluate instructional events by recording structural characteristics about an activity such as its duration, whether special resources are needed, and whether students need to spend time first learning special rules to participate. This kind of information should be available to teachers since they are better judges of the costs and benefits of a design for instruction in their local situation. As our metaphor reflects, DOCENT is designed to be a knowledgeable guide and assistant, not a dictator.


## CONCLUSIONS

Novice teachers and teachers on the job share a keen interest in making their teaching as effective as possible. Due to a host of factors, however, the help which teachers would welcome in approaching this goal is too rarely available. We are attempting to close this gap in pre-service and in-service teacher education through DOCENT.

To date, efforts have focused on developing a scheme which can represent knowledge about instruction. The product, ELI, is still undergoing testing, revision, and implementation, and is being extended in preliminary design work on KATI. While this work has been successful, much is yet to be accomplished. Ultimately, we intend that DOCENT will provide teachers with means for expanding their knowledge about teaching and for casting it in terms of a design. It would be a mistake, however, to imagine that DOCENT will provide direct answers either to education's short-term or long-range problems. Instead, our objectives will have been met if DOCENT can serve teachers as an expert consultant whose perspective and advice helps them take steps which raise the quality of education by improving their teaching.

## REFERENCES

Berliner, D.C., Clarridge, P.B., Cushing, K., Sabers, D., & Stein, P. (1988, April). *Expert, novice, and postulant teachers: Perspectives and research.* Symposium presented at the meeting of the American Educational Research Association, New Orleans, LA.

Clark, C.M. (1988). Asking the right questions about teacher preparation: Contributions of research on teacher thinking. *Educational Researcher, 17*(2), 5–12.

Clark, C.M., & Peterson, P.L. (1986). Teachers' thought processes. In M. Wittrock (Ed.), *Handbook of research on teaching* (3rd ed., pp. 255–296). New York: Macmillan.

Corno, L. (1986). The metacognitive control components of self-regulated learning. *Contemporary Educational Psychology, 11,* 333–346.

Dallöf, U.S. (1971). *Ability grouping, content validity, and classroom process analysis.* New York: Teachers College Press.

Dunkin, M.J., & Biddle, B.J. (1974). *The study of teaching.* New York: Holt, Rinehart, & Winston.

Elawar, M.C., & Corno, L. (1985). A factorial experiment in teachers' written feedback on student homework: Changing teacher behavior a little rather than a lot. *Journal of Educational Psychology, 77,* 162–173.

Evertson, C.M., & Green, J.L. (1986). Observation as inquiry and method. In M. C. Wittrock (Ed.), *Handbook of research on teaching* (3rd ed., pp. 162–213). New York: Macmillan.

Gage, N.L. (1985). *Hard gains in the soft sciences—The case of pedagogy.* New York: Teachers' College Press.

Holley, C.D., & Dansereau, D.F. (Eds.). (1984). *Spatial learning strategies: Techniques, applications, and related issues.* Orlando, FL: Academic Press.

Hook, C.M., & Rosenshine, B. (1979). Accuracy of teacher reports of their classroom behavior. *Review of Educational Research, 49*(1), 1–12.

Joyce, B., & Weil, M. (1986). *Models of teaching* (3rd ed.). Englewood Cliffs, NJ: Prentice-Hall.

Kramer, L.L., & Winne, P.H. (1988). Representing knowledge about instruction in

DOCENT. In P.H. Winne (Ed.), *Project DOCENT: Interim summary report on Phase I*. Burnaby, BC: Instructional Psychology Research Group, Faculty of Education, Simon Fraser University.

Leinhardt, G., & Greeno, J.G. (1986). The cognitive skill of teaching. *Journal of Educational Psychology, 78,* 75–95.

Perkins, D.N. (1986). *Knowledge as design*. Hillsdale, NJ: Lawrence Erlbaum.

Peterson, P.L., & Comeaux, M.A. (1987). Teachers' schemata for classroom events: The mental scaffolding of teachers' thinking during classroom instruction. *Teaching and Teacher Education, 3,* 319–331.

*Pride and promise: Schools of excellence for all the people.* (1984). Washington, DC: American Educational Studies Association.

Weinstein, C.E., Goetz, E.T., & Alexander, P.A. (1988). *Learning and Study Strategies: Issues in Assessment, Instruction, and Evaluation*. San Diego, CA: Academic Press.

*WHAT WORKS: Research about teaching and learning.* (1986). Washington, DC: U.S. Department of Education.

Winne, P.H. (1985). Steps toward promoting cognitive achievements. *Elementary School Journal, 85,* 673–693.

Winne, P.H. (1987). Why process-product research cannot explain process-product findings and a proposed remedy: The cognitive mediational paradigm. *Teaching and Teacher Education, 3,* 333–356.

Winne, P.H. (1990). Project DOCENT: Design for a teacher's consultant. In P. Goodyear (Ed.), *Teaching knowledge and intelligent tutoring*. Norwood, NJ: Ablex.

# 9
# Using Multiple Teaching Strategies in an ITS*

Fiona Spensley
Mark Elsom-Cook
Paul Byerley
Peter Brooks
Massimo Federici
Claudia Scaroni

This chapter describes the DOMINIE system (DOMain INdependent Instructional Environment). DOMINIE is a tutoring system which operates in a number of domains and supports multiple teaching and assessment strategies. The strategies implemented in DOMINIE are described individually, and then the way in which the current system chooses between strategies is discussed with reference to future directions for research on multiple teaching strategies in intelligent tutoring systems.

Ohlsson (1987) and Elsom-Cook (1987) have stressed the importance of variation in teaching strategy in Intelligent Tutoring Systems (ITS). The potential for providing an adaptive program of instruction depends upon having a variety of presentation techniques to select from. Only with sufficient variety can the system respond to the cognitive needs of each individual student. This chapter will focus on the formalization of and selection between teaching strategies as embodied in DOMINIE, which is a fully implemented system, and then discuss the system in relation to theoretical desiderata. As background, the first part of the chapter summarizes the major points about the knowledge representation and student model used in the system, since this information is necessary for fully understanding the strategies which the system uses.

## BACKGROUND

The DOMINIE system has been developed as a joint project between Standard Elektrik Lorenz A.G., The Open University and Datamat SpA. Standard Elektrik Lorenz first produced a prototype domain-independent tutoring system which

---

* The project was funded under the European ESPRIT program. Esprit project no. 1613: "Evaluation of an Intelligent Tutoring System Shell for Industrial/Office Training".

was field-tested, and the results of this field test were used in totally redesigning the system. It is the redesigned system which is described here. This system has just been field-tested in three domains and the results from these trials will be evaluated and used to respecify the system once more before the project is completed.

The development of the system was driven by the need for a tool to support users learning to use computer-based interfaces. As such interfaces are often constantly being updated the project aimed to produce a domain-independent system. This makes intelligent tutoring economically feasible for industry, as dedicated machines would quickly become outdated. The system allows for major or minor changes in an interface to be accommodated, or for the teaching of completely unrelated interfaces. DOMINIE has a "trainer interface"[1] which is designed to support people who are not programmers to enter their own domains. The advantages of having a domain independent system are much reduced if a consultant has to be called to update or replace the knowledge representation. This interface requires no knowledge other than of the target software. It automatically checks that a complete and consistent domain representation is being generated. This aspect of the system is not central to this chapter; more details of the "trainer interface" can be found in Spensley (1988).

Complete domain independence is not feasible, so a restricted range of computer interface tasks were selected. The DOMINIE system was designed to teach computer-based procedural skills, that is, goal-directed tasks whose goal is achieved by executing a sequence of actions on a computer interface. The system represents the interface actions and the goal structure of tasks in considerable detail. The underlying system upon which the interface operates is represented more shallowly. The current domains in which the system has been operated are electronic telephone exchange maintenance, customization procedures for an office automation system, and system administration activities on an Apollo Domain© workstation.

## KNOWLEDGE REPRESENTATION

The main goal of the system is to teach people to carry out certain tasks using computer-based interfaces. In its simplest form this could be done by presenting the user with a sequence of actions upon the computer which they must memorize. This is not very constructive educationally, and does not help the user gain an understanding of the system which would allow generalization of experience and tackling new situations. The other extreme would be to provide a complete simulation of the system upon which the interface operates (e.g., an electronic

---

[1] So called because it was envisaged that the DOMINIE system would be used in industrial setting through training departments. However, its use is in no way specifically restricted to trainers.

telephone exchange) and teach this to every student. Apart from the difficulty of producing such a simulation, it is not clear that this deep procedural knowledge is needed by most users.

Instead, the tutor takes a midway position and focuses on the goal structure of someone using the interface. Given a task (i.e., a high-level goal to be achieved with the interface) the tutor uses a planner to generate a goal hierarchy that will achieve that high level goal. Each procedure in this plan is composed of a goal, zero or more conditions (or subgoals), zero or more actions, and links to related conceptual information. Where a procedure represents a choice point between disjunctive goals the action component is replaced with a posttest. The posttest is the question that provides the rationale for following one path rather than the other(s). Posttests cover decisions that the user must make that do not involve explicit actions on the computer interface, for example, following one procedure if an item occurs on a list and another if it does not.

The plan representation and the associated skills of problem decomposition are what the tutor attempts to teach, but the system also requires two other sources of knowledge. The first is basic knowledge about the sorts of actions which can be performed on the interface. Each action is described in terms of six elements: the type of action (e.g., selecting with the mouse or typing on the keyboard); the object on which the action takes place (e.g., an icon or a menu) and a name for that object which is meaningful to the student; the location of the action on the screen; the parameters of the action (e.g., alphanumeric characters, literal command, or one of a set); and a verbatim record of any typed input. This format allows for the description of any action in any computer interface task. Each of the action descriptions for a specific domain is associated with a "screen snapshot"[2], these sources of information can then be composed to illustrated to the student any sequence of operations on the interface for that specific application. These interface actions, either singly or grouped into larger interface tasks, constitute the action component of the plan representation (see Figure 9.1).

The second additional knowledge source required is conceptual information about the domain on which the interface operates. This is stored as a network of high-level declarative knowledge about the underlying system. It does not provide a procedural model, nor a deep representation of the system. Each concept has a textual description, and text associated with the links between the concepts (the links being roughly characterized as generalize/specialize relations), and text associated with links to any relevant procedures in the plan representation.

Figure 9.1 shows the relationship between these knowledge sources. Interface tasks appear in the action part of the goals in the plan, and there is a two-way linkage between the procedures and concepts in the underlying domain. Further

---

[2] These screen snapshots are collected automatically during the domain specification phase by the "trainer interface". For more details see Spensley, 1988.

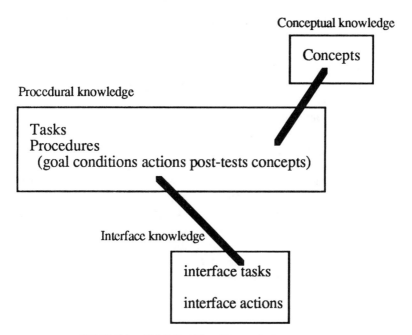

**Figure 9.1. Relationship of knowledge sources.**

details of the knowledge representation can be found in Elsom-Cook and Spensley (1988).

## STUDENT MODEL

The student model is a numeric overlay model. That is, a number of components in the system have numeric tags associated with them which are intended to represent the system's beliefs about the knowledge of the student. The student is represented as a subset of the total knowledge within the system. The scale used is bipolar (i.e., varying from "confident the student does not know this" to "confident the student knows this"). These numeric tags are associated with basic interface actions (e.g., selecting an icon), goals (both in particular contexts and in general), and concepts in the underlying domain. The system also models the short-term states of the student (e.g., bored, confused) based on self-reports and the successes of the different teaching strategies. This modeling technique is simple and well understood. It offers no contribution to research in this field. The system also uses a "dialogue history" which is a record of the interaction. This is used to provide the context for teaching and assessment decisions. The relationship between student modeling and the use of multiple teaching strategies will be discussed later in the chapter, after the strategies represented in Dominie have been outlined.

## TEACHING STRATEGIES

Dominie has eight teaching and assessment strategies which will be described in detail in this section. In broad terms the teaching strategies correspond to all the plausible domain-independent presentation formats for the procedural plan hierarchy. In broad terms these are bottom-up (cognitive apprenticeship), top-down (successive refinement), using analogies (discovery learning), and generalization (abstraction). The assessment strategies cover the monitoring of procedural performance both with (discovery assessment) and without elaborate feedback (practice), assessment of declarative knowledge (direct assessment), and a diagnostic strategy (Socratic diagnosis). In addition to these eight strategies the student has the facility to revise material that has been previously presented or to browse forward to unpresented material on demand.

### Cognitive Apprenticeship

There has been a lot of interest recently in a teaching technique known as "cognitive apprenticeship" (Collins & Brown, 1987). This is based on the idea that cognitive skills can be learned in the way that crafts were learned from an expert in that craft. The apprentice commences by watching the expert in action and asking questions. As time passes the expert allows the apprentice to perform small parts of the whole task. These parts will gradually increase in size until the pupil is able to perform the whole of the task in question. The claim for cognitive apprenticeship is that this technique operates beyond the level of manual skill acquisition. Problem solving, reasoning, and other cognitive processes are claimed to be amenable to this approach. In domains such as electronic fault finding, the pupil is expected to learn the fundamental concepts of the area by observing the actual activity and (with the aid of a few questions) inferring the reasoning process of the expert. This approach relies on the expert having reasoning techniques which are meaningful to the pupil. In the case of a computer-based tutor, the computer must reason using glass-box (psychologically valid) techniques if it is to attempt to teach in this style.

As far as DOMINIE is concerned, it is a working assumption that the "reasoning" which it uses (i.e., the goal structures generated by the planner) are meaningful to the users. Since these structures are input by experienced human users this is a reasonable assumption, but one which is to be investigated in the analysis of the recent field trials. Providing a meaningful goal structure for the domain was a major influence in moving away from representations based upon task analysis or state-transition models.

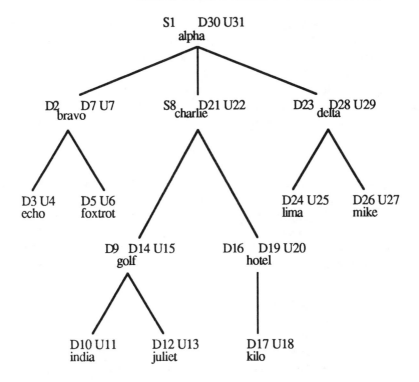

Numbers indicate sequence
U  indicates user performs task
S  indicates summary
D  indicates demonstration by system

**Figure 9.2.   Cognitive Apprenticeship Strategy.**

To illustrate this approach within DOMINIE consider the plan tree represented in Figure 9.2. The tutor must select an appropriate part of the domain and teach it to the student using a mixture of demonstrations and exercises for the user. In selecting an area to teach, our assumption is that the area should be slightly beyond the current state of knowledge of the pupil (as inferred from the student model). There should be enough material to give the exercise a structure and purpose, but no so much that the pupil is overwhelmed. In terms of our plan tree this is represented by choosing to teach a goal within the tree for which all sub-subgoals (if they exist) are already known to the pupil, but the majority of the subgoals are not. If we assume that the student currently knows nothing about the task, an example of such a goal is "bravo" in Figure 9.2.

DOMINIE would actually teach that goal by demonstrating it (which includes a demonstration of the subgoals "echo" and "foxtrot"). The tutor then explicitly breaks the goal into subgoals, and for each subgoal demonstrates it and then asks the pupil to carry out the same subgoal. If any of the subgoals are already known to the user, the tutor simply asks for them to be carried out (rather than demonstrating them). Finally, the tutor demonstrates the overall goal again and asks the pupil to perform the whole task. At any point during this process the pupil can ask for an explanation in terms of the role of this action within the overall plan, or for details of any of the domain concepts with which this plan is associated.

Figure 9.2 shows how the strategy would be applied to the whole of area "alpha." Numbers give the order in which nodes are tackled, "s" means that the tutor gives a brief summary of the node, "d" means that the tutor demonstrates the node, and "u" means that the user is requested to carry out the actions of the subtree containing that node. Monitoring of the student's performance is carried out by the practice assessment strategy.

**Successive Refinement**

Successive refinement is a top-down approach to teaching. It derives from the work of A.N. Whitehead (1932). The basic principle is that a good teacher should be able to explain a topic at a number of levels of detail, always providing an interaction at a level which is meaningful to the pupil in her current state of knowledge. In particular, a domain which contains an overwhelming number of details should be initially taught at a very general global level, telling a coherent story but omitting the full ramifications of the topic. This provides the pupil with an overview and a systematic framework into which subsequent teaching of the domain can be fitted. As the pupil becomes more sophisticated, a more powerful model of the domain may be taught. This is likely to involve explicitly highlighting erroneous simplifications which the tutor made for pedagogical purposes and actively supporting the construction of new, restructured models of the domain.

In the case of DOMINIE we do not support reconceptualization of the domain at the lower levels, but simply provide a more detailed account of the activities and concepts involved. Successive refinement is an important strategy for introducing concepts in relation to procedural knowledge.

DOMINIE selects the highest level untaught goal in the plan. It then uses information about the concepts associated with each goal in that tree to generate "weighted subnets" of the declarative knowledge of the system. These nets identify relevant concepts and assign them an importance in terms of the current plan. The subnets are generated by tracing the links from the procedural representation to conceptual network to highlight various concepts. Each concept then highlights all the more general concepts (by tracing its network links) until a more general concept is found which is marked as known in the student model. These subnets are then amalgamated to eliminate duplications and form one or more subnets for presentation. The concepts are then presented to the student from the most general to the most specific. When the concepts linked to a procedure have already been presented and are marked as known in the student model, just a brief summary of that concept will be provided.

Starting from the highest procedural goal, the tutor presents the major concepts associated with that goal and briefly summarizes the subgoals and actions which are involved in achieving the goal. On subsequent passes the subgoals are presented in a similar fashion. This process is repeated recursively through the plan tree. The level of explanation given at each point depends on the importance of the concepts within the weighted subnets and the level of understanding of the concepts and procedures which the pupil already has.

## Discovery Learning

The nature of discovery learning remains a subject for debate. Some educationalists (e.g., Papert, 1980) see such learning as implying a completely free activity on the part of the pupil. At the other extreme (e.g., Rousseau, 1762) the pupil has the impression of discovering new material for herself, but the task is actually carefully structured by a teacher who knows in advance the sequence of discovery which the pupil will make. In our model of this style, a teacher is necessary to set up an appropriate environment in which the learning can take place, and to provide guidance to the pupil when requested or when the pupil is in difficulty. A major part of the teacher's action is to assess the current state of knowledge of the pupil, and to select a task for the pupil to explore which is slightly beyond the current state of her knowledge, but not so much so as to be too difficult for her to achieve. Choosing such a task can be extremely complex and may involve finding similar situations in which the learner has made an appropriate cognitive leap, or identifying knowledge which the learner can bring to bear on the task. In our case we only attempt to model the selection of one type of area appropriate to discovery learning: that is, an area which is new to the student but which has a structure analogical to something which the student has already learnt. The student is then encouraged to attempt to perform the procedure and is presented with the appropriate screens for the execution of that procedure.

Identifying analogous areas is possible by using the goal information within plans to find subplans which are identical but occur in different contexts, and by using the parameter information in the action descriptions to recognize different parameterization of the same procedure or plan. By searching top-down for analogies the system captures them at the highest level within a plan. All the subgoals will necessarily be analogous due to the plan generation procedure.

## Discovery Assessment

Discovery assessment always and only follows discovery learning so they could be visualized as one strategy. However due to the control of structure of the system outlined later the teaching and assessment components have been separated. Having identified an appropriate area for discovery learning the tutor must monitor the student working in that area. If the student gets into difficulty or asks for help then the tutor will provide it. In general this help could take any of a number of forms. Since we are restricting ourselves to analogical reasoning the help can be similarly restricted. The tutor offers guidance by a sequence of progressively more detailed hints which give information about the analogy with previous knowledge. In terms of our knowledge representation this is fairly simple. An appropriate area for discovery learning by analogy is one in which the student knows most of the skills involved in a task, but does not know some part which is analogical to something previously learned. In our usage two goals are analogical if they involve the same procedure or a different parameterization of the same procedure in different problem contexts with different parameters. The first level of hint which the tutor offers is identifying the context in which the analogous procedure arose. Subsequent hints identify individual parameters in the two contexts were appropriate.

## Abstraction

Abstraction focuses on providing students with a global view of the tasks which can be carried out with the system, rather than teaching specific activities. This is achieved by explicitly pointing out the conceptual links between activities which have been separated in the teaching so far. This facilitates two major learning methods: allowing students to elaborate their model of the task (deeper processing and longer retention of skill), and generalising across task boundaries. Abstraction makes explicit links between all the known procedures, from the conceptual perspective. Unlike other strategies, it operates only on procedures which the student has already learned.

The strategy operates by tracing the links from all the procedures within the current task to the conceptual representation, and generating a weighted net (in a similar fashion to that generated in successive refinement). This net is then given an additional weighting in terms of the number of individual procedures (from any task) that are linked to the individual concepts.

Presentation will start from the node in the declarative representation which has the most procedures associated with it. The strategy presents concepts from this point in order of decreasing generality. At each node the abstraction strategy will present the conceptual information in summary or expanded form (depending on whether the student knows that concept) and then outline the links between that concept and the procedure types.

**Socratic Diagnosis**

Socratic diagnosis is a technique which has been much used in tutoring systems. It is often the case, however, that the interpretation which system builders place on this method varies immensely and has little to do with the technique as originally described by Plato. In the original form, the technique relies on the pupil already having some model of the domain which she is learning. This model is flawed in some respect, embodying one or more misconceptions about the nature of the domain. The teacher identifies these misconceptions and then takes the pupil through a series of educational interactions designed to make the pupil realize that there is an error in her model because it makes incorrect predictions. The educational interaction should also guide the pupil into recognizing the misconception(s) in her model and correcting them for herself.

In Why (Stevens, Collins, & Goldin, 1982) the strategy used was one which is commonly described as Socratic, but which omits a vital component. The technique may better be described as concept decomposition. The student makes a mistake at a level involving some concept and the tutor then switches to a sequence of questions regarding subconcepts of the errorful concept. If the student makes an error with one of these, that is broken into its constituent concepts in turn. The major difference from true Socratic tutoring is that the tutor does not know in advance where the misconception lies. The diagnostic and remedial actions have been mixed together.

Trill (Cerri & Elsom-Cook, 1988) on the other hand, detects an error and explicitly builds a push-down stack of concepts which are likely to have contributed to that error. It then guides the pupil down this misconceptions stack with a sequence of questions. The diagnostic strategies are not sufficiently powerful, however, to be certain that this path is the actual one leading to the misconception.

DOMINIE uses a technique between the two. It does not actively engage in diagnosis prior to the questioning phase, but on detecting an error it builds a "likely path" to the error by selecting those subcomponents which the user model suggests are least understood. This likely path is then used to guide the order of the questioning.

To illustrate this, let us assume that the pupil has incorrectly attempted the procedure associated with *alpha* in figure 9.3. Let us further assume that this is due to one misconception about the basic procedure *juliet* and a second misconception about the procedure *golf.* We will also take the left-to-right ordering of the tree as indicating the level of confidence that the tutor has about the student's knowledge. Items on the left of the tree are believed to be less well understood than those on the right.

The tutor will ask the student a question about *alpha* which she will fail to answer correctly. The tutor then asks about *bravo,* which the student deals with correctly, and then *charlie* which the student answers incorrectly. The next

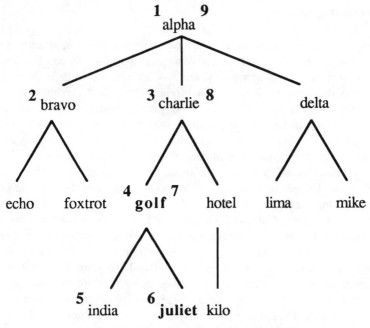

Figure 9.3. Socratic Search Strategy.

question is about *golf* (which is answered wrongly), then *india* (which is answered correctly) and finally *juliet* which is answered incorrectly. Since this is a basic procedure, the tutor reteaches it and updates the student model accordingly. Returning to *golf*, another question is asked which still leads to an error. The children of this node have been assessed, so the node is retaught and the system returns to ask a question about *charlie* and then *alpha*.

**Practice**

The practice strategy is simple. It involves presenting the pupil with the interface by means of the stored screen snapshots and asking them to carry out some task. While the student is engaged in this activity the tutor is monitoring the student actions in the background. This is achieved with a technique very like Anderson's model tracing (Anderson & Skwarecki, 1986). The plan for the task is generated and the actions of the student are checked for their correspondence with that plan. If the student deviates from the plan the tutor immediately provides remedial feedback. If the student has taken the wrong path at a disjunctive point in the plan then the tutor identifies the disjunction and the conditions which decide on the appropriate branch. Otherwise the tutor reminds the student of the appropriate goal structure at this point and indicates the appropriate action.

This form of assessment always follows cognitive apprenticeship. Correct execution of a procedure in this context, immediately following a demonstration of the task, is not the basis for a high confidence rating. However, successful "practice" in other contexts provides the ultimate test of the students ability to perform the procedural skill.

## Direct Assessment

Direct assessment allows for the assessment of students declarative knowledge using the traditional question and answer format. Only multiple choice and slot-filling questions have been used to avoid the natural language and typing error problems associated with constructive responses. For the conceptual information this is the only method of assessing student knowledge, but it is also used for procedural material. Some of the questions used by this strategy will be entered explicitly by trainers others will be automatically generated from the tutorial text and from the plan structure when the domain is being specified (see Spensley, 1988).

## Strategy Selection

Given the eight strategies described above, DOMINIE must decide which is most appropriate at a given point. This decision is based upon a number of factors. These factors are: achieving a balance between teaching and assessment; the appropriateness of the strategy to a given area; the students prior success with the different strategies; and the student's personal preferences.

The primary decision which the tutor takes when it considers a strategy change is the balance of teaching and assessment in its activity. Obviously the tutor wants to present new material to the student, but it also has goals of ensuring that the student has understood the material and checking that its model of the student is still accurate. The system therefore starts by teaching when it has a new pupil. This is based on the assumption that the pupil knows nothing about the area which is being taught.[3] As the interaction progresses the decision as to whether to teach or assess depends on the strategy used. For example, the successive refinement strategy is not designed to be frequently assessed, whereas the cognitive apprenticeship strategy works by having each step follows by a practice of the skill.

DOMINIE has a fine granularity in its control structure, making a strategy decision after each step in the interaction. The student model is updated (if

---

[3] If the pupil may already know something about the area, it would make sense to start with a diagnostic phase aimed at building an accurate student model. The current version of DOMINIE does not include this.

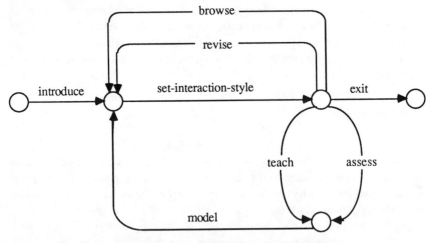

**Figure 9.4.   Control structure in DOMINIE.**

required) after every interaction step. The control structure is illustrated in Figure 9.4. The student is also given the opportunity of influencing the interaction at any point. The student can choose to be taught or assessed or to exit, they may also choose to revise previously presented material or browse forward through unpresented material. Revision involves presentation of the material using the strategy by which it was last presented. Material to be browsed is presented by using the cognitive apprenticeship method. Neither of these interactions is modeled, as the reasons for using them may vary. Revision may indicate confusion or a strategic recap; browsing may be due to boredom or used for creating an overview. Within revision students have the facility to enter "reteach flags" and DOMINIE will then respond to the student's self-identified problems. This facility in conjunction with the diagnosis strategy allows for flexibility in the student modeling, once a procedure is marked as known with a high degree of confidence it is not unmodifiable.

The control structure of a tutoring system which uses multiple teaching strategies involves making a decision as to which area to teach and which strategy to use. These decisions are not independent, and in order to obtain maximum flexibility in DOMINIE these are subdivided into general and specific decisions, and then interleaved. The initial decision made is whether to teach or assess; this restricts the range of possible strategies, and allows the student to express a performance at this level. The next decision made is which task should be taught, a task being a broad area within the domain. This decision encompasses teaching new material, reteaching old material, and assessing or reassessing the student's understanding. Then the specific teaching or assessment strategy is selected, the choice being restricted by the task chosen in the previous step and the student's interaction history. For example, discovery learning can only be used for new

1. In order to find an appropriate procedure to teach, given a broad task area, search the plan tree using top down, left to right, breadth first search.

2. A procedure is appropriate if it is untaught and it is analogous to a goal which is already known.

2a Two goals are considered analogous if they are identical or if they are represented by different parameterisations of the same planning procedure

3. To present the problem to the student, present an introduction to the strategy, present the problem context, present the appropriate screen and then ask them to execute the task.

3a Presenting the strategy involves presenting a motivating text and an explanation of what the student should do. If it is the first time the student has encountered the strategy, or the student has not previously been successful with this strategy, present a detailed explanation. Otherwise present a brief summary.

3b Presenting the context involves presenting the goal of the problem and its position in relation to the broader task context.

4. To carry out discovery assessment monitor the students performance.

5. At any time while monitoring performance the student can ask for a hint or demonstration of the correct next step.

6. If the student asks for a demonstration, only give one if all the hints have been used.

7. If the student ask for a hint then:
7a If the user tried an action associated with the procedure but omitted an action associated with a condition (subgoal) of that procedure then remind the user what the procedure is and state the omitted precondition.
7b If the user is in one branch of a disjunct and has executed an action from the other branch, then tell the user the critical post-test which should determine the branch to choose.
7c Otherwise, if this is the first time the user has asked for a hint then identify the context of the analogy.
7d Otherwise identify a parameter of the procedure and give it's old value.
8. Monitor student performance by generating a solution to the problem from the planner and seeing if it matches the student actions.
8a If the match is complete, increase confidence in the student model and present the student with a summary of what she did.
8b If the student moves away from the correct solution, decrease confidence in the student model and offer the hint menu.

Figure 9.5.    Strategy specific rules in discovery learning.

material, and reteaching should always use a different strategy. The final decision is which specific procedure should be taught; this is determined by strategy specific rules applied to the chosen task. An example of the rules for discovery learning is shown in Figure 9.5. The system can backtrack on any of these decisions as it is implemented in Prolog. It is possible that there is no appropriate procedure within the chosen task (given a strategy), so in this case DOMINIE will backtrack to try another strategy. The backtracking is limited so that the initial teach/assess decision is never revised, as the student may have specifically requested this option.

**Discussion**

DOMINIE provides a prototype system for using multiple teaching strategies. There are many directions in which to improve the system, but it provides a good basis for development as it is one of the few fully implemented intelligent tutoring systems. The use of multiple teaching strategies promises to be a very productive area for ITS research.

As outlined in the introduction, a tutoring system needs multiple strategies in order to be able to be responsive to the student's needs. In order to be responsive the system also needs to be able to switch effectively between the strategies. To do so effectively, the system needs a good idea of the state of the student coupled with a model of the teaching/learning process to inform the selection. To have a good idea of the state of the student also requires multiple assessment techniques. This section will discuss how far DOMINIE fulfills these ideals and discusses possible extensions of the system.

DOMINIE does not explicitly embody a model of the teaching/learning process, although it approaches the overarching tutorial style of "decreasing intervention" (Peters, 1966). With a system like DOMINIE the user is learning to operate an interface about which she knows nothing; the starting point for this interaction should clearly be one in which the tutor provides a lot of structure and controls the interaction to a large extent. In the final state we wish the user to be able to use the interface without the presence of the tutor. The tutor, while initially directing the interaction, must be constantly assessing the value of switching to a teaching strategy which involves less control on the part of the tutor. In addition to this overall style, the tutor must continuously assess the appropriateness and effectiveness of the strategy which is currently being used. This ideal of "decreasing intervention" is particularly appropriate for teaching procedural skills, but due to the restrictions involved in producing a working system the current version of DOMINIE takes a somewhat simpler approach in its strategy selection.

The implementation of multiple teaching strategies is clearly an essential basis for implementing the "decreasing intervention" approach. To the extent that "decreasing intervention" is employed in DOMINIE, it is implicit in the strategy selection rules. The teaching strategies in Dominie vary in their supportiveness and prescriptiveness, and through careful strategy switching the student could be moved from a very structured teaching approach toward independent activity where the system merely observes the student's performance. The sensitivity of the 'decreasing intervention' style is limited in DOMINIE by the domain independence of the system, and the fact that it must have a very general (and therefore impoverished) student model. The mechanisms for implementing "decreasing intervention" are discussed in detail in Elsom-Cook (1988).

The rules for selecting a teaching strategy depend on the state of the very limited student model, and the interaction history, without reference to any model of the learning process. There is a lot more scope for research into learning processes, and we certainly have no accounts that could be used to support a domain independent system such as DOMINIE. The problem of switching between strategies is a novel one emerging, obviously, from the novel use of more than one strategy. It is not clear what theoretical basis exists for this choice procedure as it is not clear that human teachers employ multiple strategies, and because current teaching practices do not often involve extended one to one interactions. Intelligent tutoring systems using multiple teaching strategies could potentially provide a more responsive educational interaction than human teachers if a sound basis for strategy change could be established. The most productive extension for research on strategy selection and student modeling using the DOMINIE system would be to concentrate on one particular domain and thus be able to produce a more sophisticated model of the teaching process and of the state of the student. Sally Douglas (personal communication) has suggested that text processing is such a domain.

The student modeling in DOMINIE is very basic with a confidence level associated with procedures, concepts, teaching strategies, and short-term states. In the current version of the system there are multiple assessment strategies feeding this student model, but the information they produce is stored in this simple format. A more sophisticated student model would need a variety of assessment approaches including those implemented in DOMINIE. Using one domain would allow for a more targeted assessment component for student behavior, where the learning processes is modeled. The approaches implemented in Dominie (i.e., question and answer, performance monitoring, diagnostic, and self-report) are all likely to be involved in such a system.

The teaching strategies embodied in DOMINIE are fairly coarse-grain, but this again is unavoidable with a modular, domain-independent system. The strategies had to be implemented as content-independent approaches to the general knowledge structures. The system is not able to make minor shifts in presentation style when it encounters problems, but must make severe shifts in strategy. With a teaching style such as "decreasing intervention" the system would want the facility to produce gentle changes of emphasis as well as more distinct

204 SPENSLEY, ELSOM-COOK, BYERLEY, BROOKS, FEDERICI, AND SCARONI

changes of strategy. The broad strategy shifts in DOMINIE do not seem to have caused too much of a problem for the students tested in our field trials, although the fact that we are teaching a procedural skill rather than something more conceptual may be important in this respect. Concentrating on a single domain would allow for a larger variety of less coarse teaching strategies. Also, by eliminating the need for modularity the range of strategies could be extended to include specific teaching approaches appropriate for only small parts of the domain. Another variation could be using multiple viewpoints on the knowledge representation. Both of these increasing the potential for subtle shifts in presentation.

## CONCLUSION

This chapter has described a tutoring system which operates across a number of related domains and supports multiple teaching strategies. It is based on some theoretical work and an empirical study of a prototype system. The system described here has undergone field tests, and will be reimplemented to take into account the results of those tests. It was implemented in LPA Prolog on an IBM PC-AT. The most interesting point about the system is its explicit formalization of multiple teaching strategies and reasoning about the choice of strategy. The strategies described here are still somewhat primitive, although they capture the essence of the styles they are intended to represent. Refinement and sophistication of these strategies, along with the extension of the strategy selection to reflect global styles such as "decreasing intervention," are major goals for further research.

## REFERENCES

Anderson, J.R., & Skwarecki, E. (1986). The automated tutoring of introductory computer programming. *Communications of the ACM, 29*(9), 842–849.
Cerri, S., & Elsom-Cook, M.T. (1990). Trill: The rather intelligent little lisper. In R. Lawler & M. Yazdani (Eds.), *AI and education* (Vol. 2). Norwood, NJ: Ablex.
Collins, A., & Brown, J.S. (1987). Cognitive apprenticeship: Teaching students the craft of reading, writing, and mathematics. In L.B. Resnick (Ed.), *Cognition and instruction.* Hillsdale, NJ: Lawrence Erlbaum.
Elsom-Cook, M.T. (1987). Guided discovery tutoring and machine learning. In J. Self (Ed.), *Artificial intelligence and human learning: ICAI.* London: Chapman & Hall.
Elsom-Cook, M.T. (1988). Decreasing intervention. *Proceedings of Third Windermere Workshop on ICAI.* Windermere, UK.
Elsom-Cook, M.T., & Spensley, F. (1988). *DOMINIE: Knowledge Representation.* (CITE Tech. report 36). Milton Keynes, UK: Open University.
Ohlsson, S. (1987). Some principles of intelligent tutoring. In R. Lawler & M. Yazdani (Eds.), *AI and Education* (Vol. 1, pp. 203–237). Norwood, NJ: Ablex.

Papert, S. (1980). *Mindstorms*. Brighton, UK: Harvester.

Peters, R.S. (1966). *Ethics and education*. London: Allen and Unwin.

Rousseau, J.J. (1974). *Emile*. Everyman Edition. London: Dent. (Original edition published 1762).

Spensley, F. (1988). *DOMINIE: Trainer Interface*. (CITE Tech. report 44). Milton Keynes, UK: Open University.

Spensley, F., & Elsom-Cook, M.T. (1988). *DOMINIE: Teaching and Assessment Strategies*. Milton Keynes, UK: Centre for Information Technology in Education, The Open University, Number 37.

Stevens, A., Collins, A., & Goldin, S.E. (1982). Misconceptions in students understanding. In D. Sleeman & J.S. Brown (Eds.), *Intelligent tutoring systems*. London: Academic.

Whitehead, A.N. (1932). *The aims of education*. London: Benn.

# 10
# Finding Errors by Overlooking Them*

## Warren Sack

### INTRODUCTION

For the past few years our group has been engaged in the development, implementation, and evaluation of automatic program debuggers for novices (e.g., MENOII [Soloway, Rubin, Woolf, Bonar, & Johnson, 1983], PROUST [Johnson, 1986]). One of our goals is to develop an automatic debugger that can serve as a programming expert in a programming tutoring system for novices; such a tutoring system would also include a pedagogical expert (Littman & Soloway, 1986).

In this chapter we focus on techniques for automatically identifying two important classes of programming errors: *detail* and *coordination* bugs. The techniques we have developed to identify these classes of errors are one outgrowth of a two year empirical study to determine the efficacy and accuracy of the automatic debugger PROUST. In the empirical study (Sack & Soloway, 1989) we describe the weaknesses of PROUST. In this chapter we will concentrate on an error identification method, called the *overlooking* method, that overcomes the weaknesses of the bug identification and bug representation techniques used in PROUST and many other existing automatic debuggers. This chapter is a description of the design of the *overlooking* method. We are currently working on an implementation of the design presented in this chapter: We are building our newest automatic debugger, CHIRON, which will use the *overlooking* method to identify bugs in novices' programs.

*Error identification* is an understanding problem that most AI understanding theories avoid. Most AI *understander* programs assume that the input correctly represents either the user's intentions (e.g., via an English sentence) or a real world situation (e.g., a photograph of a cup and saucer) and are constructed solely to disambiguate the input and fill in information implied by, but not explicitly stated in the input. Some understanding systems handle noise. For

---

\* Elliot Soloway has been the main source of guidance, support, and advice behind this research. Thanks to Stan Letovsky for discussions on program understanding and plan representation, and to Jim Spohrer and David Littman for ideas about programming errors and the programming process. Thanks also to Harald Wertz for allowing me to continue my research in his laboratory at the University of Paris VIII. This research was funded by the NSF grand MDR-875-1361 and a 1988/89 Chateaubriand Scholarship for the Exact Sciences, Medicine, and Engineering awarded by the French Embassy to the United States.

example, many speech understanding systems deal with noise at the phonetic level and many vision systems deal with noise at the edge-detection level. But most understanding systems are built on the assumption that the high level structure of the input is "correct" (i.e., the sentence/paragraph and 3D-objects respectively are correctly described). Program understanders like Letovsky (1987), Waters (1978), and Wills (1986) assume that the programs input are free of bugs. An understander that can assume that the input is error free can also assume that any discrepancies that arise during the analysis process can be attributed to errors in its understanding of the input. The understander does not have to entertain the possibility that all (or some) of the discrepancies are due to errors in the input.

Theories of understanding developed for application in Intelligent Tutoring Systems (ITSs) cannot avoid the extra complexities raised by errors in the input. By and large, the understander programs used in ITSs are used to analyze the buggy solutions input by students. In this paper we are concerned with the issues involved in understanding buggy computer programs.

The rest of this chapter can be summarized as follows. First, we describe two classes of bugs that account for over 70% of novices' programming errors (and, which we speculate, account for many of the bugs made by expert programmers as well): *detail* and *coordination* errors. We give a quick example of how the *overlooking* method of bug identification can be used to find such bugs in a particular Pascal program. Then, we characterize the bug identification technique used by most other existing automatic program debugging systems (including our debugger PROUST); we dub this technique the *mal-rule* method and describe its weaknesses. Next we present our programming knowledge representation language and then we devote two sections to the specification of new techniques for identifying *detail* and *coordination* programming errors. These techniques characterize the bug identification method that we call *overlooking*. We explain how the *overlooking* method of bug identification solves the weaknesses of the *mal-rule* method. A section on our implementation of the *overlooking* method is included, and we briefly discuss the relevance of *overlooking* to the general problem of automatically inferring student models. The conclusion is a simple rap-up of the vices of the *mal-rule* method of bug identification, the virtues of the *overlooking* method, and a synopsis of implementation concerns regarding the *overlooking* method.

## DETAIL AND COORDINATION ERRORS

### Definitions of Detail and Coordination Errors

In this chapter we focus on techniques for identifying programming errors due to programmers' struggles with *detail* and *coordination* difficulties. We speculate

```
PROGRAM Average(INPUT, OUTPUT);
VAR Count: INTEGER;
    Sum, New, Avg: REAL;
BEGIN
  Sum := 0;
  Count := 0;
  WRITELN('Input a number');
  READLN(New);
  WHILE (New <> 99999) DO BEGIN
    Sum := Sum + New;
    Count := Count + 1;
      READLN(New);
      WRITELN('Input a number');
  END;
  IF (Count > 0) THEN BEGIN
    Avg := Sum / Count;
    WRITELN('The average is ', Avg);
  END;
END.
```
**Bug**

**Figure 10.1. Program reads before it prompts user for input.**

that these two classes of bugs can occur in the programs of expert and novice programmers regardless of the programming language used.

*Detail.* Programming is difficult because of the number and types of low level details that a programmer must keep track of. *Detail* bugs are errors made by programmers typing, ordering, or defining syntactic pieces of a program. For example, typing Sverage instead of Average, ordering the expression X − Y as Y − X, or defining the expression X − Y as X + Y. All of these examples are on the statement level, but *detail* errors are also found in larger segments of a program. Figure 10.1 contains an example of a *detail* bug that involves more than one statement. We call the bug shown in Figure 10.1 a prompt-after-read-bug: the program will prompt the user to input a value *after* the user has already input a value (the program should query the user for a value *before* the program tries to read a value).

*Coordination.* Putting the pieces together is hard to do. Stepwise refinement (Dahl, Dijkstra, & Hoare, 1972) of a programming problem is only one leg of the journey from problem specification to coded implementation. After the problem has been decomposed into subproblems, and subsolutions to the subproblems have been written, the programmer must interlock the subsolutions together into a single program that solves the complete problem. Specific programming language control and data flow contructs (e.g., the WHILE statement from Pascal) and conventions can ease *coordination* difficulties for the programmer. However not all *coordination* difficulties can be solved by programming language designers. For example, in writing a program to handle withdrawals from a bank account, it is important that the program checks the balance of the account before dispensing the cash. In short, *coordination* difficulties are often domain dependent.

Our studies of novice Pascal programmers (Johnson, Soloway, Cutler, & Draper, 1983; Spohrer, Pope, Lipman, Sack, Freiman, Littman, Johnson & Soloway, 1985; Spohrer & Soloway, 1986; and especially Spohrer, 1989) has revealed that *detail* and *coordination* difficulties account for over 70% of the bugs made by novices. Our studies of the errors made by expert programmers and programmers working in languages other than Pascal are not as complete as our studies of novice Pascal programmers' errors. However, with the observations we do have (e.g., Adelson & Soloway, 1985; Littman, Pinto, Letovsky, & Soloway, 1985; Soloway, Letovsky, Loerinc, & Zygielbaum, 1984) we speculate that *detail* and *coordination* difficulties plague programmers of all languages and levels of expertise.

## AN EXAMPLE OF FINDING DETAIL AND COORDINATION BUGS USING THE OVERLOOKING METHOD

### The Example

Figure 10.2 contains a buggy solution to the following programming problem:

*Averaging Problem.* Read in numbers until 99999 is input. Prompt the user before each number is read. Calculate and output the average of all of the numbers input excluding the 99999.

All of the bugs illustrated in Figure 10.2 affect the *count plan;* that is, the method that the programmer has implemented to count the numbers input by the user.

*Bug 1* is a *detail* error. The programmer has typed Count := Count − 1 instead of Count := Count + 1.

*Bug 2* is an *intra-coordination* error. The programmer has corrupted the data flow within the count_plan by duplicating the Count update. By the term *intra-coordination* we mean to denote the coordination within a single plan. This is in contrast to the term *inter-coordination* which we use to describe coordination between a number of plans.

*Bug 3* is an *inter-coordination* error. The programmer has forgotten to guard the average_calculation against division by zero; that is, the case where Count = 0. To describe this error more in terms of the symptoms rather than the cure we might say that the count and average plans are not coordinated correctly.

```
PROGRAM Average(INPUT, OUTPUT);
VAR Count: INTEGER;
    New, Avg, Sum: REAL;
BEGIN
  Count := 0;
  Sum := 0;
  WRITELN('Input a number');
  READLN(New);
  WHILE (New <> 99999) DO BEGIN
    Sum := Sum + New;                    ──────Bug 1
    Count := Count - 1;
    Count := Count - 1;──────────────────Bug 2
    WRITELN('Input a number');
    READLN(New);
  END;
  Avg := Sum / Count;──────────────────Bug 3
  IF (Count > 0) THEN BEGIN
    WRITELN('The average is ', Avg);
  END;
END.
```

**Figure 10.2.** (1) Detail, (2) intra-, and (3) inter-coordination bugs.

## The Method

The *overlooking* method for bug identification depends upon *abstraction* (Michalski, 1986). Namely a debugger's ability to abstract away necessary, but often erroneously implemented or neglected details or aspects of a programming plan. Figure 10.3 contains paraphrased definitions for a count_plan and an average_plan (later we will more carefully describe our plan representation language).

Consider the problem of finding a statement in Figure 10.2 that matches the constraints assigned to the update of the count_plan-template defined in Figure 10.3; there are *no* statements in the program of Figure 10.2 that meet all of the data_flow and template constraints of the count_plan. In order to find a likely candidate we can abstract away some of the constraints. Firstly we ignore completely the data_flow constraints, and, secondly we abstract the + operator into something more general like <arithmetic_operator>. By overlooking these constraints (and keeping track of what we have overlooked), candidates for the update statement can be found and diagnosed; i.e., the two Count := Count − 1 statements.

Bug 2 can be diagnosed by abstracting away all of the constraints specified in

count—plan =
    template =
                result—variable = ?Count
                initialization = ?Count := 0
                update = ?Count := ?Count + 1
                positional—constraints = *The* initialization *preceeds the*
                update.
    data—flow =
                *There should be data flow from*
                        *the* initialization *to the* update, *and from*
                        *the* update *back to the* update
    input—output =
                *The variable* ?Count *should be declared intege*r
average—plan =
    template =
                result—variable = ?Average
                avg—calculation = ?Average := ?Sum / ?Count
                sum = *is a* sum—plan *with*
                        result—variable = ?Sum
                        update = ?SumUpdate
                count = *is a* count—plan *with*
                        result—variable = ?Count
                update = ?CountUpdate
    data—flow =
                *There should be data flow from*
                        *the* ?SumUpdate *to the* avg—calculation, *and from*
                        *the* ?CountUpdate *to the* avg—calculation
    input—output =
                *The value of* ?Count *used in the* avg—calculation *must*
                *not be equal to* 0.

**Figure 10.3.   Definitions for Count and Average Plans.**

the template aspect of the count_plan. (In this manner Bug 1 is overlooked, so that the analysis process can concentrate on the data_flow properties of the program in Figure 10.2.) A data flow analysis of the program shows immediately that Count is being redefined twice, when the count_plan specifies that it should only be redefined once.

Bug 3 is diagnosed later in the analysis process when the debugger is looking for an instance of the average_plan in the program. The first two aspects of the average_plan can be identified without any problems. The third aspect, the input_output aspect, the *value of* ? Count *used in the* avg_calculation: *must not be equal to* 0, is not a property of the program of Figure 10.2. Consequently, the program is diagnosed as missing a guard around the average calculation.

The *overlooking* method of bug identification works by loosening, or abstracting away, certain constraints. By overlooking certain constraints, a debugger can infer what various pieces of a program are suppose to do even if the pieces are not functionally correct.

## MAL-RULE DEBUGGERS

### What is a Mal-rule Debugger?

The programming knowledge bases of most existing debuggers can be be simplistically characterized as grammars: nonterminals signify intermediate states of program development, terminals stand for implemented code, and productions denote a step in the program development process. (Incidentally, this is almost exactly the way Ruth (1976) wrote his debugger's knowledge base and the LISP-TUTOR's (Farrell, Sauers, & Anderson, 1984) knowledge base is written in GRAPES production rules (which can be easily reformulated as grammar productions). The knowledge bases of most other debuggers can also be described as simple syntactic variations of grammars.) For example, PROUST's knowledge base is written using goals, plans, and subgoals, but these names for the grammar productions were picked to draw a specific analogy between the contents of PROUST's knowledge base and the findings of psychological experiments regarding human program understanding (e.g., Soloway & Ehrlich, 1984) This gross characterization allows us to compare the performance and bug representation schemes of a wide variety of existing debuggers.

Most debuggers have two kinds of productions in their programming knowledge base: a set of *correct* productions and a set of *mal* productions.[1] Used in a generative manner, exclusive use of the set of correct rules results in a correct solution to a given programming problem: a correct program. The specification of the programming problem serves as the start symbol of the grammar.

*Mal* productions are paired with correct productions. Use of one or more mal productions instead of their correct siblings will ultimately result in a buggy program solution. Mal-rules applied soon after the start symbol will, of course, have farther reaching disastrous consequences than mal-rules that are used closer to the leaves of the implementation process.

The mal-rule method of bug identification is as follows. The source program is parsed using the correct set of productions. If an impasse in the parsing occurs using a correct production, its mal pair(s) are tried. If one of the mal productions succeeds, the debugger corrects the source program by deleting the results (i.e., the bugs) of the mal-rule and inserts the expected results of the correct production. The parsing continues until each piece of the source program has been explained by either a correct or a mal-rule.

### Some Examples of Mal-rule Debuggers

Debuggers that use the *mal-rule* approach to representing and identifying bugs include PROUST (Johnson & Soloway, 1985), LISP-TUTOR/GREATERP

---

[1]Sleeman (1979) developed mal-rules to explain high frequency bugs in the domain of algebra.

(Reiser, Anderson, & Farrell 1985), SNIFFER (D. Shapiro, 1981), LAURA (Adam & Laurent, 1980), Ruth's system (Ruth, 1976), and numerous others. For the purposes of this paper the main difference between these systems regards the respective representations used to express the *correct* productions. For example, PROUST uses a cognitively based plan representation while the representation used in LAURA is a data flow representation. However, all of these systems use the same methodology for representing bugs. They all use mal productions. Bugs are the results of specific deviations from the correct code or correct methods that should be followed by the programmer to produce correct code. For example plan-differences are used in PROUST and graph differences are used in LAURA.

*Mal-rule* debuggers have also been built for other domains (e.g., arithmetic (BUGGY, Brown & Burton, 1978); (DEBUGGY, Burton, 1982)[2]; geometry (GEOMETRY-TUTOR, Anderson, Boyle, & Yost, 1984); and algebra (LMS, Sleeman, 1984). We conjecture that the researchers in automatic programming debugging have been encouraged by the success of mal-rule bug models in these other domains and that is the reason why so many mal-rule debuggers for programming have been built to date.

### The Weaknesses of the Mal-rule Method

There are four major weaknesses with the mal-rule method of representing and identifying bugs:

*1.   All bugs are equal:* All bugs are represented as mal productions. Cognitively plausible bugs are just as difficult to represent as cognitively implausible bugs. In order to allow the mal-rule debugger to recognize a new bug, the knowledge engineer must add a new mal production. We pointed out that two types of bugs, *detail* and *coordination* bugs, account for over 70% (Spohrer, 1989) of the bugs made by novice Pascal programmers. Intuitively it would be preferable to use a knowledge representation that allowed us to represent high frequency bugs more easily than low frequency bugs. Mal-rules are simply an awkward way of representing *detail* and *coordination* errors. We can summarize this weakness by comparing it to the representation inadequacies of certain conventional programming languages. For example, PROLOG is a bad choice for representing procedural information; similarly mal-rules are a bad choice for representing high frequency programming errors.

*2. Mal-rules are idiosyncratic:*   Most mal-rule debuggers do not allow the knowledge engineer to define "super-bug-rules," that is, mal-rules that could be used to represent and identify sets of highly related bugs. For example, to cover

---

[2]The theory behind the mal-rules used in DEBUGGY is significantly more sophisticated than the theory behind the mal-rules used in existing program debuggers. Brown and VanLehn (1980) have a theory of how mal-rules are formulated by students learning procedural skills.

Bug 1 of Figure 10.2 in PROUST's knowledge representation we would have to write a special purpose mal-rule that corresponds to something like this:

. *Found:* Count := Count − 1;
  *Expected:* Count := Count + 1;

In order to represent the bug in which the programmer has written * instead of + we would have to write yet another special purpose mal-rule and so forth, ad infinitum, for every possible operator the programmer might mistakenly replace the + with.

Even some automatic program debuggers that are *not* mal-rule debuggers rely on large amounts of idiosyncratic information that is peculiar to specific bugs. For example, both TALUS (Murray, 1986) and APROPOS2 (Looi, 1988) match students' code against correct reference code. In order to find the best match to the reference code, both of these systems rely on *heuristic best-first matching* routines that make use of arbitrary weighting functions to determine the "best" match. Examples of arbitrary weights assessed for mismatches from Murray's (1986) system include

    2 * (sprog − rprog)
    where
            sprog = number of PROGNs in student's code, and
            rprog = number of PROGNs in reference code
and
    0.5 if not(sname = rname)
    where
            sname = name of student's function, and,
            rname = name of reference function. (Murray, 1986, pp. 104–105)

*3. Derivative bugs cannot be represented:* Mal-rule debuggers parse programs into representations that essentially capture only one *aspect or viewpoint* (Bobrow & Winograd, 1977) of the program. For example, LAURA parses programs into a data flow graph, and PROUST parses programs into a representation that captures the textual and structural elements of the program. It is difficult, if not impossible, to write mal-rules representing bugs that are best described in a vocabulary derivative of the vocabulary the debugger parses the source program into. For example, in using a data flow vocabulary it would be difficult to describe the bug of leaving out the parentheses in an algebraic expression (e.g., writing A + B / C instead of (A + B) / C) because the preprocessing has washed-out the original textual arrangement of the expression. In PROUST, such a bug would be easy to represent, but a bug in the data flow of the program is almost impossible to represent in a nonidiosyncratic manner. For example, to incorporate Bug 2 of Figure 10.2 into PROUST's knowledge base we would have to write a mal-rule that said something like

IF an assignment statement with *?Count* as the left-hand-side variable immediately follows the *?Count* update,
THEN signal an error.

However, we would also have to write a second, third, fourth rule (and so on) to take care of the cases in which Count was reassigned two, three, or four times.

4. *Program parts are assumed to be independent:* Imagine another buggy solution to the Averaging Problem in which the programmer has used the variable Sum in the left-hand side of the counter update rather than the variable Count. That is, the programmer has defined the counter update as Sum := Count + 1 instead of Count := Count + 1. This is a difficult bug to diagnose because fixing the sum_plan might damage the count_plan. Consider the case in which the mal-rule debugger has not yet found the count_plan, and, at this moment, is identifying the sum_plan. If the mal-rule debugger is capable of finding data flow errors it might at this time discover that Sum is being overwritten by the Sum := Count + 1 statement. There are a number of things that the mal-rule debugger might do with the Sum := Count + 1 statement in order to fix the sum_plan and continue the parse; e.g., remove it, or move it below the loop. However, if either of these fixes are performed the mal-rule debugger will detect an extra error in the count—plan that the mal-rule debugger itself has introduced! This is another example of an *inter-coordination* bug. Most existing debuggers have difficulties identifying *inter-coordination* bugs for three reasons: (a) most debuggers need to correct a bug as soon as they find it so that they can continue to parse the program, and (b) most debuggers do not systematically keep track of the modifications that they have made to the buggy program, and (c) most debuggers cannot reason about interactions between nonlocal pieces of a program. These three difficulties are usually avoided in one of three ways: (a) ignore the inherent difficulties of correcting inter-coordination bugs (e.g., MENOII, Soloway et al., 1983), (b) attach a lot of idiosyncratic "demons" to pieces of the knowledge base to look for specific interactions (e.g., PROUST, Johnson & Soloway, 1985; this approach amounts to side-stepping the question of identifying *inter-coordination* bugs for any programming problems outside of the system's current repertoire). Or, (c) only reason about about a restricted number of interactions by constraining the programming language that the programmer is allowed to work with (for example, this is the approach taken in PDS6 (Shapiro, 1983): PDS6 remembers its modifications but only works on functional programming languages containing nonside-effecting procedures); this approach seems to be the most fruitful of the three, but we believe that the programming languages used so far to this end have been *too* constraining and therefore techniques for detecting usual *inter-coordination* bugs made by novices in less constrained languages (e.g., standard PASCAL) have not been discovered.

In the following sections we explain how the *overlooking* method of bug identification addresses the above described four weaknesses of mal-rule debuggers: (a) All bugs are equal, (b) mal-rules are idiosyncratic, (c) derivative bugs cannot be represented, and (d) program parts are assumed to be independent. We first present our representation for programming knowledge and then solutions to these four weaknesses are woven around our main points of discussion: how to identify *detail* and *coordination* errors.

## REPRESENTING PROGRAMMING PLANS

### PANGLE

In our debugger, CHIRON, programming plans are written using a frame-like notation that we call PANGLE (for Plan ANd Goal LanguagE). In this chapter we will use a syntax that looks like this:

```
mammal = {
    name = ?Name
    blood_temperature = ?Temp: warm
    skin_color = ?Color
    number_of_appendages = ?NumOfAppendages: greater_than_two
}
```

The above denotes the type *mammal*. A mammal structure has four slots: name, blood_temperature, skin_color, and number_of_appendages. The question-marked variables shown in the slots represent the contents of the slot; this allows us to mention the contents of one slot in any of the other slots. (The question marked variables can be left out if we don't need to mention the slot contents elsewhere.) The contents of a slot can be restricted using constraints that follow the question-marked variables (or are alone if no question-marked variable appears). For example, the contents of the blood_temperature slot, ?Temp, is constrained to be warm. To create a subtype we simply apply more restricting constraints to the contents of the slots. To name the subtype we also include an is-a statement. For example, we might want to say

```
elephant ⇐ mammal          ;;; An elephant is a mammal.
elephant = {
    name = african_name
    skin_color = gray
    number_of_appendages = ?LegsAndTrunk: equal_to_five
}
```

Notice that we have left out the blood_temperature slot in the elephant structure; this is a shorthand way of specifying that elephant structures inherit the blood_temperature slot and constraints from mammal. One more thing to notice is that the constraints on the slot contents are themselves typed and that it is illegal to create a subtype with a slot that contains an incompatible or more general constraint on a slot. So, for example, it would be illegal to define the subtype, Clyde the blue elephant,

$$elephant(name = clyde \ skin\_color = blue)$$

because the color blue is not a sub-type of gray. (Clyde is probably not an African name either.) Consequently, our inheritance is inheritance without exceptions (Touretzky, 1984).

## Template, Flow, and I/O Aspects of Programming Plans

PANGLE is primarily just the syntax of our programming plan language. Here we describe the contents of programming plans. Figure 10.3 contains a paraphrased definition of an average plan. All of the programming plans in our debugger's knowledge base have three *aspects*: (a) template, (b) flow, and (c) i/o. An *aspect* of a plan is a piece of a plan formulated in a special purpose vocabulary.

In our plan language the *template aspect* is described with syntactic structure and position descriptors: this vocabulary allows the syntactic form of the plan to be specified. The *flow aspect* is specified with a vocabulary of data and control flow terms. (The current knowledge base of our debugger, CHIRON, contains a set of rules that, given the abstract syntax tree of a Pascal program, can make assertions about data and control flow relations between different parts of the program. This is done using standard flow analysis techniques (Aho, Sethi, & Ullman, 1986).) The *i/o aspect* is essentially a description of the symbolic values that can can be used and produced by a plan and other parts of the program that use the objects produced by a plan. (Our debugger also has a set of rules that allows it to symbolically execute Pascal programs).[3] This representation for programming plans is very similar to the representation used in the Programmer's Apprentice Project (e.g., see Rich, 1981).

Plans are divided into aspects in many sophisticated AI planners (e.g., the steps and preconditions of HACKER's plans [Sussman, 1975]). Aspects do *not* define multiple isomorphic representations of the plan. Rather aspects help the debugger create *slices* (Sussman & Steele, 1980) or *views* (Bobrow & Winograd,

---

[3]CHIRON's powers of symbolic execution are currently limited to reasoning about explicitly stated guards in the code (e.g., a sequence of nested IF statements) and explicitly stated type declarations (e.g., VAR Count: INTEGER;). In order to show equivalence between boolean expressions in the guards, CHIRON uses a skeletal theorem prover that does not use any inferred type knowledge about the variables in the expressions. CHIRON does use type knowledge in its analysis of the student program, it just doesn't use type knowledge when comparing boolean expressions.

1977) of a program so that the program can be "seen" by the debugger from a variety of perspectives: "The way that slices do their job is *by providing redundant paths* for information to travel in the process of analysis," (Stallman & Sussman, 1979). Loosely, the template aspect allows our debugger to identify *details* of a plan, the flow aspect is used to identify *intra-coordination* information, and the i/o aspect allows it to reason about *inter-coordination* information.

One of the main advantages in defining a debugger's library of programming knowledge with plans that have several aspects, is that it frees the debugger from having to reason about derivative properties of a program; for example, reasoning about data flow using only knowledge about the syntactic structure of a program. Giving the debugger the power to parse a program into more than one vocabulary allows the debugger multiple views (i.e., *slices*) of the program; certain things that are hidden in one view are visible in others. Defining plans with multiple aspects is our answer to avoiding the mal-rule debuggers' impotence to represent derivative bugs. Plans with multiple aspects can be used to find bugs associated with the various aspects' views.

## FINDING DETAIL BUGS

Consider the problem a debugger faces in trying to identify the template for a count_plan in the program shown in Figure 10.2. The template pieces for the count_plan are shown in Figure 10.3. On searching the program in Figure 10.2 for the count_plan-template-update pattern, the debugger would come up empty handed. To find viable buggy candidates using the mal-rule method, the debugger would have to search the buggy productions, find the production

> *count_plan-template-update* → *Count := Count − 1*

and then try matching again using the buggy rule found. Instead we propose that such idiosyncratic mal-rules can be done away with by having the debugger automatically generate plausible alternative patterns.

The basic idea behind automatic generation of alternative patterns is to take the correct pattern apart, find a piece that can be generalized using the is-a hierarchies defined in the debugger's data base of *correct* programming knowledge, and replace the piece with its generalization. This kind of process is normally called *instance-to-class generalization* in machine learning (Michalski, 1986). In effect, this is one operation that many learning and inductive inference (Angluin & Smith, 1983) algorithms perform on a current hypothesis if the current hypothesis is not in concordance with a new piece of data.

In the count_plan-template-update case, + would be replaced with the pattern <arithmetic_operator>, the debugger would search the code again and find two candidates in the program shown in Figure 10.2: the two Count := Count − 1

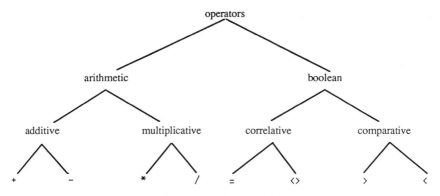

**Figure 10.4.   A hierarchy of operators**

statements. If the resulting generalized pattern had also failed, the debugger could recursively apply *instance-to-class generalization* (see Figure 10.4). By keeping track of the generalizations made to the original pattern, the debugger formulates a description of the bug. In this case the description is that: *The count_plan-template-update uses an <arithmetic_operator> that is not the expected <+> operator.*

The process of instance-to-class generalization can be used to find bugs that are more interesting than + for −. For example, Figure 10.1 contains a prompt-after-read-bug (this bug was explained in the section in which detail and coordination errors were described: the section immediately following the Introduction). An input plan's template contains two pieces: a ?Prompt and an ?Input (which in Pascal will usually just be a READLN statement). Also the template will specify positional constraints, i.e., immediately_precedes(?Prompt ?Input). The positional constraints on the pieces of the input_plan can be generalized using the following is-a definitions:

;;; precedes is a generalization of immediately_precedes
immediately_precedes ⇐ precedes
;;; precedes is a specialization of some_kind_of_ordering
precedes ⇐ some_kind_of_ordering

To identify the prompt-after-read-bug in Figure 10.1, using instance-to-class generalization, the immediately_precedes(?Prompt ?Input) term would be generalized into a some_kind_of_ordering(?Prompt ?Input), the debugger could then find the ?Prompt and ?Input in the program, and the debugger could report: *The program does not prompt_for_input before read_the_input.*

*Detail* errors can be found using *instance-to-class generalization*. Instance-to-class generalization addresses the need fulfilled by idiosyncratic mal productions in mal-rule debuggers. Intuitively, instance-to-class generalization allows the debugger to figure out what the pieces and arrangement of a programming plan might look like without all of the details that the programmer has more than likely messed up or forgotten. Instance-to-class generalization is one way of *overlooking* errors.

## FINDING COORDINATION ERRORS

**Plan Aspects are Part-to-Whole Generalizations of Programming Plans**

*Coordination* errors can be found with the power of instance-to-class generalization and a second type of generalization: *part-to-whole generalizations* (Michalski, 1986). In the last section on the identification of *detail* errors we concentrated exclusively on the template aspects of the count and input plans. Our discussion implicitly illustrated the idea of *overlooking* the problems associated with identifying the other aspects of programming plans: All but one aspect of a programming plan are ignored in order to search for bugs associated with the chosen aspect; once the bugs in one aspect have been identified each of the other aspects of a plan are chosen in turn. Abstracting away all but one aspect of a plan is an example of *part-to-whole generalization*.

Our debugger, CHIRON, is designed to accept a problem specification (a list of abstract plans that must be present in concrete form in a student's program solution) and a student program. First it will try to find the template aspects of the plans mentioned in the problem specification. We say that it *overlooks* the other aspects until it has matched the templates or some *instance-to-class generalizations* of the templates. The debugger corrects any *detail* errors and then it will attempt to identify the flow aspects of the plans from the problem specification. Similarly it overlooks the template and i/o aspects (and any bugs associated with those aspects) as it looks for the flow aspect. And so forth for the i/o aspect of the plans in the problem specification.

Intuitively there are two good reasons for dividing a debugger's work up into an aspect-by-aspect identification process:

1. *Smaller search spaces*: The more aspects programming plans can be divided into the better, because then, at any given point in the analysis, the debugger only has to reason with a very constrained *view* of the buggy program. All of the other *views*, or *slices*, of the program can be overlooked.

2. *Local bugs can be found first*: *Detail* bugs are usually more localized to specific sections of code, more so than *intra-coordination* bugs. Likewise *intra-coordination* bugs usually involve more localized pieces of a program than *inter-coordination* bugs. Dividing the program analysis task according

to the three aspects of our programming plans allows our debugger to correct the most local bugs first.[4]

## Search for Confusable Plans at the Same Time

It is difficult to separate the search for *intra-coordination* errors from the search for *inter-coordination* errors. Plans that look a lot alike (e.g., a sum _plan and a count _plan) can easily be confused with one another especially if there are bugs in the plans. Consider again the bug in which the programmer has used the variable Sum in the left-hand side of the count _plan-template-update rather than the variable Count. The debugger might easily "repair" a piece of the count _plan assuming that it is a piece of the sum _plan.

The *overlooking* method of bug detection requires that bugs found in one aspect of a plan be corrected before the analysis proceeds to the next aspect. This is better than the *mal-rule* method in which a bug usually needs to be corrected immediately after it is found. But, the *overlooking* method is still prone to error. "Repairs" made to correct one aspect of a plan might damage another aspect of the plan or might damage another plan. To solve the general problem of avoiding destructive repairs the debugger must keep track of what it has modified and why. Implementing such a record keeping capability requires the use of reason maintenance type machinery (Doyle, 1977).[5] In this chapter we will not discuss how CHIRON keeps track of its corrections; that is the subject of another paper (Sack, 1989).

However, the *overlooking* method of error identification does incorporate one method that can help a debugger to avoid destructive repairs. The abstract plans of a problem specification are partitioned into groups that "look alike" (i.e., plans included in a partition are all those plans that can be *instance-to-class generalized* into the same object type). We call this partitioning process *plan factoring*.[6] Once the plans of the spec have been factored in this manner,

---

[4]The strategy of correcting local bugs first was used by Goldstein (1975) in his debugger MYCROFT.

[5]Shrobe (1979) has a good discussion of many of the relevant issues even though he is concerned with maintenance and enhancement rather than correction of programs.

[6]Burns and Kitchen (1987) factor their database of 3D geometrical objects into a single combined is-a and part-of hierarchy so that the work of matching similar objects can be efficiently shared: shared parts and general properties of objects are looked for only once. Letovsky (1987) factors his program understander's knowledge base of programming plans into is-a hierarchies so that when the understander matches a piece of code that is shared by many plans it need not immediately decide which plan the code belongs to; instead his program understander can postulate a general plan and, later after the understander has gathered more information, can specialize the general, vague plan into a more specific plan (via a process Letovsky calls *abductive specialization*). Although, with respect to our debugger, we are concerned with both efficient plan recognition and the process of abductive specialization, our primary concern in factoring the debugger's database of programming knowledge using is-a and part-of hierarchies is to gather plan *confusability* information to help prevent destructive repairs.

CHIRON will be able to look for similar plans at the same time. For example, the sum and the count plans of the Averaging Problem specification would be abstracted into an accumulator[7] plan. The student's program would first be searched for all instances of accumulators; those found would then be further scrutinized to see if they were sums or counters.

*Plan factoring* is *not* a general solution to the problem of separating the *intra-coordination* analysis process from the *inter-coordination* analysis. However, plan factoring can provide the debugger with information about groups of plans mentioned in the problem specification that might be confusable with one another in a programmer's code. This information can be used by the debugger to help it make its decisions about what code to correct and at what point in the analysis code should be corrected.

## IMPLEMENTATION CONCERNS

In the above we have tried to argue that automatic program debuggers can accomplish the task of bug identification without bug catalogues (as the *mal rule* debuggers do) and without an arbitrary large number of idiosyncratic weighting functions to perform heuristic best-first matching to a canonical correct solution (as do TALUS, Murray, 1986; and APROPOS2, Looi, 1988). Instead, the techniques of the *overlooking* method can be employed to identify buggy parts of a student's program. In the above we have discussed the pragmatic, bug identification advantages, of using the techniques of the *overlooking* method (e.g., no need for predefined, idiosyncratic bug rules); these advantages will be restated again in the *Conclusion*. In this section we will discuss the more mundane issues of what it takes to actually incorporate the techniques of the *overlooking* method into a bug identifier. We are currently attempting our second implementation of the *overlooking* method. Our first attempt was flawed in several ways that will be discussed below.

### General Knowledge Base and Control Structure Requirements

From an implementation point of view, the *overlooking* method can best be understood as two requirements that prescribe how a knowledge base of programming plans should be written and two requirements that that prescribe how the student program should be searched for bugs:

---

[7]An *accumulator* is any process that accepts a sequence of values, combines the values in some way, and then returns a result (see Abelson & Sussman, 1985). Sum_plans and count_plans can both be viewed as specializations of the general type accumulator.

## Knowledge Base Requirements

*KB Requirement 1: Simple representation language.* The knowledge base of programming plans is written in a language whose algebraic structure makes *instance-to-class* and *part-to-whole generalization* computable for any given term written in the language (the machinery necessary to compute generalizations are called *derefinement operators* in the inductive inference literature [e.g., Laird, 1987].) Because PANGLE is a representation language that uses only inheritance *without* exceptions, theoretically it should be possible to map PANGLE terms into first-order logic (Touretzky, 1984). This possibility is worth considering, not because we have or will attempt such a proof, but because it is necessary to convince oneself that one is using a representation language simple enough that

1.  useful derefinement operators can be constructed for it that will be applicable to all the terms in the knowledge base (and to intermediate terms generated by the derefinement operators themselves); and, so that,
2.  plan factoring can be performed by instance-to-class generalizing similar terms into single terms.

*KB Requirement 2: Plans are divided into aspects.* Programming plans are divided into numerous aspects (e.g., template, flow, and i/o) so that

1.  The knowledge engineer can change vocabularies to express different properties of a plan; and,
2.  An automatic bug identifier can take advantage of the multiple aspects of plans by using the plans' divisions into aspects to divide the search space (i.e., the student's program can be searched for the template aspect before the flow aspect of the plans is considered).

## Control Structure Requirements

*CS Requirement 1: Search for similar plans at the same time.* If two or more pieces of a problem specification can be *plan factored* together, then a least common generalization of them should be built and searched for only once in the student program (e.g., if the problem specification includes a count_plan and a sum_plan, then the student program should be search for all existing accumulators only once). This has two advantages:

1.  It increases efficiency of the search through the students' code
2.  A bug identifier can use precomputed plan factoring results to insure that it

doesn't accidently damage a plan by "repairing" a similar looking second plan (this advantage is not discussed in this chapter, but rather in another, forthcoming paper, [Sack 1989]).

*CS Requirement 2: Search for the least complicated plan aspects first.* Specifically, in CHIRON this means that the template aspect is searched for before the flow, and the flow before the i/o. This is a good thing to do because cheap operations (e.g., the straightforward pattern matching used to identify template properties) can be used to narrow down the search space before expensive operations are used. For example, if a count_plan-update has already been identified by the template analysis, the data flow analysis need only query to see if the found update has the correct data flow connection to other parts of the program (e.g., the count_plan-initialization); it does not need to query to see which, of all possible pieces of the student program, have the necessary count_plan, data flow connections. In other words, CHIRON uses the template aspects of plans as the *beacons* (Brooks, 1983) or *focal segments* (Rist, 1986) to direct its search through the students' programs. A plan's template aspect should specify the plan's most characteristic, syntactic features so that the pieces of the student program that make up the plan can be discovered using cheap matching operations.

## Algorithms That Incorporate the Overlooking Method Can Be Machine Learning Algorithms

The techniques of the *overlooking* method do not specify an algorithm for identifying buggy parts of a student program. Instead, as we have stated above, the *overlooking* method can be viewed as 4 (2KB + 2CS) prescriptions to be followed when building an automatic program debugger. One way to understand the utility of these prescriptions (from an implementation point of view) is if the bug identification problem is rephrased as an inductive inference identification *problem* (Gold, 1967):[8]

• The initial hypothesis of a description of a given student program is the problem specification (written in PANGLE).

• Each piece of the problem specification is checked against the student program; failures and successes are recorded.

• If a piece of the problem specification failed to match against the student program, then that piece of the problem specification serves as a contradiction to

[8]Simply put, the problem solved by *inductive inference* systems built to solve the *identification problem* is this: given a sequence of examples, derive a general procedure that is capable of identifying all objects from the class of objects that the examples were taken from.

the current hypothesis and the problem specification (current hypothesis) is revised by generalizing (e.g., using *instance-to-class* or *part-to-whole generalization*) a piece of the current hypothesis.

• After all failed pieces of the problem specification have been processed (and the necessary generalizations made for each failure), the generalized specification derived by this process is output. It represents what is correct about the student program. The difference between it and the problem specification (i.e., a series of specific generalization operations) specifies what is not correct about the student program.

We can now see that the knowledge base and control structure prescriptions given above insure that a generalized problem specification can probably be found (because the representation language is simple), and insure that a generalized problem specification is searched for in a manner that is more efficient than simply a generate-and-test algorithm that enumerates all possible generalizations of the problem specification and then tests them against the student program. The algebraic structure of the knowledge representation language, similarities between parts of a problem specification, and the costs of performing different checks against the student program are all used to advantage in the prescriptions given above. It is a bit of a distortion to view the bug identification problem as an inductive inference identification problem (simply because there is only one example: the particular student program currently being examined). Nevertheless, we have found that some of the research concerns of those involved in machine learning seem to be relevant to our efforts in designing an algorithm to incorporate the techniques of the *overlooking* method (e.g., the design of derefinement operators).

## The Difference Between Overlooking and E. Shapiro's Methods

We hasten to add the *overlooking* method is different from other work on automatic program debugging that has been done using inductive inference methods (specifically the work of Shapiro [1983]). Shapiro's (1983) system, PDS6, is designed to find three types of errors: termination with incorrect output, termination with a missing output, and nontermination (as opposed to the *detail* and *coordination* errors that CHIRON is being designed to find). It would be interesting to know if the three types of errors that PDS6 is designed to diagnose are high frequency errors common for either novice or expert programmers. We do not know of any empirical studies that would support this conjecture.

Also, PDS6 uses a programming problem representation language that only allows the user one vocabulary (input/output pairs, as opposed to the three vocabularies used in CHIRON: template, flow and i/o). Most of the benefits of the *overlooking* method are directly or indirectly dependent on having a multiple-aspect representation language. We don't think input/output pairs are a very practical language for describing programming knowledge simply because explicit knowledge of program syntax and data and control flow and seems indispensable to human programmers who are attempting to understand programs (e.g., Littman, Pinto, Letovsky, & Soloway, 1986), and because the hierarchical structure of well designed programs cannot be described using input/output pairs.

Finally, Shapiro applied his inductive inference algorithms in an effort to change the program under examination and *not* the problem specification (i.e., the input/output pairs given as a specification). On the other hand, we are suggesting the use of machine learning techniques to modify the problem specification and *not* the student program under examination: we want the output of CHIRON's bug identification module to be a specification (written in PANGLE) that describes what the student's program does correctly plus the sequence of generalization operations that were applied to mutate the original, desired, correct problem specification (we describe in the upcoming *Overlooking's Relevance to the Automatic Construction of Student Models* section why this is a good type of output for CHIRON's bug identification module to construct).

Nevertheless, we feel that E. Shapiro's system is notable for the fact that it defines a mechanism that can identify classes of bugs rather than specific instances of bugs and his more theoretical results (e.g., E. Shapiro, 1981; Banerji, 1987) are invaluable contributions that shed light on the foundations of all inductive inference systems (Banerji, 1987).

## Experience with Implementing the Overlooking Method
## The Derefinement Operator

We are currently implementing a version of the *overlooking* method that uses the following derefinement operator to generalize parts of the problem specification that cannot be matched to a student program. The operator is defined by three cases of generalization:

1. *Instance-to-Class_for_Variables*: Given a PANGLE term, make two instances of a variable unique.

Example: times(arg1 = ?X, arg2 = ?X) becomes times(arg1 = ?X1, arg2 = ?X2)

2. *Instance-to-Class_for_Terms*: Replace the root of a PANGLE term with the type that has been predefined as the root's generalization.

Example: times(arg1 = number, arg2 = number) becomes arithmetic_operator(arg1 = number, arg2 = number).

Comment: This operator also allows constants to be replaced with patterns because constants are treated as PANGLE terms with zero arguments; for example, 99999 written as a PANGLE term would be 99999() and could be generalized to number; also, number should properly be written as number(). Further, by default all terms that do not have a predefined generalization are generalized to the most general term (called TOP) that can be matched to anything (i.e., all the type hierarchies are arranged into one large lattice); for example, operator(arg1 = ?X1, arg2 = ?X2) generalizes to TOP().

3. *Part-to-Whole_for_Plans*: In addition, our implementation will implicitly include one more type of generalization: *Part-to-Whole_for_Plans* (plans are simply compound PANGLE terms). This type of generalization is implicitly included because the bug identifier searches for each aspect of a plan (template, flow, and i/o) independently of the other aspects.

Example: count_plan(template = ?T, flow = ?F, i/o = ?I/O) is first analyzed as count_plan(template = ?T), then as count_plan(flow = ?F) and finally as count_plan(i/o = ?I/O).

Note that the first two cases (instance-to-class_for_variables and instance-to-class_for_terms) work together to serve as a fourth type of generalization, another type of *part-to-whole generalization*, because they can be combined to essentially drop a slot out of a PANGLE term: If the variables of a particular slot are renamed to unique names (so that they aren't mentioned in any other slots) and then, if the constraints on the slot are eventually replaced by TOP(), the slot can match anything, and, therefore is trivially matched.

Our first implementation did not use an instance-to-class_for_variables generalizer. Consequently, its derefinement operator was incomplete; for example, it wasn't able to identify misspelled variable names.

## Control Structure

A match failure causes the creation of a generalization of the failed term or a related term. It is possible that more than one of the generalization cases (defined in the derefinement operator given above) is applicable after some given failure. Consequently, we want our implementation to split the analysis at that point and pursue all possible generalization possibilities. The final output will be, therefore, a list of possible generalizations of the original problem specification and not simply one possible generalization.

When a failure occurs, the problem might be with the particular term that failed to match, or the problem might be with a term, that has already been successfully matched, that bound one or more of the variables mentioned in the current term.[9] The algorithm to implement the *overlooking* method must investigate all possibilities (i.e., that the failed term should be generalized, or that other, previously matched, terms that use the same variables should be generalized, or all terms involved should be generalized).

---

[9] This is a problem not unlike the one faced by programmers using a logic programming language in which the declarative reading of the program can be correct, but the program might not work due to the ordering of the conjuncts.

Our first implementation of the overlooking method did not investigate all of the possibilities: Only the current, failed term was generalized. However, because everything can eventually be generalized to TOP, the worst thing that could happen with our first implementation was that it eventually came up with a description that was not the minimal possible generalization of the correct problem specification.

Note that both our first implementation, and our intended second implementation, are incomplete. That is, since instances of plans are searched for by independently searching for each of the aspects, there is no possible way to blame a match failure in the Nth aspect on variables bound by a match in the N-i aspect. This means that bug identifiers using the *overlooking* method cannot consider all possible generalizations of the original problem specification.

## Plan Factoring

Our first implementation did not do any plan factoring. In our second implementation we intend to *plan factor* using a fairly simple operation:

- if the roots of two terms are equal or have a common ancestor in the generalization hierarchy, then group the two terms together.

The most general pattern of each group is then fetched from the student program, the successful matches cached, and the cache used by each of the terms in the group when they are to be matched against the student program. This information is also used in the bug correction part of CHIRON (Sack, 1989).

## OVERLOOKING'S RELEVANCE TO THE AUTOMATIC CONSTRUCTION OF STUDENT MODELS

An *overlay* model of a student skills, as defined by Goldstein and Carr (1977) (and used in a number of intelligent tutoring systems—e.g., Clancey, 1982)—represents a given student's skills as a particular subset of a canonical set of expert skills. In CHIRON, expertise is represented as a list of PANGLE terms (i.e., a programming problem specification). A student's program is modeled, as was discussed above, as a generalization of the correct problem specification. Since the generalization operations employed by CHIRON (e.g., *instance-to-class* and *part-to-whole*) involve either dropping constraints on a slot of a PANGLE term, dropping a slot, or dropping a term, CHIRON's model of the student program is essentially an *overlay* model of the correct specification: It is a subset of the constraints specified in the correct problem specification.

However, the use of generalization operators is a very particular way of generating a subset of the expert model. The use of generalization operators takes advantage of the fact that the expert model is written using a set of hierarchically defined concepts (e.g., a count_plan is a type of accumulator). Goldstein (1982) has called student models that employ, among other things, generalization/specialization relations *genetic graph* models. Consequently, it would be more precise to say that CHIRON's output is a special kind of overlay model that is a genetic graph model defined using the correct problem specification and the application of of a series of generalizations.

We hope that the *overlooking* method will have applications within the field of intelligent tutoring systems beyond just the diagnosis of programming errors. It is encouraging to know that the form of the output of an *overlooking* debugger already has a name in the ITS literature (genetic graph); and, that some of the concerns discussed in this chapter are shared by other researchers in the field (e.g., the use of generalization hierarchies in diagnosis, Greer & McCalla, 1988).

## CONCLUSIONS

In this chapter we have pointed out four weaknesses present in most existing automatic program debugging systems. We have outlined a new method for identifying three kinds of high frequency programming errors: *detail* errors, *intra-coordination* errors, and *inter-coordination* errors. We call our bug identification method the *overlooking* method. We are currently implementing a program debugger, CHIRON, that employs the *overlooking* method of debugging and that we hope will not suffer from the same weaknesses most existing debuggers have:

*(Weakness 1) All bugs are equal.*

Solution: The *overlooking* method is geared toward the identification of high frequency programming errors: *detail* and *coordination* bugs.

*(Weakness 2) Mal-rules are idiosyncratic.*

Solution: Instance-to-class generalization and part-to-whole generalization allow the debugger to automatically generate many similar, but slightly different patterns.

*(Weakness 3) Derivative bugs cannot be represented.*

Solution: The *overlooking* method of bug identification supports multiple vocabularies. Many different *slices* or *views* of a program can be constructed using rules that support special purpose vocabularies and plans that have multiple *aspects*. This allows the debugger to avoid having to reason about derivative properties of a program; instead the debugger can simply change vocabularies. CHIRON's knowledge base currently has vocabularies that will allow it to reason about template(*detail*), flow(*intra-coordination*) and i/o(*inter-coordination*) aspects of Pascal programs.

*(Weakness 4) Program parts are assumed to be independent.*
Solutions: Bugs associated with any one aspect (e.g., template) aren't corrected until all of the templates of the plans in a problem specification have been identified in the program being analyzed. Consequently, an *overlooking* debugger can "glance" through a program before it makes corrections. The first aspect of all of the plans in the problem specification are matched before the matching of the second aspect of any of the plans is begun. Also, the *overlooking* method of bug identification looks for similar looking plans at the same time by *plan factoring* the programming problem specification before the analysis of a program begins.

We also discussed some of the issues involved in implementing the *overlooking* method. We pointed out that an algorithm that incorporates the prescriptions of the *overlooking* method could be a machine learning algorithm. Specifically we drew an analogy between bug identification as it is handled by the *overlooking* method, and the *identification problem* as it is handled by *inductive inference* systems. From an implementation point of view, the *overlooking* method can best be understood as two requirements that prescribe how a knowledge base of programming plans should be written and two requirements about control structure that prescribe how the student program should be searched for bugs:

• *KB Requirement 1: Simple representation language*: The knowledge base of programming plans should be written in a language whose algebraic structure makes *instance-to-class* and *part-to-whole generalization* easy to compute for any given term written in the language.

• *KB Requirement 2: Plans are divided into aspects*: Programming plans are divided into numerous aspects (eg., template, flow, and i/o).

• *CS Requirement 1: Search for similar plans at the same time*: If two or more pieces of a problem specification can be *plan factored* together, then they should be searched for at the same time.

• *CS Requirement 2: Search for the least complicated plan aspects first*: Specifically, in CHIRON this means that the template aspect is searched for before the flow, and the flow before the i/o.

We also mentioned, in the final section of this chapter, what relevance the *overlooking* method has to the larger issue of student modeling. The output of an *overlooking* debugger can be shown to be a *genetic graph* (Goldstein, 1982).

## REFERENCES

Abelson, H., & Sussman, G., with Sussman, J. (1985). *Structure and interpretation of computer programs.* Cambridge, MA: MIT Press.

Adam, A., & Laurent, J-P. (1980). LAURA, A System to ebug Student Programs. *Artificial Intelligence, 15,* 75–122.

Adelson, B., & Soloway, E. (1985). The role of domain experience in software design. *IEEE Transactions on Software Engineering, SE-11*(11), 1351–1360.

Aho, A., Sethi, R., & Ullman, J. (1986). *Compilers: Principles, techniques, and tools.* Reading, MA: Addison-Wesley.

Anderson, J.R., Boyle, C.F., & Yost, G. (1985). *Acquisition and Automated Instruction of Geometry Proof Skills.* Paper presented at the IICAI Proceedings.

Angluin, D., & Smith, C. (1983). Inductive inference: Theory and methods. *Computing Surveys, 15*(3), 237–269.

Banerji, R. (1987). A discussion of a report by Ehud Shapiro. *Computational Intelligence, 3,* 295–303.

Bobrow, D., & Winograd, T. (1977). An Overview of KRL, a Knowledge Representation Language. *Cognitive Science 1*(1), 3–46.

Brooks, R. (1983). Towards a general theory of the comprehension of computer programs, *International Journal of Man-Machine Studies, 18,* 543–554.

Brown, J.S., & Burton, R. (1978). Diagnostic models for procedural bugs in basic mathematical skills. *Cognitive Science, 2,* 155–192.

Brown, J.S., & VanLehn, D. (1980). Repair theory: A generative theory of bugs in procedural skills. *Cognitive Science, 4,* 379–426.

Burns, J.B., & Kitchen, L. (1987). Rapid recognition out of a large model base using prediction hierarchies and machine parallelism. *6th SPIE Conference on Intelligent Robots and Computer Vision.*

Burton, R. (1982). Diagnosing bugs in a simple procedural skills. In D. Sleeman & J.S. Brown (Eds.), *Intelligent tutoring systems* (pp. 157–183). New York: Academic Press.

Clancey, W.J. (1982). Tutoring rules for guiding a case method dialogue. In D. Sleeman & J.S. Brown (Eds.), *Intelligent Tutoring Systems* (pp. 201–225). New York: Academic Press.

Dahl, O.-J., Dijkstra, E., & Hoare, C.A.R. (1972). *Structured programming.* New York: Academic Press.

Doyle, J. (1977). *Truth maintenance systems for problem solving* (Tech. Report No. 419). Massachusetts Institute of Technology, Artificial Intelligence Laboratory.

Gold, E.M. (1967). Language identification in the limit. *Information and Control, 10,* 447–474.

Goldstein, I. (1975). Summary of MYCROFT: A system for understanding simple picture programs. *Artificial Intelligence, 6,* 249–288.

Goldstein, I., & Carr, B. (1977, October). The computer as coach: An athletic paradigm for intellectual education. *Proceedings of the 1977 Annual Conference* (pp. 227–233). Association for Computing Machinery, Seattle, WA.

Greer, J., & McCalla, G. (1988). *Exploiting granularity for strategy recognition* (Unpublished Working Paper). Saskatoon, Canada: University of Saskatchewan, Department of Computational Science, ARIES Laboratory.

Johnson, W.L. (1986). *Intention-based diagnosis of novice programming errors, research notes in artificial intelligence.* Los Altos, CA: Morgan Kaufmann.

Johnson, W.L., Soloway, E., Cutler, B., & Draper, S. (1983). *Bug Catalogue I* (Technical Report No. 286). New Haven, CT: Computer Science Department, Yale University.

Laird, P. (1987). *Learning from good data and bad* (Technical Report No. 551). New Haven, CT: Department of Computer Science, Yale University.

Letovsky, S. (1987). How abstraction can reduce ambiguity in explanation problems.

*Proceedings of the First International Conference on Expert Database Systems*, pp. 413–421. Menlo Park, CA: The Benjamin/Cummings Pub. Co., Inc.

Littman, D., Pinto, J., Letovsky, S., & Soloway, E. (1986). Mental models and software maintenance. In E. Soloway & S. Iyengar (Eds.), *Empirical studies of programmers* (pp. 80–98). Norwood, NJ: Ablex.

Littman, D., & Soloway, E. (1986, October). Toward an empirically-based process model for a machine programming tutor. *IEEE International Conference on Systems, Man, and Cybernetics*. Atlanta, GA.

Looi, C.-K. (1988). APROPOS2: A program analyzer for a PROLOG intelligent teaching system. In C. Frasson (Ed.), *Proceedings of the 1988 International Conference of Intelligent Tutoring Systems* (pp. 379–386). Montreal, Canada.

Michalski, R. (1986). Understanding the nature of learning: Issues and research directions. In R. Michalski, J. Carbonell, & F. Mitchell (Eds.), *Machine learning: An artificial intelligence approach, Volume 2*. Los Altos, CA: Morgan Kaufmann.

Miller, M. (1982). A structured planning and debugging environment for elementary programming. In D. Sleeman & J.S. Brown (Eds.), *Intelligent tutoring systems*. New York: Academic Press.

Murray, W.R. (1986). *Automatic program debugging for intelligent tutoring systems* (Tech. Report No. 86–27). Austin, TX: Artificial Intelligence Laboratory, University of Texas at Austin.

Murray, W.R. (1987). Automatic program debugging for intelligent tutoring systems. *Computational Intelligence, 3*, 1–16.

Reiser, B., Anderson, J.R., & Farrell, R. (1985). Dynamic student modeling in an intelligent tutor for Lisp programming. *IJCAI Proceedings*, pp. 8–14.

Rich, C. (1981). A formal representation for plans in the programmer's apprentice. *IJCAI Proceedings*, pp. 1044–1052.

Rist, R. (1986). Plans in programming: Definition, demonstration, and development. In E. Soloway & S. Iyengar (Eds.), *Empirical Studies of Programmers* (pp. 28–47). Norwood, NJ: Ablex.

Ruth, G. (1976). Intelligent program analysis. *Artificial Intelligence, 7*, 65–85.

Sack, W. (1989). *Fixing bugs by remembering them: Knowledge based program correction*, in preparation.

Sack, W., & Soloway, E. (1989). From PROUST to CHIRON: Its design as iterative engineering; Intermediate results are important! In J. Larkin, R.W. Chabay, & C. Scheftic (Eds.), *Computer assisted instruction and intelligent tutoring systems: Shared issues and complementary approaches*. Hillsdale, NJ: Lawrence Erlbaum.

Shapiro, D. (1981). *SNIFFER: A system that understands bugs* (Tech. Memo No. 638). Cambridge, MA: Artificial Intelligence Laboratory, MIT.

Shapiro, E. (1981). *Inductive inference of theories from facts* (Tech. Report No. 192). New Haven, CT: Department of Computer Science, Yale University.

Shapiro, E. (1983). *Algorithmic program debugging*. Cambridge, MA: MIT Press.

Shrobe, H. (1979). *Dependency directed reasoning for complex program understanding*. (Tech. Report No. 503). Cambridge, MA: Artificial Intelligence Laboratory, MIT.

Sleeman, D. (1979). Some current topics in intelligent teaching systems. *AISB Quarterly, 33*, 22–27.

Sleeman, D. (1984). An attempt to understand students' understanding of basic algebra. *Cognitive Science, 8*, 387–412.

Soloway, E., & Ehrlich, K. (1984). Empirical studies of programming knowledge. *IEEE Transactions on Software Engineering, SE-10*(5), 595–609.

Soloway, E., Letovsky, S., Loerinc, B., & Zygielbaum, A. (1984). The cognitive connection: Software maintenance and documentation. In *Proceedings of the 9th Annual NASA/Goddard Workshop on Software Engineering.* NASA/Goddard, Atlanta, GA.

Soloway, E., Rubin, E., Woolf, B., Bonar, J., & Johnson, W.L. (1983). MENOII: An AI-Based programming tutor. *Journal of Computer-Based Instruction, 10*(1&2), 20–34.

Spohrer, J. (1989). *MARCEL: A generate test and debug impasse/repair model of student programmers* (Tech. Report No. 687). New Haven, CT: Computer Science Department, Yale University.

Spohrer, J., Pope, E., Lipman, M., Sack, W., Freiman, S., Littman, D., Johnson, W.L., & Soloway, E. (1985). *Bug Catalogue II, III, IV* (Tech. Report No. 386). New Haven, CT: Computer Science Department, Yale University.

Spohrer, J., & Soloway, E. (1986). Novice mistakes: Are the folk wisdoms correct? *Communications of the ACM, 29*(7),624–632.

Stallman, R., & Sussman, G. (1979). Problem solving about electrical circuits. In Winston & Brown (Eds.), *Artificial intelligence: An MIT perspective, Volume 1.* Cambridge, MA: MIT Press.

Sussman, G., & Steele, G.L., Jr. (1980). CONSTRAINTS—A language for expressing almost-hierarchical descriptions. *AI Journal, 14,* 1–39.

Sussman, G. (1975). *A computer model of skill acquisition.* North Holland, Amsterdam: Elsevier.

Touretzky, D. (1984). *The mathematics of inheritance systems* (Tech. Report No. CMU-CS-84-136). Pittsburgh, PA: Computer Science Department, Carnegie-Mellon University.

Waters, R. (1978). *Automatic analysis of the logical structure of programs* (Tech. Report No. 492). Cambridge, MA: Artificial Intelligence Laboratory, Massachusetts Institute of Technology.

Wills, L.M. (1987). *Automated program recognition.* (Tech. Report ). Cambridge, MA: Artificial Intelligence Laboratory, Massachusetts Institute of Technology.

# 11

# 20 Years in the Trenches: What Have We Learned?*

Beverly Woolf

## RESEARCH AND ENGINEERING

We have been working in the trenches now since Carbonell (1970) built SCHOL-AR 20 years ago. We have designed, built, and tested many intelligent tutoring systems. What has this work taught us? What have we achieved? This chapter attempts to answer some of these questions. It does not provide a complete survey, see for example, Wenger (1987) and Woolf (1988). Instead it focuses on how engineers and researchers interact with each other to keep the vision strong and the products flowing.

Before addressing these issues, we need to distinguish between our role as engineers and our role as researchers. As engineers, we solve real problems: We utilize current technology, abide by hardware and software constraints, and produce working systems. As researchers we are not constrained by technology: We can give full rein to our vision, setting long-term goals, and asking unanswerable questions. We can remain open to change, and make suggestions about how the technology might unfold. Seymour Papert once said that it is important for children to have powerful ideas (Papert, 1980). This is also true for researchers. Both engineers and researchers are important to the field and they interact in useful ways. One example comes from the 13th century when society was making a transition from medieval times to the Renaissance. At that time the construction industry used bricks, mortar, and architecture (as the term has been more traditionally employed). Strong analogies exist between those artifacts and the ones used today in computer science.

During the Renaissance, society moved from concerns about the mystical and the cosmos, typified in medieval times, toward the rational and concepts about the unity of society. The Renaissance had as a goal the conquest of space and the

* This work was supported in part by National Science Foundation grant MDR-8751362. Partial support was also received from the Air Force Systems Command, Rome Air Development Center, Griffiss AFB, New York, 13441 and the Air Force Office of Scientific Research, Bolling AFB, DC 20332 under contract F30602-85-C-0008. This contract supports the Northeast Artificial Intelligence Consortium (NAIC). Partial support also provided by ONR University Research Initiative Contract N00014-86-K-0764.

The author thanks architect Stephen Woolf for his contribution of drawings and insight.

achievement of human supremacy over natural elements. In keeping with this goal, architects of the 13th century tried to build lofty and spiritual spaces for their houses of prayer. Specifically, they wanted large structures that reflected the increased religious fervor of the day and the increasing power of the Catholic Church. However, construction technology, based on bricks and mortar, did not provide easy solutions. For example, brick tends to buckle when built to extreme heights. Thus, the predominant church form of the period remained the simple Roman Basilica, in which a central vault was flanked by two side aisles (Figure 11.1).

Yet researchers of the day, the artisans and architects, dreamed of loftier, more spiritual spaces. They tried many solutions. For instance, they tried to raise the walls of the central vault which would just buckle out and collapse since exterior forces were needed to stabilize them (Figure 11.2). Another solution was to build wide stone piers to buttress the walls (Figure 11.3). However, this was unsatisfactory as it precluded side aisles. Then cathedral ceilings were built by

**Figure 11.1.   Older Roman Basilica Church.**

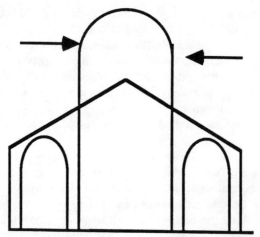

**Figure 11.2.   Tall walls needed additional support.**

removing the traditional horizontal ceiling beam (Figure 11.4). However, this solution necessitated that the walls be spread apart at the base, clearly limiting how high the walls could be built.

As the engineers experimented, architects and researchers kept true to their

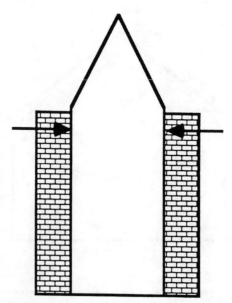

**Figure 11.3.   Wide stone piers supported tall walls.**

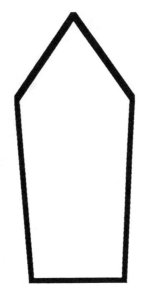

**Figure 11.4. Cathedral ceilings provided another solution.**

goal: They continued to search for solutions that would provide tall walls and unrestricted spaces. At the time, few people knew which artifact would actually satisfy this goal. For instance, a researcher would not say: "I am inventing the flying buttress" or "I will build a vaulted arch." Rather, he or she could describe the goal to build tall spaces. Researchers persisted without knowing which individual technology would allow a solution.

Today, as builders of intelligent tutoring systems, our position is similar to that of the craftspeople and architects of medieval times. As engineers we implement systems constrained by current technology, yet as researchers we dream of more powerful systems. We cannot say what form the ideal and ultimate intelligent tutor will take, yet we know some of the functionality we might want to include (see next section). Given this long-term view and our persistence, we need to continue, as did medieval architects, to design, experiment, and have powerful ideas.

In medieval times, after years of trial and error, the solution of a flying buttress and vaulted arch did emerge (Figure 11.5). This solution used the traditional materials of bricks and mortar, yet allowed for creation of very large central spaces as well as sideways vaults. Walls could be developed to unprecedented heights, long uninterrupted spaces could be provided in the central and side vaults, and the general structure could be applied to solve other building problems.

Modern technological advances improved on this solution. For example, since bricks can take only one force, compression, they require a vertical force,

Figure 11.5.   Section of a flying buttress and vaulted arch.

such as gravity, to hold them in place. New materials, such as steel and pres-
tressed concrete technology with internal tensile strength, emerged which take
tension as well as compression. These materials can withstand strong horizontal
forces and permit the enclosure of far larger buildings without the use of outside
supports such as flying buttresses. In modern times, three- and four-story high
unrestricted spaces are regularly designed by using steel and concrete beams.
Structures such as the Astrodome, whose construction would have been unthink-
able in medieval times, are now easily constructed throughout the world.

The point is that the flying buttress was an elegant solution for that day and
that technology. When viewed across time and in light of the technological
advances of this day, it is but a data-point within a large space of possible

solutions. The technology of building materials continues to evolve even today as newer building construction technologies give way to better solutions.

As researchers in intelligent tutoring systems we cannot know how our computer technology will evolve nor even which data point we are working on. We cannot say we are building a specific artifact any more than a Gothic architect could say he was building a flying buttress. We can only persist with the vision and can push the technology until new solutions emerge. Our goal is to continue to experiment and to remain open to new possibilities.

The 20 years we have spent as engineers and researchers pursuing development of intelligent tutoring systems are full of successful data points. We can identify problems that have been solved and problems for which a solution is imminent as a result of advances in hardware and software technology. Being cognizant of the limitations of the current technology helps clarify the larger goal and allows us to realize which achievements have already evolved. Both long-term goals and recent achievements are described in the next two sections.

## LONG-TERM GOALS

Workers in the field of intelligent tutoring systems have created what might be considered a modest structure (Figure 11.6). We have built more of a log cabin than a gothic cathedral, sort of a "handyman's special." Much work is required to bring this structure in line with the long-term goals (Figure 11.7). Remodeling this structure might include achieving several long-term goals. A few are suggested below:

• Develop artificial intelligence mechanisms that model the thinking processes of domain experts, tutors, and students.

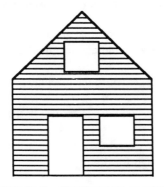

Figure 11.6.  Handyman's special.

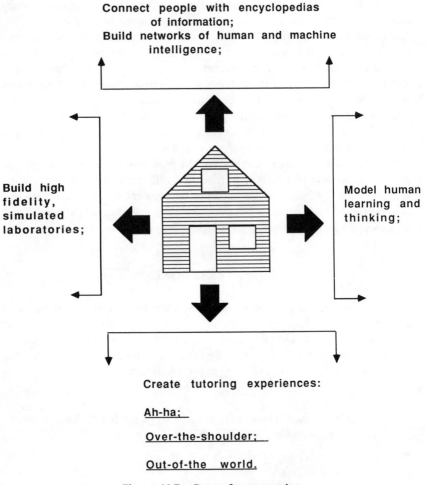

Figure 11.7.   Room for expansion.

- Produce intelligent environments that supply students with world-class laboratories within which they build and test their own reality.
- Provide students with
  - the *ah-ha* experience, in which the machine recognizes the student's intention
  - the *over-the-shoulder* experience, in which the machine aids and advises the student
  - the *out-of-the-world* experience, in which the machine provides an environment rich enough for discovery.

To fully achieve our goal, we would also like to have use of the following:

- Stores of knowledge easily accessible for joint human-machine problem solving.
- Widely available encyclopedias of information and knowledge bases which contain the sum of human knowledge.
- Computational intellects that enable networking of human and machine problem solvers.

Obviously few of these goals have been achieved and possibly the available hardware and software technology does not allow for them at this time. Remember, engineers could not have used bricks and mortar to build the Astrodome. Yet the above description provides a feeling for the vision that might be held while awaiting suitable technology.

How can we solve the myriad of problems that will emerge en route to these goals? The answer lies in the same methodology adopted by Renaissance builders: continued research and experimentation. Solutions do not necessarily emerge as a result of explicit and preformed plans; often they result from risk taking, frequent mistakes, and persistent exploration.

## RECENT ACCOMPLISHMENTS AND REMAINING PROBLEMS

Given a high-level description of the goals, what have we accomplished after nearly 20 years in the trenches? We have asked many of the right questions and have solved many problems. For instance, we have successfully identified four types of knowledge required in these systems and have developed many artifacts that provide good solutions in each area (Figure 11.8). Our solutions are still modest by the high standards (goals) set out in the previous section, but nevertheless they begin to provide habitable structures from which we can pursue our goal. The accomplishments now begin to look more like town-house condominiums, though they do not yet provide elegant and spacious environments.

In terms of goals, we have clarified some conventional fears (nonproblems) about development of these systems, have solved some problems, and have left many problems unsolved, awaiting a possible technology shift.

*Conventional fears.* Nonproblems have disappeared. For example, it was suggested that intelligent tutoring systems would be too expensive to build. Experience at Carnegie-Mellon suggests that once a framework is established, several tutors can be produced in a rather efficient manner (Anderson, 1988). Thus an algebra, geometry, and LISP tutor were produced from a common framework (Anderson, Boyle, & Yost, 1985; Anderson & Reiser, 1985). Bonar was able to leverage work done on an earlier economics tutor to build an electronics and an optics tutor using the same "bite-sized" framework (Bonar, Cunningham, & Schultz, 1986).

Professional nay-sayers also suggested that development time for these sys-

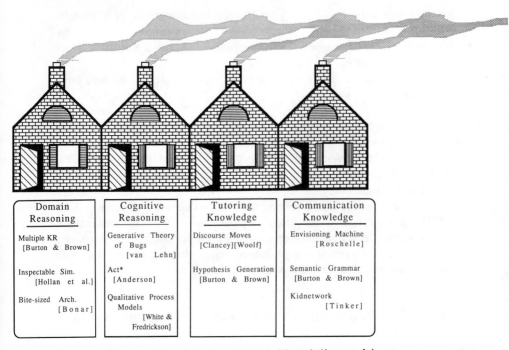

| Domain Reasoning | Cognitive Reasoning | Tutoring Knowledge | Communication Knowledge |
|---|---|---|---|
| Multiple KR [Burton & Brown] | Generative Theory of Bugs [van Lehn] | Discourse Moves [Clancey][Woolf] | Envisioning Machine [Roschelle] |
| Inspectable Sim. [Hollan et al.] | Act* [Anderson] | Hypothesis Generation [Burton & Brown] | Semantic Grammar [Burton & Brown] |
| Bite-sized Arch. [Bonar] | Qualitative Process Models [White & Fredrickson] | | Kidnetwork [Tinker] |

**Figure 11.8.  Respectable solutions exist.**

tems would be excessively long. In fact, it now appears that two person-years is a convenient estimate for practical development of these systems and that time is decreasing as expert system shells and authoring systems emerge (Anderson, 1988; Woolf, Blegen, Verloop, & Jensen, 1986).

Anderson has suggested that 60 person-hours of preparation time is needed per hour of training (Anderson, 1988). This is not excessive when compared with that of designing and writing a textbook. If such a system does in fact cover a semester's worth of material, then development time is not unreasonable.

Others have claimed that these systems would not be any more effective than conventional teaching media. In fact, Anderson has shown these systems can be one standard deviation more effective than lecture-style teaching methods (Anderson, 1988). For example, in a programming course at Carnegie-Mellon University, an intelligent tutor improved learning results, as measured by test performance, by 43% and reduced learning time by 30%. Using traditional lecture-style environments, students spent about 40 hours covering the first six lessons of a LISP course. Using the intelligent tutoring system and the lectures, students completed the lessons in only 15 hours.

*Problems remaining to be solved.* Obviously many real problems still exist. In terms of AI technology we have not effectively included student models, qualitative reasoning, machine learning, hypertex (Yankelovich, Meyrowitx, & van Dam, 1987), or multimedia (e.g., AI systems which include videodisc, speech, or film) into our tutors, Additionally, one standard deviation learning improvement for intelligent tutors as compared with lecture-style teaching is not good enough. Given the resources put into development of these systems, they should produce two standard deviation improvement over lecture-style teaching just as one-on-one human tutoring produces.

Other problems awaiting solutions arise from educational and societal issues such as:

- Limited number of powerful AI-based computers available to education and industrial training sites. Increased memory size and reduced prices on general-purpose machines should eliminate this problem.
- A generation of entrenched and unusable computers in the classroom.
- Public school resistance.
- The difficulty of integrating intelligent tutors into existing curriculum and educational systems.

Each of these problems require a combined, that is, integrated, effort from computer scientists, instructional scientists, and educators.

*Solved problems.* Some very real milestones have been accomplished. For example, intuitive communications models have been built employing state-of-the-art tools, such as high resolution graphics, windows, icons, and pop-down menus. Cognitive results have been used to inform systems based on models of thinking and learning. Domain and reasoning knowledge have been codified for teaching a multitude of domains, from radiology and second languages to mathematics and science. Real accomplishments include the fact that AI techniques are now being studied by a large community of educators and cognitive scientists. Knowledge about representation strategies, control structures, and symbolic languages, essential for building intelligent educational computer systems is now available.

Another real accomplishment is rooted in work done by electrical and computer engineers. Expensive and complex machinery is now being replaced by cheaper and more powerful hardware. For example, at the University of Massachusetts, we have built intelligent tutors on special-purpose $50,000 AI workstations donated by Hewlett-Packard. These same tutors can be ported and further developed on Macintosh II systems at one-fifth the cost. The interface is substantially cleaner and easier to use in the smaller machine. We use Allegro Common

Lisp on the microcomputer, and are enjoying a development environment that rivals that of special-purpose Lisp machines selling at 2–3 times the price.

## ARCHITECTURE FOR DISCOURSE

The accomplishments described above are rather general in nature; specific results could have been provided demonstrating how specific goals have been accomplished. In this section, I describe a technology developed to satisfy one goal, namely that of modeling the tutoring process of an expert teacher. Since I began this chapter by describing an architectural challenge, I provide an analogous computer architecture challenge: Build human-like tutoring discourse into a machine tutor.

Discourse in an intelligent tutoring system should be effective, responsive, and customized for the individual user. The tutoring system should reason dynamically about selection of its response and should show genuine flexibility in its choice of topics, presentation, examples, and response. For example, it should reason about an abstract directive provided by the author, such as:

"When the student is *confused*, present a *less complex* example."

To do this, the system should decide when the student appears confused, and then should know how to construct a less complex example, for instance, by weakening features along a specific dimension. This directive is to be contrasted with the use of situation-specific rules, such as "If the student answers the question correctly, present example #32." This latter kind of specification, frequently used in conventional teaching systems, is responsive only to local information, i.e., to which problem was presented and how the student responded. It ignores situation abstractions derived from a sequence of interactions. It also forces the programmer into a tedious level of detail.

### Layers of Discourse Control

We have built a four-layered control structure for dynamic control of discourse at four levels of granularity (Figure 11.9). The goal is to build a system which is sensitive to the current tutoring strategy as well as to the history of the user. I sketch this architecture here; a more complete description can be found in Woolf et al. (1988) and Woolf and Murray (1987).

The discourse control architecture is designed to show flexibility in its choice of goal, topic, presentation, and response. The control component can also choose the tutoring strategy, which in turn parameterizes how the choices in the other four layers are made. For example, the Lessons level of control makes decisions about which set of issues will be the focus of the session. The next

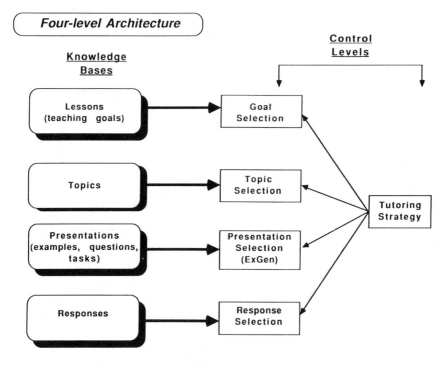

Figure 11.9.   Four-layered control of discourse.

level makes decisions about which topic to discuss, concept to tutor, or misconception to remediate. The Presentation level instantiates the chosen topic into various ways of interacting with the student, such as giving examples of a concept, asking questions, providing descriptions and definitions, and so on. The Response level interprets the chosen presentation, and generates informative and motivational feedback according to the tutoring strategy. The interactions are recorded in the student and discourse models and used to drive diagnosis of misconceptions.

Tutors based on this architecture are responsive to a tutoring strategy and are beginning to automate their selection of tutoring strategies. Each strategy specifies the values for various control parameters at each of the four levels of control. Changing control behavior will be simply a matter of changing which strategy is designated as current. We are ready to address the more difficult aspect of implementing strategic metacontrol: knowing when to change the current strategy.

The three levels described below are defined by the choices available at each level and how the current tutoring strategy impacts on these choices.

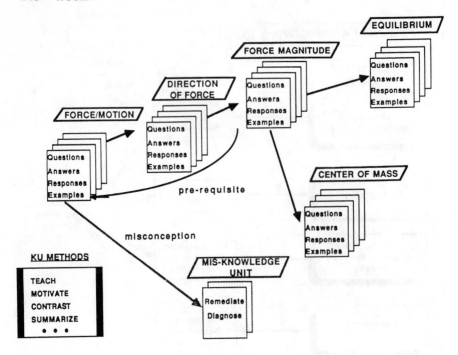

**Figure 11.10.   Hierarchy of frames.**

***Topic selection.*** Topics are represented within a Knowledge Unit network of frames which explicitly expresses relationships between topics such as prerequisites, corequisites, and related misconceptions (Figure 11.10). An important notion about the network is that is declarative; it contains a structured space of concepts, but does not mandate any particular order for traversal of this space.

The current tutoring strategy manifests itself in the control at this level by parameterizing the algorithm used to traverse the Knowledge Unit network based on classifications of and relations between these units. Several major strategies have thus far been implemented. For example, the tutor might always teach prerequisites before teaching the goal topic. Alternatively, it might provide a diagnostic probe to see if the student knows a topic. Prerequisites might be presented if the student doesn't exhibit enough knowledge on the probe. These prerequisites may be reached in various ways, such as through depth-first or breadth-first traversal. An intermediate strategy which we have used is to specialize the prerequisite relation into "hard" prerequisites, which are always covered before the goal topic, and "soft" prerequisites, taught only when the student displays a deficiency.

There are also "Mis-Knowledge Units," which represent common misconceptions or knowledge "bugs," and ways to remediate them. These are inserted opportunistically into the discourse. The tutoring strategy parameterizes this aspect of Knowledge Unit selection by indicating whether such remediation should occur as soon as the misconception is suspected, or wait until the current Knowledge Unit has been completed.

*Presentation selection.* The intermediate level of discourse control utilizes an example generation tool called ExGen (Suthers & Rissland, 1988; Woolf, Suthers, & Murray, 1989). Examples, questions, and descriptions of the concept being taught are all treated as "examples" by ExGen. A "seed" example base contains prototypical presentations of each type. ExGen's modification routine expands this into a much larger virtual space of presentations as needed. The goal is to enable the tutor to have flexibility in its presentation of examples and questions/tasks that accompany those examples, without the knowledge engineering being burdened by representing all possible presentations explicitly.

ExGen takes a list of weighted constraints called requests, and returns an example (Woolf et al., 1989). The constraints are written in a language which describes logical combinations of the desired attributes of the example, and the weights on them represent the relative importance of each of these attributes. The returned example generally meets as many of the constraints as possible in the priority indicated by the weights.

ExGen is driven by *example generation specialists,* or knowledge sources, each of which examines the current discourse and student models and produces requests (weighted constraints) to be given to ExGen. These example generation specialists may be thought of as tutoring rules, encoding such general prescriptives as "when starting a new topic, give a start-up example," or "ask questions requiring a qualitative response before those involving a quantitative response."

The tutoring strategy impacts on this layer of presentation selection by prioritizing the relative importance of the recommendations produced by each of the example generation specialists. Within a strategy, each specialist has a weight multiplied by the weight of the requests produced by the specialists. Altering the behavior of the Presentation control is simply a matter of changing the weights on the specialists by selecting a new strategy.

For instance, one specialists requests that presentations describing the current Knowledge Unit be given, and another requests that the student be questioned. These competing requests are ordered by the current tutoring strategy. We are also examining strategies for temporal ordering of the presentation of examples, such as Bridging Analogies (Brown, Clement, & Murray, 1986) and Incremental Generalization.

*Response selection.* We have begun to represent alternative responses to student actions. The choices available at this level are concerned with how much information to give the student in the interactive presentation and what motivational comments to make. For instance, the machine might decide to:

- tell the student *whether* she is correct;
- tell the student *what* the correct response is;
- tell the student *why* her response is correct or incorrect;
- give hints or leading questions;
- challenge the student's answer with a counter-suggestion; or
- provide additional information which extends the content of the current question-answer interaction.

Motivational responses may include encouragement, congratulations, challenges, and other statements with affective or prelocutionary content. As before, the current tutoring strategy specifies which of these feedback and follow-up responses will be generated. The strategy may also specify that the responses be predicated on whether the student's response was correct, or even that no response is to be given.

## FUTURE WORK

The architecture described above demonstrates only a particular engineering solution to the problem of providing customized response in an intelligent tutoring system. Clearly it does not represent a final solution. The final solution requires input from both engineers and researchers and incremental improvements as well as larger conceptual leaps. It requires a recognition of the constraints of current technology in addition to an awareness of the possibilities and the vision.

For instance, one of the next incremental improvements might be to use qualitative reasoning and planning technologies to provide flexibility and sensitivity in machine response. Another near-term improvement might be to integrate multimedia communications technology, such as film, video, sound, and networks of information sources into these systems. Both engineers and researchers will have to contribute development of such goals.

In terms of Gothic architecture, we have established a "habitable structure" but not yet a flying buttress. In a world of intelligent behavior, paradox, chance, and pattern randomness abound. Understanding and replicating this type of world involves working with the purposeful, the tangible, and, if necessary, the mystical. We need to be open to change and to accept questions with no easy answers. We need to recognize the interdependence of many themes yet remain childlike and exploratory. Again, the important thing is to have powerful ideas. From good ideas flow genuine solutions and from good solutions flow the ultimate achievement of our goals.

## REFERENCES

Anderson, J. (1988, January). NSF Principal Investigator's Meeting, Phoenix, AZ.

Anderson, J., Boyle, C., & Yost, G. (1985). The geometry tutor. *Proceedings of the International Joint Conference on Artificial Intelligence* (pp. 1–7). Los Altos, CA: Morgan Kaufmann Publishers, Inc.

Anderson, J., & Reiser, B. (1985). The LISP Tutor. *Byte, 10*(4), 159–175.

Bonar, J., Cunningham, R., & Schultz, J. (1986). An object-oriented architecture for intelligent tutoring systems. *Proceedings of the ACM conference on object-oriented programming systems languages and applications.* New York: Association for Computing Machinery.

Brown, D., Clement, J., & Murray, T. (1986). Tutoring specifications for a computer program which uses analogies to teach mechanics. *Cognitive Processes Research Group Working Paper.* Department of Physics, University of Massachusetts, Amherst, MA.

Carbonell, J.R. (1970). *Mixed-Initiative Man-Computer Instructional Dialogues.* PhD Dissertation, Massachusetts Institute of Technology, Cambridge, MA.

Papert, S. (1980). *Mindstorms: Children, computers and powerful ideas.* New York: Basic Books.

Suthers, D., & Rissland, E. (1988). *Constraint manipulation for example generation,* COINS Technical Report #88-71, Computer and Information Science Department, University of Massachusetts, Amherst, MA.

Wenger, E. (1987). *Artificial intelligence and tutoring systems, computational and cognitive approaches to the communication of knowledge.* Los Altos, CA: Morgan Kaufmann Publishers.

Woolf, B. (1988). Intelligent tutoring systems: A survey. In H. Shrobe & American Association for Artificial Intelligence (Eds.), *Exploring artificial intelligence: Survey talks from the national conferences on artificial intelligence* (pp. 1–43). Los Altos, CA: Morgan Kaufmann Publishers.

Woolf, B., Suthers, D., & Murray, T. (1989). *Discourse control for tutoring: Case studies in example generation.* COINS Technical Report. Computer and Information Science Department, University of Massachusetts, Amherst, MA.

Woolf, B., Murray, T., Suthers, D., & Schultz, K. (1988). Primitive knowledge units for tutoring systems. *Proceedings of the International Conference on Intelligent Tutoring Systems (ITS88).*

Woolf, B., & Murray, T. (1987). A framework for representing tutorial discourse. *International Joint Conference on Artificial Intelligence (IJCAI-87).* Los Altos, CA: Morgan Kaufmann, Inc.

Woolf, B., Blegen, D., Verloop, A., & Jensen, J. (1987). Tutoring a complex industrial process In R. Lawler & M. Yazdani (Eds.), *Artificial intelligence and education:*

*Learning environments and tutoring systems* (Vol. 1, p.p. 413–427). Norwood, NJ: Ablex.

Yankelovich, N., Meyrowitz, N., & van Dam, A. (1987). Reading and writing the electronic book. *IEEE Computer, 20*(9), 15–30.

# 12
# Three Current Tutoring Systems and Future Needs

## Patrick Suppes

### INTRODUCTION

In this chapter, three extended examples of tutoring systems are considered. They are interactive theorem provers, a system to handle informal calculus derivations, and a program that embodies several mathematical models of different aspects of mastery learning. The last section is devoted to what we need and what we may expect of tutoring systems in the next decade or two.

It is appropriate to being with some general remarks about the instructional use of computers. My own involvement began in 1962, and now that a quarter of a century has passed it is easy enough to see where I had incorrect ideas and especially incorrect forecasts about how the instructional use would develop. In an article written for *Scientific American* (1966a), I had this to say about the immediate impact of computer-assisted instruction.

> Before the advent of computers it was extremely difficult to collect systematic data on how children succeed in the process of learning a given subject. Evaluating tests of achievement at the end of learning have (and will undoubtedly continue to have) a place both in the process of classifying students and in the process of comparing different curriculum approaches to the same subject. Nonetheless, such tasks remain blunt and insensitive instruments, particularly with respect to detailed problems of instruction and curriculum revision. It is not possible on the basis of poor results in a test of children's mastery of subtraction or of irregular verbs in French to draw clear inferences about ways to improve the curriculum. A computer, on the other hand, can provide daily information about how students are performing on each part of the curriculum as it is presented, making it possible to evaluate not only individual pages but also individual exercises. This use of computers will have important consequences for all students in the immediate future.

My prediction of "important consequences for all students in the immediate future" was certainly too sanguine. It is not only a matter of not using data to revise and improve ordinary texts and workbooks, it is even a problem of extensive use of data to improve computer-assisted instruction. The problems of having good data feedback and good analytical and statistical methods for using the data for improvement have not really been satisfactorily solved, and we are, in terms of global results, not too much better off than we were 20 years ago. All the same, I am still hopeful. I will have something more to say about this later.

In a second article published the same year (Suppes, 1966b) I predicted that in a matter of a few years we would be able to implement, in an effective and efficient manner, instruction in a wide range of skill subjects, and I mentioned in particular elementary mathematics, instruction in reading, and the teaching of foreign language. There is now a good deal of instruction in reading and elementary mathematics by computer, but actually not very much in foreign language, in spite of the very clear possibilities.

I first consider three extended examples of application of mathematical models and artificial intelligence in computer-assisted instruction. The three examples are interactive theorem proving, informal derivations in the differential and integral calculus, and mathematics of mastery learning. Later, I try to forecast, as I did not too successfully in the past, some of the anticipated future developments.

## INTERACTIVE THEOREM PROVERS

First, I want to say something about the history of my own work and that of my colleagues. Simple uses of an interactive theorem prover for the teaching of elementary logic began more than 20 years ago. I remember well our first demonstrations with elementary-school children in 1963. For a number of years we concentrated on teaching elementary logic and algebra to bright elementary- and middle-school children. We felt at the time that this was the right level of difficulty to reach for in terms of computer capacity and resources that could be devoted to the endeavor. By the late 1960s it became clear that we could aim at something more advanced, and by 1972 I was able to convert the elementary-logic course at Stanford to a course taught entirely at computer terminals. By that time we had introduced a better and more powerful interactive theorem prover. That course is probably the longest-running show anywhere on earth having an interactive theorem prover used on a regular basis day in and day out by large numbers of persons. Access to the computer is pretty much around the clock seven days a week so that at almost any time of the day or night a routine use of our interactive theorem prover is taking place. The content of the course in elementary logic is comparable to that of my text (Suppes, 1957). It is obvious enough that the theorem-proving demands of such an elementary course are not very severe.

The most natural move up was to a course in axiomatic set theory, roughly corresponding to my text in the subject (Suppes, 1960/1972). Here there were nontrivial theorems to be proved, above all the classical organization of a mathematical subject into a long sequence of theorems, with no hope of individual theorems' being proved from scratch directly from the axioms. Since 1974 this course also has been offered every term as a course in computer-assisted instruction, with students' getting all of the instruction at terminals. The enrollment is much smaller than for the logic course. The average enrollment each term is eight or nine students, but the enrollment is greater than it was in the days before the course was computerized. The details of the set-theory course are described in several articles in Suppes (1981) and more recently in McDonald and Suppes (1984). It is organized in terms of somewhat more than 600 theorems. Depending upon the grade students seek, they prove somewhere between 30 and more than 50 theorems. Some of the theorems have proofs that are too hard to require in a course at this level. After all, one of the theorems on transfinite induction is essentially the main content of von Neumann's dissertation. I also do not want to give the wrong impression about the finished character of the setup. I think that the interactive theorem prover we are using has many good features but it is still awkward to prove the hardest theorems in the sequence. Much work remains to be done to make the proofs of these theorems as natural and easy as they really should be.

Roughly speaking, I would describe the main features of the interactive theorem prover used in the set-theory course under two headings. First, elementary available and can be used by the students. Second, students can call a resolution theorem prover that will run for a few seconds of machine time. What students give as input to the theorem prover are the definitions or previous theorems that are to be used to infer a desired formula.

There are several important remarks to be made about the way in which the students use the interactive theorem prover. First, the most frequently used rule is the use of a previous theorem to make a fairly direct inference. Second, contrast must be sharply drawn between the highly interactive nature of the way the students use the theorem prover and the way proofs can be printed out under a review function at the end. The interactive phase of creating the proof looks from the outside world like a mess. The program is acting as an intelligent tutor to help the student construct a proof. The result has the kind of highly interactive discourse structure that is not easy to follow at a glance. It is meant to be easy for the students to use and to provide considerable help to them. In contrast, the proofs that are printed out at the end under the heading of review are organized and systematic. They are put in a standard crisp form that gives much less insight into the interaction that took place in creating the proofs. Figure 12.1 shows an interactive construction of an elementary proof, and the review version of it, which is immediately understandable.

Third, when a student attempts an invalid inference the theorem prover produces a diagnostic message that says exactly why the attempted inference was not valid and therefore not acceptable. Fourth, and finally, an expert system that provides a goal and subgoal structure has been developed by Blaine (1981).

The current effort is focused on developing a theorem prover for the foundations of the differential and integral calculus—the fundamental theorem of the calculus, the mean value theorem, Rolle's theorem, and the like. The first efforts are reported in Suppes and Takahashi (in press). In the context of this conference

*SETDerive
Theorem, Lemma, or Formula *THeorem  <Name> ()  *2.4.2

Theorem 2.4.2:  ($\forall$ A,B,C) (A $\subseteq$ B & B $\subseteq$ C $\rightarrow$ A $\subseteq$ C)
*HYP
  hyp                (1)  A $\subseteq$ B and B $\subseteq$ C
*1SIMP
  Occurrences       (1)  *1
  1 simp          (2)  A $\subseteq$ B
*DEFinition  <Name> ()  *SUBset
    ($\forall$ B,C) [B $\subseteq$ C $\longleftrightarrow$ ($\forall$ x) (x $\in$ B $\rightarrow$ x $\in$ C)]
  Do you want to specify?  (yes) *yes
  Variables (B,C)  *yes
  Substitute for B?  (B) *A
  Substitute for C?  (C) *B
  definition subset
              (3)    A $\subseteq$ B iff ($\forall$ x)(x $\in$ A $\rightarrow$ x $\in$ B)
*2,3IMPLies
  2 implies using 3
              (4)    ($\forall$ x) (x $\in$ A $\rightarrow$ x $\in$ B)
*US
      ($\forall$ x) (x $\in$ A $\rightarrow$ x $\in$ B)
  Substitute for x?  (x)  *yes
  4 us           (5)  If x $\in$ A then x $\in$ B
*5HYP
  5 hyp         (6)  x $\in$ A
*5,6AA
  5, 6 aa
              (7)  x $\in$ B
*1,7VERify        (B)  *x $\subseteq\in$ C
  x $\subseteq\in$ C is not a formula.
  (B)  *x $\in$ C
  Using *DEFinition  <Name> ()  *SUBset
  Using *OK
*6,8CP
  6, 8 cp
              (9)  If x $\in$ A then x $\in$ C
*UG
  Generalize *x
  9 ug          (10)  ($\forall$ x) (x $\in$ A $\rightarrow$ x $\in$ C)
*10ESTablish    (11)  *A $\subseteq$ C
  Using *OK
*REVIEw
  Which Review?  (current context)  *yes

  Theorem 2.4.2:  ($\forall$ A,B,C) (A $\subseteq$ B & B $\subseteq$ C $\rightarrow$ A $\subseteq$ C)
              (1)  A $\subseteq$ B and B $\subseteq$ C
  So            (2)  A $\subseteq$ B
  By definition subset
              (3)  A $\subseteq$ B iff ($\forall$ x) (x $\in$ A $\rightarrow$ x $\in$ B)
  2 by 3        (4)  ($\forall$ x) (x $\in$ A $\rightarrow$ x $\in$ B)
  So that      (5)  If x $\in$ A then x $\in$ B
  Also          (6)  x $\in$ A
  5 by 6        (7)  x $\in$ B
  By 1          (8)  x $\in$ C
  cp            (9)  If x $\in$ A then x $\in$ C
  And         (10)  ($\forall$ x) (x $\in$ A $\rightarrow$ x $\in$ C)
  So          (11)  A $\subseteq$ C
*QED ok

**Figure 12.1.   Sample interaction with EXCHECK (from Suppes, 1981, p. 8).**

the most important remark to be made is about the modularity of the system. General theorem provers built on logical principles like that of resolution are very poor at doing algebraic inferences. What we have added to the interactive theorem prover to meet this difficulty is the powerful symbolic computation program REDUCE (Hearn, 1987), which will easily verify in less than 100 milliseconds on any reasonable term substitution instances of such algebraic inequalities as

$$|x - y| \leq |x| + |y|.$$

(One warning: a fairly elaborate interface is required to use REDUCE in conjunction with a theorem prover.)

## INFORMAL CALCULUS DERIVATIONS

A central component of work at Stanford on preparation of a year's computer-based calculus course is development of an intelligent program for monitoring the correctness of informal calculus derivations. It is a familiar remark that the intuitive and computationally efficient notation used in calculus courses and textbooks is not mathematically explicit and rigorous. Our problem has been to give students the command structure to produce what look like the usual calculus derivations and symbolic computations, but at the same time to check their mathematical correctness, the kind of work that an intelligent human tutor usually does with grace and speed.

The problems of development a program that comes close to what is expected of a good tutor are more subtle than they appear to be on first consideration. I necessarily limit myself here to a couple of simple examples to illustrate the nature of the problems.

1.  Using the usual rule of replacing equals by equals, from $x = y$ we infer
    $$\frac{dx}{dx} = \frac{dy}{dy}.$$
    Now take $y = 1$, and we obtain the absurdity $1 = 0$.
2.  Let $f(x) = 0$ for all x. Then the derivative $f'(x) = 0$ for all x. Also $\sqrt{x^2} - \sqrt{x^2} = 0$ for all x, but $f(x) = \sqrt{x^2} - \sqrt{x^2}$ does not have a derivative at $x = 0$, because the derivative of $\sqrt{x^2}$ does not exist at $x = 0$.

The problems raised by these two examples and others of a like nature must be solved in a computationally efficient manner if the student is going to be kept out of trouble and properly assisted by a program serving as an intelligent tutor. For those special cases that go beyond what the program can handle, methods must be introduced to join with the student in finding a solution. A classical example of the latter is that it is not automatically, that is, recursively, decidable when a given denominator is equal to zero and thus the whole expression is undefined, but in most such cases the student who has not made a real mistake should be able to show the program why his specific expression is acceptable. If he cannot, the program will require that he take another path to solve the problem at hand.

In creating intelligent programs of the type I have been describing it is important to recognize there are fundamental limits in principle to what can be done. Students can wander into problems that are not recursively decidable, or even if they are, are not computationally feasible. The computer tutor like the human tutor must be ready to make a graceful exit from situations that are computationally unmanageable. (The work on calculus is supported by NSF Grant MDR-87-51523 to Stanford.)

## MATHEMATICS OF MASTERY

What I describe under this heading is extensive work done at Computer Curriculum Corporation over the past decade on computer-assisted instruction in basic skills. I shall use as my focus elementary mathematics, but most of what I have to say applies to reading skills and also elementary language skills as well. The fundamental problem is that we want to individualize instruction and move each student forward on an individual basis as he or she masters successive skills or concepts. It is somewhat surprising how little this complex problem has been studied from a systematic or mathematical standpoint. The subject is intricate, so I shall give only a sense of the application of relatively sophisticated formal models. There are five components of mastery that I consider, some in greater depth than others. These are:

1. Curriculum distribution
2. Student distribution
3. Contingent tutoring
4. Initial placement motion
5. Application of a learning model for judging mastery

*Curriculum distribution.* Not all concepts are equal in importance, so that the expected time devoted to mastery should vary. Addition of positive integers, for example, is much less important in the fourth grade than addition of fractions. But how should the expected time be allocated and on what intellectual basis? There is, unfortunately, only a very limited literature on this important matter in the theory of curriculum. At the present time the most feasible approach is to use as initial data curriculum guidelines set by various state and local school systems, and then to count the empirical frequency of exercises in various widely used textbooks. After pooling and smoothing these data, the next step is to use latency data to convert to a time distribution. Then to smooth this distribution, and then convert back to a distribution of exercise types organized by concept.

The individual tutoring aspects come in with the next, related concept.

*Student distribution.* However thorough the curriculum analysis that lies back of the curriculum distribution, individual student differences will necessarily lead to uneven progress for students across the range of concepts and skills in a given curriculum. One student will be much better at executing the standard algorithms of arithmetic than in solving word problems, and another student will be the reverse. So to keep the position of the student at approximately the same level of achievement in all the skills of a basic course in mathematics, a second, individual student distribution is introduced, for purposes of smoothing the actual distribution of grade-level achievement across strands—the concepts and skills are organized into homogeneous strands—one for addition, one for subtraction, one for fractions, one for word problems, and so forth.

I shall try to outline the basic setup, which depends on selecting two parameters. One is the threshold parameter $\theta$ for how far behind this average grade placement student s must be to receive greater emphasis on strand i. The second is the parameter $\alpha$ for weighting the curriculum distribution $c(i)$, $\Sigma c(i) = 1$, and assigning weight $1 - \alpha$ to the student distribution $k(i,s)$. So that at a given time $t$, the actual distribution $d(i,s)$ used in selecting exercises from stand $i$ for student $s$, is defined as:

$$(5)\ d(i,s) = \alpha c(i) + (1 - \alpha)k(i,s),$$

with $0 \le \alpha \le 1$. To define $k(i,s)$, let

$$h(i,s) = \begin{cases} \bar{a}(s) - g(i,s) \text{ if } \bar{a}(s) \ge g(i,s) + \theta \\ 0 \text{ otherwise,} \end{cases}$$

where $g(i,s)$ is at the time t the grade-level achievement in strand i of student s, and $\bar{a}(s)$ is the weighted average grade-level achievement of s at time t with the averaging being across strands weighted by the curriculum distribution $c(i)$. Finally,

$$k(i,s) = \begin{cases} c(i), \text{ if } \sum_i h(i,s) = 0, \\ \dfrac{h(i,s)}{\sum_i h(i,s)}, \text{ otherwise.} \end{cases}$$

The qualitative analogue of equation (5) is used by any observant intelligent human tutor. In this instance it is easy to implement something that probably does a better job in most cases.

*Contingent tutoring.* Most computer-assisted instruction in basic skills is supplementary. It is assumed that the student has been given classroom instruction, or is simultaneously being so instructed. All the same, students in such courses often need additional instruction in particular concepts or skills. On the other hand, it is inefficient to provide instruction of a tutorial nature to a student who is exhibiting mastery of a skill by making no errors.

For these reasons we have introduced what we term *contingent tutoring*. A student is given a quick tutorial whenever he makes an error, with the tutorial focused as closely as possible on the type of error. We are in the process of analyzing data to determine the efficacy of this approach, in terms of an optimal use of the student's time.

*Initial placement motion (IPM).* Chronologically, the first problem is to determine a correct initial placement of a student. At any moment the student has a grade-level position of achievement in each strand. The purpose of IPM is to estimate the weighted average achievement level of the student at the beginning of his enrollment. As would be expected, the basis of IPM is probabilistic. The underlying model is easy to formulate. Let $X_n, n \geq 0$ denote (the student's) grade level at the end of session n, achieved under the standard curriculum motion, $X_0$ being the initial (entering) grade level prior to any estimation by IPM. Then $\Delta_n = X_n - X_{n-1}$, $n \leq 1$, will be the grade-level increment (positive or negative) achieved during session n under the standard curriculum motion. Let $Y_n$, $n \geq 1$ be the grade-level increment (positive or negative) achieved at the end of session n under the IPM motion. If $Z_n$, $n \geq 1$, denotes the grade level at the end of IPM session n, we can write:

$$Z_n = X_0 + \sum_{i=1}^{n} \Delta_i + \sum_{i=1}^{n} Y_i.$$

This means that the stochastic process $\{Z_n; n \geq 1\}$, with $Z_n$ being the grade level at the end of IPM session n, is the sum of the curriculum and IPM processes. Further mathematical details and empirical data on IPM will be given in forthcoming joint work with Mario Zanotti.

*Learning model of mastery.* Our problem is to decide when performance on a given class of essentially equivalent exercises satisfies some criterion. In many situations it is assumed that the underlying process that is being sampled is stationary—at least in the mean. The first simple model we shall consider is of this type. The third model is explained later. A more realistic assumption in dealing with student behavior is that learning is occurring—both individually and in the mean, so that the process is not stationary. The second model is of this type.

Although in the intended applications the number of possible student responses is usually large—and therefore the probability of guessing a correct answer is close to zero—we shall consider here only correct and incorrect responses. With this restriction:

$A_{0,n}$ = event of incorrect response on trial n,
$A_{1,n}$ = event of correct response on trial n,
$\quad x_n$ = possible sequence of correct and incorrect responses from trial 1 to n inclusive,

$q_n = P(A_{0,n}) = $ mean probability of an error on trial n,

$q_{x,n} = P(A_{0,n}|x_{n-1})$.

Also, $A_0$ and $A_1$ are the corresponding random variables.

For simplicity we shall assume a fixed initial probability $P(A_{0,1})$ rather than a prior distribution on the unit interval for this probability. Given the extensive knowledge of this distribution, assuming that all the weight is on $P(A_{0,1})$ is not unrealistic. In Model I the assumptions are:

(1) $P(A_{0,n+1}|A_{0,n}x_{n-1}) = (1 - w)P(A_{0,n}|x_{n-1}) + w$

(2) $P(A_{0,n+1}|A_{1,n}x_{n-1}) = (1 - w)P(A_{0,n}|x_{n-1})$.

We can easily prove the significant fact of stationarity of the mean probability $P(A_{0,n})$.

**THEOREM 1.** In Model I, for all n, $P(A_{0,n}) = q_1$.

**Proof.**

$$P(A_{0,n+1})) = \sum_x [P(A_{0,n+1}|A_{0,n}x_{n-1})P(A_{0,n}|x_{n-1})P(x_{n-1})$$
$$+ P(A_{0,n+1}|A_{1,n}x_{n-1})P(A_{1,n}|x_{n-1})P(x_{n-1})]$$
$$= \sum_x [(1 - w)P^2(A_{0,n})|x_{n-1}) + wP(A_{0,n}|x_{n-1})$$
$$+ (1 - w)P(A_{0,n}|x_{n-1})$$
$$(1 - P(A_{0,n}|x_{n-1}))]P(x_{n-1})$$
$$= \sum_x P(A_{0,n}|x_{n-1})P(x_{n-1})$$
$$= P(A_{0,n}).$$

We have at once then

**Corollary**

$E(A_{0,n}) = q_1$

$Var(A_{0,n}) = q_1(1 - q_1)$.

In Model II we generalize Model I to unequal w's on the assumption that learning is occurring during the trials, so we assume $w_1 < w_2$, and we replace (1) and (2) by (1') and (2'):

(1') $P(A_{0,n+1}|A_{0,n}x_{n-1}) = (1 - w_1)P(A_{0,n}|x_{n-1}) + w_1$

(2') $P(A_{0,n+1}|A_{1,n}x_{n-1}) = (1 - w_2)P(A_{0,n}|x_{n-1})$.

To express results compactly, we define moments:

$$V_{i,n} = \sum_x P^i(A_{0,n}|x_{n-1})P(x_{n-1}).$$

**THEOREM 2.** In Model II,

$V_{1,n+1} = (1 - (w_2 - w_1))V_{1,n} + (w_2 - w_1)V_{2,n}.$
**Proof.** By the same methods used for Theorem 1,

$$P(A_{0,n+1}) = \sum_x [((1 - w_1)P(A_{0,n}|x_{n-1}) + w_1)P(A_{0,n}|x_{n-1})$$

$$+ (1 - w_2)P(A_{0,n}|x_{n-1})$$

$$(1 - P(A_{0,n}|x_{n-1})]P(x_{n-1})$$

$$= (1 - w_1)V_{2,n} + w_1V_{1,n} + (1 - w_2)$$

$$V_{1,n} - (1 - w_2)V_{2,n}$$

$$= (1 - (w_2 - w_1))V_{1,n} + (w_2 - w_1)V_{2,n}$$

In the case of both Models I and II the asymptotic behavior is well known (Karlin, 1953). All sample paths converge to 0 or 1, with the exact distribution depending on the initial distribution, and in the case of Model II, the relative values of $w_1$ and $w_2$. Of course, in the case of Model II, detailed computations are difficult.

Here is how either model would work computationally in practice. A student is exited upward from a class when $q_{x,n} < a$, where a is the normative threshold, for example, we might set a = .15, corresponding to a probability correct of .85. Notice that both models are noncommutative, and thus give greater weight to later responses. These models are derived from learning models that have been extensively studied. For pedagogical purposes in a computer environment they are computationally simple. The history of a sequence, 001100111 for example, is absorbed in the current $q_{x,n}$, and no other data need be kept, except possibly a count of the number of exercises.

Still more suitable is a third model that has both a parameter for individual paths, such as in Model I, or possibly two such parameters as in Model II, together with a uniform learning parameter a that acts constantly on each trial, since the student is always told the correct answer. For simplicity I shall consider the two-parameter model using a and w, which are assumed to lie in the open interval $(0,1)$.

In Model III the assumptions are

(3) $P(A_{0,n+1}|A_{0,n}x_{n-1}) = (1 - w)aP(A_{0,n}|x_{n-1}) + aw$

(4) $P(A_{0,n+1}|A_{1,n}x_{n-1}) = (1 - w)aP(A_{0,n}|x_{n-1}).$

It is then easy to prove by the methods already used:

**THEOREM 3.** In Model III, for all n, $P(A_{0,n+1}) = a^n P(A_{0,1})$, or in terms of random variables:

$E(A_{0,n+1}) = a^n q_1,$
$Var(A_{0,n+1}) = a^n q_1 (1 - a^n q_1).$

A variety of methods are available for estimating the three parameters of Model III, namely, the parameters q, a, and w. One method is to use the following three equations, which are easily derived from the model:

$$E\left(\sum_{i=1}^{n} A_{0,i}\right) = N - q \frac{1 - a^N}{1 - a}$$

$$P(A_{0,n+1}) = a^n q$$

$$P(A_{0,2}|A_{1,1}) = (1 - w)aq.$$

Another good way to estimate q is simply to take for a population of students the relative frequency of an error on the first trial. Extensive data analyses using Model III will be published with Zanotti elsewhere.

## THE FUTURE

The three examples of computer-based instruction I have described go far beyond what was actually available in 1966, but still fall far short of what we should see in the next decade. Here are some features future intelligent tutoring systems should have.

*Prediction.* A feature of good human tutoring that is not discussed enough as a requirement of intelligent tutoring systems is the ability to make good global forecasts of a student's progress. The human forecasts are based upon a great variety of information about the student, integrated in ways that we cannot yet explicitly describe. For computer purposes, a more formal and systematic theory is required, but fortunately there are many ideas about forecasting in the scientific literature that can be used effectively.

A typical remark of a good human tutor to a student is "Well, you have got to spend more time on this chapter if it is going to be of any use to you in taking the final exam." Note that in this kind of analysis it is not a matter of diagnosing particular individual difficulties of the student but in having a global overview of the kind of progress the student is making, and assessing how much more time and effort the student must make in a general way in order to accomplish agreed-upon goals.

In a computer-based course, we have the opportunity to organize the structure of the course in a detailed way so that we can expect the trajectory of a student working his way through the course to be a smooth function. For the purposes of prediction, however, it is not satisfactory just to find that a smooth function will fit the data points of the student's progress. What is really desired is that from any given initial segment of data, a predictive curve can be constructed which will not be too inaccurate in predicting the actual trajectory of the student. Beyond performance in a given course we are also concerned about understanding a student's progress on a still larger time scale. At this global level there have been a great variety of studies of predicting, for example, achievement in college based on grades in the first year, based on grades in high school, etc. We know a lot about how well we can do and what the limitations are of such large-scale predictions. We do not seem to have a very good understanding of how to make predictions that run over two or three years a good deal more precise than they currently are. I have in mind, of course, that other variables than simply cognitive ones will need to be brought to bear in such long-term predictions.

The prospect of good predictions is more optimistic, as already indicated, in an individual computer-based course, that might run for the course of an academic year. A detailed theory of such trajectories for a given course was developed in Suppes, Fletcher, and Zanotti (1976) and in a number of subsequent publications that I shall not cite. Implementation of these ideas is now under way at the Computer Curriculum Corporation, and we are having reasonably good results in predicting for three to six months in advance the progress of an individual student based on his performance over an initial several months. What we will need in the future, as the theory is developed and tested more thoroughly, are explicit dynamic algorithms for adjusting the time spent by the student and, in some cases, the kind of tutoring, to his specific progress.

*Cognitive diagnosis of learning difficulties.* A number of interesting ideas have been advanced in the past decade for diagnosing the cognitive source of particular student errors. The pioneering work of John Seely Brown and his colleagues at Xerox PARC has been an important contribution. The exact source of errors in some contexts can be diagnosed with precision and efficiency. A good example would be mistakes in inference. In using the interactive theorem—provers described earlier, when the student attempts an invalid inference he receives an error message that spells out in detail the nature of the error he has made. The explicitness of the message begins to fade away as the steps the student attempts to take become larger. Moreover, although we can make a very detailed analysis of invalid elementary inferences, we do a much poorer job when the student uses, for example, the resolution theorem-prover and is not successful. In some cases, devices for identifying the source of his difficulty can be implemented, but in others the problem is well-known to be beyond the reach of systematic theory, just because of the undecidability of the theories in question. Note that undecidability holds even at the level of first-order logic, which means that a theorem-prover cannot be guaranteed to show that an attempted inference is not a valid one in all cases.

It does not take much observation of a student's work at computer terminals to realize that a real problem for any cognitive diagnosis of errors is the continual presence of errors that are not explicitly cognitive in nature but are recognized immediately by the student as what I like to call output errors. For example, a student who is doing an exercise in elementary arithmetic will touch the key for one number rather than another, and immediately recognize the mistake. Sometimes the mistakes are ones of hand-eye coordination. Some are due to momentary lapses of concentration. I have not seen a real study, nor have I or my colleagues attempted one, of the many different sources of such errors at a level of detail enabling a quantitative estimate to be made. I do think that in elementary mathematics a surprising percentage of the errors students make can be attributed to such factors, and the cognitive diagnosis can then be easily mistaken. Let me give just one personal example. I have recently watched over several months my eight-year-old daughter do more than a thousand exercises in the elementary-mathematics course described above. She is very irked to get a contingent-tutoring message when the mistake she has made is one that she clearly recognizes as a casual mistake and not as a result of not understanding the exercise. The percentage of such casual mistakes, as a portion of her total number of errors, I would casually estimate as significant, but unfortunately I have not kept the kind of data records to enable me to make a quantitative estimate. I do think there is a methodology for trying to identify such noncognitive mistakes. Perhaps the most powerful method is latency measurements, for in the case at least of elementary-school children, I would conjecture that a good portion of such errors are due to responding too quickly and too casually, especially when a multiple response (for example, a response requiring several digits) is required. I am not trying to really describe the solution here, but only to bring to the front the problem of estimating such noncognitive mistakes, a problem that I think is a significant one for any intelligent tutoring system. The student thinks the system is pretty dumb if it does not recognize when a mistake is casual and not a result of misunderstanding.

*Maintaining motivation.* Good human tutors do not simply cognitively understand the difficulties of their students but they understand at least as well what it is that motivates them, and what will keep them working. If one were to survey the great variety of work in computer-assisted instruction that has been done in the past several decades, it would be my own judgment that the absence of sustained work on motivation is perhaps the most serious omission. There are a few exceptions, for example, Tom Malone's excellent study on what makes games fun (Malone, 1984).

The difficulties at the deepest level are fundamental. How do we recognize when a student is letting his mind wander, as we like to say? Perhaps the best way is by observing his eye movements and focus of attention. Observations of this kind are subtle, and at the present time quite difficult for any computer system to make. I mentioned earlier latencies of responses as a method of detecting noncognitive mistakes. Latencies can also be used to give us information about motivation but not as directly as other measures of attention. When I work with my daughter I can tell when she is getting tired, but I do not understand very well how to convert this intuitive knowledge into a program. I can also tell when she is finding a sequence of exercises boring, and even though I know my judgment is sometimes mistaken I still have faith that on many occasions I do correctly make such judgments, but again a program to catch this aspect of her response to the work is not easy to construct.

Some systematic experimental work on motivation in the past decade or so can provide interesting and important conceptual guidelines in introducing explicitly considerations of motivation in computer-based courses. On the other hand, it is my impression from this literature that a closer and more detailed interface between schemes of motivation and schemes of instruction is required to have a real impact on student performance.

*Dialogue.* In the 1966 article in the *Scientific American* I dreamed of dialogue systems that would be the rival of fourth century B.C. tutors in ancient Athens. I have not given up hope, even though we are not there yet. Interestingly enough, perhaps from the standpoint of the ancient Greek viewpoint the most important feature is a technical one not specific to education. This is the capability of good speech synthesis and good speech recognition, so that an oral dialogue can be properly conducted. In this age of compact disks and high fidelity it may seem that there is no real problem of computers talking but only of listening. However, this is not the case. It is not a characteristic of serious dialogue that message are precanned. It is important that the content of what is to be said be synthesized on the spot. This means that synthesizers that work by rule and not by digital approximation of an entire message are essential. We still do not have high-fidelity speech based on synthesis by rule and in fact we are just beginning to have minimally acceptable quality of speech operating on synthesis by rule. The fine and subtle prosodic features that any good tutor uses in talking to a student are still some distance away, but until we have them the Greek ideal will not be realizable just at the level of speech, not to speak of the content of the speech.

But more than content is needed for good dialogue. A good tutor deeply engaged with a student builds on the spot a global model of the mind of the student. We are only beginning to understand how to build such models, and we shall not in any near future match good human performance. But there are other things that we can do in a computer framework that even the best of human tutors cannot. Here are a few examples: intimate use of detailed memory of past responses of the student, subtle quantitative use of the speed of the student's responses, the generation of a vast range of exercises tailored to the needs and interests of the student—most human tutors do not have time for this, and even at a somewhat later date, monitoring a student's eye movements to give a refinement of insight that on some points can exceed what any human tutor can be expected to do. (For some evidence of the complexity of a quantitative theory of eye movements in an instructional setting, see Suppes, Cohen, Laddaga, Anliker, & Floyd, 1983.)

The Turing test for intelligence is well known in the computer world. We need a Socratic test for dialogue systems. I doubt that any system will really pass before the end of this century, but much useful theoretical and practical work will be done on the way.

## REFERENCES

Blaine, L. (1981). Programs for structured proofs. In P. Suppes (Ed.), *Computer-assisted instruction at Stanford: 1968–1980* (pp. 81–119). Stanford, CA: Stanford University, Institute for Mathematical Studies in the Social Sciences.

Hearn, A.C. (1987). *REDUCE user's manual: Version 3.3.* Santa Monica, CA: Rand Corporation.

Karlin, S. (1953). Some random walks arising in learning models I. *Pacific Journal of Mathematics, 3,* 725–756.

Malone, T.W. (1984). What makes computer games fun? Guidelines for designing educational computer programs. In D. Peterson (Ed.), *Intelligent schoolhouse.* Reston, VA: Reston Publishing Co.

McDonald, J., & Suppes, P. (1984). Student use of an interactive theorem prover. In W.W. Bledsoe & D.W. Loveland (Eds.), *Automated theorem proving: After 25 years* (pp. 315–360). American Mathematical Society.

Suppes, P. (1957). *Introduction to logic.* New York: Van Nostrand.

Suppes, P. (1972). *Axiomatic set theory.* New York: Dover. (Original work published 1960).

Suppes, P. (1966a). The uses of computers in education. *Scientific American, 215*(3), 206–220.

Suppes, P. (1966b). Tomorrow's education. *Education Age, 2,* 4–11.

Suppes, P. (Ed.). (1981). *University-level computer-assisted instruction at Stanford: 1968–1980.* Stanford, CA: Stanford University, Institute for Mathematical Studies in the Social Sciences.

Suppes, P., Cohen, M., Laddaga, R., Anliker, J., & Floyd, R. (1983). A procedural theory of eye movements in doing arithmetic. *Journal of Mathematical Psychology, 27,* 341–369.

Suppes, P., Fletcher, J.D., & Zanotti, M. (1976). Models of individual trajectories in computer-assisted instruction for deaf students. *Journal of Educational Psychology, 68,* 117–127.

Suppes, P., & Takahashi, S. (1989). An interactive calculus theorem-prover for continuity properties. *Journal of Symbolic Computation, 7,* 573–590.

# 13
# Toward a New Epistemology
# for Learning*

## John Seely Brown

### INTRODUCTION

As we look to the future of Intelligent Tutoring Systems (ITS), the very first question we must ask ourselves—the question whose answer is crucial to all our work—is "What do we really know about learning?" And, at the moment, the simple answer is, "Not nearly enough." I do not want to suggest, however, that our current lack of understanding is a cause for pessimism, because I believe, that in the recent, innovative field of *learning* research—and I want to stress learning, not teaching, nor educational, but learning research—there is some very exciting work going on that will, inevitably, force us to reexamine our fundamental assumptions, and that will offer us tremendously powerful new paradigms and new possibilities for learning technology.

In her presidential address to the American Educational Research Association (AERA), Lauren Resnick (1987) showed that we need to expand our school-based understanding of learning and to shift, or at least broaden, the focus of research. Her subject was the distinction between "practical and formal intelligence" (p. 13), and with this distinction she was able to point to the particularly significant (and unfortunate) division between approaches to "learning in and out of school." She argued that practical, out-of-school intelligence involves a great deal of learning, and, moreover, of highly successful learning, which at present we know little about.

Now, I want to examine the nature of this division in the context of ITS for two reasons. First, technology clearly exists both in and out of school. Indeed, it pervades almost all aspects of the modern world. If, therefore, in looking at learning technology, we look only at technology for schools or training courses and other sorts of in-school learning, we risk reinforcing the division that, as Resnick shows, already exists between the problematic learning in schools, and the more successful learning encountered elsewhere. And, further, we risk automatically and blindly inheriting all the widely recognized secondary problems of

---

*Many of the ideas that I put forth in this chapter have been developed with my colleagues at the Institute for Research on Learning. Several of these ideas have already appeared in or are in preparation for papers written collaboratively with Paul Duguid, who also helped in the writing of this chapter.

transferring in-school knowledge to the out-of-school world where it is intended to be used.

If, on the other hand, we do not limit our horizons to the highly specialized situation of schooling alone, it may be possible to design technology that can support learning activity wherever it is needed, both in and out of school, and both within and beyond the years of schooling. Instead of designing micro-environments for learning in school, we could more generally design the tools with which people live, learn, work, and conduct the normal transactions of daily life—including, but not limited to those used in school—so that our *world* becomes an environment for learning. The creation of such universal learning environments is becoming increasingly necessary in the face of the accelerating pace of change in the modern world. Put most simply, as society is coming to need life-long, ubiquitous learning (Brown & Duguid, in preparation), we can no longer afford to leave learning, and, in particular learning technology, to schools and school time alone.

My second reason for exploring Resnick's distinction is motivated by the recent literature on learning out of school. The work of, for instance, Carraher, Carraher, and Schliemann (1983), Lave (in preparation, 1988a, 1988b), Scribner (1984), Hutchins (in press)—and some studies of the non-academic learning that actually goes on in school (Willis 1981; Lave 1988c; Jordan, 1989; Eckert, 1989)—challenges many assumptions about learning. This work suggests that the way people do learn (rather than either the way they are taught or the way they are thought to learn) is significantly different from the conventional paradigms that underpin the methods of didactic education (and which tend, therefore, to underpin aspects of ITS). In short, I believe that, based on observations of out-of-school learning, a new epistemology of learning is emerging.

Formulating and exploring this new epistemology call upon us to distinguish carefully between the theorists' accounts of cognition, and the actual practices of ordinary people as they engage in the activities from which they learn. Descriptions of a mental state are not the same thing as the mental state itself. Theorists' descriptions tend to focus, inevitably, on explicit renderings of "knowledge," which have thus preoccupied most of the theory of the cognitive science and AI communities, and consequently have influenced much of the theory of ITS. As a result, all three, cognitive science, AI, and ITS, tend to assume too readily that knowledge, the goal of learning, resides in the head in explicit concepts and reified, abstractions. In particular, this assumption has focused attention on formal, explicit problem solving as the central characteristic of expertise.

Evidence from actual practices, however, suggests that the theorists' view overlooks both the fine balance between the implicit and the explicit in human cognition and the essential interplay between mind and world in sense making. The contribution of the implicit and even of the nonconceptual to expertise is little understood, as is the contribution of the world, though the importance of all three is beginning to be acknowledged (Cussins, 1988; Brown, Collins, & Duguid, 1988). Certainly, we need to develop far clearer insights than we have at present into the roles they play and how they interact in human learning.

Donald Schön (1983), developing ideas of Thomas Kuhn's, argues that "reflective practice," even in the science-based professions, begins with a deeply implicit process he calls "seeing as." According to Schön, people productively develop an understanding of a little understood situation by seeing it as in some way similar to a better understood situation. This process of "seeing as," Schön notes, begins with "an unarticulated perception. . . . Only later, in an effort to account for their earlier perception, did they [the subjects of Schön's research] develop an explicit account of the similarity" (p. 185–186). We begin, it seems, with the implicit and only later, if at all, move to an explicit and explicitly representable understanding of phenomena. As Lucy Suchman (1987) suggests, explicit representations are usually produced only "when otherwise transparent activity becomes in some way problematic" (p. 50).

The process of moving beyond the implicit and ultimately acquiring explicit knowledge and formal concepts is, moreover, not a simple process of information transfer. Good learning situations and successful ITS are successful, not because they enable a learner to ingest preformed knowledge in some optimal way, but rather, because they provide initially underdetermined, threadbare concepts to which, through conversation, negotiation, and authentic activity, a learner adds texture. Learning is much more an evolutionary, sense-making, experiential process of development than of simple acquisition. We must, therefore, attempt to use the intelligence in the learning environments to reflect and support the learner's or user's active creation or co-production, *in situ*, of idiosyncratic, highly "textured" models and concepts, whose texture is developed between the learner/user and the situating activity in which the technology is embedded.

My purpose in this chapter, then, is to examine these sorts of features of human learning that obtain, regardless of whether the learning goes on in or out of school, and to argue that a new paradigm for learning technology that can support the concept of learning as sense-making activity should follow from the sort of epistemology my examination entails.

## LEARNING IN AND OUT OF SCHOOL

Resnick (1987) notes four categories in which teaching within school differs significantly from learning without: Individual cognition versus shared cognition; pure mentation versus tool manipulation; symbol manipulation versus reasoning about "stuff"; generalized learning versus situation-specific competencies (pp. 13–16).

**Individual Cognition versus Shared Cognition.**

The conventional didactic classroom and its attendant methods of working and testing tend to be designed with the assumption that learning is an individual process. This view of learning has become dominant despite the fact that almost all other human activity, and particularly all learning and working out of school, is usually highly social. Even knowledge itself is coming to be recognized as a process of social construction (Wittgenstein, 1968; Bloor, 1983; Lave, 1988a). People evidently learn communally, but they are usually taught individually. We need to develop ways to transform the pedagogical assumptions implicit in the practice of teaching and to support communal learning, wherever it is needed. ITS can of course be designed to fit into either paradigm. But Roschelle's work with the "Envisioning Machine" (Behrend, Singer, & Roschelle, 1988) shows that the shift from seeing technology as a cognitive delivery system to seeing it as means to support collaborative conversations about a topic and the ensuing construction of understanding is a significant and highly productive one.

**Pure Mentation versus Tool Manipulation**

Schools tend to endorse the belief that thought is ideally a process that goes on in heads, independent of support from the environment—either social or physical. If "props" of some sort are allowed in learning, they are usually denied in testing. This emphasis on "mental processing" completely overlooks the fact that, outside school, tools make up a significant part of the environment in which people live and work. Moreover, it ignores the innovative, useful, and productive ways in which people deploy their environment to their advantage, using unrelated artifacts and apparently inconsequential features of a particular task as tools to spread the burden of cognition (see below).

**Symbol Manipulation in School versus Reasoning about "Stuff"**

Conventional school work with abstractions tends to involve students in manipulating symbols without being able to see or make connections between the symbols and the world to which they refer. Outside school people more usually either manipulate the stuff of the world itself directly, or if that is not possible, they work on symbols closely connected to their activities and through which they might be said to look onto the world itself (see below). Thus, in ordinary activity, symbols have a sort of transparency onto and a connectedness to situations, whereas in school, the symbols tend to be opaque and disconnected, becoming ends in themselves, not tools or means to an end based in authentic activity.

## Generalized Learning versus Situation-Specific Competencies

School learning is, of course, not accidentally different. It is designed to be abstract or general in order to be maximally transferrable. Situation-specific knowledge is thought not to be transferrable. It is becoming increasingly clear, however, that abstract knowledge is not only very difficult to learn, it is also not particularly transferrable. What is learned in the classroom too often cannot be carried beyond the classroom door. Thus, for instance, students with a highly developed classroom knowledge of physics are unable to put that knowledge to use except in classroom tests (McCloskey, Caramazza, & Green, 1980; diSessa, 1982, 1983; Haertel, personal communication). Less abstract situation-specific knowledge, on the other hand, appears to be much more easily acquired (Lave 1988b). Furthermore, situated knowledge also has a certain transferability. In this, it is rather like the folk tale, which carries its generality in its particulars; the body of the tale acts as scaffolding for seeing "into" and acting in a new situation. In Schön's concept of "seeing as," knowledge developed in a series of situation-specific circumstances is redeployed in new situations through the mind's ability to intuit analogies between the two. The particulars of the second situation seem to enable the mind to make the connection with the similarities of the first situation and apply them to the second, in a way that abstraction devoid of situations may, in fact, fail to do.

The in-school activities that Resnick points to in each of these four categories are so distinct from all other activities, that, first and foremost, we must question how school can be said to prepare students for later life.

## EVERYDAY COGNITION

An examination of everyday activities reveals how people ease the burden of cognition in two particularly useful ways that are not recognized by standard teaching or AI methodology. We all use our embodied and embedded position in the world to off-load onto our environment part of the representational and the computational burden of cognition. The processes that we use to do this allow us to respond in real time to events as they unfold in the world in which we are embedded.

Let me give three examples—in order of increasing complexity—of this sort of inventive representational and computational off-loading, which perhaps forms the basis of our ability to improvise. First are the many means we deploy to help us count—and, indeed, even to help us learn to count—using fingers, toes, tallies, recurring features of the environment, and so forth.

Second is an example from Jean Lave's study of supermarket shoppers (Lave, 1988b). Lave noted that though some shoppers carried and claimed to use calculators in pursuit of "best buy" bargains in the supermarket, in fact they used much more situated and inventive means of calculation. One shopper, for instance, faced with a barrel full of variously sized lumps of two sorts of cheese with individual prices but no unit prices, wanted to find out which cheese was cheaper. Instead of trying to work out the price-per-ounce of each cheese, which would probably have involved, among other things, two fairly complex long-division sums of the sort that are not easily done in the head, the shopper dug around until she found one piece of each cheese that was almost exactly the weight she wanted, and then chose the cheaper piece. By off-loading the representational and computational task onto the cheese itself in this way, the shopper did not just end up with an answer in her head that had then to be interpreted with regard to the cheese (i.e., having first found an abstract answer, the shopper would then have to find an appropriate piece of cheese). Rather, the situated computation concluded with the very piece of cheese that she wanted in her hand. What would otherwise have taken several different steps,[1] with each one capable of introducing its own sort of error, it simply took the repetition of one step with very little room for error.

Third is an example from Olivier de la Rocha's study of computation in a Weight Watcher's class (quoted in Lave, 1988b), whose participants were preparing their carefully regulated meals

> In this case they were to fix a serving of cottage cheese, supposing the amount laid out for the meal was three-quarters of the two-thirds cup the program allowed. The problem solver in this example began the task muttering that he had taken a calculus course in college . . . . Then after a pause he suddenly announced that he had "got it!" From then on he appeared certain he was correct, even before carrying out the procedure. He filled a measuring-cup two-thirds full of cottage cheese, dumped it out on the cutting board, patted it into a circle, marked a cross on it, scooped away one quadrant, and served the rest. (p. 165)

As Lave goes on to point out, the dieter's solution path was extremely practical. It reflected the nature of the activity, the resources available, and the sort of resolution required. And it resulted from the dieter's being embedded in the context of the problem, which itself was embedded in ongoing activity. The dieter's position gave him the ability to exploit the particulars of the context in which he was embedded and a privileged access to the solution path he chose. (This probably accounts for the certainty he expressed before beginning his calculation.) He was able to see the problem and its resolution in terms of the

---

[1]For example—Step 1: convert weight of cheese A to suitable units (e.g., ounces); Step 2: ditto for cheese B; Step 3: convert price of cheese A into suitable units (e.g., pennies); Step 4: ditto for cheese B; Step 5: divide weight of A by price for A; Step 6: ditto for cheese B; Step 7: compare prices for A and B; Step 8: find requisite sized lump of cheaper cheese. The apparent certainty said to result from symbol manipulation in tasks such as these is somewhat undermined by the multiple sources of potential error this sort of calculation introduces.

measuring cup, cutting board, and knife. Apparently inconsequential parts of the environment were appropriated as computing tools. He thus could use his environment to share with him both the representational and computational burden.

The dieter's actions are not in any way exceptional and are echoed in many ordinary working practices. Scribner (1984) records, for instance, how complex calculations are performed by people using their environment directly. Scribner studied, dairy loaders used the configuration of milk crates almost like an elaborate abacus. And Hutchins's (in press) study of intricate naval navigation showed, sailors share highly complex task of navigating an aircraft carrier both with the other members of the navigational team and with the environment. The resulting cognitive activity cannot simply be abstracted; it can only be explained, as Hutchins argues, in relation to the context in which it takes place: "When the context of cognition is ignored, it is impossible to see the contribution of the structure in the environment, in artifacts and in other people to the organization of mental processes" (msp. 31).

Instead of taking problems out of the context of their creation and providing them with an extraneous framework, people seem to be particularly adept at solving them within the framework of the context that produced them. They see (or, rather, they implicitly impute) a useful structure in the environment to help them represent and calibrate their tasks, and, similarly, they see tools, not just objects, in the various features of their surroundings. It is this inventive process that allows them to share the task—of both defining and solving the problem—with the task environment, responding in realtime and in context to the issue that emerges.

## EXPERT COGNITION

It may be objected that this sort of activity, these instances of *everyday cognition,* shows more evidence of the failings of education than of anything else. It might be thought that anyone with a good grasp of abstract computation would refuse to work in this informal way. Some have suggested, for instance, that the dieter was inept because he manipulated the world itself rather than mathematical symbols (Palincsar, 1989; Wineburg, 1989). Observations of the practice (rather than the subject matter theory) of highly competent physicists (Roschelle & Greeno, 1987; Greeno, 1988; deKleer & Brown, 1983) and of equally competent electronics troubleshooters (Brown & Burton, 1987), however, argue that experts also employ thoroughly situated reasoning strategies and not just decontextualized abstractions (White & Frederiksen, in press). Indeed Schön (1983, 1987) proposes that the ability to reason in this situated way is a central component of expertise.

Roschelle's work shows how physicists "run" envisionments in order to help them reason about physical structures in the world. He presented physicists with

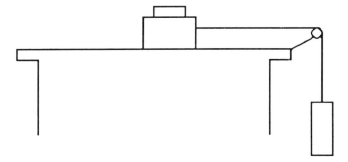

**Figure 13.1.   Physics diagram.**

diagrams such as those in Figure 13.1, and he asked them to describe the forces at work. The protocols the physicists produces included remarks such as, "This one is very interesting because it illustrates a very important point, which is that friction isn't always in the wrong direction—or the right direction" (p. 12). This physicist recounted how he had started with a force diagram "in his head," that included a friction force associated with the smallest block, pointed to the left, while envisioning that the entire system on the table moved in the opposite direction. The evidence of the envisionment contradicted the implications of his force diagram, which led him to reformulate the problem in order to resolve the contradiction: "The answer," he reported, "is . . . that friction opposes relative motion . . . so the friction's going . . . to oppose the motion between the little mass and the big mass its sitting on. And that happens to be to the right if the big mass is moving to the right" (Greeno, 1988, p. 12).

The evidence from work with physicists and troubleshooters suggests first, that experts are able to see *through* their formulae and mental models onto the world of physical objects, so for them these formulae are transparent with respect to the world; and, second, that they are able to see or impute causality or reasoning "behind" or "within" those objects. Thus, Roschelle's physicists "saw" the forces underlying the physical situation.

Similarly, in a circuit diagram, such as that for the Schmitt trigger (Figure 13.2), it becomes quite clear that standard explanations provided by textbooks employ a series of unwritten assumptions that are necessary in order for the explanation to "work." In fact, deKleer and Brown (1983) and Brown and Burton (1987) showed that, in constructing their mental models of a specific circuit, experts made a number of informal, situation-specific assumptions about questions that they could not definitively answer, which they held in abeyance while they pursued a reasoning-path around the circuit. Each of these assumptions was objectively unwarranted and simply resulted from the experts' adroitness in "seeing as." To simplify their reasoning, they were able to see transistors either as amplifiers or as switches, depending on the particular circumstances.

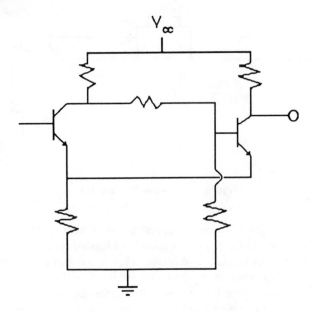

**Figure 13.2.   Schmitt trigger.**

Once they had a "causal story," the experts could then go back and make sure that each assumption cohered with the overall account. Only after these qualitative models had been developed, could the appropriate mathematical models be effectively deployed (modeling a transistor as a switch, for example, is considerably simpler than modeling it as an amplifier).

Figure 13.3 shows the sort of simplified causal pattern that the experts see "behind" the Schmitt trigger in order to explain its workings, and indeed, it suggests the way that experts off-load the task of tracing and keeping track of causality in a circuit onto the diagram itself, making annotations to help remember at what point they had made assumptions about significant voltage changes. (For a fuller account, see deKleer & Brown, 1983; Brown & Burton, 1987.)

This sort of imputation of causality—constructing a causal story—involves a great deal of informal reasoning and manipulating of assumptions that standard explications inevitably overlook. Rather than simply pondering abstractions, this essential sort of reasoning involves "seeing through" abstractions, models, and paradigmatic examples to the world they represent, and then penetrating that world to explore the causality that underlies it. It is, in some sense, a little like getting beyond the ability to read a map by looking over it, to a state in which you expertly negotiate the map by being in it.

This sort of practice is evidenced by, for instance, experienced architects who seem to see (rather than merely extrapolate to) three dimensions in a two dimensional plan. Becoming an expert, even in a formal discipline like abstract mathe-

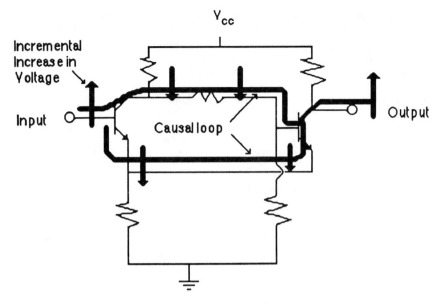

**Figure 13.3.   Causal reasoning with the Schmitt trigger.**

matics or logic, requires, in a similar way, fully entering "in" the abstract situation as opposed to merely being, like the map reader, over it. At the moment, we lack adequate computational or representational machinery to account for this form of expertise, though the work of Brian Smith (in preparation), which has inspired several ideas in this chapter, is leading us in the right direction.

## EVERYDAY COGNITION AND EXPERT REASONING

In exploring the reasoning of what Jean Lave (1988b) has called "Just Plain Folks" (JPFs) and of experts, I have tried to show the surprising similarity between their implicit reasoning *processes*. Both have a belief system that treats learning as a sense-making pursuit that grapples with ill-defined problems (Brown, Collins, & Duguid, 1989b). Both are heavily situated. Both try to produce reasonable, causal stories about their world. Both negotiate with the situations. Schön (1983), for instance, describes experts as conversing with the situation itself. Both take as much advantage as possible of their embodied and embedded position to help them make inventive and insightful assumptions and approximations. This is quite distinct from the sort of cognitive activity that, as Resnick shows, is assumed to go on in school. It is also distinct from the sort of problem solving many of our models of expertise have captured in the past.

**Table 13.1.   JPF, Expert, and Putative Student Learning Activity**

|  | JPFs | Students | Expert Practice |
|---|---|---|---|
| reasoning with: | causal stories | laws | causal models |
| acting on: | situations | symbols | conceptual situations |
| resolving: | emergent dilemmas | well-defined problems | ill-defined problems |
| producing: | negotiable meaning & socially constructed | fixed meaning & immutable understanding | negotiable meaning & socially constructed concepts understanding |

While, then, between the JPF and the expert, there appears to be a continuum, between the student and the expert—on the conventional path of learning—there is a clear discontinuity.

I try to represent both the continuum and the discontinuity in Table 13.1, which compares salient features of JPF, experts, and putative student behavior.

This table is intended to make apparent the great similarity between JPFs' and experts' activity. Beyond the explicit features I have emphasized in the examples above, it can also be argued that, unlike students, both have their activities situated in the cultures in which they work, within which they negotiate meanings and construct understanding. The issues and problems that they face arise out of, are defined by, and are resolved within the constraints of the activity they are pursuing. Students, by contrast, are generally expected to behave entirely differently. Usually, it is only in the final stages of graduate education, when students come to do independent research in the community of scholars, that they move from the in-school world of laws, symbols, well-defined problems, and so forth, to the out-of-school world that circumscribes the activities of both JPFs and experts.

## IMPLICATIONS—PARADIGMS FOR DESIGN

So, what are the immediate implications of the similarity between experts and JPFs and the disjunction between these two and putative school learning?

First of all, if formal teaching in school and the conditions of school are highly specialized and overlook the key implicit features of human learning, then, in order to take advantage of those robust, innovative features, we need to enact a fundamental shift in the focus of our research and practice.

If the options for research and practice can be represented in a matrix (Figure 13.4) that includes explicit knowledge *and* implicit understanding, and formal

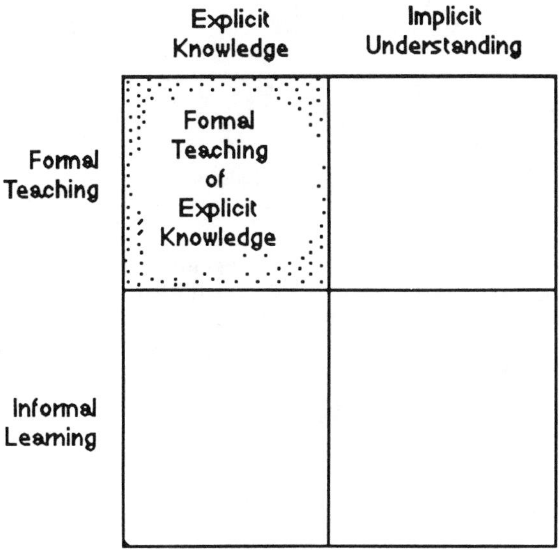

|  | Explicit<br>Knowledge | Implicit<br>Understanding |
|---|---|---|
| Formal<br>Teaching | Formal<br>Teaching<br>of<br>Explicit<br>Knowledge | |
| Informal<br>Learning | | |

**Figure 13.4.**

teaching *and* informal learning, then it is not unfair to argue that most attention is currently focused on the top left-hand quadrant—the formal teaching of explicit knowledge and in particular, of formal problem solving.

We need to break down the rigid compartmentalization of such a matrix and focus our research across continuums that stretch from the formal to the informal and from the explicit to the implicit (Figure 13.5).

Studies of experts, like Schön's (1987) or Lave's (in preparation), indicate that any account of expertise that tries to reflect only the cognitive, abstract, and abstractable content (represented in the top, right-hand quadrant of Figure 13.4) will be wholly inadequate for someone learning that expertise. Expertise involves what Schön calls a "practicum," through which a learner enters the "traditions of a community of practitioners and the practice world they inhabit. . . . [acquiring] their conventions, constraints, languages, and appreciative systems, their repertoire of exemplars, systematic knowledge, and patterns of knowing-in-action" (pp. 36–37). Thus I have referred elsewhere (Brown, Collins, & Duguid, 1989a) to learning as at core a process of *enculturation,* of entry into a culture or community of practice. The challenge for ITS, then, is to construct environments that reflect the nature of the practicum and that support the process of enculturation. These environments will have to be not simply Increasingly Complex Microworlds (Burton, Brown & Fischer, 1984), but rather, Increasingly Complex Enculturating Environments (Brown, Collins, & Duguid, 1989a).

Second, if, as I have argued, the reasoning of JPFs and experts is usefully similar, and if conventional student learning activity is a significant deviation

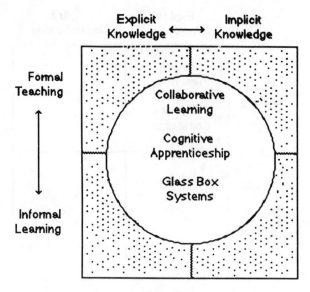

**Figure 13.5.**

from the learning norm, then concentrating our research just on the current paradigms of education might be a serious mistake. Conversely, if we concentrate instead on supporting the learning activities of JPFs, believing that they exhibit the sort of learning activity that should go on in school, then we will inevitably bridge the gap between learning in and out of school—because the two processes converge. If we can bridge this gap, then the target of rendering the world as an environment for learning may not seem as grandiose or as impractical as at first. Moreover, the current entrenched separation between learning and working may slowly dissolve as learning and working become one. As we enter an era of increasingly rapid change, the need to learn while working is becoming imperative. We, therefore, need, if it is at all possible, to design technology that can help people both learn and work, simultaneously. And the emerging epistemology of situated learning suggests that this is indeed possible.

Third, to introduce learning technology that extends across the continuums of Figure 13.5, we need new paradigms for design to reflect the new epistemology and the new focus.

According to my characterization of this new epistemology, our tools will need to honor the following salient, currently overlooked, features of learning:

• They will have to honor the way people interact with the world, sharing with their environment the representational and computational burdens of tasks.

• They will have to reflect the environment and context in which both users and tools are embedded and allow learners to deploy inventive problem-solving skills within that environment. Thus, they must not overconstrain the kinds of reasoning they support.

- They will have to honor the social construction of knowledge—supporting conversations and shared explorations rather than delivering unquestionable definitions and answers. That is, they must allow users, *in situ*, to add texture, both by talking about and experiencing the situation, in the way I described above.
- They will have to look beyond conventional problem solving and allow issues, dilemmas, and problems to emerge from authentic activity and to be resolved with regard to the constraints and demands of that activity.
- And they will have to permit the reflective, analogic process of "seeing as," which appears to be such an important feature of human understanding.

At the core of these criteria is a necessary transparency that allows users to see through the technological tools themselves so that both technological tools and conceptual tools are not ends-in-themselves, but means to an end, which is the seamless pursuit of authentic activity. Thus, these sorts of tools have been dubbed "Glass-box technology."

Another image for this sort of technology with an exalted heritage is offered by Hubert Dreyfus (paraphrasing Wittgenstein and Merleau-Ponty):

> Consider the example of the blind man's cane. We can hand the man the cane and ask him to tell us what properties it has. After hefting and feeling it, he can tell us that it is light, smooth, about three feet long, and so on; it is present-at-hand for him. But when the man starts to use the cane (when he grasps it in that special mode of understanding that Heidegger calls 'manipulation') he loses his awareness of the cane itself; he is aware only of the curb (or whatever object the cane touches); or, if all is going well, he is not even aware of that. Thus it is that equipment that is ready-to-hand is invisible just when it is most genuinely appropriated. (Suchman, 1987)

## Glass-Box Technology

The goal of design of any tool or device, therefore, should be to produce "glass boxes," which, first and foremost, connect users to the world. Further, in response to examination and investigation, they should allow users to build adequate mental models and provide a useful focus for collaborative discussions and the social construction of knowledge. Essentially, the current opaque technology or "black boxes" must become "transparent" to the user, allowing him or her to see "through" the tool (this I call "domain transparency"), or "into" the tool ("internal transparency"), or to see the relationship of the technology and its user in the larger context of the interaction between the user and the tool ("embedding transparency"). The depth and complexity of this sort of technology is being explored by Etienne Wenger (1988), and his taxonomies are richer than my quick sketch here.

1. *Domain transparency*. This transparency provides a user with a view of the domain in which he or she is working. Glass windows, archetypes of transparency, serve on the one hand to keep out cold, germs, people, and so forth. But

this is only part of their job. Unlike brick walls and wood doors, they also allow people to see through them unimpeded, to whatever is the focus of attention. Black box tools are only doing one part—the exclusionary part—of their job. Auto diagnostic aids, for instance, help an auto mechanic service the ignition, or whatever, but they generally impede any attempt to see through the tool onto the domain, to impute causality to the process and thereby understand how the instructions a mechanic carries out affect the workings of the ignition. Domain transparency is achieved by tools whose presence, like a magnifying glass is both effective and invisible. The tool remains unobtrusive while bringing the workings of the domain, into coherent focus.

2.  *Internal transparency.* For the auto mechanic, there are (at least) two complex machines—the car's black box and the diagnostic aid. Domain transparency would allow the mechanic to see through the diagnostic aid onto the workings of the engine. The diagnostic aid would thereby become invisible. But the mechanic could also usefully learn parts of how the diagnostic aid itself reasons as an expert. This would require internal transparency (which of course is also something that the car engine itself might support with respect to its own processes). The "expert reasoning" built into smart job performance aids should be accessible to people learning with those tools so that the users can build for themselves adequate models of the reasoning processes that contribute to the completion of the task (Clancey, 1986).

Internal transparency should ideally be able to support, through continuous metaphors and images, explanations and explorations of variable depth. The more one needs to know about a particular tool, the more one should be able to find out (Haertel, 1987). But simultaneously, initial understanding should not be complicated with unnecessary detail.

3.  *Embedding transparency.* Many information tools inadvertently isolate people from any understanding of the overall processes of which they are a part and to which the contribute. Tools, like rigid abstractions, can then become decontextualized, exhibiting little evident connection to the rest of the world. Technology design must concern itself with ways to remain connected with the world so that the interactions with the technology take place within the context of ongoing interactions between the user and the world.

Despite the immense latent power of the technology, it is clearly not easy to develop these sorts of transparency, for the development clearly does not depend on power alone, but on a profound understanding of the situated social elements of human learning I have been describing. Thus, as I suggested at the outset, our first task must be to recognize how little we currently do understand about learning and to endeavor to find out a great deal more.

## CONCLUSION—THE CHALLENGE FOR ITS

At present, the ITS community confronts a profound and exciting challenge. As a result of our central concern with learning, we find ourselves at the heart of an emergent epistemology. It is, therefore, members of this community who are most likely to find themselves uncovering better, and much needed, models of the architecture of cognition, because it is this community that is most closely coupled to—or situated in—the full blooded complexity of human learning activity. Thus, if we meet this challenge correctly, it may well be that, instead of ITS being merely one subset of the overall schema of AI, we will, instead, find that it is AI that becomes one subset of the overall schema of ITS.

## REFERENCES

Behrend, S., Singer, J., & Roschelle, J. (1988). *A methodology for the analysis of collaborative learning in a physics microworld.* Paper presented at ITS-88, Montreal, Canada.

Bloor, D. (1983). *Wittgenstein and the social construction of knowledge.* New York: Columbia University Press.

Brown, J.S., & Burton, R. (1987). Reactive learning environments for teaching electronic trouble shooting. *Advances in Man Machine Research, 3,* 65–98.

Brown, J.S., Collins, A., & Duguid, P. (1989a). Situated cognition and the culture of learning. *Education Researcher, 18*(1), 32–42. (Also available in a fuller version as IRL Report 88-008. Palo Alto, CA: Institute for Research on Learning.)

Brown, J.S., Collins, A., & Duguid, P. (1989b). Debating the situation: A rejoinder to Wineburg and Palincsar. *Educational Researcher, 18*(4), 10–12.

Brown, J.S., & Duguid, P. (in preparation). Innovation and organizational learning.

Burton, R., Brown, J.S., & Fischer, G. (1984). Skiing as a model of instruction. In B. Rogoff & J. Lave (Eds.), *Everyday cognition: Its development in social context* (pp. 139–159). Cambridge, MA: Harvard University Press.

Carraher, T., Carraher, D., & Schliemann, A. (1983). *Mathematics in the streets and schools.* Unpublished manuscript on file at Recife, Brazil, Universidad Federal de Pernambuco.

Clancey, W. (1986). *From Guidon to Neomycin and Heracles in twenty short lessons.* (Report KSL 86-11). Palo Alto, CA: Stanford University, Department of Computer Science.

Cussins, A. (1988). *The connectionist construction of concepts.* (SSL Research Report). Palo Alto, CA: Xerox Palo Alto Research Center.

deKleer, J. (1985). How circuits work. In D.G. Bobrow (Ed.), *Qualitative reasoning about physical systems* (pp. 205–280). Cambridge, MA: MIT Press.

deKleer, J., & Brown, J.S. (1983). Assumptions and ambiguities. In D. Gentner & A.L. Stevens (Eds.), *Mental models* (pp. 155–196). Hillsdale, NJ: Erlbaum.

diSessa, A. (1983). Phenomenology and the evolution of intuition. In D. Gentner & A. Stevens (Eds.), *Mental models* (pp. 15–33). Hillsdale, NJ: Erlbaum.

diSessa, A. (1982). Unlearning Aristotelian physics: A study of knowledge-based learning. *Cognitive Science, 6,* 37–75.

Eckert, P. (1989). *Jocks and Burnouts.* Philadelphia: Temple University Press.

Greeno, J.G. (1988). *Situations, mental models, and generative knowledge.* (IRL report 88-0005). Palo Alto, CA: Institute for Research on Learning.

Haertel, H. (1987). *A qualitative approach to electricity.* (IRL report 87-0001). Palo Alto, CA: Institute for Research on Learning.

Hutchins, E. (in press). Learning to navigate. In S. Chalkin & J. Lave (Eds.), *Situated learning*.

Jordan, B. (1989). Cosmopolitical obstetrics: Some insights from the training of midwives. *Social Science and Medicine*. (Also available as IRL report 87-0004. Palo Alto, CA: Institute for Research on Learning.)

Lave, J. (in preparation). Tailored learning: Education and everyday practice among craftsmen in West Africa.

Lave, J. (1988a). *The culture of acquisition and the practice of understanding*. (IRL report 88-0007). Palo Alto, CA: Institute for Research on Learning.

Lave, J. (1988b). *Cognition in practice*. Boston, MA: Cambridge University Press.

Lave, J. (1988c). *Word problems: A microcosm of theories of learning*. Paper presented at AERA Annual Conference, New Orleans.

McCloskey, M., Caramazza, A., & Green, B. (1980). Curvilinear motion in the absence of external forces: Naive beliefs about the motion of objects. *Science, 210*, 1139–1141.

Palincsar, A. (1989). Less chartered waters. *Educational Researcher, 18*(4), pp. 5–7.

Resnick, L. (1987). Learning in school and out. *Educational Researcher, 4*, 13–20.

Rogoff, B., & Lave, J. (Eds.). (1984). *Everyday cognition: Its development in social context*. Cambridge, MA: Harvard University Press.

Roschelle, J., & Greeno, J.G. (1987). *Mental models in expert physics reasoning* (Report GK-2). Berkeley, CA: University of California School of Education.

Schön, D. (1987). *Educating the reflective practitioner*. San Francisco: Jossey-Bass.

Schön, D. (1983). *The reflective practitioner*. New York: Basic Books.

Scribner, S. (1984). Studying working intelligence. In B. Rogoff & J. Lave (Eds.), *Everday cognition: Its development in social context* (pp. 9–40). Cambridge, MA: Harvard University Press.

Smith, B. (in preparation). *The view from somewhere*. Cambridge, MA: MIT Press.

Suchman, L. (1987). *Plans and situated actions*. New York: Cambridge University Press.

Wenger, E. (1988). *Glass-box technology and integrated learning: Information, communication, and knowledge in computerized environments*. (IRL Working Paper). Palo Alto, CA: Institute for Research on Learning.

White, B., & Frederiksen, J. (in press). Causal model progressions as foundations for intelligent learning environments. *Artificial Intelligence*.

Willis, P. (1981). *Learning to labor*. New York: Columbia University Press.

Wineburg, S. (1989). Remembrances of theories past: A response to Brown, Collins, and Duguid. *Educational Researcher, 18*(4), 7–11.

Wittgenstein, L. (1968). *Philosophical Investigations*. [Trans. G.E. Anscombe. (3rd edition; 1st English edition 1951]. Oxford, England: Blackwell.

# Author Index

## A

Abelson, H., 41, 43, 44, *53, 54,* 67, *82,* 222, 230
Achthoven, W.A., 136, *138*
Adam, A., 148, *159,* 213, *230*
Adelson, B., 209, *230*
Aho, A., 217, *231*
Aizenstein, H., 7, 30, 31, *31*
Alexander, P.A., 167, *187*
Allen, J., 65, *81*
Anderson, J.R., 2, *5,* 83, 84, 87, 88, 89, 91, 100, 104, *105, 106,* 108, *122,* 125, *137,* 140, *159,* 198, *204,* 212, 213, *231, 232,* 242, *249*
Angluin, D., 218, *231*
Anliker, J., 264, *265*
Arens, Y., 125, *138*

## B

Bauren, J.v.d., 124, *137*
Banerji, R.B., 27, *32,* 226, *231*
Barrie, J.B., 142, 149, 152, 153, *159*
Baskin, A.B., 6, 7, 20, *31, 32*
Behrend, S., 269, *281*
Bergeron, A., 35, 43, *53, 54*
Berliner, D.C., 170, *186*
Biddle, B.J., 173, *186*
Bison, P., 129, *137*
Blaine, L., 253, *265*
Blegen, D., 242, *249*
Bloom, B.S., 84, *105*
Bloor, D., 269, *281*
Bobrow, D., 44, 45, *55,* 214, 217, *231*
Bonar, J., 131, *137,* 206, 215, *233,* 241, *249*
Bordier, J., 35, *54*
Borne, I., 43, *53*
Borning, A., 34, *53*
Bouchard, L., 43, *53*
Boyle, C.F., 83, 87, 89, *105,* 125, *137,* 213, *231,* 241, *249*
Bradshaw, G.L., 36, 41, 50, *54*
Brecht, B., 142, 154, 156, *160*
Breuker, J.A., 124, 129, 130, *137, 138*
Brooks, R., 224, *231*
Brown, D., 247, *249*
Brown, J.S., 7, *31,* 56, *81,* 90, *106,* 116,
*122,* 124, 126, 133, 135, *137,* 140, 153, *160, 161,* 192, *204,* 213, *231,* 267, 272, 273, 274, 275, 277, *281*
Bundy, A., 28, *33*
Bunt, R.B., 140, *160*
Burns, J.B., 221, *231*
Burton, R.R., 7, *31,* 133, 135, *137,* 153, *160,* 213, *231,* 272, 273, 274, 277, *281*

## C

Caramazza, A., 270, *282*
Carbonell, J.R., 41, 50, *54,* 234, *249*
Carr, B., 228, *231*
Carraher, D., 267, *281*
Carraher, T., 267, *281*
Carroll, J.M., 73, 80, *81*
Cauzinille-Marmeche, E., 116, *123*
Cerri, S., 197, *204*
Chabay, R.W., 89, *106*
Chan, T.W., 6, 7, 10, 30, *31, 32*
Chin, D., 125, *138*
Clancey, W.J., 73, *81,* 114, *122,* 126, 135, 136, *137,* 228, *231,* 280, *281*
Clark, C.M., 163, 171, *186*
Clark, H.H., 136, *137*
Clarridge, P.B., 170, *186*
Clement, J., 247, *249*
Clinger, W., *54*
Cohen, M., 264, *265*
Collins, A., 56, *81,* 136, *138,* 192, 197, *204,* 205, 267, 275, 277, *281*
Comeaux, M.A., 170, 173, *187*
Conrad, F.C., 84, *105*
Corbett, A.T., 83, 91, *105*
Corno, L., 115, *122,* 167, 184, 185, *186*
Cross, D.B., 117, *122*
Cunningham, R., 131, *137*
Cushing, K., 170, *186*
Cussins, A., 267, *281*
Cutler, B., 209, *231*

## D

Dahl, O.-J., 208, *231*
Dällof, U.S., 166, *186*
Dansereau, D.F., 167, *186*
DeJong, G., 25, *32*

DeKleer, J., 7, *31*, 133, *137*, 272, 273, 274, *281*
Dijkstra, E., 208, *231*
diSessa, A., 36, 41, 43, *54*, 270, *281*
Doise, W., 8, *32*
Doyle, J., 221, *231*
Draper, S., 209, *231*
Drescher, G.L., 43, *54*
Duguid, P., 267, 275, 277, *281*
Dunkin, M.J., 173, *186*
Duursma, C., 124, *137*
Dyer, M.G., 125, *138*

**E**
Eckert, P., 267, *281*
Ehrlich, K., 212, *233*
Elawar, M.C., 184, 185, *186*
Elsom-Cook, M., 127, *137*, 188, 191, 197, 203, *204, 205*
Ennals, K., 34, 39, *54*
Erman, L.D., 141, *160*
Escott, J.A., 142, 149, 155, *160*
Evertson, C.M., 173, *186*

**F**
Farrell, R., 87, 88, 89, *105*, 212, 213, *232*
Fischer, G., 125, *137*, 140, *160*, 277, *281*
Fletcher, J.D., 262, *265*
Flowers, M., 125, *138*
Floyd, R., 264, *265*
Foss, C.L., 120, *122*
Fox, B.A., 89, *106*
Fraisse, P., 57, *81*
Frederiksen, J., 272, *282*
Freiman, S., 209, *233*
Friedland, P.E., 131, *137*

**G**
Gage, N.L., 162, *186*
Gary, G.H., 26, *32*
Gennip, A. van., 136, *138*
Gilmore, D.J., 9, *32*, 119, *122*
Glaser, R., 34, *54*
Goetz, E.T., 167, *187*
Gold, E.M., 224, *231*
Goldin, S.E., 197, *205*
Goldstein, E.P., 114, *122*, 129, *137*, 154, *160*, 221, 228, 229, 230, *231*
Goodman, K.S., 7, *32*
Gray, W., 104, *106*
Green, B., 270, *282*

Green, J.L., 173, *186*
Greeno, J.G., 166, 173, *187*, 272, 273, *281*, *282*
Greer, J.E., 152, *160*, 229, *231*

**H**
Haas, N., 26, *32*
Haertel, H., 280, *281*
Harms, J.J., 140, *160*
Hartley, J.R., 74, *81*, 125, *138*
Havilland, S.E., 136, *137*
Hayes-Roth, F., 141, *160*
Hearn, A.C., 255, *265*
Hoare, C.A.R., 208, *231*
Holland, J.H., 41, *54*
Holley, C.D., 167, *186*
Holyoak, K.J., 41, *54*
Hook, C.M., 170, *186*
Huang, X., 142, 147, *160*
Hughes, S., 74, *81*
Hutchins, E., 267, 272, *282*

**I**
Ikeda, M., 114, *122*
Iwasaki, Y., 131, *137*

**J**
Jeffries, R., 100, *105*
Jensen, J., 242, *249*
Johnson, M.L., 103, *106*
Johnson, W.L., 4, *5*, 140, 149, *160*, 206, 209, 212, 215, *231, 233*
Jordan, B., 267, *282*
Joyce, B., 166, *186*

**K**
Kakusho, O., 114, *122*
Karlin, S., 260, *265*
Kearsley, G.P., 140, *160*
Kedar-Cabelli, S.T., 27, 28, *32*
Keller, R.M., 27, 28, *32*
Kitchen, L., 221, *231*
Kolodner, J.L., 109, *122*
Kozma, R.B., 117, *122*
Kramer, L.L., 168, *186*
Kulik, C.C., 89, *106*
Kulik, J.A., 89, *106*

**L**
Labelle, M., 35, *54*
Laddaga, R., 264, *265*

Laird, J.E., 25, *32*
Laird, P., 223, *231*
Langley, P., 36, 41, 50, *54*
Lauer, S., 57, *81*
Laurent, J.-P., 148, *159*, 213, *230*
Lave, J., 267, 269, 270, 271, 275, *282*
Lawler, R.W., 41, *54*
Lehnert, W.G., 74, *82*, 125, *138*
Leinhardt, G., 166, 173, *187*
Lemke, G., 125, *137*
Lenat, D.B., 26, *32*
Lepper, M.R., 89, *106*
Lesser, V.R., 141, *160*
Letvosky, S., 207, 209, 221, 226, *231, 232, 233*
Lieberman, H., 44, *54*
Lipman, M., 209, *233*
Littman, D., 206, 209, 226, *232, 233*
Loerinc, B., 209, *233*
Looi, C.K., 140, *160, 222, 232*
Luria, M., 131, *138*

**M**

Macmillan, S.A., 127, *138*, 143, 158, *160*
Mahadevan, S., 30, *32*
Malone, T.W., 263, *265*
Mark, M.A., 152, *160*
Mathieu, J., 116, *123*
McCalla, G.I., 144, 145, 147, 152, 155, 156, 158, *160, 161*, 229, *231*
McCloskey, M., 270, *282*
McDermott, D.V., 60, *82*
McDonald, D.D., 127, 133, *139*
McDonald, J., 253, *265*
McKeachie, W.J., 117, *123*
McKeown, K.R., 131, 136, *138*
Meyrowitz, N., 243, *250*
Michalski, R.S., 26, *32*, 41, 50, *54*, 210, 218, 220, *232*
Miller, M., *232*
Miller, P.L., 30, *32*
Minsky, M., 44, *54*
Mitchell, T.M., 27, 28, 30, *32*, 41, 50, *54*
Mizoguchi, R., 114, *122*
Mobus, C., 114, *122*
Monaco, J., 59, 61, *82*
Montmollin, G. de., 57, *81*
Mooney, R., 25, *32*
Mostow, D.J., 26, *32*
Mugny, G., 8, *32*
Murray, T., 127, *139*, 244, 247, *249*
Murray, W.R., 140, 148, *161*, 214, 222, *232*

**N**

Nadeau, R., 35, 43, *53, 54*
Neves, D.M., 29, *33*
Newell, A., 25, *32*
Newman, S.E., 56, *81*
Ng, T.H., 142, 144, *161*
Nisbett, R.E., 41, *54*

**O**

Ohlsson, S., 126, 136, *138*, 188, *204*
O'Shea, T., 39, *54*

**P**

Palincsar, A., 272, *282*
Papert, S., 26, *33*, 34, 41, *54*, 195, *205*, 234, *249*
Paquette, G., 35, *54*
Parkes, A.P., 58, 59, 60, 61, 65, 72, 80, *82*
Pask, G., 115, *122*
Payne, S.J., 116, *122*
Peachey, D., 156, 158, *160*
Perkins, D.N., 168, 183, *187*
Perret-Clermont, A., 8, *32*
Peters, R.S., 202, *205*
Peterson, P.L., 171, 173, *186, 187*
Petitto, A., 8, *33*
Pinto, J., 209, 226, *232*
Pintrich, P.R., 117, *122*
Pirolli, P.L., 87, *106*
Polya, G., 26, *33, 49, 55*
Pope, E., 209, *233*
Popper, K.R., 36, *54*
Pospisil, P.R., 142, 152, 153, *161*

**Q**

Quillici, A.E., 125, *138*

**R**

Raghavan, K., 34, *54*
Reddy, D.R., 141, *160*
Rees, J., *54*
Reichman, R., 136, *138*
Reid, L., 145, *161*
Reiser, B.J., 2, *5, 83*, 84, 87, 89, *105*, 108, *122*, 140, *159*, 213, *232*, 241, *249*
Rengel, B., 129, *138*
Resnick, L.B., 116, *122*, 267, 268, *282*
Rich, C., *232*
Rissland, E., 247, *249*
Rist, R., 224, *232*
Rogoff, B., *282*

Roschelle, J., 269, 271, *281, 282*
Rosenbloom, P.S., 25, *32*
Rosenshine, B., 170, *186*
Rousseau, J.J., 195, *205*
Rubin, E., 206, 215, *233*
Ruth, G., 212, 213, *232*

**S**
Sabers, D., 170, *186*
Sack, W., 206, 209, 221, 224, 228, *232, 233*
Salamon, G., 80, *82*
Sandberg, J.A.C., 107, *123*, 124, 129, *137, 138*
Sauers, R., 87, 88, *105*, 212
Schank, R.C., 67, *82*
Schliemann, A., 267, *281*
Schneider, P.F., 145, *161*
Schoenfeld, A.H., 7, 11, 12, *33*
Schön, D., 268, 272, 275, 277, *282*
Schultz, J., 131, *137*, 241, *249*
Schultz, K., 244, *249*
Schwab, T., 125, *137*
Scribner, S., 267, 272, *282*
Self, J., 9, *32, 33*, 39, *54*, 117, 119, *122, 123*, 125, 126, *138*
Sethi, R., 217, *231*
Shapiro, D., 213, *232*
Shapiro, E., 215, 225, 226, *232*
Shauble, L., 34, *54*
Shoham, Y., 65, *82*
Shrager, J., 109, *123*
Shrobe, H., 221, *232*
Simon, H.A., 36, 41, 50, *54*
Singer, J., 269, *281*
Singley, M.K., 110, *123*
Skwarecki, E.J., 96, *106*, 198, *204*
Slavin, R.E., 119, *123*
Sleeman, D.H., 90, 92, *106*, 117, *123*, 125, 126, *138*, 140, 143, 158, *160*, 212, 213, *232*
Smith, B., 275, *282*
Smith, C., 218, *231*
Smith, M.J., 74, *81*, 125, *138*
Snow, R.E., 115, *122*
Solomon, C., 41, *55*
Soloway, E., 4, *5*, 103, *106*, 140, 149, *160*, 206, 209, 212, 215, 226, *230, 231, 232, 233*
Sowa, J.F., 66, 67, *82*
Spensley, F., 189, 190, 191, 199, *204, 205*
Spiro, R.J., 7, *33*

Spohrer, J., 209, 213, *233*
Squibb, H.R., 116, *122*
Stallman, R., 281, *233*
Steele, G.L., Jr., 217, *233*
Stefik, M., 44, 45, *55*
Stein, P., 170, *186*
Steinberg, L.I., 30, *32*
Stevens, A., 136, *138, 205*
Suchman, L., 268, 279, *282*
Suppes, P., 251, 252, 253, 262, 264, *265*
Sussman, G.J., 44, *53*, 217, 218, 222, *230, 233*
Sussman, J., 222, *230*
Suthers, D., 244, 247, *249*

**T**
Takahashi, S., 253, *265*
Thagard, P.R., 41, *54*
Thole, H., 114, *122*
Thompson, R., 84, 89, *105*
Touretzky, D., 217, 222, *233*
Turner, R., 60, *82*

**U**
Ullman, J., 217, *231*
Utgoff, P.E., 27, *32, 33*

**V**
VanCaneghem, M., 44, *55*
van Dam, A., 243, *250*
van der Pal, F., 129, *137*
Van Harmelen, F., 28, *33*
van Lehn, K., 116, *122*, 213, *231*
Verloop, A., 242, *249*
Vygotsky, L., 7, *33*

**W**
Ward, B., 156, 158, *160*
Waters, R., 207, *233*
Weil, M., 166, *186*
Weinstein, C.E., 167, *187*
Wenger, E., 90, *106*, 126, *138*, 140, *161*, 234, *249*, 279, *282*
White, B., 272, *282*
Whitehead, A.N., 194, *205*
Wilensky, R., 125, *138*
Willis, P., 267, *282*
Wills, L.M., 207, *233*
Wineburg, S., 272, *282*
Winkels, R.G.F., 124, 129, 130, 131, 136, *137, 138*

Winne, P.H., 158, *161,* 163, 166, 167, 168,
    *186, 187*
Winograd, T., 214, 217, *231*
Wittgenstein, L., 269, *282*
Woolf, B.P., 114, *123,* 127, 133, *139,* 149,
    158, *161,* 206, 215, *233,* 234, 242,
    244, 247, *249*

**Y**
Yankelovich, N., 243, *250*

Yazdani, M., 140, *161*
Yost, G., 125, *137,* 213, *231,* 241, *249*

**Z**
Zanotti, M., 262, *265*
Zygielbaum, A., 209, *233*
Zytkow, J.M., 36, 41, 50, *54*

# Subject Index

ACT* (Adaptive Control of Thought*), 83
ACT* theory and tutor design, 86–90
Actor model, 44
AlgebraLand, 57, 120
Apprenticeship model, 56–57
APROPOS2, 214, 222
Architecture; *see also* CLORIS, DOCENT
  blackboard-based, 143–146
  byte-sized, 241
  of cathedrals, 234–239
  for discourse, 243–248
  of ELI, 175–179
  for intelligent help systems, 125–128
  of SCENT-3, 143–158
ARK, 57

**B**
BACON, 50
Blackboard, 141, 143–146
BORIS (Bank of Representation of the Information in Settings), 67–69
BUGGY, 153, 213
Bugs; *see also* Mal-rule debuggers
  catalog, 90
  detail and coordination, *see* Errors
  finding detail bugs, 218–220
  overlooking method, 206–207, 209–211, 220–222, 224–226, 229
Byte-sized architecture, 241

**C**
CHIRON
  automatic debugger, 206
  finding coordination errors, 220–222
  finding detail bugs, 218–220
  implementation concerns, 222–228
  representation of programming plans, 216–218
CLORIS (Conceptual Language Oriented to the Representation of Instructional film Sequences)
  architecture, 65–71
  methodological basis, 58–65
  operation of the system, 71–80
  requirements of the system, 59–60
Coaching principles for help systems, 133–136

Cognition
  everyday cognition, 270–272
  everyday cognition and expert reasoning, 275–276
  expert cognition, 272–275
  individual versus shared, 269
Cognitive apprenticeship, 192–194
Cognitive development
  psychological studies of social interaction, 7–8
Cognitive diagnosis of learning difficulties, 262–263
Cognitive model of learning companionship, 30
Cognitive strategy, 154–155
Computer-assisted scientific discovery, *see* Scientific discovery
Conceptual clustering, 50
Conceptual graph, 66
Counseling, 30

**D**
DEBUGGY, 213
Design
  of instructional material, 11
  of intelligent discovery learning environments, 40–48
  of a Learning Companion System, 10–12
  paradigms for, 276–280
Design system
  LOUTI, 35
Didactic
  planners, 126–127
  goals, 129–130
Discourse
  architecture, 243–248
  planner, 131–132
  strategies, 130–132
Discovery
  environment, 48–52
  learning, *see* Learning
DOCENT
  architecture, 164–168
  ELI (Expression Language for Instruction), 168, 172–182
  the LIBRARY, 168–172

project, 163
DOMINIE (DOMain INdependent Instructional
  Environment)
  decreasing intervention approach, 202
  knowledge representation, *see* Knowledge
    representation
  student model, 191–192
  system, 188–189
  teaching strategies, *see* Teaching strategies
DORIS (DOmain Representation Inference
  System), 67

**E**
ELMER route planning system, 145
Empirical
  evaluation, 153
Errors
  detail and coordination, 207–211
  finding coordination errors, 220–222
  multiple, 101
EUROHELP project, *see* Project

**F**
Feedback
  student-controlled, 98, 101–105
Focusing algorithm for concept learning, *see*
  Learning

**G**
Generic software
  EXCEL, 36
  HyperCard, 36, 124
  limitations, 38–40
  SUPERCALC, 36
  TURBO-PROLOG, 36
Genetic graphs, 114–115, 129, 154, 229–230
GEOMETRY tutor, 213, 241
Glass-Box technology, 279–280
GRAPES production system, 212
GREATERP, 212

**H**
Help system for UNIX mail, 124, 126
Hierarchies
  temporal event, 65
Hypertext systems, 120–121

**I**
In and out of school learning, *see* Learning
Indefinite integration, 10–11, 27–28
INTEGRATION-KID, 10, 30

Intelligent help systems
  architecture, 125–128
  coaching principles, 133–136
  discourse strategies, 130–132

**K**
Knowledge representation
  in DOMINIE, 189–191
  granularity-based approach, 152
  object knowledge base, 45–46

**L**
LAURA, 148, 213, 214
LCS (Learning Companion Systems)
  design of a LCS for integration, 10–12
  knowledge and learning ability of compan-
    ion, 23–24
  learning companionship, 6
  learning tasks of the companion, 24–26
  role of the teacher and of the companion,
    12–18
Learning
  ability of companion, 23–24
  cognitive diagnosis, 262–263
  companionship, 6
  discovery, 41, 195
  explanation-based, 119
  focusing algorithm for concept, 119
  group, 41
  in and out of school, 266–272
  model of mastery, 258–261
  a new epistemology of, 266–268
  simulation of peer group, 29
  learning tasks of the companion, *see* LCS
Learning Companion Systems, *see* LCS
Learning environments
  based on generic software, 36–38
  design of intelligent discovery, 40–48
  High school chemistry, 49–51
  The forest, 37
  La Ville, 48–49
  Logic tutor, 112–114
  LOGO, 34
  Meteorology, 37
  Nutrition, 51–52
  Optical lenses, 38
Learning model of mastery, *see* Learning
LEX learning program, 27, 28
LISP tutor, 83–84, 140, 212, 241
LISP-Critic, 140
LMS (Leeds Modeling System), 213

LOUPE (Logiciels-Outils Utilisés Pour l'Enseignement), 35
LOUTI (L'OUTIl), 35, 42, 47–48

**M**
Machine learning, 119, 242
Machine learning approach to LCS, 26–28
Mal-rule; *see also* Student model
debuggers, 212–216
weaknesses of the mal-rule method, 213–
216
Mastery learning, *see* Learning
Mathematics of mastery, 256–261
MEMO-II, 206, 215
Mental models, 41
Microworlds, *see* Learning environments
Model tracing paradigm, 84–86, 90–92, 198
MORISS (Module Of Rules for Interpreting
the Structure of Sequences), 70–71
Multimedia, 249; *see also* Video

**N**
Natural language, 72, 114, 146

**O**
Overlay model, 91, 115, 126, 155, 191, 228
Overlooking method, *see* Bugs

**P**
PANGLE (Plan ANd Goal LanguagE), 216–
218, 227
PDS6, 215, 225
Peer interaction, 6–7
PITS, 140
Planning; *see also* PANGLE
means-ends analysis, 89
PRISME, 43–45
Problem compilation, 92–96
Programming environment, 43–44
Programming paradigms, 44–45
Project
DOCENT, 163
LOUPE, 35–40
SCENT, 140–141
EUROHELP, 124–126
Protocol analysis, 12–15
PROUST, 103, 140–141, 206–207, 212

**R**
RCS (Reading Companion System), 30–31
REDUCE, 255

Responsibility sharing, 16–17, 22–23
Rules
in discovery learning, 201
production, 87–88

**S**
SCENT (Student Computing ENvironmenT)
project, 140–141
prototypes, 141–143
SCENT-3
blackboard, 143–146
cognitive analyst, 154–155
interface, 146
student knowledge analyst
cognitive analyst, 154–155
domain knowledge analyst, 153–154
instructional planner, 156–158
strategy judges, 148–153
student model manager, 155–156
student response analyst, 146–147
SCHEME, 44
SCHOLAR, 234
Scientific activity categories, 36
Scientific discovery
computer-assisted, 35–36
Simulation
approach to LCS, 28–29
of peer group learning, 29
SNIFFER, 213
Socratic diagnosis, 197–198
SOPHIE (SOPHisticated Instructional Environment), 6
Student model; *see also* DOMINIE
automatic construction of, 228–229
bypassing the student modeling problem,
109–121
genetic graph, *see* Genetic graphs
learner style, 115
legality of, 120
mal-rule approach, 115–117
manager, 155–156
overlay, *see* Overlay model
slogans, 110, 114, 115, 118
student modeling problem, 108–109
Student-controlled feedback, 98

**T**
TALUS, 140, 148, 214, 222
Teaching strategies, 192–199
Temporal event hierarchies, 62, 65
Testing student-controlled feedback, 101–105

Theorem provers, 252–255
Theory of Learning Companionship, 30
THINGLAB, 34
Tools; *see also* LOUTI
  ExGen (Example Generation tool), 246–248
  KATI (Knowledge Acquisition Tool for Instruction), 168, 182
  T-KATI (Teacher's version of KATI), 171, 182–183
Trill, 197
Tutorial interaction, 84–86, 96–101

**V**
VOLTAVILLE, 34
Video; *see also* DORIS, BORIS, MORISS
  based apprenticeship, 57
  based ITS, *see* CLORIS
  settings structures, 61–65
  temporal event hierarchies, 65
Vygotsky's hypothesis, 7

**W**
WHY, 197